THE WORLD ALMANAC
50
YEARS OF
AMERICAN
SPORTS
A DECADE-BY-DECADE HISTORY

JAMES BUCKLEY, JR., DAVID FISCHER, JIM GIGLIOTTI,
TIMOTHY SEEBERG, MICHAEL TEITELBAUM,
JOHN WALTERS, BOB WOODS

D1530741

50 Years of American Sports

World Almanac® Books
An imprint of Infobase Publishing
132 West 31st Street
New York NY 10001

Contact the publisher for Library of Congress Cataloging-in-Publication data.

ISBN 978-1-60057-140-4

World Almanac® Books are available at special discounts when purchased in bulk quantities for businesses, associations, institutions, or sales promotions. Please call our Special Sales Department in New York at (212) 967-8800 or (800) 322-8755.

You can find World Almanac® Books on the World Wide Web at http://www.infobasepublishing.com

Produced by the Shoreline Publishing Group LLC
President/Editorial Director: James Buckley Jr.
Contributing Editor: Jim Gigliotti
Text design by Thomas Carling, carlingdesign.com
Index by Nanette Cardon, IRIS

Cover printed by Bang Printing, Brainerd, MN
Book printed and bound by Bang Printing, Brainerd, MN
Date printed: September 2010

Printed in the United States of America.

10 9 8 7 6 5 4 3 2 1

This book is printed on acid-free paper.

CONTENTS

INTRODUCTION

BY JAMES BUCKLEY, JR.

For more than 200 years, America has been an ongoing series of shared experiences. It began with the literal building of a community of citizens and states. It continued with the shared experience of pioneers and immigrants. The move of much of the nation to an urban setting created millions of closely-shared lives. Our ongoing national community experience is one that the world continues to envy. The American Dream of progress and hope. Since the years following World War II, America has also shared, with ever-increasing fervor and universality, another type of experience: the sports world. Sure, there were sports in America before 1960, when this book begins. But in the past five decades, the enormous appeal and accessibility (thank you, TV and the Internet!) of an ever-growing sports world has created one of the biggest ways that literally tens of millions of Americans share an experience with each other in one form or another. And while wins and losses, champions and goats, plays and moments big and small are among the main focuses of this shared experience of loving sports, the games we play and the people who play them have grown in the past 50 years to mythic levels. And what is more of a shared experience than a myth, whether told around a fire or via Facebook?

The ongoing history of American sports in the past fifty years encompasses and reflects just about every part of our national story.

- Working hard to achieve greatness (did a steel-worker ever work harder than Vince Lombardi?).
- The ever-growing influence of money on our society (Joe Namath's record contract in 1965:

$400,000; Alex Rodriguez's in 2000: $250 million).

- The ever-changing world of race relations (though sports' "color" barriers were broken by 1960, Alabama didn't have a black football player until 1971, for instance).
- The impact of a wired world (halftime locker-room updates from athletes via Twitter, anyone?).
- Debates on drugs? Sports has them endlessly.
- The changing role of women in society? Sports led the way in some phases of that issue.
- Changing fashion? Two words: Air Jordans.

In nearly every phase of American life, sports has found a place or served as a mirror. And you'll read how in this book.

The other thing about America's shared experience is how many choices we have these days to share. In the early days of "big" sports, you had two or three channels on broadcast TV, maybe some radio . . . and everyone tuned in together. Then came cable, the Internet, and the multiplicity of distractions, creating an infinite number of experiences to share.

Yet amid all that choice, sports somehow remains the one thing that attracts the most eyeballs, the greatest community. The Super Bowl regularly gets 100 million viewers, the Olympics half that many (in the U.S.), while other major events such as the World Cup bring in hundreds of millions. Events like this, the stories that surround them—okay, the hype from broadcasters and advertisers—those events remain the biggest shared experiences we have left. More people watched the Saints beat

1960s

1970s

1980s

1990s

2000s

the Colts in 2010's Super Bowl than watched the inauguration of President Barack Obama in 2009.

You can have a debate on a withering of our priorities, but that's for the editorial page. In here, we'll celebrate the sports pages and the many ways that they have reached out to touch every aspect of American life in the past five decades. See how many of these experiences you've shared.

Sportswriter James Buckley, Jr. has written more than 50 books on sports. He was the editorial director of the nine-volume Sports in America *reference series.*

INTRODUCTION
1960–1969

A not-so-subtle change took place in the sports world in the 1960s: Where competing—striving for a championship—was the end-all early in the 1960s, cashing in—not just making a living playing sports, but getting rich doing it—crept in toward the end of the decade.

Athletes began to see themselves as entertainers who performed for money. Some observers saw that as an end to a simpler, more innocent time. Others saw it as overdue in an arena in which owners long had prospered at the expense of the athletes. That culture clash was a reflection of life in the 1960s, a period remembered for rebellion in the lifestyles and attitudes of the younger generation— ideas that eventually crept into the mainstream and beyond.

Labor struggles were inevitable in the new sports-world order as the players organized by hiring union leaders to represent them in their dealings with team owners.

Race relations and issues of freedom were other themes of the decade. Heavyweight boxing champion Cassius Clay, who became a Muslim and changed his name to Muhammad Ali, refused to register for the military draft in 1967 and was stripped of his heavyweight title. Black competitors used athletic venues to express their views against racism, such as at the 1968 Olympics.

Instances of the social strides that prove how sport mirrors society include the Boston Celtics. In 1966, they won an unprecedented eighth consecutive National Basketball Association (NBA) championship, after which the team named Bill Russell the NBA's first African-American coach.

Commercialism invaded sports during the decade, as corporate sponsors began paying Olympic athletes to sell their products. The ideal of amateurism— competing for sheer love of the sport— became a naive notion as big business invaded sports. The struggle to maintain

Decade of Protest *Anti-war sentiment in the United States was reflected in this protest in Berkeley, California.*

one's amateur status amid the increasing prize money came to a head in the Winter Olympics in 1968, the same year that tennis began allowing amateurs and pros to compete in the same tournaments.

New leagues sprouted up during the decade like tulips in springtime, with varying success, but always upsetting the status quo.

Despite suffering through embarrassing gambling and drug scandals, the racial tension of an integrated America on and off the fields, and the corruption resulting from big dollars coming into sports, sports fans still remember the memorable performances of the decade. Magnificent athletes such as Jim Brown, Jack Nicklaus, Wilma Rudolph, Sandy Koufax, Billie Jean King, Wilt Chamberlain, and others were at their height in the 1960s. These years also featured the staying power of such dynastic teams as the Celtics, the NFL's Green Bay Packers, and college basketball's University of California at Los Angeles (UCLA) Bruins.

The 1960s were one of the most revolutionary decades in American history. In this case, sports certainly imitated life.

1960

Rozelle Takes Over

In late January, NFL owners gathered in Miami Beach to pick the league's next commissioner. Bert Bell, who had been commissioner since 1946, died of a heart attack the previous October while attending a game between the Philadelphia Eagles and the Pittsburgh Steelers (the two teams he had previously owned).

After seven days and 22 ballots, the owners failed to break a deadlock between Austin Gunsel, who had been serving as acting commissioner since Bell's death, and Marshall Leahy, an attorney for the San Francisco 49ers. Finally, on the 23rd ballot, a surprise compromise candidate was voted in: Pete Rozelle, the 33-year general manager of the Los Angeles Rams.

Rozelle (1926–1996), who became the fourth commissioner in NFL history, was an inspired choice. He went on to do more to make the NFL successful than any player or coach in the league. During his term, from 1960 to 1989, the football league grew from 12 to 28 teams and merged with the AFL to create the Super Bowl.

The First Miracle on Ice

In a huge upset, the United States ice hockey team won the Olympic gold medal at Squaw Valley, California, in February. Before the 1960 Games, the U.S. hockey team had never won a gold medal in the Winter Olympics.

First, the team beat Canada 2–1, as U.S. goalie Jack McCartan stopped 39 shots and Bob Cleary and Paul Johnson scored goals. Two days later, the United States recorded its first ice-hockey victory over a Soviet team when the Christian brothers, Billy and Roger, combined for a third-period goal that resulted in a 3–2 win.

After defeating the Soviet Union, the United States had to play Czechoslovakia at eight o'clock the next morning in the championship game. The Americans trailed the Czechs 4–3 entering the final period, but crushed the Czechs with six unanswered goals over the final 20 minutes for a 9–4 victory to take home the gold. Roger Christian scored four goals in the game. Twenty years later, Dave Christian, Billy's son and Roger's nephew, played on the U.S. hockey team that won the gold medal at the 1980 Winter Olympics, in an equally stunning upset.

Olympian Effort *American sprinter Wilma Rudolph (see page 10) shined in the 1960 Games in Rome, Italy.*

Arnie Enlists His Army

In 1960, golfer Arnold Palmer (b.1929) was at the top of his form, winning eight of the 27 tournaments he entered, including the Masters and the U.S. Open. At the Masters, he attracted a crowd of admirers, dubbed Arnie's Army, who loved his winning ways and his "regular Joe" style of play. Palmer was a risky shotmaker, and sometimes played with his shirt untucked or his hair uncombed.

Fight Night *Floyd Patterson (right) and Ingemar Johansson duke it out in New York's Polo Grounds. Patterson regained the heavyweight title with a fifth-round knockout.*

Twice Is Nice

Floyd Patterson (1935–2006) became the first boxer to regain the world heavyweight championship when he knocked out the champion, Ingemar Johansson of Sweden, in the fifth round of their bout at New York's Polo Grounds. Patterson had lost his championship belt to Johansson during a title fight one year earlier, when Patterson was knocked down seven times in one round! In the rematch, on June 20, Patterson got his revenge. The 25-year-old New Yorker outboxed his bigger opponent, avoided Johansson's powerful right-hand punch, and connected with two devastating left hooks to floor the previously undefeated Swede.

Rudolph Leads the Way

Wilma Rudolph (1940–1994) could not walk when she was a youngster because she had polio, a disease that can cause paralysis. She wore a brace on her left leg until she was 12 years old. By the time she was 20, Wilma could run so fast that she was called the World's Fastest Woman. Rudolph won three gold medals at the 1960 Summer Olympic Games in Rome. She became the first American woman to win three golds in track and field at a single Olympics, setting world records in two of the events.

In the semifinal heat of the 100-meter dash, Rudolph tied the world record of 11.3 seconds, crossing the finish line a full three yards ahead of the runnerup—a huge margin of victory in so short a race. In the final heat, Rudolph claimed her

Palmer birdied (had one shot under par) the last two holes of the Masters to win by a stroke over Ken Venturi. He followed that victory with one of the most amazing comebacks ever seen in golf. On June 18, Palmer was seven shots behind leader Mike Souchak going into the final round of the U.S. Open at Cherry Hills Country Club in Denver, Colorado. But Palmer got six birdies over the first seven holes, went on to shoot 65, and vaulted him over 14 golfers to win

Palmer, perhaps the most popular golfer ever, won 60 titles during his career and became the first player in his sport to earn $1 million. He won the Masters four times. But more important, it was Palmer who made golf a sport for television. Prizes that were $5,000 are now more than $1 million.

first gold medal by winning in 11 seconds flat, but this record was not recognized because the two-mile-an-hour wind at her back was over the Olympic limit.

In the 200-meter dash, Rudolph set a world record with a time of 22.0 seconds in a qualifying heat, the first time a woman broke the 23-second barrier. She then won her second gold medal with a time of 24.0 in the final (four-tenths of a second faster than her closest competitor), and she displayed a powerful finishing kick while anchoring the 4x100-meter relay team that set a world record.

The Rome Games were the first Olympics to be broadcast to millions of television viewers around the world and they were the first Olympics to be televised live in the United States. Rudolph's success on the track did much to help women's athletics gain overall acceptance in America. Thousands of girls, inspired to "be like Wilma," joined local track clubs and then demanded competitive athletic opportunities in their schools, just like the boys. The seeds of Title IX, the landmark 1972 legislation that would vastly expand women's sports programs, had been planted.

Friendly Rivals

The favorites in the 10-event decathlon at the Rome Olympics were Rafer Johnson (b.1934) of the United States and C.K. Yang of Taiwan. Johnson, the silver medalist in the decathlon at the 1956 Olympics, and Yang were college friends who trained together while on the track and field team at the University of California at Los Angeles (UCLA).

After nine events, Johnson led Yang by only 67 points. As they entered the final event, the 1,500-meter race, Yang knew he had to beat Johnson by at least 10 seconds to win the gold. Yang won the race, but Johnson finished in a career best time of 4:49.7, which was only two seconds slower than Yang. Johnson won the gold medal with a record 8,392 points. Yang took the silver and became the first Taiwanese athlete to win an Olympic medal.

In 1984, Johnson was chosen to light the torch at the Opening Ceremonies of the Summer Olympics in Los Angeles.

Series-Winning Homer

The 1960 World Series was one of the strangest, most exciting, unique, and entertaining in the rich and colorful history of the Fall Classic. When it was over, the N.L.'s Pittsburgh Pirates had upended the A.L.'s New York Yankees in seven games.

Looking at the statistics, the Series should have been won by the Yankees. The Bronx Bombers set a number of Series records—highest batting average (.338), most hits (91), most runs (55), and most runs batted in (54). But this October, the Yankees lost to the Pirates on one of the most dramatic endings in World Series history.

The Series was tied, three games each, after the Yankees routed the Pirates in Forbes Field, 12–0 in Game Six. In the deciding seventh game, the Yankees rolled to a 7–4 lead, but the Pirates stormed back in the bottom of the eighth inning, scoring five runs to take a 9–7 advantage. In the top of the ninth inning, though, New

1960

York's Mickey Mantle (1931–1995) singled to score one run, then made a sensational base-running play to elude a tag, allowing the tying run to score.

Pittsburgh second baseman Bill Mazeroski (b.1936) was the leadoff batter in the bottom of the ninth. Ralph Terry, the fifth Yankee pitcher in the game, threw one ball and, on the second pitch, Mazeroski swung and blasted a high fly ball that cleared the left-field wall for a home run to win the Series for the Pirates.

Mazeroski jumped up and down, waving his cap in the air. There were so many people on the field blocking his way by the time he rounded third base, he barely made it around to touch home plate. He did make it home, though, and the Pirates won, 10–9. The only other player to end a World Series with a homer is Joe Carter of the Toronto Blue Jays in game six of the 1993 Series against the Philadelphia Phillies.

California Dreaming

The NBA joined the expansion of professional sports to the West Coast, when the Lakers moved from Minneapolis to start the 1960–61 season in their new home, the 14,000-seat Los Angeles Memorial Sports Arena.

Los Angeles basketball fans were wowed by the moves of forward Elgin Baylor (b.1934), the first NBA player who seemed to defy gravity, "flying" in a way that Chicago Bulls star Michael Jordan later did in the 1980s and 1990s. The 6-foot-5 Baylor was an 11-time All-Star who averaged 27.4 points per game in the Lakers' first season in Los Angeles.

Baylor scored more than 60 points in a game three times in 1960–61, including an NBA-record 71-point performance on November 15, 1960, in the Lakers' 123–108 victory over the New York Knicks at Madison Square Garden. Baylor made 28 field goals and 15 free throws to break his own league mark of 64 points.

Football's Iron Man

With limited substiution in the 1930s and most of the 1940s, almost all NFL players were "two-way" players—that is, they played both offense and defense (and usually special teams, too). A rule change in 1949 permitted free substitution and ushered in the era of specialization. By 1960, there was one full-time, two-way player left in the NFL: Chuck Bednarik (b.1925).

"The Iron Man," as he became known, played center on offense and linebacker on defense for the Philadelphia Eagles. A hard-hitting blocker and tackler, he was chosen All-Pro at both positions.

Bednarik, at 35, was the oldest man on the Eagles in 1960, and was a symbol of durability. The length of a regulation NFL game is 60 minutes, and Bednarik never seemed to leave the field, averaging 57.8 minutes per game. In the 1960 NFL Championship Game against the Green Bay Packers, held at Franklin Field in Philadelphia on December 26, Bednarik's performance inspired his teammates to a 17–13 victory.

While playing offense in the second quarter, Bednarik blocked blitzing defenders, allowing quarterback Norm Van Brocklin time to throw a touchdown pass.

Then, while playing defense in the fourth period, he knocked down Green Bay's Jim Taylor at the nine-yard line on the final play. Bednarik's game-saving tackle gave Philadelphia its first championship in 11 years. He was on the field for nearly every play. The record book shows he played an incredible 58 minutes of the title game!

Johnny U.

Baltimore Colts' quarterback Johnny Unitas (1933–2002) extended his NFL record-setting streak by throwing two touchdown passes in a game against the Detroit Lions on December 4. That gave Unitas at least one touchdown pass in 47 straight games! The streak, which stretched over four seasons, ended the following week in the same place where it started, the Los Angeles Coliseum.

Johnny U.'s record may stand forever. The closest anyone has ever come to it was the Miami Dolphins' Dan Marino (b.1961), who threw touchdown passes in 30 games in a row from 1985 to 1987.

With his crew cut and high-topped black cleats, Unitas was the personification of leadership at the quarterback position. He set 22 NFL passing records in an 18-year career with the Colts (1956 to 1972) and San Diego Chargers (1973).

Other Milestones of 1960

✔ There was a big problem as the date approached for the 1960 Winter Olympics to begin in Squaw Valley, California: no snow. The Piute, a local tribe of Native Americans, did a snow dance to help out, and it worked. A snowstorm came and saved the Games.

✔ The Charlotte Motor Speedway in Charlotte, North Carolina, opened on June 19 to host the World 600. Joe Lee Johnson won while averaging 107.75 mph.

✔ Betsy Rawls set a women's golf record by winning her fourth U.S. Women's Open golf championship in July, scoring a four-round total of 292 for a one-stroke victory over Joyce Ziske at the Worcester (Massachusetts) Country Club. Rawls, who also won in 1951, 1953, and 1957, roared back from a seven-stroke deficit with a record-tying 68 in the third round. Mickey Wright equaled Rawls' mark of four U.S. Open victories in 1964.

✔ The United States routed the Soviet Union 81–57 in the gold-medal game in men's basketball at the Summer Olympics in Barcelona. The 12-man U.S. team featured four future Hall of Famers.

✔ Green Bay Packers halfback Paul Hornung, who also kicked, set an NFL single-season record that would stand 46 years when he scored 176 points.

✔ The year saw several baseball innovations. Bill Veeck, the maverick owner of the Chicago White Sox, was the first to put names on the back of his players' uniforms, above their numbers. Baltimore Orioles manager Paul Richards introduced an oversized mitt for his catchers' adventures with knuckleball pitcher Hoyt Wilhelm. The Cleveland Indians and Detroit Tigers made history on August 3 by trading managers. It had never been done before. Cleveland got Jimmy Dykes and Detroit got Joe Gordon.

1961

Higher and Higher

On January 29, two high jumpers on different sides of the world reached new heights, as the world indoor record was set and broken.

John Thomas of the United States and Valeri Brumel of the Soviet Union both bettered the indoor record height of 7-feet-2 1/2 inches, which had been set by Thomas less than a year earlier, in March of 1960.

At a track meet in Leningrad, Russia, Brumel jumped 7-feet-4 1/2 inches, setting a new world record. News that Brumel had added two inches to his former mark reached Thomas just as the 19-year-old student was preparing for a meet in Boston. "It must have been quite a jump," said Thomas, who then cleared 7-feet-3-inches, but did not attempt a record. Both jumpers broke the previous record. Brumel just broke it more!

Memorial Day Champion

A.J. Foyt, a 26-year-old, tough-talking Texan, drove his Formula One racecar to a five-second victory over Eddie Sachs in the Indianapolis 500 on May 30.

Foyt (b.1935) and Sachs dueled for 300 miles in the 50th anniversary of the great race. Foyt pulled ahead with just 25 miles to go, but he needed a pit stop to repair a faulty fuel line. Sachs could have breezed to the finish line, but with three laps to go, he also was forced to make a pit stop to change a tire. Foyt zipped back on the track ahead of Sachs and took the checkered flag for the win.

Foyt, who was well on his way to making auto racing a mainstream sport, repeated his Indy victory three more times, in 1964, 1967, and 1977. Foyt won the Indy-car driving championship a record seven times and ran over anyone who got in his way. In 1972, he tried stock car racing and won the Daytona 500!

The Big Kahuna

American Phil Edwards became the first person to ride the Banzai Pipeline, one of Hawaii's best surfing areas. At the Banzai Pipeline, waves hit two sets of submerged reefs that slow the bottom of the wave, making the front rise up and get steeper. Then, the top of the wave comes crashing forward, creating a tube of air inside that surfers try to ride.

Two Titans *Roger Maris (left) and Mickey Mantle chased the homer record (page 16).*

Surfing competitions became serious as surfboard designs improved and surfers' abilities improved. In 1964, the first official world championships were held at Manly Beach in Australia. And in 1966, the first Duke Kahanamoku Invitational was held in Hawaii. In 1969, the Duke Kahanamoku Invitational awarded $1,000 in prize money to the winner. (Duke Kahanamoku was a Hawaiian who won a swimming gold medal for the United States in the 1912 Olympics and later made surfing popular around the world.)

In the early 1960s, the number of surfers around the world grew from the thousands into the millions. Motion pictures and popular music helped. A series of movies featured a young California girl named Gidget who loved to surf. And people all over the country heard the Beach Boys sing songs about California and surfing, including "Surfin' USA."

1961

The Big Picture

🏆 This was a breakthrough year in the marriage of television and sports. *ABC's Wide World of Sports*, a weekly anthology show produced by Roone Arledge (1931–2002), hit the airwaves for the first time on April 29 with Jim McKay as host. The debut telecast featured two track events: the Penn Relays from Franklin Field in Philadelphia, and the Drake Relays from Des Moines, Iowa. *ABC's Wide World of Sports* began as a 20-week series; it is now the longest-running sports program in the history of television. The show, which covered such diverse fare as downhill skiing in Switzerland and figure skating in the Soviet Union, whetted Americans' tastes for nontraditional sports.

The power of television was not lost on the NFL's Pete Rozelle. He had been working on lucrative television contracts since he was elected the league's commissioner in 1960. He had seen football's future—through the television camera. Rozelle realized that if he could represent all the teams in one television package, the league would have more bargaining power with the networks.

First, Rozelle had to convince the successful team owners that it was in their best interest to share television revenues equally, even with struggling teams. In the short run, they might not make as much money. But in the long run, all the teams would benefit, making the league stronger. With this accomplished, in 1961 Rozelle helped fight for a federal law exempting football from future monopoly charges. This way the league could act as one unit instead of as individual teams.

In 1962, the NFL signed a two-year contract with CBS for $4.5 million a year. Then, during the merger with the AFL, the leagues negotiated a four-year contract with both CBS and NBC for $9.5 million. By 1969, the newly combined league signed a $150-million contract with ABC.

New Home Run King

⚾ In 1927, New York Yankees legend Babe Ruth blasted an incredible 60 home runs—more than any other *team* in the American League had. The possibility of anyone breaking Ruth's mark was almost unthinkable, but in 1961 not one, but two, Yankees launched an assault on Ruth's hallowed mark. In the end, outfielder Roger Maris (1934–1985) set a new single-season record of 61 home runs; teammate Mickey Mantle (1931–1995) finished with with 54.

Mantle started out red-hot, but injuries forced him to drop out of the race in mid-September. Maris pulled ahead in the middle of September, but the pressure of making a run at one of baseball's most cherished records was so intense that it made Maris's hair fall out in clumps.

On October 1, the final day of the season, the Boston Red Sox were visiting Yankee Stadium. In the bottom of the fourth inning, Red Sox pitcher Tracy Stallard was behind in the count with two balls and no strikes to Maris when he served up a fastball. Maris connected and stroked it into section 33 of the right-field bleachers. The hit was Maris's 61st home run for 1961—one more than Ruth hit in 1927—though the Babe did it in 10 fewer games.

Maris' home run also was the 240th of the season for the Yankees, another record. More importantly, the "M&M Boys," as Mantle and Maris were called, helped the Yankees win the world championship. New York won 109 games during the regular season, then beat the Cincinnati Reds four games to one in the World Series.

Maris held the home-run record 37 years until Mark McGwire (b.1963) of the St. Louis Cardinals hit 70 homers in 1998. His mark was broken when the San Francisco Giants' Barry Bonds (b.1964) hit 73 home runs in the 2001 season.

Bear Turns the Tide

The University of Alabama Crimson Tide football team went 11–0 and won the national title for the first time under coach Paul "Bear" Bryant (1913–1983). The man in the houndstooth hat transformed foundering programs at the University of Kentucky and Texas A & M before arriving at Alabama in 1958 to take over a Crimson Tide team that had fallen to 2–7–1 the previous season. In Bryant's 25 years at Alabama, his teams won six national titles and 15 bowl games.

Other Milestones of 1961

✔ On New Year's Day, the Houston Oilers beat the Los Angeles (now the San Diego) Chargers 24–16 in Houston to win the first championship in the American Football League.

✔ The Cincinnati Bearcats outlasted the Ohio State Buckeyes 70–65 in overtime on March 25 to win the NCAA basketball championship for the first time in school history.

✔ In May, the Chicago Blackhawks defeated the Detroit Red Wings in six games to win the National Hockey League's (NHL) Stanley Cup championship. The Blackhawks finished in third place in the six-team NHL during the regular season, then stunned the Montreal Canadiens in six games in the semifinals to end that team's five-year run as champs. Chicago won the Stanley Cup for the first time in 23 years.

✔ On May 9, Jim Gentile of the Baltimore Orioles pounded a home run with the bases loaded in the first inning of a game against the Minnesota Twins. Then he did it again in the second inning. Baltimore won the game 13–5.

✔ New York Yankees lefty Whitey Ford pitched 14 scoreless innings in his team's four-games-to-one victory over the Cincinnati Reds in the World Series. Ford ran his consecutive-innings scoreless streak in the World Series to 32. That broke the record of 29 innings previously held by Babe Ruth (set when Ruth was with the Boston Red Sox).

✔ Paul Hornung, on leave from the Army to play for the Green Bay Packers, scored 19 points—still a record for an NFL title game—as Green Bay won its seventh league title by routing the New York Giants 37–0 in Green Bay December 31. Hornung scored a touchdown on a six-yard run in the first half and kicked four extra points and three field goals. After this game, Green Bay became known as "Titletown, U.S.A."

1962

The Soaring Marine

Heading down the runway on his attempt to become the first man to vault 16 feet, John Uelses thought the height looked insurmountable. After all, it had been 29 years since the 15-foot barrier had been shattered; for a long time, 16 feet was unthinkable. But the 1960s introduced the fiberglass pole, and on February 2, Uelses soared 16 feet and one-quarter inch during competition in the Millrose Games at New York's Madison Square Garden.

The 24-year-old Marine missed on his first two attempts at the magical 16-foot height, but he easily cleared the bar on his final vault. "I just can't believe it," he said. "Even when I was pounding down the runway I was thinking, 'I'll never make it.'"

The fiberglass pole eventually replaced the wooden one, which had much less spring, and effectively rewrote the record books by enabling vaulters to soar ever higher. (By 1963, the 17-foot mark was shattered.) Three weeks after Uelses' feat, American astronaut John Glenn—really rocketing into space—successfully orbited the earth.

The Hershey Hundred

On March 2, Wilt Chamberlain (1936–1999) of the Philadelphia Warriors poured in 100 points as Philadelphia beat the New York Knicks, 169–147, in Hershey, Pennsylvania. No one else has ever come close to Chamberlain's amazing single-game record.

Right from the start, Chamberlain dominated. By the end of the first quarter, he had 23 of his team's 42 points. He had 41 points by halftime, when the Warriors led 79–68.

In the third period, Chamberlain was eight for eight from the foul line and made 10 baskets for a 28-point quarter. He had 69 points in the game's first 36 minutes. Chamberlain broke his own single-game record by reaching 79 points with more than seven minutes remaining. (He had scored 78 points in a game against the Los Angeles Lakers in December, 1961.) His tally stood at 89 points with five minutes left to play. But then he failed to score for more than two minutes! He quickly dropped in three free throws and two jumpers. Now he had 96 points. The 4,124 fans in Hershey Arena were yelling, "Give it to Wilt!"—which the Warriors did.

Century Mark *Wilt Chamberlain set an all-time record with his 100-point night.*

Chamberlain had 98 points with 1:27 to play, but the next three times he got the ball, he shot and missed. The Knicks were now stalling to avoid being embarrassed, and they were fouling other Warriors to keep the ball away from Chamberlain.

New York tried a collapsing defense around the big man (putting two or three defenders on him whenever he got near the basket). There would be no denying Chamberlain on this night, however. With 46 seconds remaining, he got the ball a few feet from the basket and slammed home a final dunk for 100 points.

In all, Chamberlain made 36 of 63 field goals. Usually a horrendous free-throw shooter, he even made 28 of 32 free throws!

1962

Lovable Losers

The Brooklyn Dodgers and the New York Giants dealt a double blow to baseball fans in the Big Apple when both teams left New York City to play on the West Coast (the Dodgers in Los Angeles and the Giants in San Francisco) beginning with the 1959 season. It was not until the arrival of the expansion New York Mets in 1962 that the void was filled.

To manage their new team, Mets owners turned to a baseball legend: 72-year-old Casey Stengel (1890–1975), who as a player and manager had been a New York fixture for almost 50 years.

"The Old Professor" had led the New York Yankees to 10 pennants and seven World Series titles in 12 years as manager, from 1949 to 1960. But with the Mets, he was the manager of one of the worst, but best-loved, teams in history. The 1962 Mets, who captured the hearts of New York baseball fans, won 40 games and lost 120. Stengel skillfully deflected any criticism as only he could. After the Mets set a major-league record for futility by losing game number 120, Stengel addressed his players in the locker room. "Men," he said, "no one person is responsible. This was truly a total team effort."

Stengel was best known for his skill as a manger and for his colorful language—a variation of English that came to be called "Stengelese."

The Green Team

The Boston Celtics, coached by Red Auerbach, won a then-record fourth straight NBA title, defeating the Los An- geles Lakers, 110–107, in game seven of the finals behind a 44-rebound, 30-point performance by Bill Russell on April 18. The Celtics surpassed the Minneapolis Lakers' record of three straight championships (from 1952 to 1954). The Celtics went on to win four more NBA titles, running their record streak to eight in a row. Nine future Hall of Famers played on Auerbach's championship teams, including K.C. Jones, Sam Jones, John Havlicek, Tom Heinsohn, and Frank Ramsey.

Nicklaus Breaks Through

Jack Nicklaus beat heavily favored Arnold Palmer in an 18-hole playoff on June 17 to become the first rookie golfer ever to win the United States Open. Nicklaus was the victor in a duel that tested emotions as well as golfing skills.

The tournament was played at Oakmont Country Club in Pennsylvania, Palmer's home state. The popular Palmer is from nearby Latrobe, Pennsylvania, and the partisan gallery constantly called "Come on, Arnie," and hooted at the 22-year-old Nicklaus. But Nicklaus was not rattled by the hostile fans. He jumped to a four-stroke lead after six holes of the playoff and coasted to a 71—three strokes better than Palmer.

Déja Vu

Eleven years to the day after Bobby Thomson's famous home run lifted the Giants (then based in New York) past the Dodgers (then based in Brooklyn), the Giants did it to their fiercest rivals again, mounting a ninth-inning rally in the third game of a playoff to win the N.L. pennant and reach the World Series.

The Dodgers (now in Los Angeles) took a 4–2 lead into the top of the ninth inning against the visiting Giants (now in San Francisco) in the deciding game of the 1962 playoff. But San Francisco utilized four walks, an error, a wild pitch, and a sacrifice fly to mount a four-run rally and win the game 6–4.

Unfortunately for the Giants, the World Series also was a repeat of 1962. Beating the Dodgers meant a date with the Yankees in the World Series, and, just like 11 years earlier, the Yankees won.

The Series went seven games, with New York winning the finale 1–0 when second baseman Bobby Richardson caught Willie McCovey's liner with two on and two out in the ninth inning.

Other Milestones of 1962

✔ In college football, the University of Southern California streaked to an undefeated record and the national title, the first for coach John McKay. The Trojans' perfect record was sorely tested in the Rose Bowl on New Year's Day of 1963 as the University of Wisconsin staged a furious comeback but fell short in USC's 42–37 win.

✔ Oscar Robertson of the Cincinnati Royals, one of the greatest all-around players in NBA history, averaged a triple-double: 30.8 points, 12.5 rebounds, and 11.4 assists—per game!—during the 1961–62 regular season. Robertson played through the 1973–74 season and was the NBA's all-time leader among guards in scoring and assists at the time of his retirement.

✔ Washington Senators pitcher Tom Cheney set a Major League Baseball record by striking out 21 Baltimore Orioles in the Senators' 16-inning, 2–1 win at Baltimore on September 12.

✔ Heavyweight boxing champion Floyd Patterson was knocked out by Sonny Liston in the first round of their championship fight at Chicago's Comiskey Park on September 25.

✔ The New York Giants' Y.A. Tittle tied an NFL record by tossing seven touchdown passes in a 49–34 win over the Washington Redskins on October 28.

✔ The National Basketball Association expanded to the West Coast, with the Philadelphia Warriors moving to San Francisco. Basketball fans near the Golden Gate Bridge were excited to watch the Warriors' star, 7-foot-1 center Wilt Chamberlain.

✔ Maury Wills, the Dodgers' speedy shortstop, set a big-league record by stealing 104 bases in 1962. Ty Cobb held the old mark with 96 thefts way back in 1915.

✔ On December 23, the Dallas Texans won the American Football League championship by overcoming the Houston Oilers after two minutes, 54 seconds of the second overtime period, 20–17. At the time, it was the longest pro football game ever played.

✔ The Green Bay Packers beat the New York Giants 16–7 at New York's Yankee Stadium on December 30 to win their second straight NFL title.

1963

Football's Ups and Downs

On January 9, Paul Brown (1908–1991), founder of the Cleveland Browns of the old All-America Football Conference and the NFL, the winner of seven league titles, and the man after which the team was named, was fired as coach and general manager by the club's new owner, former television and advertising executive Art Modell, who had purchased the club in 1961.

Under new coach Blanton Collier, Cleveland won 10 of 14 games. Browns fullback Jim Brown (b.1936) ran for a then-record 1,863 yards in 1963 while becoming the career leader in rushing yardage. Brown brought his career total to 9,322 yards, surpassing the old record of 8,378 yards set by Joe Perry, who starred for the San Francisco 49ers and the Baltimore Colts from 1950 to 1962.

In November, the NFL played while the nation grieved. Football fans were angry at the NFL's decision to play its regularly scheduled Sunday games just three days after President John F. Kennedy's assassination in Dallas, Texas. Outraged fans pointed out that games in the NBA, NHL, and AFL were cancelled, but NFL commissioner Pete Rozelle, who said, "Football was Mr. Kennedy's game," announced the games would be played. Rozelle later called this his worst decision as commissioner.

By season's end, New York Giants quarterback Y.A. Tittle (b.1926) had thrown for 3,145 yards and a single-season record 36 touchdowns. The Giants, 11–3 during the regular season, faced the Chicago Bears in the NFL Championship Game at Wrigley Field in Chicago on December 29. The Giants lost 14–10—the third year in a row they lost the title game.

Black Eye for Golden Boy

On April 17, commissioner Pete Rozelle suspended two of the NFL's top players for gambling. Green Bay Packers halfback Paul Hornung and Detroit Lions defensive tackle Alex Karras were suspended indefinitely for betting on league games. In making the announcement, Rozelle stressed that neither player bet against his own team or gave less than 100 percent during games.

Hornung was nicknamed "Golden Boy" because of his blond hair, good looks, and sparkling talent. As a quarterback at the University of Notre Dame, he won the Heisman Trophy in 1956, the only time a player from a losing team has taken home the prestigious award. He joined the Packers in 1957 and sparked the team to NFL titles in 1961 and 1962. Hornung was a triple threat, meaning he could run, pass, and kick. He led the NFL in scoring for three seasons, including a record 176 points in 1960. Karras bitterly criticized Rozelle's punishment, but Hornung admitted he was guilty and never complained publicly about his suspension. The suspensions were lifted at the end of the 1963 season, but the integrity of professional football was assured for much longer.

Hornung and Karras returned to their respective teams for the 1964 season. But for Hornung, age and the year off had taken their toll. He led the team in scoring once again, but he rushed for just 415 yards. He never again played like the Golden Boy of old, and his career ended with an injury two years later.

Karras played until the early 1970s and then became a television commentator on Monday night football from 1974 to 1976. He also appeared in films, notably the Mel Brooks comedy *Blazing Saddles*, and starred on the TV sitcom *Webster* with Emmanuel Lewis in the title role.

Big Win for Small School

The University of Cincinnati Bearcats had their third straight NCAA men's basketball title all but won, but tiny Loyola of Chicago broke through for an unbelievable overtime victory, 60–58. The Loyola Ramblers missed 13 of their

The Golden Bear *Jack Nicklaus (page 24) won two majors in 1963 (the Masters and PGA Championship) on his way to amassing the highest total of such titles in golf history.*

1963

first 14 shots and trailed by 15 points with 12 minutes to play. But the Ramblers' frenetic style eventually forced the cautious Bearcats into ball-handling errors and defensive fouls. The once-huge Cincinnati lead dwindled: 48–39, 48–43, 50–48. Loyola captain and All-American Jerry Harkness hit the tying basket with five seconds remaining to send the game into overtime. In the extra minutes, Loyola's Vic Rouse grabbed an offensive rebound and laid it in at the buzzer for a 60–58 victory.

Nicklaus Makes His Mark

Jack Nicklaus, who won his first pro golf tournament at the 1962 U.S. Open (see page 20), proved to be the rising young star on the Professional Golfers' Association (PGA) circuit. In 1963, Nicklaus added the Masters and PGA titles to his growing list of credentials. By taming the Masters' Augusta National course with a two-under-par 286 that placed him one stroke ahead of Tony Lema and two ahead of three-time-winner Sam Snead, the 23-year-old Nicklaus became the youngest winner of the prestigious tournament, a distinction he held until 21-year-old Tiger Woods (b.1975) won in 1997. To capture the first of his five PGA Championship trophies, Nicklaus posted a final-round 68 in Dallas, Texas, for a 279 total. He overcame a three-stroke deficit to win.

Although Arnold Palmer did not win a major tournament in 1963, he won enough to become the first golfer to top the $100,000 mark in single-season winnings, finishing the year with $128,230. Palmer made golf a big-time sport in

America by turning what was considered a country-club sport into one that had the tension of football and the suspense of baseball. Palmer boldly attacked every course he played; he visibly agonized over sliced drives and punched his fist into the air after sinking clutch putts. "Arnie's Army" of fans loved it, even when he was not in contention. No matter where or when he played, his galleries were the largest and loudest, cheering every birdie with a loud "Charge!"

Seventeen Is the New 16

Just 18 months after John Uelses became the first pole vaulter to clear 16 feet, John Pennel shattered the 17-foot mark on August 24 in Miami, Florida. Pennel, using a fiberglass pole that made the increasingly higher marks possible, vaulted 17-feet-0 3/4 inches at the Florida Gold Coast Amateur Athletic Union meet in his hometown. It was the sixth time in 1963 that Pennel upped the world pole-vault record.

Party Crasher

Some fighters are boxers. Sonny Liston (1932–1970) was a puncher, and his sledge-hammer right hand was as intimidating as his menacing scowl. Liston's reputation for being downright nasty was enhanced when he retained his world heavyweight championship with a first-round knockout of former champ Floyd Patterson on July 22.

But Liston hardly had time to savor this victory—his 35th win in 36 fights—when another young contender, former

Olympic champion Cassius Clay, began showboating for the ringside crowd.

Clay screamed, "I'm the uncrowned champ. Liston is the tramp, I'm the champ." The next year, Clay (who later changed his name to Muhammad Ali) pulled off one of the most shocking upsets in boxing history (see page 28).

Instant Replay

The first television instant replay occurred on December 7, during the annual Army-Navy college football game, which Navy won 21–15. Tony Verna (what other initials could he have?) was a young director for CBS who introduced the new concept of showing a play again immediately after it took place.

With a Cotton Bowl bid at stake for the winner, number-two-ranked Navy led Army 21–7 in the fourth quarter. Less than seven minutes remained when Army's Rollie Stichweh faked a handoff, scored on a bootleg (a quick run to the outside by the quarterback), and then ran for a two-point conversion, pulling Army to within six points. In its broadcast of the game, CBS made Stichweh's touchdown run television's first instant replay.

The idea of seeing a play again just seconds after it happened was so new that Lindsey Nelson, who was announcing the game, had to warn viewers. "This is not live!" Nelson said. "Ladies and gentlemen, Army did not score again!"

The touchdown was the only time that day CBS used instant replay, because the replay pictures were not very clear. Still, the innovation forever changed the way we watch televised sports.

Canton or Bust

The Pro Football Hall of Fame at Canton, Ohio, was dedicated in September with the induction of 17 charter members. The original inductees—a combination of players, coaches, and commissioners—were Sammy Baugh, Bert Bell, Joe Carr, Dutch Clark, Red Grange, George Halas, Mel Hein, Pete "Fats" Henry, Cal Hubbard, Don Hutson, Curly Lambeau, Tim Mara, George Marshall, Johnny "Blood" McNally, Bronko Nagurski, Ernie Nevers, and Jim Thorpe. Of the 17 immortalized, 12 were still alive at the time.

It's interesting to note that Cal Hubbard is also in the Baseball Hall of Fame (he is the only man in both the football

Football Shrine *The Pro Football Hall of Fame opened its doors in 1963. The first class inducted into the shrine in Canton, Ohio, included 17 former star players or significant contributors.*

1963

and baseball halls). While still playing football, Hubbard started working as an umpire in baseball games, and he became an American League umpire in the mid-1930s. He worked as an umpire for 20 years and was considered one of the best.

"I was so big," the former NFL tackle once said about the respect he garnered, "the other fellows were afraid to argue with me."

Can't Beat Koufax

Since he entered the National League in 1955, Sandy Koufax had proved to be a pretty good starter, but one who sometimes struggled with his control and who had not yet developed into a 20-game winner. In 1963, however, the Los Angeles Dodgers' left-hander put it all together for the first time in his nine sea-

Other Milestones of 1963

✔ The Boston Celtics won their fifth NBA title in a row, beating the Los Angeles Lakers in six games in the Finals. The Celtics were loaded, with stars such as Sam Jones (the team's leading scorer that year at 19.7 points per game), Tommy Heinsohn (18.9 points), Bill Russell (16.8 points and 23.6 rebounds), and John Havlicek (14.3 points). But the man who brought them all together was 34-year-old Bob Cousy (13.2 points in 1962–63). The best playmaking guard of his era, Cousy had already announced his retirement after 13 dazzling seasons. For his career, he averaged 18.4 points, 7.5 assists, and 5.2 rebounds per game.

✔ Jimmy Piersall was a one-of-a-kind baseball player. When he played outfield for the Boston Red Sox, he would bow after making easy catches. He'd also flap his arms like a seal. On June 23, Piersall, playing for the New York Mets, hit his 100th career home run. He celebrated by running around the bases backward!

✔ The United States Gymnastics Federation, now called USA Gymnastics, was formed. It supports clinics, training camps, and team competitions, including programs to determine the U.S. National Team.

✔ On September 15, the outfield was filled with Alous in a baseball game between the San Francisco Giants and the Pittsburgh Pirates. The Alou brothers—Felipe, Matty, and Jesus—all played together in the Giants' outfield for one inning. The Giants won the game, 13–5.

✔ With Ralph Baldwin in the sulky (a very light horse cart, designed for racing), Speedy Scot became only the second standard-bred horse in history to win the Triple Crown of trotting. In 1955, Scott Frost had been the winner of the Yonkers Futurity, the Hambletonian, and the Kentucky Futurity, the three legs of the Triple Crown for three-year-old trotters.

✔ In December, quarterback Roger Staubach (b.1942) of the U.S. Naval Academy won the Heisman Trophy as college football's best player. Staubach was drafted by both the NFL's Dallas Cowboys and the AFL's Kansas City Chiefs, but the pros had to wait. Because of his Navy commitment, Staubach served his country for four years before joining Dallas. He played for the Cowboys from 1969 to 1979, leading them to Super Bowl titles in 1971 and 1977.

sons and developed into a dominating ace. Koufax had a 25–5 record that included 11 shutouts, a 1.88 earned run average (ERA, the number of runs charged to the pitcher times nine divided by the number of innings he pitched), 306 strikeouts, a no-hitter, the National League Most Valuable Player award, and the first of his three Cy Young Awards (when the award was given to just one pitcher from both leagues). Koufax was the first National League pitcher since 1939 to win pitching's unofficial Triple Crown by leading the league in wins, strikeouts, and ERA.

More importantly, Koufax helped the Dodgers sweep the mighty New York Yankees in the World Series in October—the first time the Yankees had gone winless in a Series since 1922. Koufax was nearly unhittable in the Series, pitching two complete games and allowing just three runs to win the Most Valuable Player award. He twice beat Yankees pitching ace Whitey Ford—in the opener and in the final game.

Mr. Hockey

Gordie Howe (b.1928) of the Detroit Red Wings surpassed Maurice Richard (1921–2000) as the leading goal scorer in NHL history on November 10. Howe scored a short-handed goal (his team was short a player, due to a penalty) against Richard's old team, the Montreal Canadiens, for goal number 545 in his career.

Howe was known as "Mr. Hockey," and with good reason. He retired holding nearly every NHL scoring record: most goals (801), most assists (1,049), most points scored (1,850), and most games played (1,767). His records seemed untouchable—that is, until Wayne Gretzky (b.1961) came along in the late-1970s.

Howe was big and strong, and he could skate and shoot. Once he planted himself in front of the net, he was tough to move. He led the league in scoring in four straight seasons, from 1950–51 to 1953–54. He won the Hart Trophy as the Most Valuable Player six times and played on the All-Star team 21 times.

Howe first retired in 1971. In 1973, the 45-year-old Howe came back to play with his sons, Mark and Marty, for the Houston Aeros in a new league, the World Hockey Association (WHA). The move was a public-relations natural for the WHA, which was in need of a star attraction in its uphill battle with the NHL.

Howe played in the WHA until 1979, when the league merged with the NHL. By then, Howe had become a member of the Hartford Whalers. After the 1979–80 season, Howe called it quits for good. He was 52 years old and a grandfather. His combined NHL and WHA totals: 975 goals scored and 2,358 points in 32 seasons!

U.S. Tennis Back on Top

At the Davis Cup tennis finals in Adelaide, Australia, the United States squad regained the international top spot, edging the four-time defending champion Australians, 3–2, to win the Davis Cup for the 19th time, but the first time since 1958. Chuck McKinley of Missouri outlasted Australian John Newcombe, 10–12, 6–2, 9–7, 6–2, for the decisive victory on December 29. As of 2009, the United States had won the Cup a record 32 times, followed by Australia with 28.

1964

Win One, Lose One

The San Diego Chargers played in two American Football League Championship Games in 1964. Well, two in the calendar year, that is, but in two different seasons. The first came on January 5 for the 1963 title. San Diego's Keith Lincoln rushed for 206 yards in a 51–10 rout of the Boston Patriots. Lincoln had a career day, also catching seven passes for 123 yards as the Chargers showed the nation how entertaining the passing offense of the AFL could be, by rolling up 601 total yards.

In the second game, to crown the 1964 champion on December 26, the Buffalo Bills beat the visiting Chargers, 20–7.

The Greatest

Cassius Clay (b.1942)—who soon would be known to the world as Muhammad Ali—was a brash, young upstart boxer. Sonny Liston was the fearsome, hard-punching heavyweight champion of the world. Liston was heavily favored when the two squared off in the ring on February 25 in Miami Beach, Florida. But it was Clay who emerged victorious with a technical knockout in the seventh round. And when it was over, Clay exclaimed over and over to anyone who would listen: "I am the greatest!"

Clay was born in Louisville, Kentucky. People called him "The Louisville Lip" because of the way he bragged. But he backed up his boasts in the boxing ring. He had a brilliant amateur career, highlighted by winning the light heavyweight gold medal at the 1960 Olympics. At 6-foot-3 and 215 pounds, Clay was big and strong, but he was also lightning fast, and he glided around the ring, taunting his opponents to hit him. After turning pro, Clay challenged Liston for the heavyweight title. Clay was the underdog, but he attracted attention by making up poems about what he would do to Liston in the ring. One of his handlers said Clay would "float like a butterfly, sting like a bee." He stung Liston enough to pull off a major upset victory in Miami.

Clay had been deeply interested in the Muslim religion, and after winning the title he became a Muslim and changed his name to Muhammad Ali. After nine title defenses, Ali was drafted into the U.S. military in 1967, during the Vietnam War. But he refused to go on the grounds that he was a Muslim minister. He was

"I am the greatest!" *Boxer Muhammad Ali, then known as Cassius Clay, shouted after defeating Sonny Liston.*

sent to prison briefly, and boxing officials took away his title. In 1970, Ali was found not guilty of violating the draft law and allowed to box again. But his titles were not restored. He would have to get them back by winning in the ring.

In 1974, Ali knocked out the new champion, George Foreman (b.1948), and was again the heavyweight champ. He lost the title to Leon Spinks on February 15, 1978, but won it back against Spinks seven months later to become the first boxer to win the title three times. On November 9, 1996, Evander Holyfield beat Mike Tyson to join Ali as the only men to win the heavyweight title three times.

1964

The Barber of Michigan

At the Winter Olympic Games in Innsbruck, Austria, speed skater Terry McDermott from Michigan, a barber by profession, pulled off a major upset when he won the 500-meter speed skating gold medal on February 4.

To make it even better, McDermott won on skates he borrowed from his coach! It would be the only gold medal for the United States in the 1964 Winter Games. The USSR dominated the Games, winning more than twice as many gold medals (11) and total medals (55) than any other country.

Beginning of a Dynasty

The University of California at Los Angeles Bruins won their first college basketball championship in 1964. UCLA did not lose a game all season. Its 30th, and final, victory of the season came in the NCAA title game on March 21, a 15-point thumping of Duke University, 98–83. The Bruins became only the third NCAA champ to complete the season undefeated (after San Francisco in 1955–56 and North Carolina in 1956–57),

Five players started every game for UCLA: Keith Erickson, Gail Goodrich, Walt Hazzard, Jack Hirsch, and Walt Slaughter. The team was short on height—its tallest starter was 6-foot-5—but long on unselfishness.

"This team came closer to realizing its full potential than any team I have ever seen," said coach John Wooden (1910–2010). The title was the first of 10 national championships in 12 years for UCLA.

Venturi's Last Stand

Ken Venturi kept his cool as temperatures soared toward 100 degrees during play at the U.S. Open Golf tournament at the Congressional Country Club in Washington, D.C. Venturi, a once-promising pro who hadn't won on the Professional Golfers' Association (PGA) Tour in four years, had lost his swing and his confidence. But he found it in the heat, firing rounds of 66 and 70 on the 36-hole final day, June 20. It was good enough to win the tournament by four strokes over runnerup Tommy Jacobs.

Venturi was close to heat exhaustion after his morning round. At the 16th tee, overcome by the scorching heat, he said to his playing partner, Raymond Floyd, "I don't know if I can make it in." He did, but he was accompanied by a doctor, who ordered Venturi to take rest periods, swallow salt tablets, and drink iced tea during the last 18 holes. In the final round, Venturi said, "The pin at the end of each hole looked like a telephone pole."

Phillies Phold

On September 21, ace right-hander Jim Bunning beat the Los Angeles Dodgers 3–2 to give the Philadelphia Phillies a six-and-a-half-game lead in the National League race with only 12 to play. Phillies' fans could be excused for excitedly looking ahead to the World Series. After all, they had played in the Fall Classic only two times and never won a championship in the 81-year history of the franchise. Could this finally be their year? Unfortunately . . . no.

The next day, Philadelphia dropped a 1–0 decision to the Cincinnati Reds, and the lead was down to five-and-a-half. The day after that it was four-and-a-half. Then three-and-a-half. In seven days, the Phillies lost seven games, and the lead was gone. Three more losses followed, running the losing streak to 10, and the St. Louis Cardinals, who pieced together an 11-game winning streak that overlapped Philadelphia's long losing streak, won the pennant. The "Phillie Phold" was the biggest late-season collapse ever.

St. Louis, which won on the final day of the season to clinch the pennant, went on to defeat the New York Yankees in seven games in the World Series in October (see page 32).

The Wright Stuff

Mickey Wright continued to be the dominant golfer on the women's tour and added another trophy to her case when she defeated Ruth Jessen in an 18-hole playoff to win the United States Women's Open at the San Diego (California) Country Club on July 12.

Wright shot a playoff-round 70 to earn a two-stroke victory over Jessen and equal the mark of four U.S. Open triumphs first attained by Betsy Rawls (b.1928). Wright previously won the Open in 1958, 1959, and 1961, while also earning a record four LPGA Championships during that time.

In all, Wright won 82 titles in her career (second on the all-time list behind Kathy Whitworth, who had 88 victories). Wright's 13 career wins in major tournaments is second to Patty Berg's 15.

In the Swim

Swimmer Don Schollander (b.1946) of Lake Oswego, Oregon, became the first swimmer to win four gold medals at one Olympic Games, and the first American to win four Olympic gold medals since Jesse Owens (1913–1980) in 1936. In the Games held in October in Tokyo, Japan, Schollander captured individual victories in the 100-meter freestyle and the 400-meter freestyle, and team wins by swimming the anchor legs of the 4-by-100-meter and 4-by-200-meter freestyle relays. He set world re-

Good as Gold   *That's American Olympic star Don Schollander on the far left in Tokyo in 1964. Fellow U.S. swimming gold medalists Gary Illman, Roy Saari, and Steve Clark pose with him.*

1964

cords in all events except for the 100—where he set an Olympic mark.

"This was the greatest moment in American swimming history," said U.S. swimming coach James Counsilman. Schollander, who was just 18, went on to win a gold medal and a silver medal at the 1968 Olympics in Mexico City.

Big Shot

Al Oerter (b.1936), a shot putter, won gold medals at the 1956, 1960, 1964, and 1968 Olympic Games, but his most amazing Olympic performance came in 1964. He suffered from extreme back pain, and less than one week before the Olympics he tore some rib cartilage (cartilage is elastic skeletal tissue). Doctors advised him to rest for six weeks, but Oerter decided to compete anyway. Before the shot-put event, Oerter told another athlete, "If I don't do it on the first throw, I won't be able to do it at all."

But Oerter's first throw only went 189 feet, 1 inch (57.63 meters). After four rounds, he was in third place. On his final throw, Oerter gave it his all. While he doubled over in pain, his discus sailed 200 feet, 1 inch (61 meters) to set another Olympic record and earn him a third gold medal. Oerter won his fourth gold in 1968. He was the first track-and-field Olympian to win his event four straight times.

End of a Dynasty

The National League-champion St. Louis Cardinals defeated the A.L.'s New York Yankees in October to win the World Series in seven games.

The Yankees' Mickey Mantle, playing in his final Fall Classic, batted .333 with three home runs and eight runs batted in (RBI). His home run off St. Louis pitcher Barney Schultz in the bottom of the ninth inning to win game three gave Mantle 15 career World Series home runs, surpassing the mark set by Babe Ruth. Mantle played in 12 World Series and was on the winning team eight times. He holds World Series records for home runs (18), runs scored (42), RBI (40), walks (43), extra-base hits (26), and total bases (123).

The Cardinals prevailed in the 1964 Series, however, behind the overpowering pitching of Bob Gibson (b.1935), who won two Series games and struck out 31 Yankees in 27 innings.

The Series loss turned out to be an omen for the great Yankees' dynasty that started in the 1920s and peaked from 1947 to 1964. During those 18 seasons, the Yankees won 15 A.L. pennants and 10 World Series. But after never having to wait more than four years to reach a World Series, the Bronx Bombers did not make it back again for 12 years.

It was truly the end of an era. Dan Topping sold the Yankees to the CBS television network in 1964. The next year, the team, which had gone 40 years without a losing record, dropped to sixth place, and in 1966 finished dead last.

Cleveland Rocks

Jim Brown of the Cleveland Browns, playing in his eighth pro season, became the first runner in NFL history to gain 10,000 yards in his career. Brown led the league in rushing for the seventh time in 1964, and then ran for 114 yards on 27 carries in the Browns' 27–0 rout of the Baltimore Colts in the NFL title game in Cleveland December 27.

It was the last NFL title won by the original Cleveland Browns franchise. In 1996, team owner Art Modell moved the team to Baltimore (the Colts were gone to Indianapolis by then), where the franchise changed its name to the Ravens. Cleveland was left without a pro football team until 1999, when NFL expansion plans brought a new team to the city and restored the Browns' name and uniforms.

Other Milestones of 1964

✔ The American Football League received $36 million from NBC when the network agreed January 29 to televise its games for the next five years. The agreement gave each of the league's eight teams $900,000 a year to spend on players and operations. NBC's decision came after CBS won the right to broadcast NFL games for $28.2 million for two years.

✔ Bob Baun of the Toronto Maple Leafs was carried from the ice after fracturing his ankle while blocking a slap shot in game six of the NHL Stanley Cup finals against the Detroit Red Wings on April 23. In overtime, on the edge of elimination, Baun returned to the ice and scored the game-winning goal. Two days later, the Leafs won game seven with Baun still skating on a broken leg. It was Toronto's third Stanley Cup championship in a row.

✔ Ken Johnson of the Houston Colt .45s (now the Astros) threw a no-hitter against the Cincinnati Reds on April 26, but the Reds won the game 1–0. Because of two ninth-inning errors, Johnson became the first pitcher to throw a complete game no-hitter and lose.

✔ On June 21, Philadelphia Phillies right-hander Jim Bunning pitched the Major Leagues' first perfect game in 42 years. He blanked the New York Mets 6–0 at Shea Stadium in New York.

✔ On August 1, Don Garlits (b.1932), the man fellow drag racers call "Big Daddy," was the first Top Fuel driver to surpass 200 miles per hour. Garlits drove his Swamp Rat dragster to victory in 35 National Hot Rod Association (NHRA) Top Fuel events in his career.

✔ The great thoroughbred Kelso (1957–1983) retired after winning his fifth consecutive Horse of the Year title. In 63 starts, Kelso won 39 races and finished second 12 times.

✔ The first Wham-O Professional plastic flying disk, the Olympic Ring #1 model—soon to be better known as the Frisbee—rolled off the production line. By 1969, the Frisbee became such a part of American culture that astronauts took one to the moon.

✔ On October 25, Minnesota Vikings defensive end Jim Marshall famously ran 66 yards the wrong way after recovering a fumble. The play resulted in a safety for the visiting San Francisco 49ers, but Minnesota went on to win anyway, 27–22.

✔ The batting glove was introduced by outfielder Ken Harrelson of the Kansas City Athletics.

✔ In November, St. Louis Hawks forward Bob Pettit (b.1932) became the first player in NBA history to score 20,000 points in his career.

1965

Dome Sweet Dome

Baseball's Houston Astros became the first professional sports team to play its home games in a domed stadium, the Astrodome. The Astrodome was also the first stadium to have a field covered with plastic grass called AstroTurf.

The Astrodome, dubbed the Eighth Wonder of the World, opened in April to 47,876 curious fans, including the President of the United States, Lyndon Johnson, all of whom had come to watch an exhibition game between the Astros and the New York Yankees. Mickey Mantle got the park's first hit and its first home run. As if the dome wasn't enough, gimmicks included a scoreboard pyrotechnic display after each Astros' home run.

The original playing surface actually was a natural grass field, but the synthetic turf was installed in 1966 when the grass could not sustain its growth.

"Havlicek Stole the Ball!"

The scene was the Boston Garden, April 15, game seven of the Eastern Division NBA finals. The Philadelphia 76ers trailed the Boston Celtics, 110–109, with five seconds remaining in the game. The 76ers still had a chance. Philadelphia's guard, Hal Greer, attempted to pass the ball inbounds to Chet Walker, but Boston's John Havlicek (b.1940) leaped and tipped the ball to teammate Sam Jones (b.1933). The raspy radio call by Celtics announcer Johnny Most—"Havlicek stole the ball! Havlicek stole the ball!"—became one of the most famous sports broadcasts of all time.

In the championship round, the Celtics defeated the Los Angeles Lakers in five games to capture their seventh straight title.

A Gentle Giant

Lew Alcindor (b.1947) was one of the most talked-about players to come out of New York City. As a 6-foot-8 teenager, he led Power Memorial High School to a record of 95 wins and only six losses. He won All-America honors his last three years and led the school to three city championships. On May 4, Alcindor, the first basketball player to be highly recruited on a national level, announced his decision to accept a scholarship to play for coach John Wooden at UCLA.

Schoolboy Star *Lew Alcindor (33) went from a high school star to a college basketball powerhouse.*

In three varsity seasons, Alcindor's teams won 88 games and lost only two. A two-time player of the year, he led UCLA to three national titles and was named the NCAA tournament MVP all three times. UCLA won back-to-back championships in 1964 and 1965, and could now claim true dynasty status with five national titles in six years. Alcindor, who had grown to 7-foot-1, was such an unstoppable scorer that, in 1967, the NCAA outlawed dunking to slow him down. (The dunk was legalized again nine years later.)

Alcindor was the first player picked in the 1969 NBA draft, by the last-place Milwaukee Bucks. In the 1970–71 season,

1965

he averaged 31.7 points per game and teamed with Oscar Robertson to lead the Bucks to an NBA title. During the season, he changed his name to Kareem Abdul-Jabbar. He had been a Muslim since college, and he wanted to show his faith publicly. Abdul-Jabbar won six MVP awards and was a member of six NBA championship teams. In his 20-year career, he set many league records, including most points scored (38,387).

The Phantom Punch

Muhammad Ali retained the heavyweight championship when he knocked out Sonny Liston in the first round of their rematch in Lewiston, Maine on May 25. Ringside officials scored the KO at one minute, the media at 1:42, and referee Jersey Joe Walcott at 2:17.

No matter whose clock you time it by, the fight was still over in round one. No other heavyweight title bout was decided that early until Mike Tyson dispatched Michael Spinks in 91 seconds in 1988.

The ending was controversial, and some spectators yelled "Fake!" and "Fix!" Many were angered because the punch—a short right hand that sent the 215-pound Liston to the canvas for the first time in his career—did not seem to have knockout power. The press would sarcastically label the final blow "The Phantom Punch."

Koufax the Magnificent

Los Angeles Dodgers left-hander Sandy Koufax became the first pitcher in baseball history to throw four no-hitters in his career. On September 9 against the Chicago Cubs, Koufax struck out 14 and retired all 27 batters he faced for a perfect game.

Poor Bob Hendley, the Cubs' pitcher, only gave up one hit in his team's 1-0 loss. Nolan Ryan (b.1947) broke Koufax's record with his fifth no-hitter in 1981.

In 1965, Koufax put up some of the best numbers of any pitcher ever, going 26–8, with eight shutouts, an N.L.-leading 2.04 ERA, and a major league-record 382 strikeouts (until Ryan broke that record, too, in 1973). Then the southpaw from Brooklyn dominated the Minnesota Twins by pitching shutouts in games five and seven of the World Series to lead Los Angeles to victory. He wrapped up his season by winning the Cy Young Award.

Six Times Six

Chicago Bears' rookie running back Gale Sayers (b.1943) burst into the National Football League record book on December 12 when he scored six touchdowns in his team's 61–20 rout of the San Francisco 49ers at Wrigley Field. Sayers equaled the record first set in 1929 by the Chicago Cardinals' Ernie Nevers and matched in 1951 by Dub Jones of the Cleveland Browns.

Sayers was nicknamed "The Kansas Comet." After playing college football at the University of Kansas, he joined the Bears in 1965. In just his third game, he scored four touchdowns. Not surprisingly, Sayers was named the NFL's Rookie of the Year. He combined for 2,272 yards, scored more touchdowns in a season (22) than anyone before him, and scored the most points ever by a rookie (132). He led the league in scoring in 1965 and was runnerup in rushing, punt returns, and kickoff returns.

Sayers went on to lead the NFL in rushing in 1966 and 1969. He averaged five yards per carry and a record 30.6 yards per kick return for his career. Unfortunately, knee injuries forced him to retire after just seven seasons. His was among the shortest and sweetest careers in pro football history. At 34 years old in 1977, he was the youngest player to be inducted into the Pro Football Hall of Fame.

From Bills to Laws

The Buffalo Bills' smothering defense blanked the San Diego Chargers, 23–0, on the road to win the franchise's second straight American Football League title on December 26. Jack Kemp, the future Congressman from New York and a vice-presidential candidate in 1996, quarterbacked the Bills to the AFL championship in 1964 and 1965. The Bills made it to the 1966 AFL title game, but lost, 31–7, to Kansas City.

Other Milestones of 1965

✔ In the NCAA basketball championship on March 20, UCLA guard Gail Goodrich scored a title-game record 42 points (since surpassed) to lead the Bruins to a 91–80 win over Michigan and their second straight championship.

✔ The Montreal Canadiens won their record 11th Stanley Cup hockey championship in May, defeating the Chicago Blackhawks in seven games.

✔ In motor sports, race car driver Jim Clark surpassed 150 miles per hour at the Indianapolis 500 on May 31 and ushered in the era of rear-engine cars.

✔ Cincinnati Reds pitcher Jim Maloney no-hit the New York Mets for 10 innings June 14 before losing the game 1–0 on a home run in the 11th. But two months later, on August 19, Maloney no-hit the Chicago Cubs for 10 innings. This time, he was a 1–0 winner when teammate Leo Cardenas homered in the top of the 10th.

✔ On September 8, in a game against the California Angels, the Kansas City Athletics' Bert Campaneris (usually a shortstop) became the first player in modern baseball history to play all nine defensive positions in one game.

✔ The bidding war between the NFL and the AFL escalated when the AFL's New York Jets signed popular and talented Alabama quarterback Joe Namath for an unheard-of $427,000.

1966

Bigger and Better

For more than two decades, despite the sport's increasing popularity, the National Hockey League declined to expand beyond its six teams: the Boston Bruins, New York Rangers, Chicago Blackhawks, Detroit Red Wings, Montreal Canadiens, and Toronto Maple Leafs. On February 9, however, NHL owners decided that the time was right. They voted to allow six new teams—all based in the United States—to begin play in the 1967–68 season. The new franchises were the Los Angeles Kings, Minnesota North Stars, Philadelphia Flyers, Pittsburgh Penguins, Buffalo Sabres, and St. Louis Blues. (The Blues reached the Stanley Cup finals in their first season.)

Expansion changed the face of pro hockey. From 1942 to 1967, nearly all the players were from Canada, and few Americans outside of the northern parts of the United States cared much about hockey. However, much has changed over the past 40-plus years. The NHL now has 30 teams. American players have become stars. So have top players from countries all over the world, such as Sweden, Finland, the Czech Republic, and Russia.

New Era in Labor Relations

Few men who never played Major League Baseball have had such an impact on the sport as did Marvin Miller (b. 1917), who spent 17 years as executive director of the Major League Baseball Players' Association beginning in March of 1966. The former chief of the tough steelworkers' union brought that steely reserve to baseball labor relations, and his experience overmatched the team owners, whom he routinely outwitted. Miller changed the fortunes of baseball players and, by extension, all athletes, forever. By the time he retired in 1983, the average salary had skyrocketed from $19,000 to $240,000. Today, that figure is well over $2 million.

Among Miller's other miracles was an end to the reserve clause, which bound a player to his team even when his contract was up. The reserve clause had always been a part of Major League Baseball, and was upheld in 1922 by the Supreme Court as part of the game's antitrust exemption. Free agency, under which a player can freely negotiate with any team when his contract is up, resulted in much higher salaries. Miller also introduced labor disputes, the right of veteran players to veto

The Golden Jet *Chicago Blackhawks wing man Bobby Hull possessed a combination that was lethal to opponents: He was the fastest man in hockey and had one of the most powerful slapshots.*

trades, a vastly improved pension plan funded largely through percentages of television revenue, and recognition of the players' union, which led to the right to collective bargaining.

Miller may have been as unpopular with some fans as he was with the owners, because he led two player strikes—a 13-day strike at the beginning of the 1972 season and a 50-day walkout in the middle of 1981—but his tough tactics finally got the players a bigger piece of the pie in a time of baseball prosperity.

Golden Jet Takes Flight

Blond-haired Bobby Hull (b.1939) was so fast a skater that he became known as the "Golden Jet." The superstar left wing of the Chicago Blackhawks dominated the National Hockey League during the 1960s with his spectacular playing style, breaking scoring records and bringing an excitement to the game that rarely had been seen before.

Hull was electrifying as he glided across the ice at nearly 30 miles an

1966

hour—faster than any other man in his sport. His slap shot, which intimidated opposing goaltenders with its accuracy and speed, was once clocked at 118 miles an hour! Hull's straight-on shot became even scarier when he and teammate Stan Mikita (b.1940) began experimenting with different ways of curving their stick blades. With just the right curve, when Hull unleashed his slap shot, the rock-hard rubber puck was on the rise as it careened toward the goalie.

On March 12, in a game against the New York Rangers at Madison Square Garden, Hull became the first NHL player to score more than 50 goals in a season. He scored his 51st goal in the season's 61st game. Hull's record goal came on a 40-foot slap shot at 5:34 of the final period, tying the game at 2–2. The Blackhawks, who went on to win, 4–2, had set up a screen in front of Cesar Maniago, the Rangers' goalie, when Hull shot.

Hull, a 27-year-old, 5-foot-10, 195-pounder, won his second consecutive Art Ross Trophy as the league's Most Valuable Player in 1965–66. He finished his record-setting season with 54 goals and 97 points. Other players, including Hull, had scored exactly 50 in a season, but nobody had ever done that twice, so Hull was also the first player to score 50 goals in a season more than once. And he was the player with the highest single-season point total to date. Before Hull's career ended, he reached the 50-goal mark three more times, for a total of five 50-goal seasons.

Landmark Hoops Game

Texas Western College, with an all-black starting five, outplayed all-white University of Kentucky in the game that would be called the *Brown vs. Board of Education* of college basketball. (The famous Supreme Court ruling in *Brown* outlawed school segregation across the United States.) The Texas Miners (whose school eventually changed its name to the University of Texas–El Paso) defeated the Kentucky Wildcats 72–65 on March 19 to win the NCAA men's basketball title.

Although both teams entered the final game with 26-1 records, legendary Kentucky coach Adolph Rupp (1901–1977) had said, "No five blacks are going to beat Kentucky." Rupp, age 64, had won

Basketball Breakthrough *Texas Western's all-black team shocked Kentucky to win the college title.*

four national championships as coach of Kentucky, and he had never allowed a black player on his team. But on Texas Western's second possession, David Lattin sent a clear message to Kentucky when he slammed a vicious dunk over a stunned Pat Riley, the Wildcats' star player (and later a championship-winning NBA coach). Then with 10 minutes gone in the first half, the smallest man on the court, Bobby Joe Hill (1943–2002), stole the ball on consecutive Kentucky possessions and converted both steals into layups. From there, Texas Western dominated much of the rest of the game.

The game made a lasting impression on many sports fans because this was an era when few important teams started more than two or three black players. Don Haskins (1930–2002), the coach of Texas Western, said the game's historic significance didn't sink in until he received "bushelsful of hate mail." Years later, when asked if he regretted that the race issue overshadowed his team's accomplishments, Haskins said, "All I did was play my best people. It was that simple" (as quoted in his December 13, 2002, obituary in *The New York Times*).

In 1969, Rupp recruited his first black player, then he retired. More than 40 years later, the Miners' victory is still hailed as the signature moment for the racial integration of college sports.

Pro Football Makes Peace

A series of clandestine meetings between American Football League representative Lamar Hunt (the owner of the Kansas City Chiefs) and National Football League representative Tex Schramm (the general manager of the Dallas Cowboys) led to a merger between the two pro-football leagues on June 8. It ended seven years of war between the leagues.

The merger agreement called for the first combined draft in 1967, with the idea of eliminating costly bidding wars. The merger was not going to be fully in place until 1970, when the two leagues' multimillion dollar television contracts ended. But the next step, after the combined draft, was a world championship game pitting the two champions from each league against one another—the first Super Bowl (see page 44).

Ironically, the bitter feud between the AFL and NFL eventually resulted in a healthier professional football league. Because of competition between the two leagues, the AFL awarded franchises to cities where NFL teams were already established, and the NFL raced to place clubs in new territories, making football a truly national sport. With television investing in both the NFL and AFL, each team's television revenues grew as more fans turned on their TV sets. Players' salaries were growing higher, but so were the number of fans filling the stadiums.

When a Tie Equals Victory

Notre Dame coach Ara Parseghian had to know that the jokes soon would be coming—and they did. The Fighting Irish soon were derisively called the "Tying Irish" by their critics. The famous saying was no longer, "Win One for the Gipper," it was "Tie One for the Gipper." But Parseghian knew what he

1966

was doing when his top-ranked team settled for a 10–10 tie with No. 2 Michigan State in college football's biggest game of the season on November 19. The game was played in front of 80,011 frenzied fans at Michigan's Spartan Stadium and another 30 million watching at home—the largest television audience ever for a regularly scheduled college football game.

The much-ballyhooed matchup became a crisis for Notre Dame midway in the first quarter, when starting quarterback Terry Hanratty (b.1948) got knocked out of the game by a shoulder separation when Bubba Smith (b.1945), the Spartans' 283-pound lineman, fell on top of him. The Irish led the nation in scoring offense under the leadership of Hanratty, who passed for 1,247 yards on the season. But without its quarterback, Notre Dame's offense was forced to play conservatively. Still, despite its impressive offense, defense had been the key to the success of this Notre Dame team, which shut out six of its last eight opponents.

Parseghian (b.1923) compiled a record of 95–17–4 during his 11 seasons at Notre Dame beginning in 1964, and deserves credit for returning the team to its past glory. But he will forever be accused of lacking courage in the Michigan State game after he chose to run out the clock and settle for a tie to preserve his team's national ranking. The Irish had their shot at victory, but Parseghian ordered four running plays after getting the ball for the last time on his own 35-yard line with a minute and a half to play. "If it was early in the fourth quarter it would have been different," said Parseghian, "but we weren't going to give up the ball deep in our territory and take a risk of losing the game after battling like we did."

The strategy worked, as both Notre Dame and Michigan State finished the season with identical 9–0–1 records. But the Irish were named the number-one team in the polls.

Out on Top

Lots of pro athletes like to say that it's their dream to walk away from sports at the height of their glory, with their talents undiminshed by age or injury. But for whatever reason—whether it's the lure of bigger and bigger paychecks, the adulation of the fans, or simply the unquenchable desire to compete—few men (or women) who make their living playing sports retire in their prime. Pro Football Hall of Fame member Jim Brown is the exception to the rule. In 1966, Brown, considered by many observers to be the greatest fullback ever, retired from football to pursue an acting career.

At the time, Brown was only 30 years old and was coming off a season in which he had won the league's Most Valuable Player award. In nine seasons with the Cleveland Browns, from 1957 to 1965, Brown never missed a game or a Pro Bowl. By the time he retired, he held just about every rushing record imaginable, including a career mark of 12,312 rushing yards.

Besides his acting career (he appeared in *The Dirty Dozen* and *100 Rifles*, among other films), Brown has worked to help African-Americans improve their economic situation. Along with being an outspoken critic of unfairness and racism, he also works to rehabilitate gang members in the Los Angeles area. He was elected to the Pro Football Hall of Fame in 1971.

Koufax KO'd by Injury

Like Jim Brown, Los Angeles Dodgers ace left-hander Sandy Koufax still was at the top of his game when he retired on November 18. Unlike Brown, though, the 30-year-old Koufax's decision was made for him, in large part, because of injury. "I am leaving the game while I can still comb my hair," he said.

Koufax was the Cy Young Award winner as the top pitcher for the second consecutive season in 1966—at the time, the award was given to just one pitcher from both leagues. Also for the second year in a row, he topped the league in wins (27), ERA (1.73), innings pitched (323), and strikeouts (317). But he suffered from severe arthritis in his throwing arm, which caused him incredible pain. Sometimes he lost all feeling in his pitching hand. His arm swelled enormously after each game and had to be iced. He had to take countless cortisone shots, and didn't want to risk permanent damage to his left arm—or his health.

Between 1962 and 1966, Koufax was the game's most dominating pitcher. He won three Cy Young Awards and pitched four no-hitters, including a perfect game. He helped the Dodgers win four pennants and three World Series. In 1972, at the age of 36, he became the youngest man ever elected to the National Baseball Hall of Fame.

Other Milestones of 1966

✔ Nineteen years after Jackie Robinson broke baseball's color barrier, the Opening Day crowd at Washington's Griffith Stadium on April 11 watched as Emmett Ashford, baseball's first African-American umpire, took the field. Major League Baseball's first black manager, Frank Robinson, wasn't named until 1975.

✔ Tennis player Billie Jean King, at age 22, won her first major tournament, the Wimbledon singles final, after stunning the defending champion, Margaret Court, in a straight-set semifinal match on July 2.

✔ Atlanta Braves right-hander Tony Cloninger drove in nine runs—the most ever in a game by a pitcher—in his team's 17–3 rout of the San Francisco Giants on July 3 at Candlestick Park.

✔ Nineteen-year-old Jim Ryun set a new world record in the mile run with a time of 3 minutes, 51.3 seconds during a competition at Edwards Stadium in Berkeley, California.

✔ Outfielder Frank Robinson (b.1935) of the World Series-champion Baltimore Orioles was named the American League's Most Valuable Player. Robinson, who had won the MVP award with the Cincinnati Reds in 1961, became the first baseball player to win the award in both leagues.

✔ On September 13, Baltimore Colts quarterback John Unitas became pro football's all-time career leader for most touchdown passes. Six weeks later, Unitas became the leader in passing yards, too.

1967

The First Super Bowl

Little did anyone realize the enormity to which the Super Bowl would grow when the Green Bay Packers defeated the Kansas City Chiefs 35–10 in the first game between the champions of the National and American Football Leagues, held in Los Angeles on January 15.

That first Super Bowl wasn't even called the Super Bowl back then. Officially, it was called the "AFL-NFL World Championship Game." There were lots of other differences between the game then and now, too.

For instance, only 63,036 fans attended the game at the Los Angeles Memorial Coliseum. That meant more than 30,000 seats were empty. (There is no such thing as an empty seat at a Super Bowl these days.) Many of the spectators left by the fourth quarter.

The game was broadcast on two television networks. An estimated 60 million curious viewers tuned in to watch either on NBC or CBS. At least twice that many people watch the Super Bowl today.

And a ticket to the first Super Bowl cost $12. The cost of a ticket to Super Bowl XLIV, in January 2010, was $325.

Bart Starr (b.1934), the quarterback of the NFL's Packers, was the MVP of Super Bowl I. He completed 16 of 23 passes for 250 yards and two touchdowns. Both of the touchdowns went to Max McGee, a 34-year-old substitute who was in action only because starting receiver Boyd Dowler got hurt early in the game. McGee's first touchdown came on an outstanding one-handed catch of a pass thrown behind him. McGee, who caught only four passes during the regular season, had 7 receptions for 138 yards against the Chiefs.

The Packers dominated the NFL during the 1960s, but they knew they were in a challenging game against the upstart Chiefs, and led only 14–10 at halftime. Doubt about the outcome disappeared in the third quarter, when Green Bay stretched its lead to 28–10. The key play came on the fourth play after halftime. That's when all-pro safety Willie Wood intercepted a pass and returned it 50 yards deep into Chiefs' territory.

The NFL was relieved to have captured bragging rights in the first Super Bowl. And while that game may have had modest beginnings, the spectacle of the Super Bowl only got bigger and bigger.

Powerful Pack *Green Bay running back Donny Anderson follows the blocking of guard Gale Gillingham.*

New Kid on the Block

While the upstart AFL and the established NFL were on the road to peace, a war between the new American Basketball Association and the established National Basketball Association was just beginning.

The ABA began play in 1967. It had 10 teams. The league lasted only nine seasons, but it made important contributions to professional basketball. It featured an All-Star Slam-Dunk Contest, and it introduced the three-point shot more than a decade before the NBA.

The league—which played with a red, white, and blue ball—had many stars, too, most notably Julius Erving (b.1950), known as "Dr. J." Erving was the ABA's Most Valuable Player in the league's last three seasons (he shared the 1975 award with George McGinnis).

The league went out of business in 1976, but four of its teams—the Denver Nuggets, Indiana Pacers, New York (now New Jersey) Nets, and San Antonio Spurs—were invited to join the NBA. As of the 2002–03 season, the Spurs are the only former ABA team to win an NBA championship (they'd done it twice).

1967

No Dunking Allowed

UCLA, led by its new star, Lew Alcindor (who eventually changed his name to Kareem Abdul-Jabbar), forged another perfect season (30–0) in college basketball. In the NCAA championship game, Alcindor scored 20 points and grabbed 18 rebounds in a 79–64 rout of the University of Dayton on March 25. It was UCLA's third NCAA title in four years, with the promise of more to follow. Alcindor—just a sophomore—averaged 29 points and already dominated the college game like nobody before him.

Opposing coaches felt they needed to cut Alcindor and UCLA down to size. And his almost unstoppable slam dunk seemed a good place to start. Basketball traditionalists found the dunk boring to watch, and critics said the stuff shot gave an unfair advantage to the new breed of taller players. After the 1966–67 season, the National Basketball Committee of the United States and Canada (a body of college coaches) banned all dunking and stuffing. The group's stated reasons: There is no defense against the dunk, and that upsets the balance of the game; players can injure themselves; dunking breaks backboards and bends basket rims.

In reality, the Alcindor Rule, as it came to be called, was a sorry attempt by the coaching fraternity to keep UCLA from winning another national title. It was one year since an all-black Texas Western team defeated an all-white Kentucky team for the national title (see page 40), and race relations were on shaky ground. Many people saw more than coincidence in the fact that the dunk was outlawed just when Alcindor, who is black, began to dominate the college game. Others considered the rule the last desperate act of racially insensitive "basketball purists," frustrated at watching the game become an increasingly high-wire game dominated by talented African Americans.

Did the no-dunk rule work? Well, in Alcindor's two remaining college seasons, UCLA lost just two games and won two more national titles. The rule forced Alcindor to perfect his jump shot and develop a different shot that was virtually impossible to defend against—the "sky hook" (a hook shot in which he held the ball high over his head).

Ali Takes a Stand

"I ain't got no quarrel with those Vietcong." With that famous statement to reporters, boxing champ Muhammad Ali articulated the feelings of many Americans who were against the controversial, ongoing war in Vietnam.

By 1967, the Vietnam War had been raging for almost eight years. U.S. military involvement in the conflict had grown considerably in that time, while at home anti-war feelings had grown even more rapidly. Millions of Americans objected strongly to American troops being sent to Southeast Asia to fight against Communist Vietcong rebels. In addition, a high percentage of the soldiers were African American, and the ongoing Civil Rights Movement added this to their list of grievances against the government.

In the middle of this, Ali got a letter that changed his life and, in many ways, the ongoing relationship between sports and politics.

At that time, the U.S. government held an annual draft to fill the ranks of the armed forces. Young men were assigned a draft number based on their birthday, and when their number came up, they were required by law to report for duty. Ali was aware of this, and for months, had been trying to have himself classified as a "conscientious objector" (CO). COs are people who object to war or violence because of religious beliefs. Ali felt that his beliefs in Islam, specifically his membership in the American Black Muslim movement (which he had joined in 1964), prohibited him from fighting in a war.

However, the government did not want Ali to become a symbol of Black Muslim power and refused to make him a CO. The fateful letter told him that he had been drafted, and, on April 28, Ali reported to the draft board in Louisville to join the Army. In a scene that would become a noted historical moment of the 1960s, an Army sergeant called out, "Cassius Marcellus Clay, step forward." Ali refused. By refusing, Ali was committing a federal crime, evading the draft.

Reaction was swift and harsh. In June, Ali was convicted of draft evasion, sentenced to five years in prison, and fined $10,000. As the case was appealed, his passport was taken away, so he could not travel. Then, Ali was stripped of his heavyweight title by international boxing authorities. Over the next few years, however, many things would change, in America and in the world, and Ali would rise to the top again. By 1971, he was back in the ring. By 1975, the war was over.

The Impossible Dream

In 1966, the Boston Red Sox finished in ninth place in baseball's 10-team American League. But in 1967, under the guidance of new manager Dick Williams, and behind the 22 wins from pitcher Jim

Muhammad Ali, CO *After refusing to step forward when called to the draft board, Muhammad Ali (left) was arrested and led out of the Lexington, Kentucky Army facility.*

1967

Lonborg, the Red Sox turned things around. In the closest A.L. race ever, four teams, including the Red Sox, battled it out in the last week of the season.

Boston's left fielder, Carl Yastrzemski (b.1939), almost singlehandedly lifted the Red Sox to the pennant. Boston needed to win the last two games of the regular season against the Minnesota Twins to avoid a three-way tie with the Twins and the Detroit Tigers. "Yaz" had seven hits in eight at-bats, with five runs batted in, to lead the Red Sox to two victories and their first pennant in 21 years.

Yastrzemski won the A.L. Most Valuable Player award for 1967, as well as the Triple Crown, leading the league with his .326 average, 44 home runs, and 121 runs batted in. He continued his hot hitting in the World Series in October, batting .400 in the Fall Classic against the St. Louis Cardinals. But in the Series, St. Louis pitcher Bob Gibson (b.1935), who won three games, and the Cardinals were too much for the Red Sox, who lost in seven games. Boston's Fenway faithful called the 1967 season "the impossible dream."

O.J.! Oh My!

The rivalry between the University of Southern California Trojans and the UCLA Bruins is one of the fiercest in all of college football. On November 18, the two crosstown rivals met in a game at the Los Angeles Coliseum that had much at stake. On the line was a Rose Bowl bid, a possible national championship, and, perhaps, the Heisman Trophy.

UCLA came into the game undefeated and ranked number one in the nation.

Led by their senior quarterback, Gary Beban, the Bruins broke a 14–14 tie early in the fourth quarter when Beban threw his second touchdown pass of the game. But USC's Bill Hayhoe blocked Zenon Andrusyshyn's extra-point try, leaving the score 20–14. The missed conversion was critical, because USC had a star of its own, magnificent halfback O.J. Simpson (b.1947), who rushed for 177 yards and two scores. Simpson ran for the winning touchdown only moments later. It came on a dazzling 64-yard run that began with Simpson taking a handoff, faking right, and then sprinting around the left end of the field. He cut toward the middle of the field at the Bruins' 40-yard line and, sprung by a block from Earl McCullouch, outran his pursuers into the end zone. The extra point was good, giving USC a hard-fought 21–20 victory.

The Trojans went on to defeat Indiana University 14–3 in the Rose Bowl in Pasadena, California, in January. Coach John McKay's USC team finished the season with a 10-1 record and captured the national championship. Simpson rushed for 1,415 yards in 266 attempts during the season, averaging 5.3 yards per carry and scoring 23 touchdowns. But the UCLA quarterback, Beban, won the Heisman Trophy in a close race. Simpson won the award the following year as a senior.

The Ice Bowl

The Green Bay Packers and Dallas Cowboys closed the calendar year in 1967 by playing one of the most famous games in NFL history on December 31. Quarterback Bart Starr ran one yard for the winning touchdown in the closing seconds of a 21–17 victory that gave the Packers the NFL championship. The dramatic title game has come to be known as the "Ice Bowl." The temperature on the field was measured at minus-13 degrees Fahrenheit, but the frozen tundra of Green Bay's Lambeau Field made it feel like 35 below zero with the wind chill.

The Packers trailed the Cowboys 17–14 with 16 seconds left in the game, but Green Bay had the ball on the Dallas one-yard line. In the huddle, Starr called a play for a handoff to a running back, who would plow over Packer right guard Jerry Kramer into the end zone. Only head coach Vince Lombardi and Starr knew the quarterback would actually keep the ball.

On a playing field frozen rock hard, Kramer dug his foot into an unusually soft area of turf and made a critical block that allowed Starr to score the winning touchdown.

Green Bay won its third straight NFL title and advanced to Super Bowl II against the Oakland Raiders. The Packers beat Oakland in January 1968 to win their second straight Super Bowl.

Other Milestones of 1967

✔ Bobby Orr of the Boston Bruins won the Calder Memorial Trophy as hockey's best rookie player. Three years later, he became the first defenseman to lead the league in scoring. That 1969–70 season was Orr's coming-out party. He became the first hockey player to win four individual season trophies: the regular-season Most Valuable Player, league scoring leader, outstanding defenseman, and playoff MVP.

✔ In June, the San Francisco (now Golden State) Warriors' Rick Barry became the first NBA star to jump to the ABA when he signed with the Oakland Oaks. But in August, a court ruled that his contract obligated him to play one more year for the Warriors. Barry decided to sit out the season instead.

✔ Billie Jean King won the women's titles at Wimbledon and at the U.S. Open. King also teamed with Rosemary Casals and Australian Owen Davidson to win the women's doubles and mixed doubles at both Wimbledon and the U.S. Open, making her the first woman to accomplish that sweep since Alice Marble in 1939.

✔ Bowling continued to gain in popularity, and bowling alleys continued to introduce new innovations. In the 1960s, bowling proprietors helped patrons who could not figure out the sport's unique scoring method. Bowling alleys introduced the new automatic score.

✔ In December, the United States Soccer Association and the National Professional Soccer League combined to form the 17-team North American Soccer League (NASL). The NASL, which eventually attracted several big-name world stars, lasted through 1984.

✔ Richard Petty streaked through the most dominant season in NASCAR history. He set a record by winning 27 races, including 10 in a row, out of 48 starts in 1967. He also won his 55th career race, passing his father, Lee, for the most ever.

1968

Battle of the Big Men

The game between the University of Houston Cougars and the UCLA Bruins at the Astrodome on January 20 was one of the epic matchups in college basketball history. It pitted the Cougars' 48-game home winning streak against the Bruins' 47-game winning streak, the second longest in college basketball history; Houston center Elvin Hayes (b.1945) against UCLA big man Lew Alcindor; and the No. 1 team in the nation (UCLA) against No. 2.

In the end, the hometown Cougars won 71–69 before 52,693 fans in attendance and a national television audience. Hayes' two free throws with 28 seconds to play—to shouts of "E! E! E!"—made the difference.

The 6-foot-8 Hayes, known as "The Big E," scored 39 points, grabbed 15 rebounds, and blocked four shots. He also contained the 7-foot-1 Alcindor, a junior who scored only 15 points, but was playing with a scratched eyeball that had caused him to miss UCLA's two previous games.

Two months later, the Cougars brought a 32-game winning streak into the NCAA tournament, and the two teams faced off again in a much-anticipated semifinal game. This time, the Bruins turned the tables. Alcindor had 19 points and 18 rebounds while limiting Hayes to 10 points in a 101–69 UCLA rout on March 22. The next day, Alcindor scored 34 points in the final as the Bruins beat North Carolina 78–55. It was UCLA's fourth championship in five years under coach John Wooden.

The Ice Queen

The United States won only one gold medal at the Winter Olympic Games in Grenoble, France, in February, but it was a memorable one by figure skater Peggy Fleming (b.1948). Her triumph helped change the face of skating.

Fleming was a graceful skater who made tough moves look easy. She won the U.S. figure skating championship and the hearts of Americans in 1964, when she was just 15 years old. She went on to win five national titles, three world titles, and the Olympic gold medal.

Fleming's victory in the Olympics was not only a personal triumph, but also a victory of the ballet approach over the athletic approach to figure skating.

Power Pitcher   *The St. Louis Cardinals' Bob Gibson (throwing, above) was baseball's best pitcher in 1968, but the Detroit Tigers' Mickey Lolich led his team to victory in the World Series.*

Until the graceful Colorado State College skater came along, women's figure skating threatened to be dominated by skaters who stressed athletic jumping ability. But Fleming, at 5-foot-4 and weighing only 108 pounds, represented a more dance-like approach in which the elements blend smoothly as the skater flows across the ice.

Events at the 1968 Winter Games foreshadowed the struggles between the International Olympic Committee (IOC) and the athletes. The first hint of the brewing storm occurred when the president of the IOC, Avery Brundage (1887–1975), threatened to cancel the skiing events unless athletes removed the manufacturers' labels on their equipment. Although he temporarily backed away from this rigid position, he had laid the foundation for a more explosive incident in the next Olympics. Austrian skier Karl Schranz was banned three days before the 1972 Olympics opened for accepting payments from his equipment manufacturer.

1968

Politics at the Olympics

Throughout history, the Olympic Games have reflected the times in which they are played. The 1960s were an emotionally charged decade. The struggle over human rights and the Vietnam War, in particular, resulted in assassinations, civil-rights protests, and anti-war rallies. The spirit of the 60s was also reflected at the 1968 Summer Olympics in Mexico City, held in October.

The Games saw a burst of record-breaking performances in the track-and-field events, perhaps helped along by the thin air of high-altitude Mexico City. The games were also rocked by protest over racial injustice. American sprinters Tommie Smith and John Carlos caused a sensation on the victory platform after the 200-meter dash by bowing their heads and raising gloved fists during the playing of the U.S. National Anthem. Their purpose was to publicize and protest prejudice against blacks in sport and society. Avery Brundage, the IOC president, was furious over the silent, non-violent protest and expelled both athletes from the Olympic village.

Beamon Takes Flight

Waiting his turn in the finals of the Summer Olympics long-jump competition in Mexico City in 1968, American Bob Beamon had no inkling what was coming. "Don't foul. Don't foul," he said to himself. Beamon not only didn't foul, but he soared nearly six feet into the air, landing with a world-record jump of 29 feet 2.5 inches (8.9 meters). The world mark, which had increased only 8.25 inches since 1935,

had just been shattered by an astonishing 21.75 inches—nearly two feet!

Beamon's leap has been called the greatest single athletic achievement of all time. Many people predicted that Beamon's long jump record would stand forever. Instead, the record stood for an amazing 23 years. Then, on August 30, 1991, United States jumper Mike Powell flew 29 feet, 4.5 inches at the world championships in Tokyo. Beamon was not upset that his record was broken. "Mine was a jump way before its time," he said. "It almost made it into the 21st century."

Year of the Pitcher

Pitchers were so dominant in Major League Baseball in 1968—perhaps the greatest year for pitchers in baseball history—that owners had to rewrite the rule book after the season to help swing some momentum back the batters' way.

Pitchers such as the Los Angeles Dodgers' Don Drysdale, the Detroit Tigers' Denny McLain, and the St. Louis Cardinals' Bob Gibson overwhelmed opposing hitters. Drysdale pitched six shutouts in a row, McLain won 31 games, and Gibson posted a miniscule earned run average of just 1.12. The entire American League batted only .230, and Carl Yastrzemski of the Boston Red Sox won the A.L. batting title with a .301 average—the lowest average ever to qualify a player for the batting crown.

The next year, the rules changed. The pitcher's mound was lowered and the strike zone was narrowed to give hitters more of a chance against increasingly better pitching. The changes worked. Beginning in 1969, baseball seemed to put an increased emphasis on offense, which eventually led to the tremendous explosion in home runs that we see today.

Football Versus Heidi

The Oakland Raiders defeated the New York Jets 43–32 in an American Football League game in Oakland on November 17. It was an important regular-season matchup between two of the best teams in the league that season, but that's not why it deserves space here. Instead, the game had a lasting impact on tele-vised sports after most of the country missed the exciting conclusion to accommodate *Heidi*, a children's television movie. In fact, the game is still known as the "Heidi game."

When the game ran late, NBC stuck to its regular schedule and cut to the movie *Heidi*. In a thrilling finish, Oakland scored twice in nine seconds and beat the Jets, 43–32. Football fans were furious because they had missed the best part of the game. The TV networks promised never to let that happen again. Now, when football games run long, they continue covering the game.

Other Milestones of 1968

✔ The Green Bay Packers defeated the Oakland Raiders 33–14 in Super Bowl II at the Orange Bowl in Miami, Florida on January 14. It was the Packers' second straight victory in the Super Bowl and the last game on the team's sidelines for legendary head coach Vince Lombardi.

✔ In April, the Naismith Memorial Basketball Hall of Fame opened in Springfield, Massachusetts. James Naismith invented the game while a YMCA teacher in that city in 1891.

✔ At the 1968 Olympics, American Lee Evans won the 400-meter sprint in a world record time of 43.86 seconds. The record was unbeaten for 20 years, until Butch Reynolds ran 43.29 seconds. Evans also anchored the 4-by-400-meter relay team to the world record and another gold medal.

✔ Also at the Mexico City Games, shot putter Al Oerter of the United States won his fourth gold medal. He became the first track-and-field Olympian to win his event four straight times.

✔ High jumper Dick Fosbury revolutionized his sport (and won a gold medal at the Mexico City Olympics) by performing the high jump in a new way. Fosbury would leap backward over the bar, face up, as opposed to the old "Western Roll," face-down style. His new move was called the Fosbury Flop.

✔ The St. Louis Cardinals' Bob Gibson and the Detroit Tigers' Denny McLain were the headline pitchers, but it was Detroit's Mickey Lolich who won three games, including the deciding game seven, in the Tigers' victory over the Cardinals in the World Series.

✔ Arthur Ashe, competing as an amateur, became the first African-American to win the men's singles title at the U.S. Open when he beat Holland's Tom Okker in a marathon five-set final, 14–12, 5–7, 6–3, 3–6, 6–3.

1969

Namath Keeps Promise

Three days before Super Bowl III between the NFL's Baltimore Colts and the AFL's New York Jets was to be played in Miami, Jets quarterback Joe Namath (b.1943) approached the podium at the Miami Touchdown Club to accept an award. "Hey, Namath, we're gonna kick your butt," a heckler bellowed. Namath, admittedly frustrated at reading all week how his team didn't even belong on the same field as the powerful Colts, got a little hot under the collar. "Wait a minute, pal, I've got news for you," he said. "We're going to win this game. I guarantee it." When the Jets stunned the Colts 16–7 January 12, Namath's guarantee instantly became a part of pro football lore.

The NFL's Green Bay Packers had cruised to victory in the first two Super Bowls, and it seemed as if it would take years for the AFL to catch up with its older rival. And when the Colts entered Super Bowl III with a 15–1 record and a snarling defense that had shut out the Cleveland Browns 34–0 in the NFL Championship Game, the matchup didn't seem fair.

When the Jets won, though, it altered the face of pro football. The Jets' victory proved that the new league was good enough to merge with the NFL, and eased the way for three established NFL teams (the Colts, Pittsburgh Steelers, and Cleveland Browns) to move from the NFC to the AFC when the merger was complete for the 1970 season. The switch evened the conferences at 13 teams each. Each conference currently has 16 teams.

Scoring Machine

Pete Maravich (1947–1988), the Louisiana State University basketball scoring machine, finished his junior season in the spring of 1969 with 1,148 points, setting an NCAA single-season scoring record. The flashy 6-foot-5 sharpshooter known as "Pistol Pete" was even better in his senior season, which began in the fall of 1969, when he scored 1,381 points for an average of 44.5 points a game—records that still stand.

Nobody in college basketball history has ever scored like Maravich. He is the all-time leader in points scored (3,667), career scoring average (44.2), and games in which he scored 50 or more points (28, including 69 in a game in 1970). He was the NCAA scoring leader and an

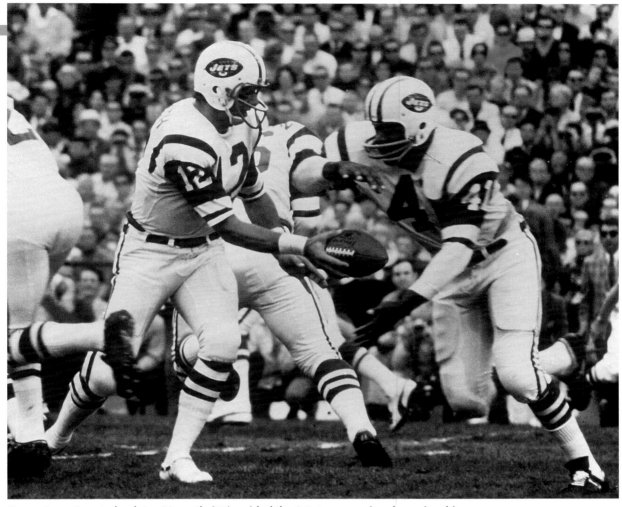

Super Joe *Quarterback Joe Namath (12) guided the Jets to a surprise championship.*

All-America selection three consecutive seasons while at LSU, from 1968 to 1970.

Maravich averaged at least 20 points a game each season during his 10-year pro career with the Atlanta Hawks, New Orleans Jazz, and Boston Celtics. He was a two-time All-Star and, in 1976–77 with the Jazz, led the league with 31.1 points a game. He retired in 1980. He died of a heart attack in 1988 at age 40 while playing pickup basketball in a church gym.

Alcindor Does It Again

In the 1960s, freshmen were not eligible to compete at the varsity level in major college sports. That might be the only reason UCLA center Lew Alcindor left school following the 1968–69 college basketball season with only three national championships instead of four. Alcindor capped his spectacular career with UCLA by leading the Bruins to a

1969

92–72 victory over Purdue University for an unprecedented third straight NCAA championship on March 22.

Alcindor, who changed his name to Kareem Abdul-Jabbar in 1971, scored 37 points and grabbed 20 rebounds in 36 minutes in the title game. He played on three varsity teams in college that recorded an amazing 88 wins in 90 games. UCLA went 30–0 his sophomore year, then the team went 29–1 in his junior year, and this year's squad was 29–1. The title was the fifth in six years for Bruins coach John Wooden.

Super Mario *Mario Andretti is all smiles after taking the checkered flag at the Indianapolis 500. Andretti went on to win the Indy car season championship for 1969, too.*

Dueling Thoroughbreds

Bill Hartack (b.1932) won his record-tying fifth Kentucky Derby by riding Majestic Prince to victory by a neck over Arts and Letters on May 3. The Derby stretch duel between Majestic Prince and Arts and Letters set the stage for a rivalry that continued into the Preakness Stakes, won by Majestic Prince by a head, and the Belmont Stakes, won by Arts and Letters by five lengths. Arts and Letters' victory in the Belmont denied Majestic Prince's bid at the Triple Crown. .

Déjà Vu All Over Again

For the seventh time in 11 years, the Los Angeles Lakers lost the National Basketball Association championship to the Boston Celtics. The Lakers, with three future Hall of Famers in their starting five—Wilt Chamberlain, Elgin Baylor, and Jerry West—were favored in the Finals, but the Celtics came through in the clutch, winning the seventh game in Los Angeles, 108–106, on May 5. Center Bill Russell, who played his final season, led the Celtics to their 11th title in 13 years. Russell, who also served as Boston's coach (he succeeded Red Auerbach in that capacity in 1966), averaged more than 20 rebounds per game in the playoffs.

The NBA awarded a playoff Most Valuable Player award for the first time, and West was the winner, although his team lost. West's form on the court was picture perfect. For proof, check out the NBA logo. The player dribbling straight at you is West. The NBA has used Jerry's silhouette on its logo for the past 30 years.

Indy, Italian Style

Mario Andretti (b.1940) drove his blazing red Hawk-Ford racing car to victory at the Indianapolis 500 on May 30. Upon reaching the winners' circle, Andretti was kissed on the lips by car owner Andy Granatelli, the president of the STP Corporation (whose initials stand for scientifically treated petroleum, an oil additive product for automobiles).

The most versatile driver racing has ever known, Andretti won races on paved tracks, road courses, and dirt tracks in the same season four different times. The 5-foot-6, 138-pounder competed successfully in all three major types of racing: Indy car, stock car, and Formula One. He is the only driver ever to win the Daytona 500 stock car race (1967), the Formula One driving championship (1968), and the Indy car racing championship (1965, 1966, 1969, 1984)!

Stock car racing gets its name because the cars used are common brands of cars, such as Dodge, Chevrolet, and Ford. Indy cars have rear engines and open cockpits. Formula One cars are the smallest in size and are made to handle the tough curves and hills of the Grand Prix courses in Europe. Each type of car requires a special skill to drive it, which makes Andretti's achievements that much more remarkable.

Andretti grew up in Trieste, Italy, before his family came to the United States and settled in Nazareth, Pennsylvania. He began racing cars in 1961, and his 52 Indy car victories ranks second on the all-time list. He also won 12 Formula One races. Andretti retired in 1994, but the Andretti name lives on in driving circles. Mario's son, Michael (b.1962) is also an Indy car driving champion (1991) and the winningest active driver on the Indy circuit. With 42 victories, Michael trails his father by just 10 wins on the all-time list.

Racing Heats Up

Beginning in 1971, any stock-car driver that won three of NASCAR's top four races in the same season earned a cool $1 million bonus. Unfortunately, that came two years too late for auto racer Lee Roy Yarbrough of Columbia, South Carolina. He made history in 1969 by becoming the first stock-car racer to win three of NASCAR's major races in the same season. Yarbrough drove his Ford into Victory Lane at the Daytona 500 and the Southern 500, and won the World 600 in a Mercury.

The R.J. Reynolds Tobacco Company, makers of Winston cigarettes, sponsored NASCAR's championship series from 1971 to 2003. The Winston Cup offered a $1 million bonus to any driver who won three of NASCAR's top four events in the same season. These races included the richest (Daytona 500 in Florida), the fastest (Talladega 500 in Alabama), the longest (World 600 at Charlotte, North Carolina), and the oldest (Southern 500 at Darlington, South Carolina). No driver won all four races, and only four drivers—Yarbrough (1969), David Pearson (1976), Bill Elliott (1985), and Jeff Gordon (1997)—won three. Yarbrough was the only one of the four to miss out on collecting the $1 million bonus.

1969

The Miracle Season

Almost all expansion teams in any professional sport struggle in their early years. But baseball's New York Mets took expansion follies to new heights—or depths—in the early 1960s. The Mets began play in 1962 in the 10-team National League and lost a record 120 of 162 games to finish last, an unfathomable 60 1/2 games out of first place. They dropped at least 109 games each of the next three seasons, too, and in their first seven years escaped the cellar only twice—both times in ninth place.

No one was prepared, then, for what came in 1969, when both the N.L. and A.L. expanded to 12 teams and divisional play began. Each league was divided into two six-team divisions, Eastern and Western. The winners of the two divisions met in a league championship series for the pennant, and the pennant winners went to the World Series.

The Mets were placed in the N.L. Eastern Division. They won 25 of 34 games in September to overtake the Chicago Cubs for first place in the division, then swept the Atlanta Braves in three games to win the N.L. pennant. Then, in October, the Mets stunned the world by beating the mighty Baltimore Orioles in the World Series in five games. It was possibly the biggest upset in World Series history. It was the Mets' first winning season, and they became known as the "Miracle Mets."

No one did more to convert the New York Mets from lovable losers to the Miracle Mets than ace pitcher Tom Seaver (b.1944). "Tom Terrific" joined the Mets in 1967. At age 23, he immediately became the ace of the Mets' staff. He won 16 games in his first year for a team that won only 61, and was named the NL Rookie of the Year. Two years later, Seaver won 25 regular-season games and lifted the Mets from their ninth-place finish in 1968 to the N.L. East title. Fittingly, Seaver started and won the first postseason game in Mets' history, which was also the first National League Championship Series game. Seaver then won one World Series game, and took home the first of his three Cy Young Awards.

Texas No Turkey

The top-ranked University of Texas Longhorns traveled to Fayetteville, Arkansas, to play the second-rated University of Arkansas Razorbacks in a Southwest Conference football showdown on December 5. It was only the thirteenth time since the Associated Press' college football poll debuted in 1936 that No. 1 played No. 2—and it produced the most exciting finish of those matchups. The Longhorns rallied from a 14-point deficit in the fourth quarter to win 15–14.

Both teams entered the contest riding high: Texas had an 18-game winning streak, and Arkansas's streak was 15 in a row. Texas' Darrell Royal, in his 15th year as coach of the Longhorns, was showing off the new Wishbone offense. The Wishbone is a variation of the T-formation in which the halfbacks line up farther from the line of scrimmage than the fullback, giving the backfield the appearance of a wishbone. Royal started using the Wishbone the season before. He made the switch in the backfield because he had three excellent running backs. With only one split end, the wishbone offense is designed for running instead of passing.

The 1969 Texas squad scored an average of 44 points per game during the season and, led by halfback Jim Bertelsmann, led the nation in rushing with an average of 363 yards per game. But against Arkansas, Texas was losing 14–0 after three quarters. With his team down by two touchdowns before 44,000 screaming Arkansas fans, including President Richard M. Nixon, Texas quarterback James Street went to work. First, he broke off a 42-yard touchdown run and sneaked in for a two-point conversion, cutting the deficit to 14–8. Then, on a short yardage, fourth-down play, with Arkansas expecting a run, Street went to the air and connected on a 44-yard pass that set up the go-ahead touchdown with 3:58 remaining.

Arkansas still had one last chance and drove into Texas territory. But the Longhorns sealed the win with an interception at the 21-yard line.

Texas beat Notre Dame in the Cotton Bowl on January 1 to finish the season with an 11–0 record and its second national title of the decade (the other was in 1963). Texas went on to win 30 consecutive games with the wishbone offense before losing to Notre Dame in the Cotton Bowl at the end of the 1970 season.

Other Milestones of 1969

✔ Boston Bruins center Phil Esposito became the first NHL player to score 100 or more points in a season when he scored two goals in Boston's 4–0 victory over the Pittsburgh Penguins at Boston Garden on March 2. The NHL had at least one 100-point scorer for the next 31 years in a row.

✔ Former Canadian prime minister Lester B. Pearson was among 29,184 in attendance April 14 for the first major-league baseball game played outside the United States. The host Montreal Expos, an expansion team, beat the St. Louis Cardinals 8–7 at Jarry Park. (The Expos moved into Olympic Stadium in 1977.)

✔ Baltimore Bullets center Wes Unseld became only the second NBA player (after Wilt Chamberlain in 1960) to earn league Rookie of the Year and Most Valuable Player honors in the same season. Although shorter than most NBA centers at 6-foot-7, Unseld ranked second in the league with an average of 18.2 rebounds per game.

✔ The Alabama International Motor Speedway, now called the Talladega Superspeedway, opened. At 2.66 miles, Talladega is the world's largest motor sports oval track. The first Talladega 500 was won by Richard Brickhouse on September 14 in a Dodge at an average speed of 153.78 miles per hour. Mark Martin set a track record in his Ford in 1997, taking the checkered flag with an average speed of 188.35 mph.

✔ Steve Carlton of the St. Louis Cardinals pitched the game of his life, and lost. On September 15, Carlton struck out 19 batters (then a record), but the New York Mets' Ron Swoboda hit a pair of two-run homers in his team's 4–3 win.

INTRODUCTION
1970–1979

The United States feted its 200th anniversary as an independent country with a year-long celebration of America's freedom in 1976. In the world of sports, freedom was the watchword there, too, as athletes sought the freedom to earn as much money as the market—and whichever market they chose—would allow, and women sought the freedom to participate on an equal playing field with the men.

First, money: Buoyed by an influx of money from ever-growing rights fees paid by network television, pro sports franchises were suddenly very lucrative enterprises. The athletes who made those leagues and teams go found themselves, in many cases, receiving a disproportionately small part of that new-found wealth. They turned, like so many Americans, to the courts for help. In baseball, the Curt Flood case in 1969 had been the first salvo in a war between players and owners that continues to this day. But it was in the 1970s that the players made their first and largest steps, beginning with the death of the "reserve clause" that bound a player to a team for life and continuing with the creation of free agency following the Andy Messersmith case (see page 105). Now baseball became a bidding war

between teams, with superstar players being offered larger and larger contracts. Similar deals were being struck in football as its own reserve system was dismantled by court cases. Basketball and hockey's salary wars were some years off, but the writing was on the wall. Success in sports would now be measured not so much in wins or losses but by paychecks.

Another part of the growing influence of money on sports was the rise of rivals to the established pro leagues. Businesspeople shut out of the existing leagues saw an opportunity to satiate the public's thirst for sports by starting their own leagues. The American Basketball Association had started in 1968, but had its heyday in the 1970s. The World Football League tried to challenge the NFL in 1974, but failed two years later. The World Hockey Association gave Wayne Gretzky his first pro job, but by the end of the decade, the National Hockey League had swallowed up the best of the upstart league. The common fate of all these leagues was their disappearance, but they gave athletes a way to leverage their services and force teams to compete on salary.

While the men's pro sports world was spending as much time in courts

Party Time! *The United States celebrated its bicentennial—200 years of independence—in 1976.*

as on them, a hugely important sports event happened in the halls of Congress in 1972. As part of the large Education Amendments Act, Congress included a section known as Title IX, which essentially forced schools to provide equal access to sports for women. Prior to the Act, college sports participation by women was a fraction of that by male athletes. In the years and decades afterward, female participation (and the attention their exploits received from the media and fans) skyrocketed. Women's pro sports, spurred by the success of Title IX and the ongoing movement for increased women's rights in all aspects of society, also experienced a boom.

Though the events of the Munich Olympics in 1972 (page 81) were not directly related to American sports, the tragedy there brought the sports world into a clash with the "real" world in what was the most public and tragic way.

While most remembered for that tragedy and the epochal changes in finances and gender balance, the 1970s also saw many memorable performances. And though sometimes dismissed as a polyester decade with bad fashion and too-long hair, events from the 1970s continue to have resonance in today's sports world. Every time a player signs another $100 million contract, he can look to the athletes of the 1970s and say thanks. And every time another girl enjoys the benefits of athletics, she can point to the pioneering work done by female athletes in the 1970s.

1970

One Happy Family

For the first time in a decade—since the 10-team American Football League (AFL) first took the field in 1960—pro football was reunited as one big, happy family in 1970. That year, four years after a monumental agreement to merge, the member teams of the AFL officially joined the National Football League (NFL). The merger formed a 26-team NFL made up of two conferences, each with 13 teams. (To even the number of teams, the Baltimore Colts, Cleveland Browns, and Pittsburgh Steelers agreed to join the 10 former AFL teams in the American Football Conference, or AFC; the remaining 13 teams made up the National Football Conference, or NFC.)

NFL play had been defense-oriented and was dominated by running plays. The AFL featured a flashier and more diverse style. The ultimate contest between these two styles of play was Super Bowl III on January 12, 1969. The Baltimore Colts of the NFL were favored over the AFL's New York Jets by anywhere from 18 to 22 points, but the game proved to be the most colossal upset in Super Bowl history. The Jets beat the Colts 16–7.

Clear-cut wins by the Jets and the Kansas City Chiefs (also of the AFL) in Super Bowls III and IV, respectively, evened the tab at two wins apiece between the two leagues. By the time of the 1970 merger, the AFL was clearly as good as the NFL. In fact, former AFL teams won five of the first seven post-merger Super Bowls, which might even suggest that the NFL had somehow absorbed the better league.

Baseball's Biggest Change

At the age of 31, star outfielder Curt Flood (1938–1997) sacrificed his career in baseball to make a point. His action—a lawsuit against Major League Baseball—is considered by many to be the pioneering act in baseball labor relations.

After a short stint as an infielder with the Cincinnati Reds, Flood was traded to the St. Louis Cardinals in 1958 at age 18. The Cardinals moved him to center field, where he played for the next 12 seasons. Flood's hitting ability and defensive skills made him one of the best all-around players in the National League. He played in the All-Star Game in 1964, 1966, and 1968.

It was off the field, however, that Flood carved a cornerstone position in

Fountain of Youth *At 43 years old, the Raiders' George Blanda (16) was still kicking—and throwing—as well as men half his age (see page 66).*

baseball's history. Following the 1969 season, the Cardinals set up a trade with the Philadelphia Phillies. St. Louis sent Flood, Tim McCarver, Joe Hoerner, and Bryon Browne to the Phillies for Richie Allen, Cookie Rojas, and Jerry Johnson.

Flood didn't want to play in Philadelphia and decided in 1970 to file a lawsuit against Major League Baseball over the reserve clause. Baseball's reserve clause, a standard part of baseball contracts since the founding of the National League in

1970

1876, said that a player belonged to the team that held his contract. Flood wanted the freedom to choose who he would play for, even though he was making $90,000 (a princely sum at the time). He compared "being owned" in baseball to "being a slave 100 years ago."

The lawsuit was a gamble for Flood. He was in the prime of his career. Still, he decided the risk was worthwhile. His challenge of the reserve clause was based on the idea that it violated antitrust legislation, which says all the business owners in an industry can't band together to control the industry. The U.S. Congress had created an exemption from this antitrust legislation for Major League Baseball.

Flood's case was heard before a Federal Court in New York. He lost his $4.1 million antitrust lawsuit, but federal judge Irving Ben Cooper recommended in his judgement that changes be made in baseball's reserve system, to be achieved through negotiations between players and owners. Within six years, the judge's recommendations forever changed the face of baseball's labor negotiations.

Flood and his lawyers appealed the case to the U.S. Supreme Court and Flood decided to sit out the 1970 season. Meanwhile, the Washington Senators made a deal with the Phillies for Flood's "reserve." After determining that accepting the assignment would not hurt his case, Flood agreed to play for the Senators in 1971. Early in the 1971 season, Flood felt he had become the target of ill will in baseball. In response, he left the Senators and moved to Denmark; meanwhile, his lawsuit continued.

On June 18, 1972, the U.S. Supreme Court upheld the lower court's ruling against Flood. This decision by the country's highest court enabled baseball to continue to be exempt from antitrust laws and maintain its reserve clause. The decision, however, was very narrow and left the door open for legislation or collective bargaining to undermine the reserve clause. By the end of the year, the Major League owners brought an end to the reserve clause by agreeing to salary arbitration, in which an impartial arbitrator would work with teams and players on contested contracts.

They Came a Long Way

"You've come a long way, baby" was the marketing slogan for Virginia Slims cigarettes in the early 1970s, which was appropriate for the first sponsor of a new women's tennis tour. (Evidence of the hazardous effects of tobacco on a person's health caused sports teams and leagues to end such cigarette sponsorships.)

Angry about the treatment of women in professional tennis and realizing the women had to separate from the men to achieve recognition and significant prize money on their own, tennis stars Billie Jean King (b.1943) and Rosie Casals (b.1948) worked tirelessly to promote the idea of a tour separate from the men to fellow players, the public, and the media, and to secure corporate sponsorship. Their efforts resulted in tobacco giant Phillip Morris' financial support for, and *World Tennis* magazine publisher Gladys Heldman's management of, the Virginia Slims Championship.

The first tournament, held on September 23 and 24, paved the way for the next year's launch of a complete Virginia Slims circuit, which included 14 tournaments and quickly became an extremely profitable and popular tour. By the end of the decade, the total annual prize money on the Virginia Slims Tour jumped from $250,000 to more than $6 million. Women's tennis had come a long way, indeed.

Offense on Defense

In 1970 Bobby Orr (b.1948) of the Boston Bruins radically redefined the role of a National Hockey League (NHL) defenseman. As the first "offensive" blueliner (a nickname for a defenseman, who normally plays behind the blue line on the ice that denotes a team's defensive zone), he set a single-season record with 87 assists, led the league with 33 goals, and was named MVP. His famous "flying goal"—scored as he leaped horizontally above the ice—in overtime of game four clinched the Bruins' Stanley Cup sweep of the St. Louis Blues in April.

The 6-foot-1, 200-pound Orr, arguably hockey's greatest defenseman ever, struck fear into the hearts of opposing players and coaches with his superior vision and uncanny knack for finding the puck in wide open ice. In the 1966–67 season, Orr scored 13 goals and 41 total points, which earned him the Calder Trophy as the NHL's best rookie. Beginning with the 1969–70 season, Orr posted point totals of 120, 139, 117, 101, 122, and 135 for the next six seasons, an awesome feat at the time for any player, but particularly remarkable for a defenseman.

The Best Defense Is a Good Offense *Hockey legend Bobby Orr heads up the ice after taking the puck behind his own net. Orr revolutionized how a defenseman plays the game.*

Orr led the "Big Bad Bruins" to two Stanley Cup championships, in 1970 and 1972. After his tenure with the Bruins ended, Orr signed with the Chicago Blackhawks in June 1976. However, a series of knee injuries limited his playing time in his final three seasons and he retired in 1978 at the age of 30.

Orr's legacy of "offensive defenseman" continues today, and nearly every NHL team boasts all-around players at every position.

1970

A New Night for Football

After overseeing the merger between the National and American Football Leagues and the beginning of the Super Bowl in the 1960s, NFL commissioner Pete Rozelle (1926–1996) began exploring new avenues to broaden the league's audience. His idea to play on Monday nights before a national audience would mark the beginning of the most successful prime-time show in history.

September 21 marked the debut of ABC's *Monday Night Football*, a show that would have a lasting impact on the way television presents sporting events to the public. (For the record, the Cleveland Browns beat the visiting New York Jets 31–21 in that inaugural game.)

Monday Night Football was not about football as America had come to know it. Pioneering ABC producer Roone Arledge recognized that sports events are dramas, with a beginning, middle, and end. However, there was no narrator carrying the plot. There was no depth to the characters. There was no "middle man" helping the audience connect with the players on the field. Arledge took care of all those shortcomings with one move. He invited Howard Cosell (1920–1995) to the announcers' booth and let him change sports television forever.

Cosell was a lawyer and a broadcaster with a grating, nasal voice, and a melodramatic style. His opinions were unlike those of any other sportscaster, and he challenged the audience to think about more than just the action on the field. Almost overnight, what he said and did during *Monday Night Football* re-energized sports television. He became the most-loved and most-hated voice in sports.

Over the next three decades, *Monday Night Football* was among the most-watched television programs every year. Sports had been brought into America's prime time, and it would never leave.

Never Too Old

The long, gray, thinning hair, the deeply lined face—George Blanda (b.1927) looked old. But he never got old. He just got better. Over 26 incredible professional seasons, he posted a record 2,002 points and an impressive 236 touchdown passes as a kicker and quarterback. But the real legacy of George Blanda is the magic he created as an American folk hero who continued to deliver clutch performances in his fourth decade playing football, until the age of 48.

Blanda was a scoring machine for 10 years as a Chicago Bears kicker, an icy competitor when he finally got his first call as a long-term starting quarterback and led the Houston Oilers to championships in the AFL's first two seasons, 1960 and 1961. With Oakland from 1967 until his 1975 retirement, he became a silver-haired legend. One season helped cement that legend. In 1970, at age 43, Blanda came off the bench in five straight games to deliver a dramatic kick or a touchdown pass that produced a win or a tie.

Blanda was a popular, sometimes testy, leader. He retired as the NFL's all-time leading scorer with 2,002 points (since surpassed by several players) and was elected to the Pro Football Hall of Fame in 1981.

Other Milestones of 1970

✔ Perhaps the most important innovation in tennis scoring, the tiebreaker was invented by Jimmy Van Alen and instituted at the 1970 U.S. Open. Previously, sets could last hours, because players had to win by at least two games to capture the set. The tiebreaker shortened and enlivened matches and soon reformed the scoring system everywhere.

✔ Former AFL star quarterback Jack Kemp (1935–2009) was elected to the United States Senate, representing New York. After a highly successful career in which he led his teams to five AFL Championship Games and two league titles, Kemp started on a long career in politics, including stints in Congress and as Secretary of Housing and Urban Development under the first President Bush.

✔ The Pittsburgh Pirates started a fashion trend that eventually swept through all of baseball. In the first radical departure in the design of baseball uniforms, the Pirates wore form-fitting uniforms made of double-knit polyester. Players welcomed the new material because it weighed far less than the traditional wool uniforms, was cooler, and allowed better freedom of movement.

✔ On September 13, 55 runners finished the first New York City Marathon, which was produced with a total budget of $1,000. From this humble beginning, the race has grown to become a weeklong, worldwide celebration. The event now includes 30,000 athletes, 12,000 volunteers, thousands of city employees, more than 2 million spectators lining the course, and tens of millions more television viewers around the globe.

✔ Gary Gabelich, driving a rocket-powered car, set the world land speed record of 622.407 miles per hour on October 23.

✔ On November 8, New Orleans Saints placekicker Tom Dempsey not only beat the Detroit Lions with the game-winning field goal, but put himself in the NFL's record books. His 63-yard field goal surpassed the previous record by a full seven yards and remained unmatched until 1998, when Denver's Jason Elam tied the mark. Amazingly, Dempsey was born without a right hand and with no toes on this kicking foot.

✔ Margaret Smith-Court became the second woman to win the Grand Slam of tennis, capturing the U.S., French, and Australian Opens, and Wimbledon in the same year. In her career, Smith-Court won 24 Grand Slam singles titles.

✔ Larry Mahan became the first rodeo cowboy to win five consecutive titles as All-Around Cowboy Champion at the National Finals Rodeo in December.

1971

Return of "The Greatest"

Three years after his boxing license and World Boxing Championship (WBC) heavyweight title had been stripped following his refusal, based on his Islamic beliefs, to be drafted into the army, Muhammad Ali got both his boxing license and his WBC title back. On June 29, the U.S. Supreme Court overturned his 1967 conviction for evading the draft. However, while Ali had been prohibited from fighting, the World Boxing Association (WBA) had given its heavyweight title to Joe Frazier (b.1944).

Never before had two active fighters simultaneously had a legitimate claim to the same title. Ali's return to the ring for a decisive bout against Frazier would leave only one champion. Appropriately, their titan matchup, billed as "The Fight of the Century," attracted 300 million viewers via satellite and closed-circuit television—more viewers than any boxing match in history.

On March 8 at New York's Madison Square Garden, the smaller Frazier wore down Ali with relentless left hooks, even knocking Ali down for only the third time in Ali's career. Frazier retained—and became the sole owner of—the heavyweight title.

But Ali was far from finished. Over the next three years, he won 12 of 13 fights, half by knockout. In 1974, Ali got his chance for a long-awaited rematch with Frazier. Although no longer the heavyweight champ, Frazier was still one of the world's best fighters. Ali proved to be better, winning the fight by a unanimous decision.

Later that same year, Ali regained the heavyweight crown, using his "rope-a-dope" strategy to let George Foreman tire himself out by throwing countless punches against Ali's body, but none that did damage. By the eighth round, Foreman was clearly exhausted. Ali threw a knock-out punch to win the fight, and he became only the second man in boxing history to regain the world heavyweight championship.

In 1975, Ali defended his title three times. But the bout that will always be remembered from that year was "The Thrilla in Manila," the third and final fight between Ali and Frazier, and still considered one of the greatest fights ever. After 14 grueling see-saw rounds, Frazier's trainer called off the fight, seeing that his

Fight of the Century *Joe Frazier (in the green trunks) stunned Muhammad Ali in an epic heavyweight title bout.*

man was unable to go another round. Immediately after this, his final and perhaps most spectacular victory, Ali said it was the "closest thing to dying I know of."

NHL: Bigger Is Better

The World Hockey Association (WHA) was formed in April 1971. After initially being dismissed by the NHL, the new league quickly proved to be the first legitimate rival to the NHL in 55 years. But ultimately, this competition—for the attention of hockey fans, the talents of the world's best hockey players, and the dollars of corporate advertisers and sponsors—resulted in the NHL becoming bigger, stronger, and more American.

In November 1971, the WHA announced it had 12 teams, eight in the United States and four in Canada. Unlike the NHL, the WHA allowed its teams to

1971

Hockey's Growth Extends Beyond the Ice

In 1971, the Mississauga (Wisconsin) Ball Hockey Association was founded. Reflecting the increasing worldwide passion for hockey, this league was the first organized street hockey (or roller hockey) league in the United States. The first plastic orange ball, used instead of a traditional black rubber puck, was introduced by Arnold Herka, of Viceroy Rubber, the same year. The street version of this exciting sport has never looked back.

sign junior league players younger than 18. The most notable result of that decision was the beginning of the career of the greatest hockey player ever. At 17, Wayne Gretzky (b.1954) took the ice as one of the WHA's Indianapolis Racers.

The WHA also led the way in scouting and recruiting European players. This changed the professional game, introducing a new style and strategy that placed more emphasis on speed, stickhandling, and passing, and less on brute force.

The new league also went after established NHL stars. The WHA's Winnipeg Jets signed the NHL's legendary Bobby Hull to a million-dollar contract. Other teams offered contracts sometimes three or four times larger than NHL salaries.

To combat the WHA threat, the NHL added two teams: the Atlanta Flames to offset the WHA's presence in the South, and the New York Islanders to regain the NHL's prominence in that big-market region. The NHL also settled a WHA-led antitrust lawsuit out of court, agreeing with the WHA to honor one another's player contracts and paying the WHA a settlement fee of almost $2 million. In effect, the WHA had defeated the reserve clause in professional hockey, which had bound players for life to NHL teams.

After growing to as many as 14 teams in 1974–75, the WHA was back down to 12 by 1976. After the 1978–79 season, only six teams remained. At that point, the WHA merged with the NHL. Four WHA teams—the Edmonton Oilers, New England (later Hartford) Whalers, Quebec Nordiques (now the Colorado Avalanche), and Winnipeg Jets (now the Phoenix Coyotes)—survived the merger intact. The other clubs' players were free to sign with NHL teams.

Ping-Pong Diplomacy

In April of 1971, the American table tennis (ping-pong) team traveled to Nagoya, Japan, to compete for the World Table Tennis Championship. The result had little to do with table tennis but much to do with international relations.

While in Nagoya, the American team received an unexpected invitation from their Chinese colleagues. For the first time since the Communists took control of China in 1949, a group of Americans were invited to the People's Republic. The invitation was accepted, and four days later history—not sports history, but diplomatic history—was made.

No one from outside the People's Republic of China could have been prepared for what awaited them at the airport in Beijing. After more than two decades of mutual hostility, Chinese Premier Zhou En-Lai personally greeted the surprised American delegation of "ping-pong diplomats." As the Chinese Premier later said, "Never before in history—and possibly never since—has a sport been used so effectively as a tool for international diplomacy."

It was a savvy gesture. Without making commitments, or even suggestions of any kind, China's gesture promised an easing of tensions in Asia and the possibility of improved trade relations between the two countries. In fact, this move also opened the door for talks with the Soviet Union on crucial matters such as arms control. And only hours after the Premier welcomed the table tennis players, President Richard Nixon announced other initiatives for trade and travel between the United States and the People's Republic of China.

The American table tennis players, led by team captain Jack Howard, faced off against their Chinese opponents at Qinghua University. The Chinese won the

Political Ping-Pong Ball   *A table-tennis match helped thaw frigid relations between the United States and communist China.*

Long Overdue *The inimitable Satchel Paige (see page 73) was the first player elected to the National Baseball Hall of Fame by the new Committee on Negro Baseball Leagues.*

Good Night, Knight

In 1971, when Bobby Knight took the job as head coach of the Indiana University men's basketball team, he was only 30 years old, but he was more than ready for the intense spotlight that would very quickly be pointed in his direction.

The team Knight inherited had come to be known as the "Hurryin' Hoosiers," a team that for years had fit perfectly in the Big Ten—a conference that was popular for its fast, high-scoring style of basketball. Rather than adapt his strategy and style to fit what crowds and players had come to love, Knight instituted the game-slowing, score-reducing man-to-man defense that had been so successful for him as coach at West Point.

It did not take long for the Hoosier fans—and even opposing coaches—to warm up to Knight's more deliberate style of play. More important to Hoosier players and fans was the consistently high level of play Knight demanded—and received—from his teams. In his first 20 years as Indiana's head coach, Knight led his team to 10 conference championships and three NCAA titles. He also amassed more victories more quickly in his career than almost any other coach at any level of the game.

As part of his fame, however, Knight's success is second only to his controversial tactics and behavior. Fear and intimidation were key elements of Knight's coaching style. His methods have been widely acknowledged by former players, assistant coaches, faculty members, and school administrators as dehumanizing. Many of his public indiscretions, such as throwing

men's games 5–3 and the women's game's 5–4. Afterward, the teams exchanged gifts and walked off together hand-in-hand.

Soon after the U.S. team's trip, Secretary of State Henry Kissinger went to Beijing to arrange a presidential visit to China. Seven months later, in February of 1972, President Nixon's journey became one of the most important events in the United States since World War II. One year later, the Chinese team visited the United States.

a chair across the court during a game, assaulting a police officer, and taking his team off the floor because of his lack of respect for the officiating, heightened his players' fear of him. The seemingly endless string of questionable behavior also brought tremendous criticism upon Knight, the university, and even college basketball in general.

Nonetheless, Knight was tolerated, even accepted because of the results he produced, both on and off the court. Knight was just as unforgiving of mistakes or apparent lapses in commitment by officials, assistant coaches, and his players. And he was entirely intolerant of inappropriate support from wealthy or influential boosters. As a result of this and other Knight standards, the Hoosiers during Knight's tenure boasted one of the best records of compliance with NCAA rules in Division I-A basketball.

Knight's relentless demand for perfection is the one common denominator found in the tremendous number of Knight's former coaches and players who have gone on to achieve great personal and professional success, in the improved officiating in the Big Ten, and in the elevation of Indiana to a college basketball champion and perennial powerhouse.

Ultimately, though, Knight's behavior became too much. He lost his job in Indiana in 2000, after his volatile temper resulted in a series of incidents. He wasn't out of work long, though, and coached at Texas Tech University from the 2001–02 season until midway through 2007–08.

Baseball Begins Righting a Wrong

Some of pitcher Satchel Paige's claims are beyond believable—such as winning more than 2,000 games and pitching more than 150 no-hitters. But Paige's legendary braggadocio is part of the charm of one of the most colorful personalities in baseball history. And almost anyone who ever saw him play would say that he was one of greatest pitchers ever.

Trouble is, a lot of folks didn't get to see Paige play because of the color barrier that existed in Major League Baseball until 1947. Paige, an African-American, spent his heyday pitching in the Negro Leagues. He didn't join the Major Leagues until 1948, when he made his debut for the Cleveland Indians two days after his 42nd birthday (some say he was even older).

Paige had enough left in him to earn two All-Star berths in the Majors, but that wasn't enough to warrant inclusion in the National Baseball Hall of Fame. Still, his overall body of work—as well as that of other Negro Leagues stars who never got a shot at the Majors—did. So in 1971, Paige was the first player elected to the Hall by the Committee on Negro Baseball Leagues.

Since Paige's induction, more than two dozen Negro Leagues players have joined him in the Hall of Fame. From 1971 to 1977, the Committee on Negro Baseball Leagues elected legendary stars such as Cool Papa Bell, Oscar Charleston, and Josh Gibson. In 2006, the Special Committee on Negro Leagues elected 17 more Negro Leaguers.

1971

The Longest Day

Christmas Day 1971 was "The Longest Day" in NFL history, and saw one of the greatest games ever played. In a double-overtime AFC playoff game, the Miami Dolphins beat the Kansas City Chiefs 27–24 when Garo Yepremian kicked a 37-yard field goal. The kick ended a tense drama after 7 minutes and 40 seconds of the second overtime—82 minutes and 40 seconds of game action in all. It remains the longest game in the history of the NFL.

The Dolphins forced the overtime sessions when they tied the game at 24–24 on quarterback Bob Griese's five-yard touchdown pass to tight end Marv Fleming with one minute, 36 seconds left in regulation. Chiefs' running back Ed Podolak returned the ensuing kickoff 78 yards to set up a potential game-winning

Other Milestones of 1971

✔ With a 2,495-game winning streak on the line on January 5, the Harlem Globetrotters, basketball's "clown princes" and most entertaining ambassadors, lost to the New Jersey Reds, 100–99. With their next game, the Globetrotters began a new winning streak, which lasted until 1995 and spanned 8,829 games.

✔ Tyler Palmer recorded the United States' first World Cup victory in alpine skiing in St. Moritz, Switzerland, on January 23.

✔ A young graphic designer, Carolyn Davidson, created the swoosh that became the official logo for Nike and, over the next 10 years, a trademark for a society increasingly focused on health and athletics.

✔ On August 10, Harmon Killebrew of the Minnesota Twins joined baseball's 500 home run club. Killebrew homered on his 6,671st at-bat, the fewest since 1929, when Babe Ruth hit his 500th on his 5,801st at-bat. Killebrew went on to play through the 1975 season and to finish with 573 career home runs.

✔ ABC televised a USA–Cuba volleyball match from Havana in August. This was the first time an American television network sports department covered a sporting event in Cuba since Fidel Castro came to power in 1959. Castro's love of sports meant that athletics would continue to help thaw relations.

✔ Pittsburgh outfielder Roberto Clemente hit .414 to earn MVP honors and lead the Pirates past the Baltimore Orioles in seven games in the World Series. In Game Four of the Series, on Wednesday, October 13, the Pirates beat the visiting Orioles 4–3 in the first World Series night game. NBC called for the later start, figuring it could get higher television ratings at night than during the day—an argument that easily persuaded Major League Baseball, which had been experiencing declines in ratings and stadium attendance over recent years. Within a few years, the majority of baseball's regular-season and post-season games were played at night. Much to the chagrin of young fans, they remain that way.

field-goal attempt by Jan Stenerud, but he missed from 31 yards with 35 seconds to go. Stenerud, normally a reliable kicker who eventually made the Hall of Fame, also missed from 42 yards in overtime when his try was blocked. Yepremian also missed a long try (52 yards) in the first overtime, but won it when he got another chance in the second overtime.

Podolak, his red-and-white Chiefs' uniform caked with mud, blood, sweat, and grass, amassed 350 yards and scored two touchdowns in the game. Podolak's total still ranks as the top mark for combined net yards (the combined total of rushing yards, receiving yards, and return yards) in playoff history, and it ranks third in all games in NFL history.

Derby Days

In August 1971, the 37-year-old All-American Soap Box Derby let young girls compete for the first time. In the annual race, children hand-build small, motorless cars and then race them on a downhill course. Gravity provides the only power.

The event had begun almost accidentally when a Dayton, Ohio, newspaperman helped some local kids find a place to race their go-karts in 1933. The next year, the first official competition was held in Dayton. One year later, the derby moved to Akron, Ohio. Over time, the event grew to sponsor races in dozens of cities, with local winners advancing to Akron. At first,

Go, Speed Racers! *The All-American Soap Box Derby, a tradition since 1933, was open to young women for the first time. Five of the 272 participants in 1971 were girls.*

only boys were allowed to race, but a flowering women's movement in the 1960s and 1970s helped break this tradition.

Five of the 272 contestants in 1971 were young women. By the next year more than 10 percent of these finalists were girls, two of whom finished among the top 10. Finally, in 1975, 11-year-old Karen Stead became the first girl to win the All-American Soap Box Derby.

1972

Strike One

In 1972, when team owners tried to reduce their payment to the Major League Baseball players pension fund by $500,000, the players decided to fight back: For the first time in baseball history, the players went on strike.

The Major League Baseball Players Association, the players' labor union had been around for more than 35 years, but its sole purpose was to collect and administer a meager pension. Concerned about getting a piece of growing television revenues, the players sought to strengthen their union in 1965. They hired Marvin Miller (b.1917), a veteran labor organizer. When Miller came on board and saw what the conditions were, he knew much more was at stake than adding broadcasting money to the pension fund.

For one thing, the minimum salary was $6,000, just $1,000 more than it had been in 1947. As he began to collect data, the players were surprised at how poorly they were being paid. This education paved the way for the first collective bargaining agreement between owners and players in 1968. It provided some modest improvements, but most importantly, it gave the players some leverage. For nearly 100 years, team owners had a "take it or leave it" relationship with players. The union could (and did) file complaints with the National Labor Relations Board when they were treated unfairly. Players also won the right to have their grievances heard before an independent arbitrator.

The owners did not like the union interfering in their business, and they especially bristled at the players standing up to them. Curt Flood filed a lawsuit against baseball commissioner Bowie Kuhn in 1970 (see page 62). Flood argued that the reserve clause, which gave teams the absolute right to renew a player's contract for one year, was illegal and, consequently, he should be allowed to negotiate freely with other teams.

Although Flood lost his case, his effort had energized the other players. The volatile situation led to the strike. It lasted just over a week, from April 6 to April 14, wiping out 86 of the season's first games. The owners settled by giving the players everything they asked for. More significantly, the players learned that through collective action, they could force the owners to make changes. Baseball would never be the same.

Perfect! *Running back Jim Kiick and the Miami Dolphins (shown here in Super Bowl VII in January of 1973) posted the first unbeaten and untied season in NFL history in 1972 (see page 83).*

Equal Rights

The Education Amendments Act of 1972 grew out of the Civil Rights and feminist movements of the 1950s, 1960s, and early 1970s. The act was intended primarily to improve the quality and equality of educational opportunities for all Americans. Almost accidentally, one specific part of it brought about one of the most significant changes in American sports.

American society had always put tremendous pressure on women to choose either marriage or a college education and a career. As a result, female athletes were rare and were considered abnormal. Physical education for girls and women was grudgingly offered, but strenuous exercise was discouraged and considered unsafe and unbecoming for a lady. Women in high school and college had few opportunities to compete in sports, and pro sports for women were limited mostly to golf and, just barely, tennis.

On July 1, when the Education Amendments Act of 1972 went into effect, Title IX of that act said, "No person in the United States shall, on the basis of sex, be

Baseball's Labor Wars

The players went on strike for the first time in baseball history in 1972. Briefly, here are key dates in baseball labor issues over the next two decades:

1972: The players walked out for 12 days beginning April 1. They gained the right to salary arbitration.

1973: The owners locked out the players from February 8 to February 25, but the season started on time. The owners eventually increased minimum salaries and pension contributions.

1975: Pitchers Dave McNally and Andy Messersmith refuse to sign contracts, battling the reserve clause again (see page 105). An arbitrator upheld these two players' cases in the offseason prior to 1976 (when a 17-day lockout interrupted spring training), and free agency was born.

1980: The players went on strike the final eight days of spring training, but the season started on time after a new working agreement was in place with free-agent compensation a key issue.

1981: A 50-day strike forced the owners to agree to a plan that let players who were not yet eligible for free agency (an earlier agreement had put that time at six years), still have their salaries decided by an arbitrator.

1985: Another player strike, this time only two days long, forced owners to change the way arbitration was arranged.

1988: An arbitrator ruled that baseball owners had unfairly and illegally "colluded," or secretly worked together, to not offer high-paying contracts to free agents. The players were awarded damages from the owners of more than $102.5 million.

1990: Spring training was delayed more than a month when the owners locked out the players, largely over salary cap and arbitration issues.

1994: A terrible impasse between players and owners forced the owners to lock the players out, ending the 1994 season in August and canceling the World Series for the first time in 92 years. A temporary agreement was reached in April 1995 and that season started a few weeks late. Baseball's current labor deal began in 2007 and runs through 2011.

excluded from participation in, or denied the benefits of, or be subjected to discrimination under any educational program or activity receiving federal aid."

In other words, women count equally with men. That statement has, too slowly for some and perhaps too rapidly for others, continued to find support throughout society. In the classroom, in the workplace, and in leadership, Title IX continues to effect changes in the opportunities available to women.

Title IX's effect on female participation in athletics at the high school and college levels has gained the most public notice. Figures from the National Federation of State High School Associations show that the more than 3 million females in sports in 2007–2008 is about 10 times the number of female participants pre-Title IX in 1971. According to the *Chronicle of Higher Education*, there were about 30,000 female athletes at the college level in 1972. By 1991, that number was 92,778; by 2008, it was more than 200,000.

Title IX's effect has been global—women from all over the world attend college and participate in sports in the United States. From professional leagues in basketball and soccer, to the recent inclusion of women in several formerly exclusively male Olympic sports, such as bobsled, basketball, and pole vault, women are receiving more of the sports spotlight previously reserved for men. The change is obvious on the local level, too, as girls in organized leagues and neighborhood pickup games enjoy soccer, baseball, basketball, and more.

Even with all the evidence of Title IX's success, athletic department spending, especially at the Division I collegiate level, remains uneven. Some schools have cut men's sports in an effort to slow growing budgets. The National Wrestling Coaches Association filed suit against the Education Department in United States District Court in 2003, alleging that Title IX was not being properly interpreted. (The lawsuit eventually was dismissed.)

Title IX advocates, however, point to alarming spending on football and men's basketball. Even more vigorously, they say the majority of universities are not close to compliance with Title IX. Men still get considerably more funding in athletics than women, and the elimination of some men's programs has not resulted in a meaningful shift toward equity. According to the NCAA's Gender Equity Report for 2005–06, Division I schools' overall expenses for men's teams averaged more than $8.6 million per institution—nearly double the almost $4.5 million for women's teams.

Neither the objective of Title IX nor the broader objectives of the entire Education Amendments Act have yet been met. Title IX is not perfect. But it has been—and will continue to be—a force that shapes athletics and our society.

Swimming's Golden Boy

Mark Spitz (b.1950) won seven gold medals—all of them in world-record time—in men's swimming at the 1972 Olympics. Not until fellow American

Opportunities for All   *Title IX quickly had an effect on women's college sports. By the end of the decade, athletes such as Old Dominion basketball player Nancy Lieberman (above) were stars.*

79

1972

Michael Phelps in 2008 did any other swimmer so dominate his competition.

Spitz's first Olympic experience was in the 1968 Olympics. Leading up to those Summer Games in Mexico City, Spitz had boasted several times that he would win six gold medals—a feat no one in any Olympic sport had ever accomplished. His cocky statements alienated him from his teammates. Those statements also proved to be more than he could live up to in 1968. He returned to the United States with only two gold medals, both of which he won in relay competitions. On his own, he won a silver medal in the 100-meter butterfly event and a bronze in the 100-meter freestyle. In the 200-meter freestyle, he came in last.

Disappointed and humbled, the 18-year-old Spitz entered Indiana University on a swimming scholarship. Again, he made more enemies than friends because of his attitude. More often than not, however, his performances in the pool backed up his words. In his four years at Indiana, he led the men's swimming team to four NCAA national championships. He also won more individual and team events than any swimmer in NCAA history.

Then, at 22, Spitz made Olympic history. At the Munich Games, Spitz won the 100-meter butterfly, the 200-hundred meter butterfly, the 100-meter free-style, the 200-meter free-style, the 400-meter free-style, the 800-meter free-style, and the 400-meter medley relay—all in world record time.

Sadly, Spitz was unable to celebrate his accomplishments among his fellow athletes. In the aftermath of the terrorist attack on the Israeli team (see box), many Jewish athletes—including Spitz—were quickly removed from the Olympic Village. Just a few hours after winning his last race, Spitz was flown back to the United States, where he was greeted like the hero he had become.

The Day Time Stood Still

The Soviet Union won the gold medal in men's basketball at the Summer Olympics by stunning the United States team 51–50 on September 10. It was the first time than an American men's basketball team ever lost a game in the Olympics.

The United States looked as if it might escape a close call when Doug Collins made a pair of free throws for a 50–49 advantage with just three seconds to go.

The Americans had not led before that point. That wasn't entirely a surprise. The United States team was its youngest ever in Olympic competition and was playing a seasoned Soviet squad. The

---

Title IX: Off the Field

Since Title IX was enacted on June 23, 1972, women have made substantial progress in athletics, education, and employment. The number of female college athletes has increased more than sixfold since 1972, while the number of high school athletes who are girls has increased from about 300,000 to more than 3 million.

But the act had perhaps farther reaching consequences off the playing fields. In 1972, fewer than 10 percent of medical, law, and other doctoral degrees were awarded to women. In recent years, those numbers have risen considerably. Today, about half of all of these advanced degrees are earned by female students.

The Games Must Go On

International terrorism collided for the first time with sports at the Summer Olympic Games in Munich, Germany. On September 5, Arab terrorists infiltrated the Olympic Village, home of the Games' athletes, and kidnapped 11 members of the Israeli Olympic team. A two-day standoff stunned and transfixed the world, as the Olympic Games were put on hold.

Tragically, all 11 athletes, five terrorists, and one policeman were killed during an attempt to rescue them as they boarded a helicopter. Even though numerous competitors and officials strongly called for the remainder of the Olympics to be cancelled, the IOC decided to let the Games continue. This decision was based largely on the wishes of the Israeli government and team, who refused to give in to terrorist pressure. Avery Brundage, IOC president, said he would not allow the peaceful spirit of the Olympic movement to be ruined by "a handful of terrorists."

The Munich tragedy signaled an end to the innocent notion that sports could be separate from the cares and troubles of the wider world. Today, heavy security accompanies every major sporting event, and security provisions are a major consideration when the IOC decides what cities host the Games.

Americans had very little experience. Most members were in college, none had played professionally, and as a team, they had been together for only 12 exhibition games before the Olympics and then for the eight games leading up to this point in the Olympic tournament. (Until the 1990s, professional players were barred from participating in Olympic events, so Dream Teams were still decades away.)

By comparison, the Soviets were significantly bigger and much more experienced. They were brilliantly coached and came into the Olympics having already played approximately 400 games as a team. The Soviets were hardly the underdog. In fact, they promised to be the stiffest competitions the Americans had ever faced.

From the opening tip-off, the Americans were surprised to find themselves playing against a team that was better than they had imagined. By halftime, the United States was down by five points. With less than 10 minutes remaining in the second half, that deficit had doubled to 10. But the Americans battled back. With 38 seconds left, the young squad had closed to within one point. Then, with three seconds left in the game, Doug Collins of the United States team was fouled as he drove to the basket. Standing up to the incredible pressure, Collins sank both free throws.

And then time seemed to stop. In fact, that very short span of time kept repeating itself. After Collins' free throw, the Soviets in-bounded the ball. Immediately, the referees stopped the game with one second remaining.

In response to an argument from the Soviet bench, the officials put three seconds back on the clock. The Soviets in-bounded the ball a second time. Almost immediately, the horn sounded signaling the end of the game and, apparently, an American victory. But again, the teams were ordered back on the floor.

1972

Upon Further Review   *U.S. players celebrate an apparent gold medal in basketball before officials put three seconds back on the clock. The Soviet Union won after the reset.*

The officials indicated the clock had not been properly reset to show three seconds remaining before the Soviets had in-bounded the ball.

Order was restored on, the clock was again reset to show three seconds remaining and, for a third time, the Soviets in-bounded the ball. Soviet center Alexander Belov caught the full-court pass and scored the winning lay-up as the clock ran out. The Soviets had won.

Immediately, the controversy exploded. Convinced that it had been wronged, the United States team filed a formal protest with the International Basketball Federation and refused to accept their silver medals.

Later that afternoon, a five-member panel ruled in favor of the Soviets. American dominance of amateur basketball had, officially, finally, and controversially ended.

Perfect

The Miami Dolphins forged the first unbeaten and untied year in NFL history (including the postseason) when they won all 17 games they played in the 1972 season. The capper came when they beat the Washington Redskins 14–7 in Super Bowl VII in January of 1973.

The 1972 season was head coach Don Shula's third with the Dolphins. Under his strict, no-nonsense approach, the Dolphins gelled into a cohesive unit. The potent offense featured five future Hall of Famers: running back Larry Csonka, guard Larry Little, quarterback Bob Griese, center Jim Langer, and wide receiver Paul Warfield. But it was the unparalleled effectiveness of its mostly unknown defense—the "No-Name Defense"—that made the Dolphins famous to fans across the country, and to all the other teams throughout the league.

Unsuspecting heroes also surfaced from the Dolphins' bench. In week five, with starting quarterback Bob Griese injured, 38-year-old Earl Morrall stepped in to keep the unbeaten streak alive. Morrall, in fact, directed Miami's offense for the remainder of the regular season and to their 20–14 victory over the Cleveland Browns in the first round of the playoffs.

Against the Pittsburgh Steelers on December 31, it was Griese who came off the bench to direct a thrilling 21–17 victory for the AFC title. Two weeks later, on January 14, Griese started and finished Miami's Super Bowl victory over Washington.

Since 1972, only the 2007 New England Patriots have won all their regular-season games. But after going 16–0 in the regular season, and then winning two playoff games, the Patriots' suffered an upset loss to the New York Giants in Super Bowl XLII.

Other Milestones of 1972

✔ After more than two months without a defeat, the Los Angeles Lakers of the NBA lost to the Milwaukee Bucks 120–104 on January 10. At 33 games, the Lakers' winning streak shattered the previous record of 20, which had been set by the Bucks the season before.

✔ In the WHA's second season (see page 69 for details on the young league), the Houston Aeros signed 45-year-old Gordie Howe, who had retired from the NHL two years earlier after legendary career with the Detroit Red Wings. The Aeros teamed him with his two sons, Mark and Matt Howe. Gordie won the league's MVP award, Mark was named rookie of the year, and the Aeros won the WHA championship.

✔ On April 20, the Naismith Memorial Basketball Hall of Fame in Springfield, Massachusetts, inducted Bob Douglas (1882–1979), the first African American to be enshrined. Douglas, who organized, owned, and coached the first African-American professional basketball team (the New York Renaissance) beginning in the early 1920s, is considered to be the father of black pro basketball.

1973

Mush!

Each year before the winter turns to spring, 65 or so mushers (dog-sled drivers) and their teams of 12 to 16 dogs begin a long race from Anchorage in south central Alaska. The finish line: Nome, Alaska, on the western Bering Sea Coast, some 1,150 grueling miles away, over often rugged terrain. It is the Iditarod Dog Sled Race, also known as the "Last Great Race on Earth."

The first Iditarod began on March 3, 1973. The first winner, Dick Wilmarth, needed almost three weeks to reach Nome. Today, the winner typically takes from 10 to 17 days, although some of the best mushers have managed the trip in less than than 10 days.

Westwood Wizardry

There has never been another college basketball dynasty like the one that head coach John Wooden (b.1910) built at the University of California at Los Angeles (UCLA) in the late 1960s and early 1970s. On March 26, the Bruins won their seventh consecutive NCAA men's basketball tournament. UCLA downed the Memphis State Tigers 87–66 in the title game behind a dominating performance from center Bill Walton (see the box on page 86.)

Earlier in the 1972–73 season, the Bruins had shattered the record for the most consecutive wins—previously held by San Francisco, who won 60 straight games from 1955–57. When the NCAA Tournament started, UCLA had won 71 consecutive games, dating back to the 1971 season.

The championship game in St. Louis, Missouri, was the first to be televised in

Alone in Front *Secretariat breezes to victory in the Kentucky Derby, first leg of the Triple Crown (see page 88).*

prime time, and a record viewing audience tuned in to watch college basketball's reigning dynasty. UCLA was formidable, but the Memphis State Tigers thought they had a good chance if they could shut down Walton. Memphis State fronted Walton (positioning a defensive player on both sides of an opponent) in an effort to deny him the ball, but the strategy backfired. The Bruins simply lobbed passes above the defense to the 6-foot-11 Walton, who easily converted them into baskets.

Still, Walton spent some of the first half on the bench with three fouls, and the Tigers shot well enough to reach halftime tied at 39–39. But the big man scored 14 points during a crucial 20–10 run in the second half, and the Bruins never looked back. When Walton left the game with a sprained ankle with just under three minutes remaining, the game was no longer in doubt, and he had scored a championship-record 44 points. He also set a record by making 21 of 22 shots.

"Big Red" Leads the Blue and Gold

In the second half of the 1973 NCAA championship game against Memphis State University, UCLA head coach John Wooden silently presided over his team's huddle during a timeout. Finally, Bruin guard Greg Lee asked Wooden if the Bruins should try some different plays. Wooden looked at Lee and replied, "Why?" The fact was, the one play the Bruins had relied on all game had been unstoppable: get the ball to junior center Bill Walton.

Walton earned national player of the year honors for the second straight season and was again named the NCAA Tournament's Most Outstanding Player after scoring 44 points, a title-game record. Walton even became the first basketball player since Bill Bradley in 1964 to win the Sullivan Award as the nation's best amateur athlete.

Knicks Do It Again

While UCLA was dominating college basketball, several teams were competing for the title of best in the pros. In 1973, the New York Knicks won their second NBA title in four years (they had won in 1970), with one of the most decorated teams in NBA history. The Knicks knocked off the Lakers in the Finals in five games, neatly wrapping up a five-year period in which its main starters were all future Hall of Fame members.

At center, Willis Reed was the heart of the team, a powerful rebounder and inside force who was just as strong a floor leader. Just before the final game of the 1970 Finals, which he was supposed to miss with a severe leg injury, he had famously limped onto the court to the cheers of the Madison Square Garden crowd. Though Reed scored only four points in that game, his "comeback" was the inspiration for the Knicks' first title. In 1973, he helped the defense-oriented Knicks shut down high-scoring Wilt Chamberlain and the Lakers.

Helping Reed on the front line were forwards Dave DeBusschere, a hard-working scorer, and Jerry Lucas, a solid scorer and defender. (Lucas would later go on to a career as a memory coach, teaching people how to use their memories better. While on plane trips with the Knicks, Lucas put his prodigious memory to use by keeping track of the winnings of the various card games going on around him.) In the backcourt, the Knicks boasted a terrific tandem of Earl "The Pearl" Monroe and Walt "Clyde" Frazier. Monroe was an outstanding ballhandler, while Frazier was a sweet shooter known as much for his somewhat outlandish off-the-court wardrobe as his clutch jumper.

Amazingly, all five of these, plus coach Red Holzman, would eventually be inducted into the Basketball Hall of Fame in Springfield, Massachusetts.

Have Bat, Will Travel

For a century, pitchers in baseball were like every other position player—they batted. Then in 1973, the New York Yankees' Ron Blomberg stepped to the plate in the first inning on Opening Day on April 6 against the Boston Red Sox' Luis Tiant at Fenway Park. Blomberg hit three more times during the game. He never took a position in the field.

Blomberg's at-bat marked the American League's official debut of the designated-hitter (DH) rule, which allowed teams to designate a non-position player to bat instead of the pitcher without affecting the pitcher's status on defense. The debate about the merits of the DH has raged ever since. Purists believe it detracts from the game, while others welcome the extra offense it provides.

The 1973 introduction of the DH was part of a two-year experiment approved by the American League as an attempt to bolster its attendance, which was lagging behind the National League. The new rule increased offense—the Kansas City Royals put the world of baseball on notice on Opening Day when they knocked ace pitcher Nolan Ryan out of the game in just the third inning with the first of three consecutive home runs hit against the California Angels—and did bring more fans to the ballpark.

In 1976, Rule 6.10(b) was made permanent, but it still applies only to baseball's American League. The National League is still virtually the only organized baseball league that does not use the DH in its games. High schools, colleges, minor-league teams, and international

Designated Hitter *The Yankees' Ron Blomberg made history when he became the first DH in big-league annals.*

The Ryan Express

Every pitcher's dream is to throw a no-hitter, and approximately 98 percent of them never accomplish that dream. Nolan Ryan managed to do it seven times, and no pitcher in the history of the game has even come close.

In 1973, the first year of the designated hitter (see page 86), Nolan Ryan, pitching for the California Angels, threw the first two of his seven no-hitters. He blanked the Kansas City Royals on May 15 for a 3–0 victory. He then no-hit the Detroit Tigers 6–0 on July 15 while striking out 17 batters. He was only the fourth pitcher to throw two no-hitters in one season.

Ryan closes out no-no No. 1.

A fireballing righthander, Ryan struggled with his control throughout his career. But when he was pitching around the plate, he was virtually unhittable. Ryan set a new single-season record in 1973 by striking out 383 batters.

Ryan later played for the Houston Astros and the Texas Rangers and kept winning and striking players out. He ended his remarkable career in 1993 at age 46, with 324 victories, and he is the all-time leader in no-hitters, strikeouts, and walks. He also pitched for more seasons (27) than any other player in the history of the game.

baseball associations have all adopted the DH rule.

Over the years, designated hitters have tended to be used primarily to add power to the lineup. A couple of DHs, however, have added some speed. Paul Molitor of the Milwaukee Brewers became the first DH to steal more than 20 bases in 1987, when he had 23. He broke his own record with 24 in 1992. His record was broken in 1998 when Jose Canseco, the Toronto Blue Jays' DH, stole 29 bases.

Big Fun and Big Business

The beginning of windsurfing can be traced to 1965, when two good friends, Hoyle Schweitzer and Jim Drake, wanted to combine surfing and sailing. They realized that the major problem with surfing was that you had to wait for the waves. By the end of 1968, they patented the first windsurf board, called the Windsurfer. In 1973, they licensed their concept to the Ten Cate Company, and for the next five years Windsurfers took American thrillseekers by storm.

Horse Racing's New King

When Secretariat won the Kentucky Derby and the Preakness Stakes—the first two legs of the Triple Crown—his performances amazed even those who had predicted greatness for the colt when he was named Horse of the Year as a two-year-old. At the Derby on May 5, he rallied from last place to win in record time. Two weeks later, at the Preakness Stakes, Secretariat won again by two and a half lengths, and only a clock malfunction prevented him from breaking another official race record.

Only the Belmont Stakes stood between Secretariat and the first Triple Crown in 25 years. On June 9, 70,000 fans packed Belmont Park in New York as Secretariat and four other horses were led to the gate. Secretariat shared the early lead with Sham, who had finished second in the Derby and the Preakness, but the pace quickened as they neared six furlongs. Secretariat pulled away, and his trainer, Lucien Laurin, worried that the horse could not maintain his speed all the way to the end of the race. His lead, however, continued to increase as Secretariat reached the third turn. He just kept getting faster.

The roar of the crowd welcomed Secretariat as he thundered home. There was no horse within 31 lengths when Secretariat crossed the finish line in a time of two minutes, 24 seconds—almost three full seconds faster that the previous track record and one of the most decisive victories in horse racing history. Secretariat had won not only the first Triple Crown in 25 years, but also the hearts of a nation and a permanent place in horse racing history as one of its greatest champions.

The Juice

These days, former NFL star O.J. Simpson has been shunned by society after a string of legal woes. In 1994, he was arrested on suspicion of murdering his ex-wife and her friend. Although he was acquitted of criminal charges, he later was found liable for the murders in civil court. In 2007, Simpson was arrested on several felony charges involving robbery, assault, and kidnapping in an incident in a Las Vegas hotel room. He was convicted in 2008 and sent to jail.

In the 1970s, however, America embraced O.J. Simpson, then a running back for the Buffalo Bills, as it had few other black athletes. Simpson (known as "the Juice" because of his initials) was breaking records on the football field, running through airports for the Hertz rental car company—as the first black celebrity to be featured in a national ad campaign—and deflecting praise to his offensive line. In less than a decade, he'd become the most popular figure in American team sports—a black hero whom white kids adored.

On the field, from his first game for the University of Southern California (USC) Trojans in 1967, it was apparent that he not only was taller, stronger, and heavier than most running backs of the period, but he was also faster than virtually all of his peers. In fact, he became the prototype running back of the next generation. In addition to winning the Heisman Trophy in 1968, Simpson led the Trojans to a national title in 1967, thanks to his memorable 64-yard touchdown run to beat cross-town rival UCLA, 21–20.

Selected by the abysmal Bills as the first pick of the 1969 NFL draft, he languished for three years in a pass-oriented offense. But Lou Saban arrived in 1972 as the Bills' head coach, and he quickly realized that he should not just be using the game's best running back as a decoy. As a result, Simpson made history. In 1973 he broke Jim Brown's all-time single-season

1973

rushing record, finishing with 2,003 yards in 14 games, the first player ever to top 2,000 yards in a season (only five other players have since gone over the 2,000-yard mark; the Rams' Eric Dickerson holds the single-season record of 2,105 yards in 1984). Simpson might have been even better in 1975, when he accounted for 2,243 combined yards (rushing and receiving), scored 23 touchdowns.

Simpson retired in 1979 after two seasons with the San Francisco 49ers, with 11,236 rushing yards and 2,142 yards more on 203 career receptions.

Monster of the Midway

He was a grunting, snarling defensive machine, dedicated to creating football mayhem and destroying offensive game plans. Dick Butkus' road to the Pro Football Hall of Fame was paved with blood, sweat, pain—and the intense anger that coursed through the veins of the celebrated middle linebacker.

The 6-foot-3, 245-pound Butkus served as the Chicago Bears' defensive leader and enforcer from 1965 to 1973, when the almost-constant physical

Other Milestones of 1973

✔ On January 22, less than two weeks after his 24th birthday, George Foreman defeated Joe Frazier to win boxing's heavyweight title. Foreman needed only until midway through the second round to pull off the stunning upset in Kingston, Jamaica.

✔ On March 1, Robyn Smith became the first woman jockey to win a stakes race (a race for which an owner pays an entry fee for his or her horse; that fee usually is part of the total prize money for the race) when she rode North Sea to victory at Aqueduct.

✔ On September 20, Billie Jean King beat former Wimbledon men's champion Bobby Riggs in the "Battle of the Sexes." Her victory was seen by a television audience estimated at more than 50 million people worldwide, a huge number at the time.

✔ Steve Prefontaine became the first major track athlete to wear Nike shoes. "Pre," who never lost a race in four years at the University of Oregon, embodied the competitive spirit of the new brand. His success and personality helped convert several athletes to Nikes, including Jon Anderson, who won the Boston Marathon, and Romanian tennis player Ilie Nastase, the top-ranked pro.

✔ Johnny Unitas was the most celebrated football passer in history when he retired in 1973 after one season with the San Diego Chargers. The longtime Baltimore Colts quarterback was inducted into the Pro Football Hall of Fame in 1979.

✔ The first Iditarod sled-dog race began on March 3, 1973. The first winner, Dick Wilmarth, needed almost three weeks to reach Nome, Alaska, 1,150 miles from the start in Anchorage. Today, the winner typically takes from 10 to 17 days.

✔ Buffalo BIlls running back O.J. Simpson became the first NFL player to top 2,000 rushing yards in a season, ending with a total of 2,003 yards.

pounding finally took its toll on a body that had been pushed to full throttle on every play. He was both loved and hated for the mean, take-no-prisoners style he brought to the field, but his success was fueled by a consuming drive to be the best and a relentless dedication to his profession.

The burly Butkus combined surprising speed with a fearsome strength that he used to fight off powerful blockers. A ball carrier who fell into the grasp of his long, thick arms could expect to be squeezed into helpless submission.

Other runners and offensive linemen were constantly amazed by the ferocity of his hits. Butkus could run down ball carriers from sideline to sideline, shadow running backs in pass coverage, and make the right calls for coach George Halas' complicated defense.

Butkus' misfortune was that he played for weak Chicago teams that never challenged for NFL superiority. But he played in eight Pro Bowls, and the notoriety he gained beyond his hometown of Chicago made him a legend. Butkus' incredible instinct for the ball can be documented by the 25 opponents' fumbles he recovered and the 22 interceptions he recorded in 119 professional

Monster of the Midway *Middle linebacker Dick Butkus was a ferocious defender for the Chicago Bears in a career that eventually led to the Hall of Fame.*

games. He also is known as one of best ball-stripping tacklers in league history, having the uncanny ability to make a tackle with one arm and knock the ball free with the other.

1974

Day of the Dolphins Part II

A funny thing happened to the Miami Dolphins on the way to another NFL championship in the 1973 season: They lost a regular-season game. (Two, actually.) Still, while the Dolphins weren't perfect like they were in 1972, they clearly were still the best team in the NFL. They won their second consecutive Super Bowl with a decisive 24–7 victory over the Minnesota Vikings in Super Bowl VIII in Houston on January 13, 1974.

After winning 12 of 14 games during the regular portion of the schedule, Miami routed the Cincinnati Bengals and the Oakland Raiders in the AFC playoffs. The Vikings also won 12 regular-season games, then ousted the Washington Redskins and the Dallas Cowboys in the NFC playoffs to reach the Super Bowl.

Once they reached the league title game, however, the Vikings were no match for the bulldozing ground attack and suffocating defense of the experienced Dolphins. Miami drove 62 and 56 yards to touchdowns the first two times it had the ball, and the Dolphins never looked back. The score was 24–0 before Minnesota scored in the fourth quarter.

Streak Stoppers

The Notre Dame Fighting Irish staged an incredible rally to stun UCLA 71–70 on January 19 and end the Bruins' NCAA-record, 88-game men's basketball winning streak. Two months later, UCLA's record seven-season run as NCAA basketball champions was ended by the North Carolina State Wolfpack 80–77 in two overtimes in the national semifinals.

At Notre Dame, the Bruins appeared well on their way to win number 89 in a row when they held a 70–59 lead with just 3:32 to play. But UCLA did not score again.

Meanwhile, the Irish capitalized on five Bruins' turnovers, and took a 71–70 lead when Dwight Clay sank a jumper from the corner with 29 seconds left. UCLA missed several shots at a potential winning basket in the closing seconds, and Notre Dame held on for the one-point victory.

In the NCAA Tournament, UCLA had a seven-point lead in the second overtime before North Carolina State rallied. The Wolfpack went on to beat Marquette 76–54 in the title game.

Company for the Babe *Atlanta Braves slugger Hank Aaron connects for career home run No. 714 to tie the legendary Babe Ruth for the most in baseball history. Four days later, Aaron hit another to take over the top spot.*

Aaron's Historic Blast

Atlanta Braves slugger Hank Aaron (b.1934) became baseball's all-time home run leader when he hit his 715th career blast in a game at Atlanta Stadium on April 8 (see page 95).

"Hammerin' Hank" belted a fastball from Los Angeles Dodgers left-hander Al Downing over the left-field fence in the fourth inning of the Braves' home opener. Aaron broke legendary Babe Ruth's ca-reer mark of 714 home runs, which stood nearly four decades.

The Braves' outfielder had ended the 1973 season at 713 career home runs. Atlanta opened the 1974 season on the road at Cincinnati, where Aaron tied Ruth's mark with number 714 off the Reds' Jack Billingham on Opening Day. Aaron did not play in the Braves' next game, then failed to homer in the third game, thus giving him a chance to break the record in front of the home fans.

1974

Broad Street Bullies

The NHL's Philadelphia Flyers got the nickname "Broad Street Bullies" for their intimidating ways and the street on which their home arena, The Spectrum, was located.

In May, the Broad Street Bullies won the Stanley Cup championship by beating the Boston Bruins four games to two in the Finals.

Philadelphia sealed its first Cup title in typical Flyers' fashion. Rick MacLeish scored a power-play goal in the first period of game six, and goalie Bernie Parent made it stand up for a hard-fought, 1–0 victory over the high-scoring Bruins.

Celtics Back on Top

It was a tumultuous year in 1974. The Watergate drama led to President Richard Nixon's resignation. (Briefly, Nixon and men working for him had tried to cover up a break-in at Democratic Party headquarters; the resulting scandal ended Nixon's presidency and sent several members of his staff to prison.) The energy crisis sapped the nation's spirit. Heiress Patty Hearst's kidnapping was a real-life drama.

In the NBA, though, everything was back to normal. That's right, the Boston Celtics were champions again. Boston, which won 11 league championships from 1957 to 1969, returned to the top after a four-season hiatus.

The Celtics won 56 of 82 regular-season games, then breezed past the Buffalo Braves and the New York Knicks in the playoffs before taking a seven-game

Finals series against the Milwaukee Bucks. Center Dave Cowens (b.1948) was the star in the decisive game, when he scored 28 points and grabbed 14 rebounds in Boston's 102–87 victory on May 12.

Girls Play, Too

On June 12, a New Jersey court paved the way for girls to play Little League Baseball. Girls had played Little League as far back as 1950—although it was a girl disguised as a boy. That prompted Little League Baseball to officially ban girls. More than 20 years later, in 1972, Maria Pepe played several games for a team in Hoboken, New Jersey. Little League Baseball refused to lift its ban, however, and the National Organization for Women (NOW) sued.

After the court ruled in favor of NOW, Little League Baseball opened to girls as well as boys. (Later in the year, Bunny Taylor became the first girl to pitch an official Little League no-hitter.) Today, Little League Baseball boasts that more than 50,000 girls play its game.

Also in 1974, minor-league baseball's Portland Mavericks hired baseball's first female coach, Lanny Moss. The next year, Moss became the general manager of the Northwest League club, which was not affiliated with a Major League team.

By the way, Portland really was a maverick franchise. In 1974, its manager, Frank Peters, orchestrated an unusual stunt. He had his players rotate each inning so that they each played one position during a nine-inning game. It worked, too! The Mavericks won 8–7.

Hammerin' Hank

Hank Aaron approached Babe Ruth's career home run record the same way he approached just about everything in his life: quietly. Aaron always did things at his own pace, and he seemed to view reaching the record as nothing more than a part of his job. The steadiness of his character was reflected in his extraordinary consistency at the plate. For 23 years, Aaron averaged nearly 33 home runs a year, yet he never hit more than 47 in any one season. When he finally retired in 1976, Aaron had 755 career home runs.

It is difficult to separate Aaron's career from its historical context. He began his professional career in 1952 with the Indianapolis Clowns of the Negro League, and his career unfolded along with the civil-rights movement. As a minor leaguer in the Deep South, Aaron encountered racial prejudices that would shadow his career but helped him forge the quiet, dignified approach that was to prove his greatest asset in the Majors.

After he joined the Milwaukee Braves in 1954, Aaron demonstrated the sweet stroke that earned him two batting titles and four home run crowns. Still, many fans were surprised when it became obvious that Aaron was going to break Ruth's record. Some Americans did not want a black man to break the mark, and others could not conceive that someone they perceived as ordinary would eclipse the larger-than-life Ruth. They tainted Aaron's pursuit of the record with hundreds of angry and bigoted letters. Reflecting on the experience, Aaron has said that, although this should have been the most enjoyable time in his life, it was, instead, "hell."

In the end, the letters were about as effective as opposing pitchers. Aaron continued to hit, and the records continued to fall. In addition to the home run record, he set career records for runs batted in and total bases. His final career total of 755 home runs ensures that he will always be included among baseball's all-time greatest players.

Love Match

Everyone knows Paris is for lovers. So, too, is Wimbledon, even if you are a player. Although in the past Wimbledon honors had occasionally gone to husband and wife or brother and sister teams in the doubles events, true singles romance hit the headlines in 1974. On July 5 and 6, Jimmy Connors (b.1952) and Chris Evert (b.1954) celebrated their engagement by winning the singles titles on Centre Court.

Connors, aged 21, and Evert, 19, were both playing at Wimbledon for the third time. A quarterfinalist in both 1972 and 1973, the third-seeded Connors reached the finals this time. He lost only six games while defeating veteran Ken Rosewall (b.1934) in straight sets in the final.

Evert, who reached the semifinals during her debut in 1972 and made it to the finals the following year, beat Russia's Olga Morozova 6–0, 6–4 to win the first of her three Wimbledon singles crowns.

Connors and Evert were engaged to be married in November. Although the engagement eventually was called off, Wimbledon was the background to three other relationships. Bjorn Borg (b.1956) married Romanian player Mariana Simionescu a month after winning his fifth consecutive Wimbledon title in 1980 (they had first met at the French Open four

Mixed Doubles *Chris Evert gives a peck on the cheek to fiancee Jimmy Connors at Wimbledon in July. The two stars, who were engaged to be married later in the year, each won singles titles.*

Mustachioed relief pitcher Rollie Fingers was the star for Oakland. Fingers won the Series opener, then closed out each of his team's next three victories. Oakland batted only .211 in the Series and managed only eight extra-base hits, but one of them was Joe Rudi's home run to break a 2–2 tie in the bottom of the seventh inning of game five. Fingers made the run stand up for a 3–2 victory that ended the Series (four of the five games were decided by that same score; the A's won the fourth game 5–2).

Oakland became the first club to win three consecutive World Series since the New York Yankees won five in a row from 1949 to 1953.

Ali Outfoxes Foreman

Former heavyweight boxing champion Muhammad Ali (b.1942) made his mark as a dancer in the ring, often taunting his opponents to come after him. He'd "float like a butterfly," as he liked to put it. But on October 29, in the "Rumble in the Jungle" in Zaire against George Foreman (b.1949), the reigning champ, Ali dramatically changed his tactics.

For most of the early rounds, Ali backed up to the ropes and let Foreman flail away. Foreman was known for his powerful punches, but his shots fell harmlessly against Ali's arms. By the eighth round, the champion was exhausted. Ali, sensing his chance, went on the offensive and knocked Foreman out.

The stunning strategy made Ali the heavyweight champion for a second time. In 1967, he had his title stripped after he refused induction into military service.

years earlier), and Evert dated another tennis player, Britain's John Lloyd, for the first time at Wimbledon in 1978. They married a year later.

There was, alas, no happy ending for the marriages of Borg and Evert. Both marriages ended in divorce.

California Dreamin'

Baseball's World Series was played entirely in California for the first time, with the American League-champion Oakland A's taking on the National League-champion Los Angeles Dodgers. The A's won their third championship in a row by taking the Series in five games.

The End of One Dynasty. . .

The Miami Dolphins' string of three consecutive AFC titles and their bid for a third consecutive Super Bowl championship ended when Oakland Raiders running back Clarence Davis made a miraculous catch to give his team a 28–26 victory in a divisional playoff game at Oakland on December 21.

The game marked the end of the Dolphins' dynasty. The next season, star running backs Larry Csonka and Jim Kiick, plus wide receiver Paul Warfield, bolted to the World Football League.

Miami missed the playoffs in 1975 for the first time since 1969.

. . . Beginning of Another

Just as one dynasty was ending in Miami, another was beginning in Pittsburgh, where the Steelers qualified for their first Super Bowl by beating the Oakland Raiders 24–13 in the AFC Championship Game on December 29.

Even as several significant NFL rules changes opened up offenses around the league, the Steelers' defense proved to be remarkably stingy. Led by future Pro Football Hall of Famers such as defensive tackle "Mean Joe" Greene, linebacker Jack Lambert, and cornerback Mel Blount, the "Steel Curtain" allowed opponents an average of only 13.5 points per game.

Other Milestones of 1974

✔ With the United States in the midst of a fuel shortage, NASCAR shortened the Daytona 500 to 450 miles. Richard Petty won the race.

✔ Speedster Ivory Crockett ran the 100-yard dash in nine seconds flat to set a new world record during a meet in Knoxville, Tennessee, on May 11.

✔ The University of Southern California (USC) Trojans capped an unprecedented string of five consecutive NCAA titles in baseball by beating Miami (Florida) 7–3 in the final game of the College World Series in Omaha in June. Through 2009, USC had a record 12 titles.

✔ The first commercially sponsored beach volleyball tournament took place in San Diego, California in the summer of 1974. Winston Cigarettes was the event's title sponsor.

✔ St. Louis Cardinals outfielder Lou Brock stole a big-league-record 118 bases. He shattered the old mark of 104, set by Maury Wills in 1962.

✔ The first World Series held entirely in California pitted the N.L.-champion Los Angeles Dodgers and A.L.-champion Oakland Athletics. The A's won in five games to become only the second team since the 1953 Yankees to win three straight Series.

✔ On December 20, a federal judge ruled that the NFL's player reserve system was illegal. The ruling opened the door for eventual free agency in professional football.

✔ Spurred by a stunning come-from-behind win over Notre Dame (they scored 55 points in 17 minutes in the second half), USC went on to win the national college football title.

1975

Happy New Year for USC

When Shelton Diggs made a diving, two-point conversion catch late in the fourth quarter to give the University of Southern California (USC) an 18–17 victory over the Ohio State Buckeyes in the Rose Bowl on New Year's Day, the Trojans figured they had simply put an exclamation point on an already exciting season. What they didn't realize was that the play delivered USC a share of college football's national title.

The Trojans had little reason to believe they had a chance at the championship after finishing the regular season 9–1–1 and ranked fifth in the country. But they beat the third-ranked Buckeyes when Pat Haden lofted a 38-yard touchdown pass to John McKay, then Diggs made his catch on the conversion.

That night, top-ranked Alabama was upset by Notre Dame in the Orange Bowl, and the Trojans vaulted to number one in the United Press International poll. The Associated Press champion, the Oklahoma Sooners, already had been determined before the bowls. That school was on probation and ineligible to play in a bowl game or compete for the UPI crown.

Steelers' First Title

There were tears in NFL commissioner Pete Rozelle's eyes when he presented the Vince Lombardi Trophy to Pittsburgh Steelers owner Art Rooney (1901–1988) in the locker room following Super Bowl IX in New Orleans on January 12. "No man ever deserved it more," Rozelle said. Rooney's Steelers had just beaten the Minnesota Vikings 16–6 at Tulane Stadium, giving Pittsburgh its first league championship.

The 73-year-old Rooney had founded the franchise in 1933, but the club enjoyed little success in its first four decades. The Steelers won a club-record 11 games in 1972, however, and began a string of eight consecutive playoff appearances.

It was the Steelers' defense that carried the club to its first Super Bowl appearance. Once there, the "Steel Curtain" didn't let up. Pittsburgh permitted the Vikings only 119 total yards (just 17 of them on the ground), intercepted three passes, recovered two fumbles, and recorded a safety.

On offense, Pittsburgh running back Franco Harris carried 34 times for 158 yards and was named the game's MVP.

Welcome Home! *Carlton Fisk (27) leaps into the arms of his teammates after hitting a home run to win one of the greatest World Series games ever (see page 103).*

Going-Away Present

After his University of California at Los Angeles (UCLA) Bruins edged Louisville 75–74 in overtime in the NCAA men's basketball tournament semifinals on March 29, head coach John Wooden announced his retirement. The "Wizard of Westwood," who won more than 80 percent of his games in 27 years as a college coach, decided that the title game against the Kentucky Wildcats on March 31 in San Diego would be his last.

The Bruins' players sent their coach out in style. With center Richard Washington (28 points) and forward Dave Meyers (24 points) combining for 52 points, UCLA beat the Wildcats 92–85. It was the Bruins' 10th national championship in 12 seasons.

Another Barrier Broken

Frank Robinson (b.1935) became the first African American to manage a Major League Baseball team when he took the reins of the Cleveland Indians for the 1975 season.

Actually, the superstar outfielder (he won baseball's Triple Crown in 1966 when

1975

he led the American League in batting average, home runs, and RBI) and designated hitter had been named the Indians' player-manager back on October 3, 1974, at the conclusion of the previous season. But his on-field debut came in the 1975 season opener against the New York Yankees on April 8. Robinson the manager penciled in Robinson the designated hitter into the lineup that day. And in his first at bat in the first inning, he belted a solo home run off New York's Doc Medich. Robinson's blast helped the Indians beat the Yankees 5–3 in his debut. Cleveland struggled, however, to a 79–80 record and a fourth-place finish in the American League East by season's end.

Women in the Sports Headlines

Title IX—the landmark ruling that prohibits institutions that receive federal funding from discriminating against women in educational programs or athletic activities—originally was written in 1972 but officially went into effect on June 21 of this year. With or without Title IX, however, women were making big headlines in sports in 1975:

- Women's college basketball powers Immaculata and Queens played at Madison Square Garden on January 27. It was a first at the Garden and drew nearly 12,000 fans. Immaculata won 65–61.

- American distance runner Francie Larrieu, who already held several world indoor records, set another in the 1,500 meters in a race in Toronto on February 14.

- Dorothy Hamill won the second of three consecutive United States figure skating championships. She eventually would complete an impressive triple in 1976 with a world figure skating title and an Olympic gold medal (see page 108).

- Chris Evert outlasted Evonne Goolagong-Cawley in three sets to win the U.S. Open tennis championship for the first time at Forest Hills in September. Evert began a string of four consecutive national titles.

Warriors Win NBA Title

The most telling moment of the NBA Finals came early in Game Four on May 25, when Baltimore Bullets guard Mike Riordan nearly tackled Rick Barry when the Golden State Warriors' star drove to the basket. The heavily favored Bullets were clearly frustrated after losing the first three games of the series, and the Warriors believed Riordan's rough foul was an attempt to get the volatile Barry to lose his cool and earn an ejection from the game. Instead, Barry stayed calm and led his team to a series-clinching, 96–95 win.

Barry ranked among the league leaders in scoring (at 30.6 points per game, he was second only to Buffalo's Bob McAdoo) and assists (6.2 per game, which was sixth) during the regular season while leading the Warriors to the Pacific Division title. But they won a relatively modest 48 of 82 games, and were decided underdogs against a Bullets' team that won 60 times and waltzed to the Central Division championship by 19 games. "No one took us very seriously," Warriors head coach Al Attles said.

As expected, the Finals did turn out to be a mismatch—but in Golden State's favor. Though the games were close,

Barry was the difference. The Warriors' forward was named the most valuable player of the Finals after averaging 29.5 points per game.

One footnote to the series: For the first time in major sports history in this country, both head coaches in a championship matchup (the Warriors' Attles, and the Bullets' K.C. Jones) were African-American. It was a tribute to the diversity of the NBA, however, that this was only a footnote, and not a major media story.

Coming to America

International superstar Pelé breathed life into the North American Soccer League (NASL) by signing with the New York Cosmos. He made his debut with New York in an exhibition match against the Dallas Tornado on June 15 in New York.

In the days before the Internet and instant communication, Pelé was perhaps the world's most famous athlete. The Brazilian combined speed, athletic ability, and power to become what many experts would call the greatest soccer player in history.

Pelé retired from international competition after leading his country to the World Cup in 1970. (He also played for the Brazil teams that won in 1958 and 1962.) He was brilliant in the 1970 final against Italy, scoring 1 goal and assisting on 2 others in Brazil's 4–1 victory.

Pelé came out of retirement to play for the Cosmos and increase the public presence of soccer in the United States, where it long has lagged behind its presence in the rest of the world.

International Star *Brazilian soccer star Pelé, the hero of his country's World Cup victory in 1970, signed with the New York Cosmos of the North American Soccer League.*

All Four None

For the first time in baseball history, four pitchers combined on a no-hitter during the Oakland A's 5–0 victory over the California Angels on the last day of baseball's regular season. More than 22,000 fans were on hand at the Oakland-Alameda County Coliseum on September

1975

28 when the A's, who were readying themselves for the playoffs, made history.

Vida Blue started and pitched five hitless innings before giving way to reliever Glenn Abbott. He didn't allow a hit in the sixth, and neither did Paul Lindblad in the seventh. Closer Rollie Fingers shut the door in the eighth and ninth innings.

Ali Outslugs Frazier in a "Thrilla"

 Thirty-something boxing greats Muhammad Ali and Joe Frazier (b.1944)

stepped into the ring in Manila on October 1 and delighted a large crowd that included Philippine President Ferdinand Marcos with an exciting bout. Ali eventually defended his heavyweight crown when Frazier could not come out of his corner for the 15th round.

Ali and Frazier had split two prior meetings in the ring. Frazier won the first, a unanimous 15-round decision in 1971 in New York's Madison Square Garden to defend his title and hand Ali his first loss in 32 fights. Ali came back to win the rematch, a non-title bout also in New York

Rubber Match *Muhammad Ali (right) made it two out of three against Joe Frazier in the "Thrilla in Manila."*

in 1974 to earn a shot at champion George Foreman (see page 96).

In this one, Ali and Frazier slugged it out toe-to-toe right from the start. Frazier, the title challenger, had the upper hand in the middle rounds. "I hit him with punches that would bring down the walls of a city," Frazier said. But Ali stood his ground, then closed with a flourish, pummeling his opponent the final three rounds. By the end of the 14th round, Frazier was visibly exhausted, and his manager threw in the towel. The championship fight has come to be known as the "Thrilla in Manila."

Prior to beating Frazier, Ali also defended his heavyweight crown in 1975 against challengers Chuck Wepner (in Richfield, Ohio, on March 24) and Joe Bugner (in Malaysia on July 1).

A Classic Fall Classic

The Cincinnati Reds beat the Boston Red Sox 4–3 in the seventh and deciding game of the World Series October 22 at Boston's Fenway Park. Thus, the Reds outlasted the Red Sox four games to three in what is widely regarded as one of the greatest World Series ever.

Boston went home for Game Six on October 21 trailing three games to two. The next two games packed enough drama to keep baseball fans talking about the Series to this day. First, the Red Sox clawed their way from the brink of elimination by winning the sixth game 7–6 in 12 innings. Boston trailed 6–3 until pinch-hitter Bernie Carbo launched a three-run home run to tie the game in the bottom of the eighth inning.

The Curse of the Bambino

Pitcher-outfielder Babe Ruth (1895–1948) helped the Boston Red Sox win three World Series titles in four seasons from 1915 to 1918. But after the 1919 season, Ruth was sold to the New York Yankees to help owner Harry Frazee cover mounting theatrical losses. That watershed deal proved to put the two franchises at a crossroads of epic proportions.

Before acquiring Ruth, the Yankees had not won a World Series. But Ruth turned the franchise into a power, and its 27 world championships are far and away the most in baseball history.

Before trading Ruth, the Red Sox's five World Series titles were more than any other team in baseball. But it was a long time before they won another championship. Boston ended its 86-year title drought by winning the World Series in 2004.

Neither team scored again until the bottom of the 12th. That's when Boston catcher Carlton Fisk blasted a solo homer to end the game. The dramatic television footage of Fisk anxiously watching his long drive, arms raised, waving the ball to stay fair, is one of baseball's most memorable scenes ever.

Fisk's heroics carried the Red Sox to the brink of their first world championship since 1918 (see box). But Boston could not shut the door on the Reds in Game Seven despite taking a 3–0 lead early on. First baseman Tony Perez narrowed Cincinnati's deficit to one run with a two-run home run in the sixth inning, and the Reds tied it with another run in the seventh. In the top of the ninth inning, Morgan blooped a single to center field to plate Ken Griffey with the winning run. Reliever Will McEnaney retired the Red Sox in order in the bottom of the ninth to save it, and the "Big Red Machine" captured the franchise's first World Series since 1940.

1975

Twice Is Nice

For its first 40 years, the Heisman Trophy (given annually to the nation's premier college football player) had been awarded to 40 different players. But on December 2 at the Downtown Athletic Club in New York City, Ohio State running back Archie Griffin became the first player ever to win the award twice.

Griffin finished his college career with a then-record 5,176 rushing yards (the mark would last only one year before Pittsburgh's Tony Dorsett shattered it). Before Griffin in 1974, four juniors—Army fullback Doc Blanchard (1945), SMU

Captain Comeback *Quarterback Roger Staubach rallied Dallas in the NFL playoffs.*

Other Milestones of 1975

✔ Golfer Jack Nicklaus drained a 40-foot birdie putt on the 16th hole to help give him his record fifth Masters title on April 13. He edged Johnny Miller and Tom Weiskopf each by one shot. Nicklaus eventually stretched his record to six Masters championships when he won at the age of 46 in 1986. He won that year by posting a dramatic six-under-par 30 on the back nine on Sunday.

✔ The Philadelphia Flyers defeated the Buffalo Sabres in six games in the NHL finals to win their second consecutive Stanley Cup.

✔ Distance-running star Steve Prefontaine died at 24 in a car accident in Eugene, Oregon on May 30.

✔ California Angels pitcher Nolan Ryan equaled Sandy Koufax's big-league record by tossing his fourth career no-hitter. Ryan shut down the Baltimore Orioles 1–0 on June 1.

✔ Two firsts for men's and women's tennis: Players at the Wimbledon tournament that concluded in July were allowed to rest on chairs during changeovers, and lights were installed to accommodate night matches at Forest Hills for the U.S. Open that concluded in September.

✔ The World Football League failed in its challenge to the established NFL, folding in October before it could complete its second season. It remains the last real challenger to NFL dominance.

✔ An arbitrator's ruling December 23 opened the door for widespread baseball free agency in later years and, subsequently, skyrocketing salaries. Labor arbitrator Peter Seitz ruled that pitchers Andy Messersmith and Dave McNally were free to sign with any team. McNally retired, but Messersmith went on to play for three teams the next four seasons.

✔ Ohio State running back Archie Griffin became the first player to win player to win the Heisman Trophy, given to college football's top player, twice. He remains the only player with two of the trophies.

halfback Doak Walker (1948), Ohio State halfback Vic Janowicz (1950) and Navy quarterback Roger Staubach (1963)—had won the coveted Heisman. But Griffin was the first, and still only, player to duplicate the feat as a senior.

Answered Prayer

With his team trailing the Minnesota Vikings 14–10 and time running out in an NFC Divisional Playoff Game in Bloomington on December 28, Dallas Cowboys quarterback Roger Staubach (b.1942) dropped back to pass from midfield and heaved the ball as far as he could. "I closed my eyes and said a Hail Mary," Staubach told reporters later.

Staubach's prayer was answered. Cowboys wide receiver Drew Pearson caught the ball at the five-yard line, cradling the ball on his hip despite close coverage from a pair of Vikings' defenders. He fell into the end zone with 24 seconds left to give the Cowboys a 17–14 victory.

A desperation heave at the end of football games has been around a long time, of course. But Staubach's miracle officially launched its designation as a "Hail Mary pass."

1976

Steelers Super Again

The Pittsburgh Steelers edged the Dallas Cowboys 21–17 in a thrilling Super Bowl played at the Orange Bowl in Miami on January 18. The Cowboys led a tense battle 10–7 in the fourth quarter before the Steelers took command by scoring 14 points in unusual fashion: on a safety, two field goals and a touchdown (while missing the extra point).

The safety came when Pittsburgh backup running back Reggie Harrison blocked a punt out of the end zone early in the fourth quarter to trim the Steelers' deficit to one point. After Roy Gerela kicked field goals of 36 yards and 18 yards to give Pittsburgh a 15–10 advantage, Steelers wide receiver Lynn Swann (b.1952) hauled in a 64-yard touchdown pass from Terry Bradshaw (b.1948) for the clinching touchdown with 3:02 remaining. The Cowboys closed within four points with a late touchdown, then held the Steelers on downs, but safety Glen Edwards sealed Pittsburgh's second consecutive Super Bowl win with an interception in the end zone on the final play.

Swann's fourth-quarter touchdown capped a brilliant day. He caught just four passes, but they went for 161 yards and earned him the game's most valuable player award. His ballet-like, 53-yard, fingertip grab in the second quarter is one of most remarkable catches in NFL history.

While the game turned on Harrison's blocked punt, the most important play may actually have been a failed field-goal attempt in the third quarter. With his team trailing by only three points, Gerela misfired on a 36-yard try. Dallas safety Cliff Harris mocked him by applauding the miss and patting him on the helmet. That bit of gamesmanship infuriated Steelers linebacker Jack Lambert, who tossed Harris to the ground. "The Pittsburgh Steelers aren't supposed to be intimidated," Lambert growled afterward. "We're supposed to do the intimidating. I decided to do something about it."

Momentum swung to Pittsburgh's side, and the Steelers controlled the action much of the way after that.

Pearson Crawls to Finish

NASCAR drivers flew around the two-and-a-half-mile oval at the Daytona 500 on February 15 at speeds

Swann Dive *Pittsburgh's Lynn Swann makes a diving, acrobatic catch against the Dallas Cowboys in Super Bowl X. Swann was named the most valuable player of the Steelers' 21–17 victory.*

averaging more than 152 miles per hour—and sometimes nearly 200 miles per hour. In the end, though, David Pearson's car limped home at less than 20 miles per hour to take the checkered flag ahead of Richard Petty. It was one of the most bizarre, but exciting, NASCAR races ever.

Pearson and Petty often raced side-by-side toward the finish throughout their careers. Pearson, in fact, won more career races than anyone else in NASCAR history—anyone else except Petty, that is.

They called Petty "The King," and for good reason (see the box on the opposite page). He won 200 races in all. This one got away from him on the last lap, however.

Petty was in front until Pearson sped by on the backstretch. That was no problem for The King, who immediately dove down inside to try to retake the lead. For a short time, the legendary drivers zoomed side-by-side, pedal to the metal. But coming out of the last turn, the two cars bumped. Pearson went careening into the

Richard Petty: The King

Richard Petty may have lost the Daytona 500 in a wild finish in 1976, but that hardly tarnished his crown. He'll forever be known as "The King" to NASCAR fans around the country.

Petty, the son of Hall of Fame driver Lee Petty, won his first NASCAR title in 1964. Then he left little doubt that he was destined to be known as one of the greatest drivers of all time with a dominating season in 1967. That year, he won an unbelievable 27 of the 48 races he entered, including 10 in a row in one stretch.

In a 35-year career from 1958 to 1992, Petty won a record 200 races—nearly double the total of David Pearson's runnerup 105. Petty also holds all-time NASCAR records for the most career starts, poles, top-five finishes and top-10 finishes, and he shares the mark for the most season championships (he and Dale Earnhardt, Sr. each won seven titles).

But Petty's influence goes well beyond the statistics. He is arguably the most popular driver in NASCAR history, and his trademark grin beneath a cowboy hat and dark sunglasses is recognized around the country even by non-racing fans. He remains a popular product spokesman more than a decade after his retirement from competitive racing. He's hardly retired altogether, however, because he remains active with Petty Enterprises, a car owner on the current NASCAR circuit.

wall. Petty spun wildly, then started going backwards toward the finish line before his car gave out only 50 yards away.

Pearson, meanwhile, bounced off the wall and hit another car, keeping him on the track. His front end was mangled, but his car still worked. He slowly headed toward the finish line while Petty frantically tried to get his car started again. "It took forever to get there," Pearson said. Eventually, he did.

Winter Olympics

Dorothy Hamill, a 19-year-old from Riverside, Connecticut, won the gold medal in women's figure skating at the 1976 Winter Olympic Games at Innsbruck, Austria. She also won over Americans with her charm, beauty and emotion.

Hamill and speed skater Sheila Young, who won three medals, were the American stars of the Winter Games. Hamill's gold medal was punctuated by dozens of flowers tossed on the ice by admiring fans. She fought tears before several young girls helped her gather the flowers, and again when the gold medal was placed around her neck. "I probably remember most all the flowers raining down at the end of my performance," she said. "It was quite a shock and a warm feeling."

The gold medalist's signature wedge haircut soon was named for her as young women all over the country went to their stylists to request a "Dorothy Hamill."

Flag Day in Los Angeles

In the midst of the United States' year-long bicentennial celebration, Chicago Cubs star Rick Monday became a contemporary hero. Monday grabbed an American flag from two men who were trying to set it on fire in the outfield at Dodger Stadium during a game on April 25.

Monday had taken his position in center field for the fourth inning when he noticed the men come out of the stands in possession of the flag. Once he realized what they were trying to do, he sprinted toward them and snatched the flag before their lighter could set it on fire. "They couldn't see me coming from behind, but I could see that one had lit a match," Monday said.

Monday safely delivered the flag to the bullpen, and the trespassers were arrested. Ironically, the outfielder was traded to the Dodgers the following year and played in Los Angeles for the last eight seasons of his 19-year, big-league career.

Lucky 13 for the Celtics

The Boston Celtics outlasted the Phoenix Suns in six games to win an NBA Finals series that featured one of the greatest contests in league history. It came in Game Five with the teams tied at two apiece. The Celtics outlasted the Suns 128–126 in three overtimes at the Boston Garden on June 4. After that, Boston's 87–80 victory in Phoenix two days later was almost anticlimactic. Boston's championship was its second in three seasons and its NBA-record 13th overall.

Over in the ABA, the New York Nets won the final title of the league's nine-year existence. The ABA was down to seven teams by the end of the 1976 season. Four of them—the Nets, Denver Nuggets, Indiana Pacers and San Anto-nio Spurs—officially joined the NBA on June 17.

Before the start of the following NBA season, flashy forward Julius Erving (b.1950), the Nets' superstar, was traded to the Philadelphia 76ers. Erving was sold to Philadelphia for $3 million on October 21. He signed a $3 million deal with his new club.

Woman Driver

A lot of male drivers didn't think a woman had any business racing dragsters, but Shirley Muldowney proved she belonged. At the Spring Nationals on June 13, Muldowney became the first woman to win a National Hot Rod Association (NHRA) event.

Muldowney had been racing dragsters professionally since 1971. She began in Funny Cars, then moved to Top Fuel—the biggest and most powerful dragsters—in 1974. By 1977, she became the first woman to win a season championship.

The Summer Olympics

Decathlete Bruce Jenner (b.1949), swimmers John Naber and Shirley Babashoff, and the American boxing team stood out in an otherwise lackluster Summer Olympic Games for the United States in Montreal. Jenner earned the distinction as the World's Greatest Athlete when he set a world record for points in the 10-event track and field competition. Naber and Babashoff each won five medals (four of Naber's were gold and four of Babashoff's were silver), while the boxers combined for five golds.

1976

After winning his gold medal, Jenner jogged around the Olympic Stadium track carrying an American flag. He quickly became a household name who was in great demand as a product endorser and television personality. Sugar Ray Leonard (see page 133) and brothers Leon and Michael Spinks (see Leon's victory over Muhammad Ali on page 121) all went on to become pro boxing champions.

Overall, the Montreal Games were dominated by the squad from the Soviet Union, while East Germany also had a strong presence. The biggest star, however, may have been 14-year-old Nadia Comaneci (b.1961), a gymnast from Romania. She won three gold medals and delighted fans around the world.

Bedlam in the Bronx

Few scenes in baseball history have been as wild as the one at Yankee Stadium in New York on October 14. That night, New York Yankees first baseman Chris Chambliss sent the hometown fans into a frenzy with a dramatic, pennant-winning home run in the bottom of the ninth inning of the fifth and final game of the American League Championship Series against the Kansas City Royals.

The teams were tied at two games apiece and were even at 6–6 in Game Five when Chambliss stepped in to face Kansas City reliever Mark Littell to open the last of the ninth. Chambliss belted Littell's first pitch into the right-field bleachers, touching off a wild celebration at Yankee Stadium.

New York fans had grown accustomed to seeing their Yankees win pennants almost at will over the years. But New York's 11-season drought from 1965 to 1975 was its longest since winning its first A.L. title in 1921. And so, when Chambliss' blast cleared the wall, thousands poured onto the field in celebration. Chambliss, in fact, was knocked to the ground by overzealous fans between second and third base. "I was in the middle of a mass of people, and when I fell to the ground, it was scary," he said. Chambliss was shuffled off to the clubhouse, then returned later to touch home plate.

World's Greatest Athlete *American Bruce Jenner earned that distinction for winning the gold medal in the decathlon at the Summer Olympic Games in Montreal, Canada.*

Big Red Machine Rolls On

While Chris Chambliss' dramatic home run delivered a pennant to New York, the world championship remained in Cincinnati. The Reds had little trouble dispatching the Yankees in four games in the World Series.

Cincinnati second baseman Joe Morgan (b.1943) homered in the bottom of the first inning of game one, and the Reds never looked back. They went on to win that game 5–1, and outscored the Yankees 22–8 in the series.

Reds catcher Johnny Bench (b.1947) was the star of the World Series, batting .533 with two home runs and six runs batted in. Morgan was the star during the regular season, when he hit .320 with 27 home runs, 111 runs batted in and 60 steals. He earned his second consecutive league Most Valuable Player award.

New NCAA Rushing Mark

University of Pittsburgh Panthers running back Tony Dorsett (b.1954) tore through the NCAA record book while leading his team to an unbeaten regular season. Dorsett, a senior, rushed for 1,948 yards in Pittsburgh's 11 victories. He capped the year by running for 224 yards and two touchdowns in a 24–7 victory over Penn State on November 26.

That brought Dorsett's career total to an NCAA-record 6,082 rushing yards (he broke the record set by Ohio State's Archie Griffin the previous year; Dorsett's mark would stand until Texas' Ricky Williams broke it in 1998). Dorsett became the first player to rush for more than 1,000 yards all four years of his career.

Dorsett was named the Heisman Trophy winner on November 30 as college football's most outstanding player.

Other Milestones of 1976

✔ Darryl Sittler of the Toronto Maple Leafs scored an NHL-record 10 points when he scored 6 goals and had 4 assists in an 11–4 rout of Boston February 7.

✔ The Indiana Hoosiers blasted Michigan 86–68 in the final game of the NCAA men's basketball tournament on March 29 to cap a perfect 32–0 season.

✔ Free-agent pitcher Andy Messersmith signed a "lifetime" contract with the Atlanta Braves on April 10. But he lasted only two seasons with the club.

✔ Slugging third baseman Mike Schmidt of the Philadelphia Phillies homered in four consecutive at-bats in his team's 18–16 victory over the Chicago Cubs on April 17.

✔ The last home run of Hank Aaron's career (it was his 755th) came while he was playing for the Milwaukee Brewers against the California Angels on July 20. Aaron, who began his big-league career in Milwaukee with the Braves in 1954, hit his final blast off Angels righthander Dick Drago.

1977

Silver and Black Attack

On a team known for its boisterous personalities and high-profile stars, the Oakland Raiders' Fred Biletnikoff (b.1943) hardly attracted any notice. But the quiet wide receiver made the key plays in his team's 32–14 victory over the Minnesota Vikings in Super Bowl XI at the Rose Bowl in Pasadena, California, on January 9. Though Biletnikoff's statistics were modest—he had four catches for 79 yards—he earned game MVP honors because three of his receptions led directly to touchdowns.

Biletnikoff's big day extended the Vikings' frustration in the Super Bowl. Minnesota, which had established itself as one of pro football's dominant teams over the past decade, went 11–2–1 during the regular season to win its fourth consecutive division title and its eighth in nine seasons. But the Vikings lost the Super Bowl for the fourth time in as many tries.

Running back Clarence Davis gained 137 yards in the Super Bowl for the Raiders, who won 13 of 14 games during the regular season, then beat New England at Pittsburgh in the playoffs to reach the Super Bowl.

Courageous Effort

Before there was CNN or AOL Time Warner, before his unprecedented billion-dollar gift to the United Nations, before he married actress Jane Fonda, Ted Turner (b.1938) made headlines by guiding *Courageous* to victory in the America's Cup yacht race in January.

Because Turner had lost in the defender trials aboard *Mariner* three years earlier, some observers feared the bombastic owner of cable superstation TBS and the Atlanta Braves baseball team would become the first skipper to lose the United States' 126-year stranglehold on the America's Cup. But the 39-year-old was an experienced sailor who would earn national Yachtsman of the Year honors four times, and he easily carried *Courageous* to a four-race sweep of challenger Australia in the 1977 finals.

Turner was more successful piloting *Courageous* than he was as the Atlanta Braves' skipper the same year. After a 16-game losing streak prompted Turner to send incumbent manager Dave Bristol on paid leave, Turner stepped into the dugout to manage the club against the Pittsburgh Pirates on May 11. Atlanta lost 2–1 to

Thumbs Up *Atlanta Braves owner Ted Turner also was an experienced sailor who won the America's Cup.*

extend its losing streak to 17 games, and National League president Chub Feeney, citing a rule that prohibited managers from owning any part of a club, ordered Turner out of the dugout the next day. Vern Benson took over, and the Braves ended their long losing streak. Turner's career managerial record remains, for all time, 0–1.

Crosby's Last Clambake

Legendary singer Bing Crosby (1903–1977) hosted his last Clambake—the popular professional-amateur golf tournament in Pebble Beach, California—in January. The internationally renowned entertainer passed away in October after suffering a massive heart attack following a round of golf in Madrid, Spain.

Tom Watson (b.1949) won the Clambake with a tournament-record score of 273 for four rounds. The field was notable for two women whom Crosby invited to participate: Nancy Lopez (b.1957) and Marianne Bretton. They were the first women to play in the tournament since 1939. Another amateur in the field was former President Gerald Ford, whose

1977

errant drives kept gallery patrons on their toes.

Crosby originally started the Clambake (which was officially known as the Crosby National Pro-Am Tournament) in 1937 as a way to get together with friends and raise some money for charity. Until his death, the tournament never lost its casual atmosphere.

Although Crosby's name is no longer associated with the tournament, and corporate sponsorship has diluted some of the camaraderie of the Clambake, the event at Pebble Beach remains one of the most popular stops on the PGA Tour more than a quarter century after his death.

Tears of Joy for Al Maguire

When Al Maguire (1928–2001) announced in January that he was stepping down as Marquette University's head coach after 12 years, effective at the end of the season, he could not have envisioned the drama that still awaited him.

Maguire's Warriors lost seven games during the regular season and were one of the last teams to make it into the NCAA tournament (which at the time included only 32 teams—half the current total). But Marquette beat University of Cincinnati convincingly in the opening round of the March tournament, survived a one-point scare against Kansas State University, then upset Wake Forest University to reach the Final Four. After beating University of North Carolina at Charlotte in the national semifinals, Maguire's team upset Dean Smith's (b.1931) favored North Carolina (Chapel Hill) Tar Heels,

67–59, in the title game. Warriors guard Butch Lee scored 19 points in the final game and was named the tournament's most outstanding player, but the real star was Maguire, who openly wept as the clock ticked down to his first national championship.

Until Marquette's surge, the University of San Francisco Dons were the story of the college basketball season. Super sophomores Bill Cartwright, Winfred Boynes, and James Hardy helped carry the Dons to 29 consecutive victories and no defeats and the top spot in the polls heading into their last game of the regular season at the University of Notre Dame. But the Irish of Notre Dame rode a boisterous crowd (which was named the "player" of the game by NBC, the network that televised the contest) to an 83–72 victory that ended the Dons' hopes for an unbeaten season. Then, San Francisco's year came to a crashing halt with a 121–95 loss to University of Nevada-Las Vegas (which ended up in the Final Four) in the NCAA tournament. After starting the year 29–0, the Dons finished 29–2, losing the two games that counted most.

The Doctor Is In (the NBA)

Acrobatic forward Julius Erving (b.1950), still known to basketball fans around the world as "Dr. J," made his National Basketball Association debut in the 1976–77 season. The Portland Trail Blazers, though, stole some of Erving's thunder by beating his Philadelphia 76ers in six games in the NBA Finals. The Trail Blazers won the decisive game 109–107 victory at Portland on June 5.

As part of the merger agreement with the ABA, the NBA incorporated four teams and a host of the defunct league's stars for the 1976–77 season. The biggest of those stars was Erving, who had helped carry the New York Nets to the ABA title the season before. Although the Nets were one of the former ABA teams to join the NBA, Erving's contract was sold to the 76ers after a bitter contract dispute with New York.

Erving, the top scorer in the ABA's final season, continued to display his elegant game in his new league. He made a dramatic debut in his first NBA All-Star Game on February 13, earning most valuable player honors after scoring 30 points in 30 minutes. In the regular season, he averaged 21.6 points per game and led the 76ers to 50 victories and the Eastern Conference championship.

But Erving and the 76ers were upstaged in the NBA Finals by Bill Walton (b.1952) and the Trail Blazers. Portland had finished second to the Los Angeles Lakers in the Pacific Division during the regular season. In the conference finals, though, Portland brushed Los Angeles aside in four games. Then, against Philadelphia in the championship series, the Trail Blazers became the first team in NBA history to win four consecutive playoff games after losing the first two.

Horse Racing Winners

Jockey Jean Cruguet rode Seattle Slew to an easy four-length victory in the Belmont Stakes on June 11 to win horse racing's coveted Triple Crown. Seattle Slew became only the 10th horse

House Call *Philadelphia 76ers forward Julius Erving, better known as "Dr. J," drives to the basket. Erving carried his team to the NBA Finals, although the Portland Trail Blazers emerged as champions.*

in history to win all three races—the Kentucky Derby, Preakness Stakes, and Belmont Stakes—in the same year. He was the first to do so while never having lost a race.

The 1977 Horse of the Year shared racing's spotlight with jockey Steve Cauthen (b.1960). The 17-year-old sensation rode more than 400 winners to more than $6 million in earnings that year—no other rider ever had reached the $5 million

Mr. 59

Al Geiberger became the first golfer to score a 59 in a PGA event when he fired 11 birdies (one shot under par) and an eagle (two shots under par) in the second round of the Memphis Golf Classic on June 10.

Geiberger started the day with a birdie at the 10th hole (he played the second nine holes on the course first), made six birdies and an eagle in a seven-hole stretch from his sixth through 12th holes, then made an eight-foot birdie putt on the ninth hole to cap his round.

Three other players—Chip Beck, David Duval, and Paul Goydos—have since equaled Geiberger's feat in PGA competition. But ever since his magical day, Geiberger is the one who has been known throughout the golfing world as "Mr. 59."

mark in a single year. Cauthen won the Eclipse Award as the nation's top jockey, earned the Associated Press male Athlete of the Year award, and was named Sports Illustrated's Sportsman of the Year.

Battle Across the Pond

Tom Watson won the British Open golf tournament at Turnberry, Scotland, July 9 when he edged Jack Nicklaus (b.1940) in one of the most memorable head-to-head battles in golf history.

After both players had third-round scores of 65 to enter the final day all even, Nicklaus forged one stroke ahead after 15 holes of the fourth round. But Watson drilled a 60-foot birdie putt to pull even on hole 16, then followed with another birdie on 17 to take the lead. When Nicklaus had trouble with his drive at hole 18 and Watson put his second shot two feet from the hole, the tournament was all but over. Still, Nicklaus made a long putt

to force Watson to sink his short putt for a birdie. Watson made it to finish with a final-round 65, one stroke better than his formidable rival.

Watson also won the prestigious Masters golf tournament in 1977. Hubert Green won the United States Open, while Lanny Wadkins captured the final major of the season, the PGA Championship.

The 30-30-30-30 Club

In his final at-bat of the regular season on October 2, Los Angeles Dodgers outfielder Dusty Baker hit his 30th home run of the year off Houston Astros pitcher J.R. Richard. Baker's home run could not avert a 6–3 defeat, but it made Los Angeles the first team to have four players with 30 or more home runs in the same season.

First baseman Steve Garvey (b.1948) led the way with 33 home runs, while outfielder Reggie Smith added 32 and third baseman Ron Cey joined Baker with 30. The Dodgers won 98 games and cruised to the National League West title by 10 games. They beat the Philadelphia Phillies in four games in the League Championship Series before losing to the New York Yankees in the World Series late in October.

Pelé Retires

International soccer star Pelé, of the North American Soccer League's New York Cosmos, retired after the 1977 season. In his farewell match, an exhibition at Giants Stadium on October 1, he played one half for the Cosmos and one half for Santos, the Brazilian club with whom he started his career more than 20 years earlier.

Pelé's arrival in the United States two years earlier kicked off the first true soccer boom in the country. For the first time, fans on major television networks and in large U.S. stadiums watched a good pro soccer league. The talent level was below long-established European or South American leagues, but by bringing in top stars such as Pelé, England's George Best, and Italy's Giorgio Chinaglia, the NASL tried to bring star power to the sport.

The Bronx Zoo

Star Wars was the year's big box-office smash, but another kind of star wars debuted in New York, where the Yankees signed high-profile free agent Reggie Jackson (b.1946) to a lucrative contract. The tempestuous Jackson combined with fiery manager Billy Martin (1928–1989) and other high-profile personalities in the Yankees' organization to form a volatile mix that threatened to undermine the team's fortunes.

The clubhouse was dubbed "The Bronx Zoo" because of the constant bickering among Jackson, Martin, owner George Steinbrenner (b.1930), catcher Thurman Munson (1947–1979), and others. In the end, though, the team fed off the atmosphere to win its first World Series in 15 years.

New York, which had won 100 games during the regular season to edge the Baltimore Orioles and the Boston Red Sox in the American League's Eastern Division, outlasted the Kansas City Royals in a taut League Championship Series. The Yankees scored three runs in the ninth inning of the fifth and final game to win 5–3 and wrest the pennant from the Royals' clutches.

Jackson then made the World Series against the Dodgers his personal stage, on which he batted .450 with five home runs and eight RBI. The Yankees won in six games, and Jackson's performance in the finale (see page 118) was one of the most memorable in World Series history.

The Yankees won the final game 8–4 to take the World Series for a record 21st time, but for the first time since 1962.

Three for Three *New York Yankees slugger Reggie Jackson put on a memorable power display at the World Series when he blasted three home runs on three successive swings in the decisive sixth game.*

1977

Sweetness

They called Chicago Bears running back Walter Payton "Sweetness" for both his smooth running style and his pleasant demeanor.

It was anything but sweet for the opposing National Football League defenses that had to face Payton in his 13-season career from 1975 to 1987, however. The Pro Football Hall of Famer, who was the NFL's all-time leading rusher at the time of his retirement, combined power and speed like perhaps no other back before or since.

On November 20, Payton had the most prolific day of a prolific career. He carried the ball 40 times for 275 yards and scored the Bears' lone touchdown in their 10–7 victory over the Minnesota Vikings.

Payton's yardage total set an NFL single-game record that stood 23 years.

Lucky Green

A little wearing o' the green helped catapult the University of Notre Dame to college football's national title. So did future Pro Football Hall of Famer Joe Montana (b.1956), who took over as

Mr. October

Reggie Jackson's reputation as a star in the postseason earned him the nickname "Mr. October," and his World Series game six dramatics while playing for the New York Yankees in 1977 was a signature performance. After drawing a walk in his first plate appearance that night against the Los Angeles Dodgers, Jackson belted a two-run home run off Los Angeles starting pitcher Burt Hooton in the fourth inning to put the Yankees ahead for good. The next inning, he slugged another two-run homer off reliever Elias Sosa. Then, in the eighth, with the Yankees' title well in hand, he punctuated the night with a solo home run off Charlie Hough. All the home runs came on the first pitch. The final scorecard: three home runs in three at bats off three consecutive pitches from three different pitchers.

It was no surprise that Jackson was such a World Series star, because he thrived in the spotlight. For his

career, Jackson batted .357 with 10 home runs in 98 World Series at bats. He was the World Series MVP in 1973 (while with the Oakland A's) and 1977, set a career record for slugging percentage (.755), and played on five championship teams.

Jackson was an all-or-nothing showman who belted 563 career home runs (eighth-best all time), but also struck out an incredible 2,597 times (far and away the most in Major League history). He helped carry 10 teams to the playoffs in a 12-year span from 1971 to 1982, but he also put off teammates and fans with his bragging.

When Jackson signed a $3 million-dollar contract with the Yankees in 1977, he became baseball's highest-paid player and proclaimed himself "the straw that stirs the drink" in New York. He quickly alienated established Yankees stars with the remark. Eventually, though, he may have proved himself right.

Other Milestones of 1977

✔ Heisman Trophy-winner Tony Dorsett rushed for 202 yards and a touchdown in the University of Pittsburgh's 27–3 rout of the University of Georgia in the Sugar Bowl on New Year's Day, 1977. The Pittsburgh Panthers completed a 12–0 season and won college football's national championship for 1976.

✔ Eric Heiden won the 500-meter race en route to the all-around title at the men's world speed skating championships in the Netherlands in February. Heiden became the first American to win the crown in the 76-year history of the event. He repeated as champion in 1978 and 1979, then won five gold medals at the 1980 Winter Olympics.

✔ Golfer Tom Watson won a pair of major championships, taking the Masters and British Open titles en route to the first of four consecutive PGA Tour Player of the Year awards.

✔ Janet Guthrie became the first woman to drive in the Indy 500 on May 29. She completed only 27 laps, however, before engine trouble forced her out of the race. A.J. Foyt took the checkered flag to become the first four-time winner of the famed auto race.

✔ Golfer Al Geiberger became the first man to record a score of 59 for 18 holes in a PGA event at the Memphis Classic on April 10.

✔ St. Louis Cardinals outfielder Lou Brock became baseball's all-time leading base stealer when he stole two bases against the San Diego Padres on August 29. Brock surpassed Hall of Famer Ty Cobb, who held the previous record with 892 steals. He ended his career with a since-surpassed record 938 steals.

✔ Charlie's Angels, mood rings, and disco music were big in 1977. The year also gave us the high five. When the Los Angeles Dodgers' Dusty Baker hit his 30th home run of the season on October 2, he was met at home plate by fellow outfielder Glenn Burke. The two slapped palms high above their heads, and a new cultural phenomenon was born.

quarterback for the Irish and passed for 1,715 yards and 12 touchdowns.

The Fighting Irish carried a 4–1 record into midseason, and their fortunes surged against fifth-ranked University of Southern California (USC) on October 22, when the Irish team sprinted from their tunnel in green jerseys instead of the traditional blue. The crowd went wild—and so did the Irish. Notre Dame breezed to a 49–19 rout and was hardly challenged after that. The Irish won their last seven games by an average margin of nearly 34 points and finished 11–1.

1978

Split Decision

The fifth-ranked University of Notre Dame's 38–10 rout of the top-ranked University of Texas Longhorns in the Cotton Bowl on January 2 lifted Notre Dame to a controversial national title for 1977 (controversial because six teams, including Notre Dame, finished with only one loss). It also presaged more controversy in 1978 that fueled cries for a national playoff for college football.

This time, it was the University of Alabama Crimson Tide and the University of Southern California (USC) Trojans who were in the eye of the storm. Alabama was ranked number one when the Trojans traveled to Tuscaloosa on September 23 and emerged with a 24–14 victory. But USC, which was ranked seventh entering the game, never made it to number one because the Trojans were upset by Arizona State University three weeks later.

USC and Alabama finished the season with just the one loss, and the result was a split national championship. The Associated Press writers' poll awarded the top spot to the Crimson Tide, while United Press International's poll of coaches had the Trojans at number one.

Doomsday for Denver

Defense was the name of the game for the Dallas Cowboys, who overwhelmed the Denver Broncos 27–10 in Super Bowl XII in New Orleans.

The Broncos had reached the Super Bowl for the first time on the strength of their own defense, which was pegged the "Orange Crush" (for the color of the team's home uniforms). Dallas, though, did the crushing on Super Sunday, sacking Broncos quarterbacks Craig Morton and Norris Weese four times, intercepting four of Morton's passes, and recovering four fumbles. Denver managed only 156 total yards and, in one stretch of the second half, turned over the ball on five consecutive possessions.

Dallas' "Doomsday Defense" was so dominant against the Broncos that for the only time in Super Bowl history, two players—defensive end Harvey Martin and defensive tackle Randy White—shared game MVP honors.

Another trivia note: Super Bowl XII, held at the Louisiana Superdome, was the first to be played indoors. The NFL since has played its biggest game five more times in the Superdome.

Chin Music *Leon Spinks (left) beat Muhammad Ali in February, but Ali bounced back to win the rematch.*

Ali: Down then Up

Muhammad Ali was perhaps past his prime, and some felt he should have retired. But he fought on, and on February 15 suffered perhaps the most stunning defeat of his career. Leon Spinks, an Olympic gold medalist as well-known for his gap-toothed grin as his punching power, defeated the champion in a huge upset in Las Vegas. Suddenly, Spinks was the heavyweight champion.

On September 16, in a hugely hyped rematch, the two men fought again in New Orleans, where the 36-year-old Ali became the first man to win the heavyweight title for a third time.

It would be Ali's last boxing win. He retired in 1979, although he eventually came out of retirement to try (and fail) to regain the heavyweight crown a fourth time. His victory over Spinks was the culmination of perhaps the most influential career of any athlete in sports history.

New Venue, Same Result *The U.S. Open moved to Flushing Meadows, but the Women's Singles champ was the same as the previous three years in Forest Hills: Chris Evert.*

Givens Goes Wild

The University of Kentucky Wildcats capped a 30–2 season with a 94–88 victory over the Duke University Blue Devils in the championship game of college basketball's NCAA tournament on March 27 in St. Louis.

Guard Jack "Goose" Givens was the star for the Wildcats in the final game. Givens poured in 23 points, many of them from long range, to help Kentucky build a seven-point halftime lead. The Wildcats never looked back. Givens finished the game with 41 points. Center Rick Robey added 20 points and 11 rebounds.

Kentucky became the fifth school in as many seasons to win the NCAA championship, since UCLA's record run of seven straight titles ended with its 1973 crown. The Wildcats had won their first national championship since 1958.

Cinderella Series

A professional basketball season that began with a black eye—literally—ended with a feel-good story when a pair of Cinderella teams, the Washington Bullets and the Seattle SuperSonics, played a thrilling, seven-game NBA Finals. The Bullets won in seven games, with the last a 105–99 decision on June 7.

Early in the season (on December 9, 1977), a vicious punch from the Los Angeles Lakers' Kermit Washington put the Houston Rockets' Rudy Tomjanovich in the intensive care unit of the hospital for several days. At the same time, the Super-Sonics were suffering through a miserable start that resulted in 17 losses in their first 22 games. But then former playing star Lenny Wilkens (b.1937) stepped out of the front office and onto the bench as coach. Wilkens revamped Seattle's lineup, sparking a turnaround that produced a 42–18 record the rest of the way.

Meanwhile, back East, the Bullets' veteran center Wes Unseld and electrifying forward Elvin Hayes (b.1945) took their team to the conference championship. In the finals, the SuperSonics held a three games to two lead and headed home for games six and seven. But the Bullets breezed to a 35-point rout to tie the series, then became just the third team in history to win a seventh game on the road.

Tennis' Girl-Next-Door

The United States Open tennis tournament moved from Forest Hills to Flushing Meadows, New York, but the change in venue had little effect on Chris Evert (b.1954), the three-time defending champion. Evert closed out a record-tying fourth consecutive title with a 7–6, 6–2 victory over Wendy Turnbull on August 29. It was the first time in more than four decades that a women's tennis player won the Open four consecutive years.

Evert was America's tennis sweetheart, the girl-next-door who first wowed the crowds at the U.S. Open as a 16-year-old amateur with a quaint two-handed backhand in 1971—the year she first reached the semifinals. Her unique combination of grace and grit made her a marketing favorite, and she earned millions in endorsements off the court.

She was a huge success on the court, too, where she amassed more than $9 million in career earnings. She won 157 singles titles, including at least one Grand Slam championship (the Grand Slam is the Australian, French, and U.S. Opens, plus Wimbledon) for 13 consecutive years from 1974 to 1986.

In 1974, she forged a 54-match winning streak and was ranked number one in the world for the first time in 1975. That began her three-year run atop the rankings. But by 1978, a new challenger was on the horizon. She was Martina Navratilova (b.1956), a 21-year-old native of Czechoslovakia who had defected to the United States during the 1975 U.S. Open.

Navratilova served notice of her arrival at Wimbledon in 1978, when she came from behind to defeat Evert 2–6, 6–4, 7–5 and win her first major singles title. The Czech would go on to win 18 Grand Slam singles titles in her career, plus a record 31 Grand Slam women's doubles titles, and 10 Grand Slam mixed doubles championships. She became number one in the world in 1978 and was number one for 331 weeks in her career, second in history only to Steffi Graf (b.1969).

Navratilova's matches with Evert highlighted tennis for years to come.

Triple Crown Is Affirmed

Affirmed won a thrilling battle against Alydar in the Belmont Stakes on July 10 to become the 11th horse to win thoroughbred racing's Triple Crown. The winner was ridden by jockey Steve Cauthen, the teen sensation who had burst onto the racing scene with a record-setting year in 1977 (see page 115).

Affirmed also edged Alydar in the Kentucky Derby and the Preakness Stakes (the first two legs of the Triple Crown). The Belmont turned out to be a two-horse match, as Affirmed and Alydar pulled away from the rest of the field and sped side-by-side down the stretch. Affirmed, racing on the inside, reached the finish line just a head before Alydar.

The Belmont winner thus became racing's second Triple Crown champion in as many years, after Seattle Slew in 1977, and its third in six years. But through 2003—despite a series of close calls—there hasn't been another Triple Crown winner.

Seattle Slew and Affirmed met in the first matchup of Triple Crown champions

1978

when they both raced in the Marlboro Cup in Belmont Park on September 16. The winner: Seattle Slew. The 1977 Horse of the Year beat the 1978 Horse of the Year by three lengths.

The Bronx Zoo, Part II

The New York Yankees beat the Los Angeles Dodgers in six games to win the World Series for the second consecutive year—but that doesn't even begin to tell the story of the Yankees' season.

There were so many story lines in New York in 1978 that it's hard to know where to start. The team overcame in-fighting in the clubhouse, a mid-season managerial change, and a 14-game deficit to the Boston Red Sox in the American League East. Almost lost amid all that was one of the most brilliant pitching performances in baseball history: Yankees left-hander Ron Guidry went 25–3 with an earned-run average of 1.74 and 248 strikeouts in 273.2 innings.

After manager Billy Martin was fired late in July, the Yankees went a remarkable 52–21 under new manager Bob Lemon. They pulled even with the Red Sox, then beat Boston 5–4 at Fenway Park in a memorable one-game playoff for the division title, famous for light-hitting Bucky Dent's game-clinching homer.

New York ousted the Kansas City Royals in the American League Championship Series for the third consecutive year to advance to the World Series. The Yankees then overcame a two-games-to-none deficit to the Dodgers by winning four straight games in October, to capture their record 22nd title.

New Game in Town

The WNBA of the 1990s and 2000s was not the first women's professional basketball league in the United States. That distinction belongs to the Women's Professional Basketball League (the WBL), which tipped off on December 9 with a game between the visiting Chicago Hustle and the Milwaukee Does. A crowd of nearly 8,000 at the Milwaukee Arena watched the Does prevail, 92–87.

The WBL's inaugural season featured eight teams: Chicago Hustle, Dayton Rockettes, Houston Angels, Iowa Cornets, Milwaukee Does, Minnesota Fillies, New Jersey Gems, and New York Stars. None of the teams proved financially sound, however, and the league lasted only three seasons. The Hustle, Fillies, and Gems were the only franchises to survive all three years.

Golfers' Earnings Soar

Long before Tiger Woods burst onto the golf scene in the late 1990s, another minority golfer dominated the sport. It was Nancy Lopez, a 1978 rookie who boosted the visibility of the LPGA and became a hero to Mexican Americans.

Lopez dominated her sport by winning nine tournaments—including five in a row in one stretch—and setting an earnings record with more than $189,000. She became the first LPGA player to win Rookie of the Year and Player of the Year honors in the same season.

On the men's side, Jack Nicklaus won the British Open at historic St. Andrews in Scotland in July. Nicklaus' third British

Open title made him the first player to win all four of golf's major tournaments (the Masters, U.S. Open, British Open, and PGA Championship) three times.

Pete Rose's Hit Parade

Long before gambling allegations sullied an otherwise brilliant career, Pete Rose (b.1941) made headlines for his hitting in 1978. On May 5, he singled off Montreal's Steve Rogers for the 3,000th hit of his big-league career. Then, on June 14, Rose, with the Reds, began a streak that would reach 44 consecutive games. Rose's hit string equaled the longest in N.L. history (Wee Willie Keeler also hit in 44 straight in 1897).

Rose parlayed his brilliant season into a lucrative contract. On December 5, he left the Reds to sign with the Philadelphia Phillies as a free agent. His four-year, $3.2 million contract was the largest in history at the time of his signing.

Rose played through 1986 and had a record 4,256 hits. But he was barred from the Baseball Hall of Fame and in 1989 was banned for life from the game by then-commissioner A. Bartlett Giamatti for allegedly gambling on baseball (allegations he long denied, but eventually admitted to in an autobiography released in January, 2004) during his tenure as a manager from 1984 to 1989. To this day, he remains on the outside of the Hall of Fame, a figure of pity to most fans.

Other Milestones of 1978

✔ The roof of the Hartford Civic Center in Connecticut collapsed from a snowstorm early in the morning hours of January 18. Luckily, no one was in the home of the World Hockey Association's Hartford Whalers. The arena had hosted a college basketball game between the University of Connecticut and the University of Massachusetts the night before.

✔ San Francisco Giants first baseman Willie McCovey hit the 500th home run of his major league career in a game against the Atlanta Braves on June 30. McCovey became only the 12th player to reach the 500 mark.

✔ Men's tennis rivals Bjorn Borg and Jimmy Connors slugged it out in singles finals at both Wimbledon and the U.S. Open. Borg won his third Wimbledon title in a row with a straight-set victory in July; Connors avenged the loss with a straight-set victory to win his second consecutive U.S. Open in September.

✔ Nineteen-year-old John McEnroe upset Bjorn Borg, the number-one tennis player in the world, to help the United States defeat Sweden in a Davis Cup tie in October. McEnroe then helped deliver the championship with two singles victories in the finals against Great Britain in December.

✔ Long-time Ohio State Buckeyes' football coach Woody Hayes was fired after he punched an opposing player during his team's 17–15 loss to Clemson University in the Gator Bowl on December 29. Hayes, famously gruff and irascible, had guided Ohio State to 205 victories, including two national championships, in 28 seasons.

1979

Super Super Bowl

The Super Bowl was turning into a Super Dud with a series of lopsided games in recent years. But the Pittsburgh Steelers and the Dallas Cowboys put on a thrilling show at the Orange Bowl in Miami on January 21, with the Steelers winning Super Bowl XIII 35–31.

This was the first Super Bowl rematch—the teams had played in the title game three years earlier, with the Steelers winning 21–17—and one of pro football's fiercest rivalries was under way. It was fueled by pregame comments from Dallas linebacker Thomas "Hollywood" Henderson, who derisively claimed that Pittsburgh quarterback Terry Bradshaw (b.1948) "couldn't spell cat if you spotted him the c and the a."

Bradshaw had the last laugh, though, passing for Super Bowl records of 318 yards and four touchdowns to earn the game's most valuable player award (he won the award again a year later after leading the Steelers past the Rams in Super Bowl XIV).

Bradshaw completed 17 of his 30 passes against the Cowboys, including a game-tying, 75-yard strike to John Stall-worth in the second quarter. Then he put the Steelers ahead 21–14—a lead they never relinquished—with a seven-yard throw to Rocky Bleier just 26 seconds before halftime.

"Go ask Thomas Henderson if I was dumb," Bradshaw told reporters after the game.

Although Pittsburgh built a 35–17 lead in the fourth quarter, the Steelers still had to survive a late rally engineered by Dallas quarterback Roger Staubach, who had mastered the art of the comeback. Staubach, who also completed 17 of 30 pass attempts for 228 yards, passed for two touchdowns in the final two and a half minutes of the game, but Pittsburgh recovered an onside kick in the closing seconds to become the first team to win the Super Bowl three times.

"The guys in the ties and dark suits [the Cowboys] against the guys in the hardhats and rolled-up sleeves [the Steelers]," was how Dallas free safety Cliff Harris described the contest. "That contrast, that was the thing between us." That "thing" was one of the NFL's classic rivalries. The Cowboys did not get their Super Bowl revenge until they beat Pittsburgh 27–17 in Super Bowl XXX in January 1996.

Super Steelers   *Quarterback Terry Bradshaw (12) led the Pittsburgh Steelers past Dallas in Super Bowl XIII.*

Road Rage

Richard Petty won the Daytona 500 for the record sixth time on February 18, but that wasn't what everyone was talking about after the race. Instead, it was a post-race skirmish involing Donnie Allison and Cale Yarborough, the leaders for much of the latter part of the race, that caught everyone's attention.

On the final lap, Allison had the lead but knew Yarborough would try to pass him down low on the backstretch. When Yarborough made his move, Allison was there to block his path. The two whacked together, sending Yarborough's car into the infield grass. When he tried to get back onto the track, the cars collided again.

Petty, who had been in third place, was the beneficiary of all this. He sped past Allison and Yarborough to take the checkered flag.

Just then, the cameras cut to the infield, where Yarborough had gotten out of his car to confront Allison. Allison's brother, Bobby, who also was in the race, stopped by in his car. Yarborough and the two Allison brothers went at each other until they could be separated by track personnel.

1979

Afterwards, Allison and Yarborough took turns blaming each other. But television viewers didn't care who was at fault. They had just witnessed the first NASCAR race ever televised from start to finish, and they were thrilled at the spectacle. NASCAR was fast on its way to becoming a national sport.

Sneak Preview   *When Michigan State and Indiana State met for the NCAA championship, stars Earvin "Magic" Johnson (33) and Larry Bird (dribbling) squared off for a title for the first of many times.*

Bird and Magic

Basketball guard Earvin "Magic" Johnson (b.1959) and his Michigan State Spartans met forward Larry Bird (b.1956) and his Indiana State Sycamores in the NCAA men's championship game in Salt Lake City, Utah, on March 26. Johnson and the Spartans won the game 75–64. The matchup was a hint of the epic battles between these two superstars that would continue for years to come in the NBA.

Johnson was a 6-foot-8 point guard who was versatile enough to play anywhere on the court. After he scored 24 points, grabbed seven rebounds, and handed out five assists in the final game, he was named the tournament's most outstanding player.

At 6-foot-9, Bird was more of a classic forward with a deft shooting touch and a nose for the ball. He scored 35 points in the national semifinal game as Indiana State improved to 33–0 by edging DePaul University, 76–74. In the final, though, he had to deal with constant double-teaming from Michigan State's defense. He led the Sycamores with 19 points and 13 rebounds, but made only seven of 21 shots.

Johnson, though only a sophomore, decided to turn pro and joined the Los Angeles Lakers for the 1979–80 season. Bird signed with the Boston Celtics, who had drafted him the previous year. Either Johnson's Lakers or Bird's Celtics won eight of the next nine NBA titles.

Batting Practice at Wrigley

 Fantasy baseball wasn't yet a national phenomenon in 1979, but the select few participating then had to be delighted with the box score from Chicago on May 17, when the hometown Cubs outlasted the Philadelphia Phillies 23–22—delighted, of course, as long as their rosters didn't include any of the pitchers involved.

Philadelphia third baseman Mike Schmidt (b.1949) hit a solo home run in the top of the 10th inning off the Cubs' Bruce Sutter to lift the Phillies to the victory. It was the 11th home run of the game, equaling the major league record. The barrage of homers was triggered by an 18-mile-per-hour wind that was blowing out to left at Wrigley Field.

Chicago's Dave Kingman slugged three home runs, while Schmidt had two. Other notes from the box score: Shortstop Larry Bowa had five hits, catcher Bob Boone drove in five runs, and center fielder Garry Maddox had four hits in four at-bats with four RBI for the Phillies; Bill Buckner drove in seven runs and Kingman added six RBI for the Cubs. Chicago starting pitcher Dennis Lamp allowed six runs in a third of an inning. Phillies starter Randy Lerch left the game after giving up five runs in a third of an inning—but he also homered to cap Philadelphia's seven-run outburst in the top of the first.

The teams combined for 50 hits and 97 total bases. The 45 runs scored were the most in a major league game since the Cubs beat the Phillies 26–23 at Wrigley Field on August 25, 1922.

NBA Rematch

 For the second consecutive year, the Washington Bullets and the Seattle SuperSonics squared off in the NBA Finals (see page 122). This time, it was the SuperSonics who emerged with their first league championship.

Seattle did not feature a big-name superstar, relying instead on a balanced scoring attack and a stingy defense to take the team to its first Pacific Division title and a team-record 52 victories during the regular season. After dispatching the Los Angeles Lakers and the Phoenix Suns in the playoffs, the SuperSonics avenged their defeat to the defending-champion Bullets.

Washington opened the finals with a 99–97 victory at home on two free throws by Larry Wright with no time left on the clock. But Seattle stormed back to win the next four games and take the title. The decisive game was a 97–93 victory at Washington on June 1.

The SuperSonics had six players who averaged double figures in scoring during the regular season, led by guard Gus Williams' 19.2 points per game. Fellow guard Dennis Johnson was an NBA All-Defensive selection, while center Jack Sikma pulled down 12.4 rebounds per game—fifth-best in the league.

A Yankee Tragedy

The New York Yankees have put together perhaps the most successful and legendary team history in sports. However, it has occasionally also been visited by tragedy. On August 2, the Yankees' catcher and team captain, Thurman Munson, only 32 years old, was killed when the private plane he was piloting crashed shortly after takeoff in Ohio.

1979

Munson had used a day off in the team's schedule to fly home to see his family.

The death of the fiery, gruff, but popular player shocked baseball and the sports world. The Yankees wore black armbands for the remainder of the season, and Munson's uniform number 15 was retired. For years after, his locker at Yankee Stadium remained unoccupied in tribute.

Youth Is Served

The country was slowed by an oil shortage in 1979, but there was no energy crisis on the men's and women's tennis tours, where an infusion of youth made headlines at the U.S. Open in Flushing Meadows, New York in September.

On the women's side, 16-year-old Tracy Austin (b.1962) became the young-

Mr. Hockey

When Gordie Howe (b.1928) took the ice for the Hartford Whalers at the start of the NHL season in 1979, he was 51 years old. It would be his 26th, and final, NHL season. Add in the six years Howe played in the World Hockey Association (Hartford was one of the teams that was incorporated into the NHL for the 1979–80 season), and that's a total of 32 years of major league hockey.

That's a remarkable record of longevity and will likely never be broken. It puts Howe in a class with legendary athletes such as George Blanda, who played pro football until he was 48, and Satchel Paige, who pitched regularly in Major League Baseball at a reported age of 47 (some experts insist he was even older).

Howe's career deserves more than just a footnote for defying the effects of aging, though. Much more. After all, they didn't call him "Mr. Hockey" for nothing.

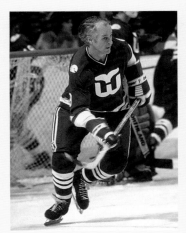

Gordie Howe

From the moment he stepped onto the ice as an 18-year-old for the Detroit Red Wings in 1946, it was clear that Howe had a unique talent. In his 26 NHL seasons, he was a first- or second-team All-Star 21 times. He won six scoring titles, six Hart Memorial Trophies as the league's most valuable player, and retired as the NHL's all-time leader for goals, assists, points, and games played. Moreover, he was one of the smartest and toughest players in history, and his abilities made his teammates better: He led his NHL teams to the playoffs 20 times, and helped the Red Wings win four Stanley Cup championships in the 1950s.

Howe also enjoyed a privilege afforded no other professional hockey star in history. While he was with the WHA's Houston Aeros in 1973, his sons Marty and Mark joined him to form the only two-generation line ever on the ice. The three were reunited on the Whalers in Gordie's last year.

est winner of the Open when she stopped Chris Evert's four-year reign as champion with a stunning 6–4, 6–3 victory. At 16 years and nine months, Austin was three months younger than "Little Mo" Connolly was when she won the Open in 1951.

"Tracy's mental toughness was scary," Evert said years later. By 1980, Austin became the top-ranked women's player in the world.

On the men's side, 20-year-old John McEnroe (b.1959) won his first Grand Slam singles title by beating Vitas Gerulaitis in straight sets, 7–5, 6–3, 6–3. McEnroe, who went on to win the U.S. Open three consecutive years and four times in a six-year span, was the youngest men's champion in more than 30 years. McEnroe would go on to win seven Grand Slam singles titles in his career and play on 12 U.S. Davis Cup teams.

We Are Family

The Pittsburgh Pirates earned a World Series title in thrilling fashion, overtaking the Baltimore Orioles by winning three consecutive games, including game seven in Baltimore on October 17. The Pirates adopted Sister Sledge's hit single, "We Are Family," as their theme song for 1979. And there was no question who was the patriarch of the family. It was veteran slugger Willie Stargell (1940–2001), better known as "Pops" to his teammates. The 39-year-old belted 32 home runs in only 126 games during the regular season, then carried his team in the postseason, when he batted .415 with five home runs, 13 RBI, and 11 extra-base hits.

Sweet Sixteen *American Tracy Austin was just 16 years old when she won the U.S. Open singles championship. She was the youngest winner of one of tennis' most coveted titles.*

Pittsburgh won 98 games during the regular season, then breezed past the Cincinnati Reds in three games in the best-of-five League Championship Series (LCS). Stargell won the first game with an 11th-inning homer, then sparked a 7–1 rout in the final game with another home run.

Baltimore, meanwhile, reached the World Series by winning a major league-best 102 games during the regular season, then outslugging the California Angels

1979

in four games in the LCS. In the World Series, the Orioles were on the verge of a title after a six-run eighth inning led to a 9–6 victory in game four for a three-games-to-one-lead.

History was not on the Pirates' side: Only three teams had rallied from a three-to-one deficit to win a seven-game World Series. But Pittsburgh won game five, 7–1, to send the Series back to Baltimore, then forced a final game when pitchers John Candelaria and Kent Tekulve combined on a seven-hit shutout in game six.

In the decisive game, Stargell's two-run home run in the sixth inning erased a 1–0 deficit and gave Pittsburgh the lead for good. The Pirates won, 4–1.

Roll Tide

The Alabama Crimson Tide began the year by beating number-one Penn State 14–7 in the Sugar Bowl on January 1. That came after USC beat Michigan 17–10 in the Rose Bowl earlier in the day. Polls the next afternoon re-sulted in a split between Alabama and USC for college football's 1978 national championship.

The Crimson Tide left little room for debate in 1979, however. Alabama opened its season with a 30–6 rout of Georgia Tech in Atlanta on September 6. The Crimson Tide rolled on to 12 consecutive victories while outscoring its opponents by a whopping 383–67 (an average of about 32–6 per game).

Alabama's 1979 national championship was the school's sixth (and last) while coached by the legendary Paul "Bear" Bryant (1913–1983).

Turnaround in Tampa

The Tampa Bay Buccaneers capped an amazing transformation by beating the Kansas City Chiefs 3–0 in a torrential downpour in Tampa on December 16 to earn the Bucs their first playoff berth in the NFL team's brief history.

Nobody expects an expansion team to be very good right away, but the Buccaneers, who had joined the league in 1976, took a new team's woes to unparalleled heights— or depths. Tampa Bay went 0–14 in its first season (no other NFL team had ever lost every game it played), then followed that up with losses in its first 12 games the next year. Such futility prompted head coach John McKay's (1923–2001) famous quip, when asked after one loss about his team's execution: "I'm in favor of it."

But by 1978, the Buccaneers showed signs of life, winning five games. Then, in 1979, Tampa Bay won its first five games of the season. McKay never abandoned his goal of combining a strong running

---

Twice as Nice

It was a banner year for the city of Pittsburgh in 1979. After the football Steelers won Super Bowl XIII in January, the baseball Pirates won the World Series in October. Only two cities have won a Super Bowl and a World Series in the same calendar year:

YEAR	CITY	TEAMS
1969	New York	Jets (football), Mets (baseball)
1979	Pittsburgh	Steelers (football), Pirates (baseball)

In the 1969-1970 season, the New York Knicks also won the team's first NBA champsionship.

Other Milestones of 1979

✔ The National Hockey League agreed to absorb four World Hockey Association teams as part of a merger agreement between the two rival leagues on March 22. The Edmonton Oilers, Hartford Whalers, Quebec Nordiques, and Winnipeg Jets joined the NHL for the 1979–80 season.

✔ Rick Swenson won the Iditarod dog-sled race for the second time in three years. Swenson, "The King of the Iditarod," went on to win the race three more times, with the last time coming in 1991.

✔ Fuzzy Zoeller won the Masters golf tournament on April 15 in a playoff with Ed Sneed and Tom Watson. Zoeller overcame a six-stroke deficit to Sneed over the final 13 holes of regulation play, then needed two extra holes to become the first golfer to win in his first trip to Augusta since Gene Sarazen did it in 1935.

✔ The Montreal Canadiens won their fourth consecutive NHL title (and their sixth of the decade) when they beat the New York Rangers in the Stanley Cup Finals in May. The Boston Bruins (1970 and 1972) and the Philadelphia Flyers (1974 and 1975) were the only American teams to capture the Cup in the 1970s.

✔ The Houston Angels defeated the Iowa Cornets in the deciding game of the Women's Basketball league championship series on May 1 to win the first women's pro basketball title.

✔ A promotional stunt went awry at a doubleheader between the Chicago White Sox and the Detroit Tigers on July 12 at Chicago's Comiskey Park. On "Disco Demolition Night," fans were invited to bring disco records to be destroyed on the field in between games. But after bedlam ensued and it took riot police to clear the field, the second game was forfeited to the Tigers.

✔ Former Olympic boxing champion Sugar Ray Leonard won the world welterweight title when he beat Wilfred Benitez in Las Vegas on November 30. Leonard recorded a technical knockout when the fight was stopped six seconds before the end. He was ahead on all the judges' scorecards as well.

attack with a stalwart defense, and he was rewarded when Ricky Bell rushed for 1,263 yards and the defense permitted only 14.8 points per game during the 1979 regular season.

A late-season three-game losing streak threatened to spoil Tampa Bay's fine start, but the Buccaneers edged the Chicago Bears for the NFC Central Division title by beating the Chiefs in the season finale. Bell rushed for 137 yards and Neil O'Donoghue kicked a 19-yard field goal to provide the only points against Kansas City.

Tampa Bay eventually reached the 1979 NFC title game. The Buccaneers fell just one victory short of qualifying for Super Bowl XIV in January 1980.

INTRODUCTION
1980–1989

It was a decade of excess. It was a time of a new "morning in America," as incoming President Ronald Reagan (1911-2004) called it after his election in 1980. Reagan served as President during some of the most financially prosperous years in American history.

The stock market soared. Peace symbols from the 1960s and 1970s were traded in for Mercedes-Benz logos, and tie-dyed T-shirts were replaced by three-piece suits. Business schools, investment banks, and Wall Street law firms were filled with a new breed of achievers, called yuppies (young urban professionals), who were making money—and lots of it.

As the money poured in, many people succumbed to the lure of illegal drugs. Cocaine use soared, not just among the desperate poor, who were devastated by the scourge of crack-cocaine, but also among those well-off enough to afford the excess. The world of sports was by no means immune to either the draw of big money or the temptations of drugs—both mind-altering substances, such as cocaine, and performance-enhancing drugs, such as steroids.

There were several unfortunate examples of this. In 1986, college basketball superstar Len Bias, a young man destined for NBA stardom, died suddenly from cocaine use, just days after being drafted by the Boston Celtics. One of baseball's great pitchers, Dwight Gooden (b.1964) was suspended for cocaine use, just one year after leading the New York Mets to a World Series win in 1986 and just two years after a Cy Young Award-winning season. In and out of rehab for the next few years, the player known as "Doc" would never again be the pitcher he was. At the 1988 Summer Olympics in Seoul, South Korea, Canadian sprinter Ben Johnson was sent home in disgrace and stripped of his world-record gold medal after testing positive for performance-enhancing steroids.

The decade in sports began with a "miracle" (see page 138) and ended with a natural disaster (see page 214).

As American citizens were held hostage in Iran, the Soviet Union invaded Afghanistan, and the cold war raged, a group of unknown college hockey players staged one of the greatest upsets in sports history, the so-called Miracle on Ice, at the 1980 Winter Olympic Games in Lake Placid, New York. It gave a boost to a nation that was burdened with double-

The Road to Washington   *Ronald Reagan and his wife, Nancy, wave to supporters at the Republican National Convention in July of 1980. Four months later, Reagan was elected the 40th President of the United States.*

digit inflation, declining productivity, and a diminished place on the world stage.

The decade drew to a shattering close as an earthquake struck San Francisco just moments before the start of game three of the 1989 World Series in Candlestick Park. In an instant, players' chief concerns switched from the best game strategies to the safety of family members in the trembling stadium. Images of play-

1980– 1989

ers hugging their wives and carrying their children from the field reminded fans that no matter how important sports are—even the World Series—they are after all, just games. This was life—real, unstoppable, and potentially deadly. The Series was an afterthought in the wake of this reminder of the raw power of nature.

All three Summer Olympics in the 1980s were tainted by outside issues such as politics, boycotts, and drug use. The line between sports and politics blurred as the United States boycotted the 1980 Summer Olympic Games in Moscow as a response to the Soviet Union's invasion of Afghanistan a year earlier. The Soviets returned the favor four years later, boycotting the 1984 Olympics in Los Angeles.

The role of business and money in sports had been growing decade by decade and reached new heights in the 1980s. Sneaker endorsements and multi-million dollar player contracts pushed the economics of sports to stratospheric levels, unthinkable a few years earlier. If baseball star Bobby Bonilla was worth $29 million, what would legendary heroes such as Mickey Mantle (1931–1995) or Ted Williams (1918–2002) be worth in the free-agent market had they been in their prime in the 1980s? If basketball player Moses Malone could be paid $13.2 million, what would 11-time champion Bill Russell (b.1934) or record-setting scorer Wilt Chamberlain (1936–1999) have been worth if they played in the 1980s?

Shaken Spectators *A major earthquake struck the San Francisco Bay Area shortly before the Giants and Athletics were to play Game 3 of the World Series.*

Television money also gained a larger influence over sports. For the first time, most major sports team owners took in more money from selling television rights than from selling tickets to fans. As the money flowed in, players demanded that more of it flow into their pockets. Both baseball and football experienced prolonged player strikes as the battle for dollars supplanted the quest for victories.

Early in the decade, AIDS, a deadly new disease, emerged, at first believed to be limited to certain groups, but soon spreading to the wider population. Movie idol Rock Hudson's death from AIDS in 1985 put a familiar face on the previously shadowy disease, and placed its sadness in the front of the American mind. A few years later, one of the 1980s' greatest athletes, Los Angeles Lakers basketball superstar Magic Johnson (b.1959), announced that he was HIV-positive (HIV is the virus that leads to AIDS).

But, as is always the case, the world of sports in the 1980s was not exclusively filled with bad news. The decade saw superstar Wayne Gretzky (b.1961) re-write the National Hockey League (NHL) record book.

The National Basketball Association (NBA), which started the decade with its popularity at an all-time low, combined the play of Johnson and Larry Bird (b.1956) with the business and marketing brilliance of its new commissioner, David Stern (b.1942), to rocket its way to new heights of success.

Pete Rose (b.1941) became baseball's all-time hits leader, although by decade's end he was banned for life from the game because of allegations that he had bet on

Court Battles *Magic Johnson (32) and the Los Angeles Lakers often went head-to-head with Larry Bird and the Boston Celtics for the NBA title in the 1980s.*

baseball. Kareem Abdul-Jabbar (b.1947) became the NBA's all-time leading scorer, Walter Payton (1954–1999) became the leading rusher in the history of the National Football League (NFL), and Joan Benoit Samuelson (b.1957) proved that women could run Olympic marathons—in many cases faster than men.

The blending of sports and business was completed during the 1980s, and the intrusion of real-life issues such as drug abuse could not be kept from locker rooms. But from the glistening miracle in Lake Placid to the rumbling stands of Candlestick, many teams and individuals reminded us that despite the real world's rude intrusion into our beloved games, America's obsession with sports would only continue to grow.

1980

The Miracle on Ice

As the final seconds ticked down in the United States' improbable 4–3 victory over the Soviet Union in the semifinals of the Olympic hockey competition in Lake Placid, New York, television announcer Al Michaels delivered the words that still reverberate more than a quarter of a century later: "Do you believe in miracles? Yes!"

The United States' victory over the Soviets was indeed a miracle by sports standards. The 1980 U.S. Olympic hockey team was made up of young college and minor league players who had never played together before the Olympic team was chosen. The national team from the Soviet Union was a powerhouse that had been playing together as a unit for many years. That squad defeated the United States team 10–3 in an exhibition game a few weeks before the Olympics, and was considered by many experts to be the best hockey team in the world.

Add to that the politically charged atmosphere of the Cold War between the United States and the Soviet Union, and the stage was set for one of the greatest upsets in sports history.

To reach the medal round, head coach Herb Brooks' American squad tied the talented team from Sweden in its opening game, then beat perennially powerful Czechoslovakia 7–3 en route to four wins and a tie in the opening round.

On February 22—which just happened to be George Washington's birthday—the United States team faced off against the Soviet Union. The 10,000 fans at the Olympic Field House screamed and chanted "USA! USA!" as an electric atmosphere filled the building. Before the game, Brooks told his team, "You were born to be players. You were meant to be here. This moment is yours."

The Soviet Union jumped out to an early 1–0 lead. But the pesky, scrappy United States team tied it. The Soviets went back up 2–1, but as the clock ran down near the end of the first period, a rebound goal by American Mark Johnson tied the contest once again.

Hard checking by the American skaters and gutsy goaltending by United States goalie Jim Craig kept the game close. The Soviets never managed to extend their lead to more than one goal, and they left the ice at the end of the second period leading 3–2.

Miracles Do Happen *Jubilant U.S. hockey players celebrate their Olympic semifinal victory over the Soviet Union.*

Johnson scored his second goal of the game—this one on a power play, while the Soviets were playing one man short—in the third period, tying the game and raising the decibel level of the crowd another notch. Halfway through the final period, United States captain Mike Eruzione found the net with a 30-foot slapshot that gave the Americans their first lead of the game.

Pandemonium broke loose in the crowd, and the chanting of "USA! USA!" continued non-stop. Now it was up to Craig and the United States' defense to hold the mighty Soviets scoreless.

Checking and swarming their opponents, the American team managed to prevent the Soviets from scoring.

The United States team had done the impossible. They had beaten the best. Two days later, in the almost anticlimactic gold medal game, the United States beat Finland 4–2 to capture the gold. The outpouring of patriotism around the United States following the victory was as great as any since the end of World War II.

1980

Heiden's Golden Games

Over the course of nine days in February, American speed skater Eric Heiden (b.1958) did what no other Olympic athlete had ever done before at either the Winter or Summer Games—he won five individual gold medals in one Olympics. The 21-year-old speed skater from Madison, Wisconsin, dominated every event in which he participated.

Although at the time his astounding performance was somewhat overshadowed by the emotional victory of the United States hockey team, time has not diminished Heiden's accomplishment.

Heiden took part in five speed skating events, and won the gold medal in all five. He broke the Olympic record in winning the speed skating competitions at 500, 1,000, 1,500, 5,000, and 10,000 meters. He completed his gold-medal sweep—the drive for five, as it was called at the time—in the 10,000-meter race on February 23. Heiden had spent the previous day watching the United States upset the Soviets in hockey. Then he went out and smashed the existing world record in the 10,000 by more than six seconds.

"He gave the most dominant performance in the history of mankind in an Olympic competition," television announcer Keith Jackson said.

Boycott

Nowhere did the worlds of politics and sports clash more blatantly than in the United States' boycott of the 1980 Summer Olympic Games in Moscow. In December of 1979, the Soviet Union invaded neighboring Afghanistan, and U.S. President Jimmy Carter called for a boycott of the Games to protest the invasion.

On April 12, the United States Olympic Committee (USOC) voted to endorse Carter's call for a boycott. The vote was taken at a meeting in Colorado Springs attended by hundreds of athletes, plus sports and business leaders. Hours of angry debate followed, along with an appeal from Vice President Walter Mondale for everyone to support the boycott.

American athletes were devastated. They had trained for years, some had been preparing for the Games their entire lives and now, through no fault of their

---

Eric Heiden's 1980 Olympics Speed Skating Results

500 meters	38.03 seconds	Olympic Record	Gold Medal
1,000 meters	1 minute, 15.18 seconds	Olympic Record	Gold Medal
1,500 meters	1 minute, 55.44 seconds	Olympic Record	Gold Medal
5,000 meters	7 minutes, 02.29 seconds	Olympic Record	Gold Medal
10,000 meters	14 minutes, 28.13 seconds	World Record	Gold Medal

The Girls Are Alright

In 1932, at the Winter Olympics in Lake Placid, New York, 21 female athletes competed in the Games. Less than half a century later, at the 1980 Winter Olympics, also at Lake Placid, 233 women competed. Figure skater Linda Fratianne was the American star, winning a silver medal in Ladies Singles.

It wasn't only at the Olympics, though, that female athletes made headlines in 1980:

- In January, Mary Decker turned in the first sub-four-and-a-half-minute mile. Decker ran the mile in 4 minutes and 21.68 seconds in Auckland, New Zealand.

- In October, Norway's Grete Waitz was the women's winner in the New York City Marathon for the third year in a row. She completed the 26-plus miles in 2 hours, 25 minutes, and 41 seconds.

- The charter class of the International Women's Sports Hall of Fame included Babe Didrikson (golf, track), Althea Gibson (tennis), Janet Guthrie (auto racing), and Billie Jean King (tennis).

Linda Fratianne

own, they would be denied the chance to compete at the Olympic level.

Twenty-five members of the 1980 United States Olympic team who were slated to go to Moscow sued the USOC. They claimed the USOC did not have the power to decide not to enter an American team in the Olympics. They also claimed the law stated that any decision to not participate in an Olympic games had to be "sports-related." The court rejected all of their claims. The boycott stood.

More than 60 other countries joined the United States in the boycott and did not send teams to Moscow.

In retaliation for the United States-led boycott, the Soviet Union refused to send a team to the Olympic Games in Los Angeles. California, in the summer of 1984 (see page 174).

It's Showtime!

In the spring of 1979, Earvin "Magic" Johnson's Michigan State University team beat Larry Bird's Indiana State University team for the National Collegiate Athletic Association (NCAA) basketball championship. That fall, both players entered the NBA as promising rookies for the 1979–80 season.

By the end of the 1980s, the rivalry between the two players dominated and re-defined professional basketball, bringing the NBA to new heights of popularity. Johnson's Los Angeles Lakers won five NBA championships during the decade, and Bird's Boston Celtics captured three NBA titles. The two teams met three times in the NBA Finals (1983–84, 1984–85 and 1986–87) during the Magic-Bird years.

No Contest *Muhammad Ali (facing camera) fought Larry Holmes, but by this point in their careers, Ali's former sparring partner was the better boxer.*

involved in the offense, creating a true team effort.

Because of his height, speed and strength, Johnson could play forward or center, as well as guard. He demonstrated his versatility in game six of the NBA Finals in 1980, when the Lakers met the Philadelphia 76ers on May 16.

Jabbar sprained his ankle in game five of the finals. The Lakers led the series three games to two, but they would have to play game six in Philadelphia without their all-star center.

Johnson, a rookie who had played all season at point guard, filled in for Jabbar at center. He scored 42 points, pulled down 15 rebounds, and dished out seven assists, leading the Lakers to a 123–107 victory to take the NBA title. Many consider it to be his finest game as a pro, stepping up when his team needed him most.

On thing was for certain: Showtime had arrived!

Marathon Tennis Match

In a match that lasted an astounding three hours and 53 minutes, 24-year-old Bjorn Borg (b.1956) of Sweden won his fifth consecutive Wimbledon singles tennis championship on July 5. His opponent in this titanic struggle was 21-year-old American John McEnroe (b.1959), who went on to win three of the next four Wimbledon singles titles.

Borg lost the first set 1–6, then came back to take the second 7–5. He grabbed the lead, winning the third set 6–3. The intense fourth set, which could have given Borg the title, ended with a marathon 34-point tiebreaker. McEnroe survived three

Johnson's arrival in Los Angeles teamed him with center Kareem Abdul-Jabbar, creating a brand of basketball that came to be known as "Showtime."

At 6-foot-9, Johnson was the tallest point guard in NBA history. He ran the offense, scoring and passing. At a time in the league when individual performances dominated, Johnson got all his teammates

match points and eventually won the tie-breaker 18–16, giving Borg a 6–7 defeat.

In the fifth and final set, Borg's serve overpowered McEnroe, giving the Swede 19 straight points and an 8–6 win. The victory represented Borg's fifth straight Wimbledon title and his 35th consecutive victory in a Wimbledon match—a tournament record.

Holmes Stops Ali

Muhammad Ali (b.1942) was a three-time heavyweight boxing champion of the world, but he never had much of a chance in his bid for a fourth crown, falling to Larry Holmes (b.1949) in a one-sided fight in Las Vegas, Nevada, on October 2.

Holmes, who at one time had been a sparring partner of Ali's and who counted the former champ among his personal heroes, was the younger, faster, and stronger fighter, and Ali was in trouble from the start. Holmes danced and punched, showing the type of power and speed that were Ali's trademarks in his prime. Ali gamely hung on through 10 rounds, but at that point, the referee stopped the fight, and Holmes retained his title.

For Ali, it was clear his storied career was nearing its end. In 1960, Ali had won the gold medal at the Olympics. In 1964, at the age of 22, he shocked the world by beating heavily favored Sonny Liston to capture the heavyweight championship. In 1967, when he refused to be drafted into the military because of his religious beliefs, the title was taken away from him. Then, in 1974, the 32-year-old Ali stunned the boxing world again by beating the previously invincible George Foreman (b.1949) to capture the heavyweight title for a second time.

In 1978, Olympic gold medalist Leon Spinks beat Ali to take his title. Six months later, Ali won the rematch to grab the championship for a third time. After two

Victory at Last! *Bjorn Borg won his fifth consecutive men's singles championship at Wimbledon, but it wasn't easy. He needed five sets to beat up-and-coming John McEnroe in an epic struggle.*

1980

years in retirement, the Champ tried for one more comeback against Holmes, but was totally overmatched.

Ali would fight just one more time in his career, but was beaten by Trevor Berbick in a non-title fight in the Bahamas in 1981 (see page 150).

"No Mas" for Duran

They could not have been more different in personality or boxing style. Welterweight champion Sugar Ray Leonard (b.1956) was a fast-moving, quick-legged dancer in the ring. He borrowed his boxing style and moves from Muhammad Ali and from his namesake, Sugar Ray Robinson, a welterweight and middleweight champion in the 1940s and 1950s. Leonard's good looks and charming personality captured a legion of fans, and in many ways he filled the vacuum left by Ali's retirement. "I studied Ali, I studied Sugar Ray Robinson, I watched them display showmanship, personality, and charisma," Leonard said in an interview on *ABC's Wide World of Sports*. "I wanted to transcend the sport. I wanted to be considered not just a fighter or a champion, but someone special."

Roberto Duran (b.1951), on the other hand, was a powerful puncher who destroyed opponents with his "hands of stone." Duran was already a great lightweight champion when he fought Leonard for the welterweight title, and he had much more experience. Their meeting on June 20, in Montreal, Canada, was perhaps the most eagerly anticipated non-heavyweight fight in history.

Duran was famous for his psychological intimidation. When he ran into Leonard on the street shortly before the fight, Duran made rude gestures, threats

Other Milestones of 1980

✔ On February 29, hockey great Gordie Howe (b.1928) scored his record 800th regular-season NHL goal, at the age of 51. Howe, playing for the Hartford Whalers, scored one more time before retiring at the end of the season.

✔ Nineteen-year-old NHL rookie Wayne Gretzky of the Edmonton Oilers won the first of his eight consecutive Most Valuable Player awards (also called the Hart Trophy). Gretzky, who led the league with 137 points scored, became the youngest player ever to receive this honor.

✔ George Brett came closer to batting .400 than anyone else in Major League Baseball since Ted Williams did it in 1941. Brett stayed right near the .400 mark until late September, and ended the season with a .390 average.

✔ Jack Nicklaus won the U.S. Open (at Baltusrol Golf Club in New Jersey) and the PGA Championship (at Oak Hill Country Club in Rochester, New York) to up his record number of men's major golf titles to 17. Nicklaus eventually won one more major in his storied career, at the 1986 Masters (see page 188).

and insults to Leonard and his wife. By the time the fight began, Leonard's trainer, Angelo Dundee—who had also trained Ali—recalled that Leonard was so angry at Duran about the insults that he was ready to go after him as if in a street brawl. Dundee reminded Leonard that his skills were superior and that he should outbox Duran, as they had planned.

But Leonard came out brawling, trying to beat Duran at his own game. After a 15-round slugfest, Duran won a unanimous decision, taking the welterweight title away from Leonard. A rematch was quickly scheduled.

In an interview with ABC Sports, Dundee explained Leonard's mind-set going into the second fight. "He was embarrassed that he lost the first fight," Dundee said. "He realized what he was supposed to do the first time. And the first time, he was supposed to box. Ray was a premier boxer. What beats Duran, I knew, was a premier boxer."

In the rematch on November 25 at the New Orleans Superdome, Leonard stuck to the plan, outboxing and outdancing Duran for seven rounds, controlling the fight from the outset.

Then, in the eighth round, Duran threw up his hands and uttered the now-famous phrase, "No mas, no mas," which is Spanish for "No more." He quit the fight, claiming that he had stomach cramps, and Leonard regained his title.

Many spectators at the fight said Duran appeared to lose heart, baffled by Leonard's shuffling feet and rapid-fire jabs. On that day, the skillful boxer beat the hands of stone.

1981

Wild Card Winner

The Oakland Raiders won the NFL championship by easily dispatching the Philadelphia Eagles 27–10 in Super Bowl XV at the Louisiana Superdome in New Orleans on January 25. It was the Raiders' second league title in five seasons; the Eagles were playing in the Super Bowl for the first time.

Oakland quarterback Jim Plunkett completed 13 of 21 passes for 261 yards and three touchdowns and was named the game's most valuable player. Plunkett came a long way from the beginning of the regular season, when he was on the Raiders' bench—a spot with which he was quite familiar.

Plunkett won the Heisman Trophy—college football's highest honor—in 1970. He was the No. 1 overall pick (by the New England Patriots) in the 1971 NFL Draft, and became an immediate starter. But his career never really took off as expected, and he was traded to the San Francisco 49ers in 1976. He joined Oakland in 1978, but had been a rarely used backup during his first two years with the Raiders.

In the fifth game of the season, Raiders starting quarterback Dan Pastorini was injured. Plunkett took over and finished the season, leading Oakland to an 11–5 record and the wild-card spot in the playoffs. (The wild-card spot went to the second-place team in the conference with the best record; that team got to join the division winners in the playoffs.)

In the postseason, Plunkett led the Raiders to victories over the Houston Oilers, Cleveland Browns, and San Diego Chargers, leading the team to its third Super Bowl. Oakland lost Super Bowl II to the Green Bay Packers in the 1967 season, and beat the Minnesota Vikings in Super Bowl XI in the 1976 season.

Plunkett took control of Super Bowl XV right from the start. He threw three touchdown passes. The first was a two-yard toss to Cliff Branch in the first quarter. Then, just minutes later, Plunkett tossed a pass to running back Kenny King, which turned into an 80-yard score—the longest pass play in Super Bowl history at the time. Plunkett's final scoring pass was a 29-yarder to Branch in the third quarter.

Linebacker Rod Martin intercepted three Eagles' passes as the Oakland defense played tough. The Eagles did not reach the end zone until they trailed 24–3 in the fourth quarter.

Strike Two *Baseball's second strike was the first to stop play in the middle of the season (see page 149).*

Two for Every One

Wayne Gretzky's journey to re-write the NHL record books continued in his sophomore season, when Gretzky became the first player in the history of the league to average two points per game. His 1981 total was 164 points (goals plus assists) over an 82-game season. He had 55 goals and a record 109 assists.

These were just among the first of the mind-boggling statistics Gretzky posted during his NHL career. From the moment he first skated onto the ice, he was the best passer and the best scorer in the NHL's history. In 1981 he captured his second league MVP award, but the best was yet to come.

Gretzky would go on to play through the 1998–99 season and finish with a host of league records, including most points (2,458), most goals (803), and most assists (1,655). His league scoring championship in 1980–81 was his first of a record nine scoring titles in his career.

Gretzky won the Hart Memorial Trophy as the league's most valuable player a record nine times, too.

1981

Hoosiers Win

At the NCAA basketball championship game on March 20, the University of North Carolina jumped out to an 8–2 lead over Indiana University, and later led by a score of 16–8. But Indiana's Randy Wittman helped close the gap, and his team led 27–26 at halftime.

As the game resumed in the second half, Indiana guard Isiah Thomas (b.1961) singlehandedly put the contest away.

During one seven-minute stretch at the beginning of the second half, the 6-foot-1 sophomore took over, leading Indiana to a 63–50 victory. He scored 10 of his game-high 23 points, consistently fed his teammates the ball, and pulled off key steals anytime it appeared that

North Carolina was poised to get back into the game.

Earlier that same day, President Ronald Reagan was shot in an assassination attempt. It looked as if the game would be postponed. But when it became clear that the President was out of danger, the game proceeded. Still, a dark mood hung over the arena, dampening the usual frantic championship atmosphere.

The King of Daytona

Richard Petty's (b.1937) father, Lee Petty, began racing even before there was a National Association for Stock Car Automobile Racing (NASCAR, which began in 1949). And Richard slipped behind the wheel himself in 1958, beginning an unparalleled 34-year-career as a race car driver. His record 200 wins may never be surpassed, and his record of seven driving championships has been equaled only once (by the late, great Dale Earnhardt). Petty's nickname, appropriately enough, was "the King."

The Daytona 500 is the biggest, most well-known stock car race of the season. In the first Daytona 500, in 1959, Richard Petty ran into engine trouble and had to leave the race. His father ended up winning that day. Richard won his first Daytona 500 race in 1964.

He opened the 1981 racing season with his record seventh and final victory at the Daytona 500 on February 15. He averaged 169.651 miles per hour in his Buick over the course of the race. Petty's seven victories at Daytona came in 1964, 1966, 1971, 1973, 1974, 1979, and 1981. Petty retired from racing in 1992.

The King *Richard Petty's trademarks included his hat, dark glasses, and engaging grin—plus a record 200 career NASCAR victories. Seven of those wins came at the prestigious Daytona 500.*

Lewis Jumps to a Record

At the time, it was a huge achievement. Carl Lewis (b.1961), an extremely talented sophomore at the University of Houston, broke the world indoor long jump record in a meet on February 20. In retrospect, it was the first baby step for a man who would redefine the sport of track and field, picking up 10 medals in four Olympics—nine of those gold—over the next 16 years.

Lewis came into the Southwest Conference Indoor Track and Field Championship at Fort Worth, Texas, that February day as the NCAA champion in both the indoor and outdoor long jump.

The tall, 19-year-old from Birmingham, Alabama, broke the previous indoor record of 27 feet, 6 inches, set by Larry Myricks of Mississippi State in 1980. Lewis' personal best in the indoor long jump had been 27 feet, 4 inches. But this day he shattered both his own mark and the world record with a jump of 27 feet, 10.25 inches. To top off his record-breaking day, Lewis also won the 60-yard sprint, posting a time of 6.06 seconds—the third fastest time in history!

Strike Out!

Baseball, like all professional sports, is a diversion. For the fans, the games are a small break from the realities of life. But on June 12, the harsh reality of baseball as a business intruded, as the players went out on strike, stopping play and jeopardizing the season.

This was not the first baseball strike, nor would it be the last. On April 1, 1972,

Carl Lewis:
The Best Ever

The 1984 Olympics were not supposed to be Carl Lewis' first, but the United States team boycotted the Games in 1980 (see page 140), so the track and field star had to wait four years. At the 1984 Games in Los Angeles, he won four gold medals. Some athletes might have stopped there, but for Lewis it was only the beginning.

He won gold medals in four Olympics (1984, 1988, 1992, and 1996), capturing 10 Olympic medals in all. Nine of them were gold, with the last medal coming at the age of 35 in Atlanta in 1996.

"He was the Babe Ruth and Michael Jordan of our sport," Pete Cava of the United States Track Federation told writer Michael Point.

"You always tried harder when Carl was competing," said American sprinter Leroy Burrell. "Part of it was the natural urge to win, but a lot of it was because you didn't want to get embarrassed."

Tom Tellez, Lewis' coach at the University of Houston, put it very simply: "He's the greatest athlete I've ever seen."

the first Major League Baseball strike in history began. Players walked out over a pension dispute. The strike was settled on April 13, and the season began on April 15, 10 days late.

As more players became free agents (that is, they had the right to negotiate with any team when their contract expired), salaries soared sky high. At the same time, television revenues grew increasingly more important in the financial structure of the game. Labor disputes between players and owners became what seemed like an annual event.

The 1981 strike was different. It was baseball's first midseason strike. Never

Ali's Last Fight

In the end, Muhammad Ali sat slumped on the stool in his corner, overweight, out of shape, and beaten badly by a Jamaican fighter named Trevor Berbick. It was an ignominious end to boxing's most storied career.

Ali had gone to the Bahamas to fight Berbick on December 11 because, with the three-time heavyweight champion's health declining, no place in the United States would sanction another fight. Berbick, who lost a title fight to Larry Holmes in April of 1981, easily won a unanimous 10-round decision.

The loss was only the fifth in 61 career fights for Ali, but it was his third defeat in his last four fights. He knew his career was at the end. The next day, he retired. "Father Time has caught up with me," he said. "I'm finished."

That was only partially true. While he was undoubtedly finished in the ring, Ali remained in the public eye as a goodwill ambassador the world over. A popular, but controversial figure, during his career, his popularity continued to grow in his post-boxing days without the accompanying controversy.

He remained an active public figure despite being diagnosed with Parkinson's Syndrome, brought on by the years of hits he took while boxing.

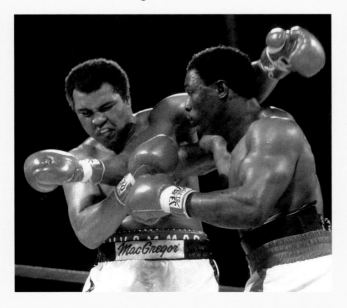

before had the game been wrenched away from fans just as the pennant races were heating up. By the time it ended, the 1981 work stoppage was the longest strike in American sports history, shutting down the game for 50 days and wiping out more than a third of the season.

The main issue of the dispute was compensation for free agents. Today's baseball fan is used to seeing players leave their team when a contract is up to sign with a new team as a free agent—and the team they left receives nothing in return. But in 1981, the idea and practice of free agency was still very new. Owners felt that when a player left their team, some type of compensation was in order.

The players had fought for and won, at the bargaining table and in the courts, the right to become free agents without any compensation going back to the team they left. But the owners wanted to take back the players' victory, feeling they deserved something in return for players they lost to free agency.

To the players, this was totally unacceptable. After fighting for years to obtain free-agent status, they were not about to give up that hard-fought victory. And so the strike dragged on. Although they had called the strike, the players grew bitter, blaming the owners for the lost baseball games. Older players grew frustrated as they tried to add to their career statistics. Younger players wanted to play a full season so they could continue developing their skills and establishing themselves.

And fans lost, perhaps most of all. For a baseball fan, the games are an inseparable part of the summer. Not being able to go to ballpark, or catch a game on

Other Milestones of 1981

✔ Mike Bossy of the New York Islanders became only the second player in NHL history to score 50 goals in the first 50 games of the season, tying Maurice ("Rocket") Richard, who pulled off the feat in the 1944–45 season. Bossy finished the season with a league-leading 68 goals in 79 games played. It was the second time in three years that he led the NHL in goals scored.

✔ On April 12, boxing great Joe Louis (1914–1981) died at age 66. Louis, who was known as the Brown Bomber, reigned as the heavyweight champion from 1937 to 1949. He won 65 of 68 career fights, including 51 by knockout.

✔ Jockey Bill Shoemaker won his record 8,000th race on May 27, far more than any other jockey in history.

✔ The longest game in baseball history was finally completed two months after it began. On April 18 the Pawtucket Red Sox and the Rochester Red Wings of the International League (a minor league) played 32 innings before the game was finally stopped at 4:07 the next morning. The game was completed on June 23, when Pawtucket scored in the 33rd inning for a 3–2 victory.

✔ In a September 26 game against the Los Angeles Dodgers, Houston Astros pitcher Nolan Ryan (b.1947) threw his record breaking fifth no-hitter, surpassing former Dodger Sandy Koufax's mark of four. Ryan eventually finished his baseball career with an astounding seven no-hitters.

✔ Pat Riley (b.1945) took over as coach of basketball's Los Angeles Lakers and led them to four more NBA titles in the 1980s. Riley, who played on the Lakers' 1971–72 league championship team, took Los Angeles to the NBA Finals seven of his first eight seasons as coach.

---

television or radio, caused bitterness and anger toward both players and owners.

With the season approaching the point of cancellation, Marvin Miller, head of the Players' Association (the players' labor union), finally worked out a complex agreement that extended baseball's Basic Agreement, signed in 1980 between players and owners, without actually resolving the free-agent compensation issue.

All told, the strike caused the cancellation of 706 games (38 percent of the season), and cost the players $28 million and the owners $116 million. The owners, however, had taken out strike insurance, which made up for some of that loss.

The decision was made to turn 1981 into a split season. The teams that were in first place in their respective divisions on June 11, when the last games were played, were declared winners of the first half of the season. A new "second season" began on August 10. All teams started with a 0–0 record. The teams that finished in first place over the second half of the season would meet the teams that won their divisions in the first half, in a best-of-five playoff series.

The unusual split season set 1981 apart from all other baseball seasons. No team was hurt more by the split season than the Cincinnati Reds, who finished with the best overall record in baseball but didn't make the playoffs. They finished a close second in each half of the split season.

1982

Playoff Marathon

After the San Diego Chargers had finally outlasted the Miami Dolphins 41–38 in overtime of their AFC Divisional Playoff Game on January 2, tight end Kellen Winslow's San Diego teammates had to help him to the locker room. It has become one of the most iconic images in NFL history—a fitting snapshot of one of the most dramatic, exciting and memorable games ever.

Winslow, a future member of the Pro Football Hall of Fame, literally was exhausted after helping his team pull out the victory. He caught 13 passes for 166 yards and a touchdown, and blocked a field-goal try in the final seconds of the fourth quarter that could have won it for the Dolphins. "Thank God it's over," he told his teammates. "It's the closest to death I've ever been."

Indeed, the game ended up pushing the physical, mental and emotional limits of the players, coaches, and even the fans.

San Diego jumped out to a 24–0 lead in the first quarter and appeared to be unstoppable. The Chargers racked up the points on a 32-yard field goal by Rolf Benirschke, a 56-yard punt return by Wes Chandler, a one-yard touchdown run by Chuck Muncie, and an eight-yard touchdown pass from quarterback Dan Fouts to running back James Brooks.

In the second quarter, Miami coach Don Shula replaced starting quarterback David Woodley with Don Strock. Strock brought Miami back into the game, engineering a long drive that resulted in a field goal, then tossing three touchdown passes to tie the game in the third period.

Fouts came right back with a 25-yard touchdown pass to Winslow, but Miami tied the score again when Strock connected with Bruce Hardy on a 50-yard touchdown pass. Early in the fourth quarter, Miami took its first lead of the game on a 12-yard touchdown run by Tony Nathan. Then, with 58 seconds left in the fourth quarter, Fouts forced an overtime period by finding James Brooks with a nine-yard touchdown pass to tie the game at 38–38. As time expired, Miami's Uwe von Schamann attempted a potential game-winning field goal, but Winslow blocked it.

In overtime, where the first score meant victory, Schamann had another field-goal attempt blocked by the Chargers. San Diego's kicker, Rolf Benirschke,

Working Overtime *San Diego Chargers tight end Kellen Winslow (80) is helped off the field by his teammates after a marathon NFL playoff victory over the Miami Dolphins.*

missed a field-goal try in the overtime period, as well. Finally, after 13 minutes, 29 seconds of overtime play, Benirschke kicked a 29-yard field goal to give San Diego the victory.

Both quarterbacks were amazing in a game that, unfortunately, someone had to lose. Fouts threw for 433 yards and three touchdowns, while Strock racked up 403 yards and four touchdowns.

1982

Montana Looks Super

The San Francisco 49ers, the worst team in the NFL in the late 1970s, completed an amazingly quick turnaround by winning the league championship for the first time in the 1981 season. They capped their resurgence with a 26–21 victory over the Cincinnati Bengals in Super Bowl XVI at the Silverdome in Pontiac, Michigan, on January 24.

San Francisco quarterback Joe Montana (b.1956) was named the game's most valuable player. Although Montana's statistics were not spectacular in this game—he passed for 157 yards and a touchdown and ran for another touchdown—he operated the 49ers' offense efficiently and flawlessly. In fact, there arguably has never been a quarterback who operated with as much calm and grace in the most pressure-filled situations as Montana. It's almost as if he preferred to have the game or the season on the line with under a minute to go, 80 yards away from the winning touchdown. At the very least, he thrived on those high-pressure situations. By the time the decade ended, his would be a familiar face peering over center, coolly barking out signals, doing whatever needed to be done to bring victory in the biggest games.

The 49ers went on to win a total of four Super Bowls in the 1980s under Montana's leadership, clearly establishing themselves as the team of the decade. In his and the team's first Super Bowl, they faced another first-time entry in the Bengals. Both San Francisco and Cincinnati won only six games in the 1980 season before winning division titles in 1981.

San Francisco was fresh off a dramatic 28–27 victory over the Dallas Cowboys in the NFC title game. To pull that one out, Montana had tossed a six-yard touchdown pass to a leaping Dwight Clark in the back of the end zone with 51 seconds left in the game. Cincinnati routed San Diego 27–7 for the AFC title.

Although both teams were in the big game for the first time, Cincinnati really looked like the rookie squad, committing three turnovers in the first half, which the 49ers converted into 17 points en route to a 20–0 halftime edge. The first two turnovers—a Dwight Hicks interception and a Lynn Thomas fumble recovery—occurred deep in the 49ers' own territory. Both led to long scoring drives.

In the second half, Cincinnati quarterback Ken Anderson brought the Bengals back to within six points, but a couple of San Francisco field goals sealed the 49ers' first Super Bowl victory. They took the game by a score of 26–21.

The championship marked a tremendous turnaround for Montana and the 49ers, led by coach Bill Walsh.

Walsh inherited a team that had been 2–14 in 1978 when he took over in 1979. The 49ers went 2–14 again that year but were much improved offensively. Then, the season before their Super Bowl victory, the team finished with a 6–10 record. But in 1981, Walsh made Montana, a third-round draft pick in 1979, his full-time starting quarterback. Montana passed for 3,565 yards and 19 touchdowns, and the 49ers finished the regular season with a 13–3 record—the best in the league—which they followed up with their victory in the Silverdome.

The Shot

Although their future NBA battles would dominate the league in the 1990s, when Michael Jordan (b.1963) and Patrick Ewing (b.1962) faced off in the NCAA championship game on March 29, they were both just college freshman.

Ewing's Georgetown University team counted on the seven-foot-tall center's tough inside defense, rebounding and scoring. Jordan's University of North Carolina teammates looked to him to consistently hit his jump shots, racking up points.

Georgetown had a 32–31 lead at half-time. The second half featured fiercely competitive play, and neither team built up more than a four-point lead. Eric Smith and Sleepy Floyd added offense to Ewing's effort for Georgetown, while Jordan's jumpers and James Worthy's hard drives and defense kept North Carolina in the game.

Floyd gave Georgetown its last lead of the game when he hit a jump shot to put his team up 62–61 with 57 seconds left. North Carolina ran 25 seconds off the clock, then called a timeout to set up one final play.

Everyone in the building expected the play to go to Worthy, a junior and the team's leader. But North Carolina coach Dean Smith surprised Georgetown and showed great confidence in his freshman player by designing a play for Jordan.

With 15 seconds on the clock, Jordan did what he would come to do so many times during the years in which he dominated the NBA. He calmly hit a 16-foot jump shot, which proved to be the game winner.

Air Apparent *Before he became an international superstar, Michael Jordan led North Carolina to an NCAA championship.*

Looking for the ball with the game on the line and coming through in the clutch became Jordan's trademarks while helping the Chicago Bulls dominate the NBA in the 1990s. But he set the pattern way back in his freshman year at North Carolina, in the first of his many championship games.

1982

The Great One

Some athletes redefine what people thought was possible in a sport. In hockey, Wayne Gretzky rewrote the record books in the 1980s.

Gretzky scored an unheard-of 212 total points (goals plus assists) in the 1981–82 season, breaking his own NHL single-season record by 51 points.

In addition to his record for total points, Gretzky set a slew of other NHL single-season records: most goals (92), most assists (120), most hat tricks (three goals in a single game—he had 10), and highest points-per-game average (2.65).

On his way to 212 points, Gretzky passed Phil Esposito's 76 goals in one season record, as well as his own assists record of 109. He scored five goals in one game, and four goals in a game three times. In an 82-game season, Gretzky was held scoreless only eight times. His team, the Edmonton Oilers, had the second best record in the NHL.

Gretzky, at the age of 21, won the MVP award, his third in three years.

Women's Hoops

In March 1982, the NCAA held its first women's championship basketball tournament. This was not, however, the first basketball championship for women. In 1972, the Association for Intercollegiate Athletics for Women

Born to Skate

Wayne Gretzky learned to skate at the age of two. Growing up in Brantford, Ontario, in Canada, young Gretzky learned the fundamentals of hockey from his father, Walter. By the age of six, he was already considered a prodigy, playing against 10-year-olds. At the age of eight, he scored 104 goals in a season, playing against 13-year-olds. At age 10 he scored 378 goals in 82 games.

When Gretzky reached the age of 15, he was already playing top level junior league hockey, always the youngest, yet always the best on his teams. He signed his first professional contract at age 17, playing for the World Hockey Association's Indianapolis Racers, who traded him to the WHA's Edmonton Oilers.

In 1979, the Oilers were accepted into the NHL and Gretzky began changing what was possible to achieve in hockey, setting new records with each passing season.

Oilers coach Billy Harris said of Gretzky's 212-point 1981–82 season, "That's like rushing for 3,000 yards or hitting 80 home runs in a season."

It wasn't his overpowering physique that intimidated opponents. Gretzky was not particularly strong, nor fast, nor did he have a devastating slap shot. What he had was uncanny instinct for seeing what was going to happen before it happened, for knowing where a teammate would be and getting a pass there, and for avoiding hard hits from the defense.

"Gretzky sees a picture out there that no one else sees," Boston Bruins executive Harry Sinden told ESPN. "It's difficult to describe, because I've never seen the game he's looking at."

(AIAW) held the first national women's college basketball tournament. At that time, the NCAA was not involved in women's sports. But by 1981, the NCAA began to stage a number of championships for women in tournaments that competed with the AIAW.

This year's tournament started with a 32-team field. Eventually, Louisiana Tech University beat Cheyney University of Pennsylvania by a score of 76–62 for the title. That first NCAA championship game drew 9,351 fans. The entire tournament brought in 56,320 people. Within a few years, that number had doubled, as women's college sports began to come into their own in the 1980s.

Before the NCAA got involved with women's college basketball, most of the best teams came from small, unknown colleges, like the two that made it to the finals that year. With the NCAA's involvement, many larger schools began taking their women's athletic programs more seriously.

We're Number One! *Forward Ann Pendergrass and her Louisiana Tech teammates won the first NCAA women's basketball championship by beating Cheyney University in the final game.*

Watson's Day at the Beach

Tom Watson beat Jack Nicklaus in a dramatic duel in the final round of golf's U.S. Open in June at Pebble Beach, California. Watson won with one of the most memorable shots in golf history.

After 16 holes of the last round, Watson and Nicklaus were tied atop the leaderboard. Then, on the par-three 17th, Watson's tee shot landed beyond the green in heavy, treacherous rough. He was only about 15 feet from the hole, but a delicate pitch shot could have cost him the tournament if not executed properly—too short, and he's still in the rough; too long, and he could bogey the hole. "Get it close," Watson's caddy told him. "No, I'm going to make it," Watson replied.

And he did. As Watson's pitch trickled into the cup, he danced around the green in joy. Watson went on to birdie the 18th hole also to win by two shots.

The next month, Watson completed a rare feat when he followed his U.S. Open triumph by winning the British Open.

1982

The Specter of Drugs

More and more as the decades of the 20th century unfolded, sports came to reflect what was happening in the rest of American society. As drug use increased, the dark specter of substance abuse raised its terrifying head in the world of sports.

How much was known of cocaine use in the NFL in the 1980s is hard to say. Did players hide it from each other? From coaches? From team officials? Or was there an unspoken "look the other way" policy?

When the July 14 issue of *Sports Illustrated* magazine hit the newsstands in 1982, a bright light was shed on this dark secret. Don Reese, a retired defensive end who had played for the Miami Dolphins (1974–76), the New Orleans Saints (1978–80) and the San Diego Chargers (1981), told the magazine that cocaine "now controls and corrupts" NFL football, because so many players in the league used it.

Reese himself was sentenced in 1977 to one year in prison for selling cocaine. He called the problem a growing cancer in the league. "Cocaine can be found in quantity throughout the NFL," Reese said in the article, which he co-wrote with *Sports Illustrated* staff writer John Underwood. "It's pushed on players, often from the edge of the practice field. Sometimes it's pushed by players. Prominent players. A cocaine cloud covers the entire league. I think most coaches know this or have a good idea."

Reese told of his own drug use, which included free-basing (inhaling cocaine in a smokable form) with several other members of the Saints. At the time of the article, Reese still owed $30,000 to drug dealers and said he had been threatened by these dealers several times.

In 1980, the NFL had introduced a voluntary program to enable players with drug and alcohol problems to find help. As of 1982, 17 players had taken advantage of the program. As cocaine use spiraled out of control in America during the 1980s, its effect on sports grew as well, and could no longer be ignored.

Decker: Another Record

Mary Decker already owned the world record for the fastest time in the women's 5,000-meter race, the 3,000-meter race, the 2,000-meter race, and the 800-meter race when she took off in the 10,000-meters at Hayward Field in her hometown of Eugene, Oregon, on July 16.

One week earlier at an international meet in Paris, Decker set a new women's world record in the mile, turning in a time of four minutes, 18.08 seconds. Now, with the hometown crowd cheering her on, she set a world record in the 10,000, finishing in 31 minutes, 35.30 seconds. The 10,000-meter race had been dominated by Soviet women, who held the nine fastest times in the event, before Decker's world-record run.

As "Little Mary Decker" (she was only 4-foot-10, 86 pounds), she burst onto the international track and field scene in 1973 at a United States-Soviet meet in Minsk. Her breakthrough year was 1980, when she set three world records. Later, she went on to win the 1,500- and 3,000-meter races at the 1983 World Championships in Helsinki, Finland.

But 1982 was the finest year of her career, when she set records in the 2,000-, 3,000-, 5,000-, and 10,000-meter races, as well as her triumph in the mile. For her achievements, Decker was voted the Women's Sports Foundation's Amateur Sportswoman of the Year. She also won the Jesse Owens Award, which is presented annually to the best U.S. track and field athlete. She became the first woman to win that prestigious award.

Magical Mark

A total of 300 victories is the magical number for Major League Baseball starting pitchers, only 23 of whom reached that plateau through 2009. No relief pitchers ever reached 300 career saves, however, until the Milwaukee Brewers' Rollie Fingers reached that mark on August 21. That night, Fingers pitched the final two innings of the Brewers' 3–2 victory over the Mariners at the Kingdome in Seattle.

Fingers was in his 15th big-league season then and was just five days short of his 36th birthday. The American League Cy Young Award winner and Most Valuable Player the previous season for Milwaukee, Fingers first came to prominence as an All-Star for the powerful Oakland A's teams of the 1970s. He also pitched four seasons for the San Diego Padres, and in 1985 finished his career in Milwaukee with a record 341 saves.

As relief pitchers have taken on a greater role in today's game and closers are used almost exclusively in the ninth inning, 300 saves no longer is such an unattainable milestone. Some 21 relief pitchers in all have reached the mark entering 2010, although Fingers' total still ranks No. 10 all-time.

King of Steals

The Oakland Athletics' Rickey Henderson (b.1958)—baseball's all-time stolen base leader and the man considered by many to be the greatest leadoff hitter the game has ever seen—broke the single-season stolen base record on August 27 in a game at Milwaukee against the Brewers.

Henderson broke the record that had been set by St. Louis Cardinals' great Lou Brock, who stole 118 bases in 1974. Henderson stole base number 119 in the third inning, after drawing a walk from Brewers pitcher Doc Medich. Medich tossed over to first four times to chase Henderson

Top Base-Stealing Seasons of the 20th Century

PLAYER	TEAM	SEASON	STOLEN BASES
Rickey Henderson	Oakland Athletics	1982	130
Lou Brock	St. Louis Cardinals	1974	118
Vince Coleman	St. Louis Cardinals	1985	110
Vince Coleman	St. Louis Cardinals	1987	109
Rickey Henderson	Oakland Athletics	1983	108
Vince Coleman	St. Louis Cardinals	1986	107
Maury Wills	Los Angeles Dodgers	1962	104
Rickey Henderson	Oakland Athletics	1980	100
Ron Leflore	Montreal Expos	1980	97
Ty Cobb	Detroit Tigers	1915	96

Other Milestones of 1982

✔ Carl Lewis broke the world record in the long jump in January. He leapt a distance of 28 feet, 1 inch, in the United States Olympic Invitational track meet.

✔ On January 26, Cheryl Miller, future NCAA basketball great, scored 105 points in a high school game for Riverside Polytechnic in California. Miller went on to play college basketball at the University of Southern California, where she led the Women of Troy to a pair of national championships in the 1980s.

✔ Martina Navratilova (b.1956) began her incredible run in women's tennis by winning 90 of 93 matches.

✔ Sugar Ray Leonard retired from boxing due to an eye injury. His record was 32–1, with 22 knockouts. His only loss came at the hands of Roberto Duran (see page 144).

✔ Lorri Bauman of the Drake University Bulldogs scored 50 points in a West Regional basketball game against the University of Maryland. Although Maryland won that game 89–78 to advance to the Final Four, Bauman's total still stands as the most points ever scored in an NCAA women's tournament game.

✔ Steve Carlton of the Philadelphia Phillies, who won 23 games at age 37, became the first pitcher to win four Cy Young Awards.

✔ Shirley Muldowney won her third National Hot Rod Association points title—the first driver, male or female, to ever win three.

✔ Kathy Whitworth was inducted into the World Golf Hall of Fame. Her 88 career victories are the most by an American.

✔ The Supreme Court ruled that Title IX covers coaches and other school employees as well as students. Title IX is a federal regulation that mandates equal funding for boys' and girls' programs, including athletic programs, at schools in the United States.

✔ Tear-away jerseys appeared for the first time in college football. A tear-away jersey easily tears off when grabbed by an opposing player, so that the wearer can't be pulled down by his jersey.

---

back to the bag. He then threw a pitchout to catcher Ted Simmons as Henderson started for second. The throw by Simmons to Brewers shortstop Robin Yount was a good one, but Henderson slid in under the tag and was safe at second.

The game was stopped and members of both teams and the media gathered around Henderson at second base. The Oakland speedster pulled the base from the ground and held it over his head triumphantly. Henderson went on to steal three more bases in that game, and finished the season with 130, still the modern single-season record. He eventually played through the 2003 season, and ended his 25-year career with 1,406 thefts, another record. He was inducted into the Baseball Hall of Fame in 2009, giving a memorable speech at the ceremony.

NFL Strike Is the Longest

For the first time in NFL history, players staged a strike that interrupted the regular-season schedule. The strike began on September 21, two games into the 1982 season. By the time it ended 57 days later, on November 16, it had become the longest strike in professional sports history, surpassing the baseball strike of 1981 by seven days. (The baseball strike of 1994, which led to the cancellation of the playoffs and World Series, is the current record holder. It lasted 234 days.)

As with the 1981 baseball strike, the issue was money. And once again, as would happen more and more frequently in the 1980s and beyond, fans turning to the sports page would come to read about labor negotiations, team revenues, and player salaries, instead of games won and lost. Sports was business, and the business of sports had grown so big by the 1980s that at times the games seemed secondary to financial deals and labor disputes.

One major issue in this strike was the fact that before 1982 the NFL Players Association (the players' labor union) was not allowed to receive copies of players' contracts. After the strike, contracts and salaries were a more open issue, as the union was allowed to receive all contract information. Minimum salaries were established, and free-agency was expanded.

When the strike was finally settled, the decision was made to reduce the number of games in the 1982 season to nine—the two played before the strike, plus seven more after. In addition, 16 teams qualified for the playoffs (six more than usual), and the regular season ended a week later than originally scheduled.

The strike cost the league $240 million in lost ticket and television money, and wiped 112 games from the schedule. The resulting agreement was set to last until 1986 and brought the players $60 million in bonuses, plus $1.3 billion in salaries and benefits for the years 1983–86.

Attendance for the games played after the strike was down greatly, and it took almost a full year for fans to return to the NFL in pre-strike numbers.

Bye-Bye Oakland

Controversial Oakland Raiders owner Al Davis wanted to move his team from Oakland to Los Angeles. The NFL said no. As was becoming the case more and more often in sports in the 1980s, the two sides ended up in court.

Davis sued, claiming an antitrust violation, saying the league had no right to tell him where he could or couldn't move his team. Following a long and bitter court battle, a jury awarded Davis the right to move his team to Los Angeles.

And so, before the 1982 season, Davis moved his Raiders about 500 miles south. The team began playing its home games in the Los Angeles Coliseum instead of the Oakland Coliseum. (The franchise eventually reversed course in 1995 and went back up north to Oakland.)

The ruling shook up the NFL, which saw moves by the Cleveland Browns, Los Angeles Rams, and Houston Oilers in the years that followed this decision.

1983

Riggins' Run

The Washington Redskins' John Riggins capped a remarkable postseason performance with one of the most memorable runs in Super Bowl history on January 30. Riggins raced 43 yards for the go-ahead touchdown in the fourth quarter of his team's 27–17 victory over the Miami Dolphins in Super Bowl XVII at Pasadena, California.

Riggins, the Redskins' burly fullback, carried his team through the longest postseason in NFL history. Because of the strike-shortened regular season (see page 160), the postseason was expanded to include 16 teams in a single-elimination tournament. Riggins rushed for 610 yards and four touchdowns in Washington's four postseason wins, including 166 yards and the key fourth-quarter score against the Dolphins.

Washington trailed Miami 17–13 until Riggins' decisive run came on a fourth-down-and-one play with 10:01 remaining in the game. The Redskins added an insurance touchdown late in the fourth quarter.

Riggins was named the game's most valuable player.

Big Name to New League

The United States Football League (USFL) began play in 1983. Playing a 16-game schedule in the spring, so as not to go head-to-head with the NFL's fall season, the new league featured colorful owners and competed with the NFL for top college players.

Founded by David Dixon, a New Orleans art and antiques dealer, the USFL announced its formation on May 11, 1982. The USFL started with 12 teams in major markets across the country: New Jersey, Los Angeles, Chicago, Detroit, Boston, Tampa, Oakland, Denver, Washington, Philadelphia, Birmingham, and San Diego (that franchise moved to Phoenix). The games were shown on ESPN and ABC.

Shortly before the start of their inaugural season, the New Jersey Generals signed University of Georgia tailback Herschel Walker, 1982's Heisman Trophy winner (the Heisman Trophy is awarded annually to the best college football player in the nation). Walker left college a year early to turn pro, and the highly touted rookie gave credibility to the new league. During his college career, Walker rushed for 5,259 yards and set 10 NCAA records.

Super Run *Washington Redskins running back John Riggins sheds a would-be tackler and breaks free on the go-ahead touchdown run in the fourth quarter of Super Bowl XVII in Pasadena, California. The Redskins beat the Miami Dolphins 27–17.*

Walker's contract with New Jersey made him the highest paid player in football history. He received $1.5 million, compared to Chicago Bears running back Walter Payton (a future member of the Pro Football Hall of Fame), who had the top NFL salary of $700,000.

Although the USFL's level of play was not up to NFL quality, the teams averaged more than 24,000 fans a game. The ratings were also good. But huge player salaries put many teams into financial trouble—trouble that would plague the USFL throughout its entire existence.

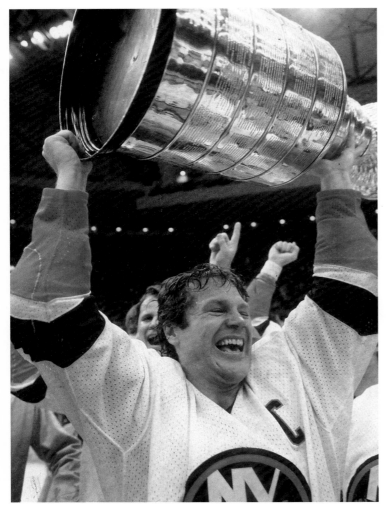

Their Cup Runneth Over and Over and . . . *Winning the Stanley Cup championship was getting to be old hat for captain Dennis Potvin and the New York Islanders, who won their fourth straight NHL title.*

Islanders Win Again

Since the formation of the NHL in 1917, no team has dominated the league the way the Montreal Canadiens have. In hockey, the word "dynasty" usually means Montreal. The Canadiens have won the Stanley Cup championship 23 times since then (that's by far a league record; the next closest, the Toronto Maple Leafs, stand at just 13 championships). Between 1955 and 1960 the Canadiens won five consecutive Stanley Cups, a feat that has never been equaled. Then, from 1975 to 1979, the Canadiens won four straight Stanley Cups.

In 1983, the New York Islanders became just the second team in NHL history to win four Stanley Cups in a row, creating their own dynasty and joining Montreal in the record books.

The streak began with a Stanley Cup Championship in the 1979–80 season, when the Islanders beat the Philadelphia Flyers in six games in the finals. In 1980–81, the Isles (as their fans call them) beat the Minnesota North Stars in five games in the finals. The 1981–82 finals saw the Islanders sweep the Vancouver Canucks in four straight games.

New York took its fourth straight Cup in May, completing another four-game sweep in the 1982–83 finals by beating the Edmonton Oilers, who were led by the Great One, Wayne Gretzky. During the regular season, Gretzky scored 71 goals and had 196 points on the way to his fourth straight MVP award. But in the Stanley Cup finals, the Islanders tough defense shut down Gretzky and his Oilers' teammates.

The Oilers were held to just six goals in the four-game series, and they didn't score off Islanders goaltender Billy Smith in seven of the 12 periods played. Islanders Bryan Trottier and Butch Goring stuck close to Gretzky, limiting him to just four assists.

The Islanders' offense was led by Mike Bossy and Clark Gillies.

Watson Wins Fifth Open

American golfer Tom Watson won his fifth British Open golf championship in July. This achievement is unique in recent times, and places Watson second only to Harry Vardon, who won six British Opens between the years 1896 and 1914.

Watson took the Open with a combined four-round total of 275 at the Royal Birkdale course in England. His other victories in the British Open came in 1975, 1977, 1980, and 1982.

Watson joined the PGA Tour in 1971, and was the leading money winner on the Tour in 1977, 1978, 1979, 1980, and 1984. He was voted PGA Player of the Year six times (1977, 1978, 1979, 1980, 1982, and 1984), and was a member of four United States Ryder Cup teams (1977, 1981, 1983, and 1989). He served as captain in 1993.

Watson also won the Vardon Trophy (named for Harry Vardon) three years in a row (1977–79). The Vardon Trophy is awarded by the PGA of America to the PGA Tour regular with the lowest average score for the year.

Malone Leads 76ers

Center Moses Malone scored 24 points and grabbed 23 rebounds to lead the Philadelphia 76ers to a 115–108 victory over the Los Angeles Lakers on May 31 in Los Angeles. The 76ers' victory capped a four-game sweep in the NBA Finals and ended the Lakers' reign as the league champions.

It was fitting that Malone was the key player in the decisive game because he was the man that the 76ers tabbed in free agency to team with Julius Erving, the 76ers' perennial All-Star, for the 1982–83 season. In these days of high-priced free agents, it doesn't seem unusual for a pro team to go out and spend millions to land the player they need. But in the 1980s, the concept was still new.

The Philadelphia 76ers had not won an NBA title since 1967. Team owner Harold Katz decided to go out and buy a top star to team with Erving.

The 6-foot-10 Malone had been the first player to go straight from high school into pro basketball, without going to college. Like Erving, Malone began his pro career in the American Basketball Association (ABA), a rival league that eventually merged several of its teams into the NBA.

From 1974 to 1976, Malone was a dominant center, a powerful rebounder, and a prolific scorer for the ABA's Utah Stars and St. Louis Spirit. When the two leagues merged in 1976, Malone joined the Buffalo Braves, then later played for the Houston Rockets, where he continued to be among the league leaders in scoring and rebounding. Following the 1981–82 season, he became a free agent.

Determined to bring a championship home to the loyal fans in Philadelphia, Katz gave Malone a contract worth $13.2 million over four years, an unheard-of figure in the NBA at that time. But it paid off. During the regular season, Malone averaged 24.5 points and a league-leading 15.3 rebounds per game. Those numbers only improved during the playoffs, when Malone averaged 25.8 points and 18.5 rebounds per game while leading the 76ers to 12 wins in 13 postseason games.

1983

The Pine Tar Incident

It was surely one of baseball's strangest and most controversial moments. On July 24, the Kansas City Royals were at Yankee Stadium, playing just another regular-season game against the Bronx Bombers. With two outs and nobody on base in the top of the ninth inning, the Yankees led 4–3. The Royals' U.L. Washington hit a single, bringing up Kansas City third baseman George Brett.

Brett smashed a two-run homer off Yankees relief pitcher Goose Gossage, giving the Royals a 5–4 lead. Or so everyone in the stadium thought.

Once Brett crossed home plate and had gone into the Kansas City dugout, however, Yankees manager Billy Martin walked up to home plate umpire Tim McClelland and handed him Brett's bat, complaining that the bat was illegal because it had too much pine tar. Pine tar is a dark, sticky substance that players put onto their bat handles to get a better grip. While use of the pine tar is legal, the amount a player may use is specified in the rules. A player may not place any substance on his bat to improve the grip that extends more than 18 inches from the end of the bat handle.

The umpires all met around home plate, measuring the amount of pine tar on the bat against the front side of home plate (which they knew to be 17 inches long). The umpires ruled that there was more than 18 inches of pine tar on the bat, and so McClelland signaled that Brett was out and the home run did not count.

The Royals' third baseman sprang from the dugout, racing toward McClelland, his eyes bulging with rage, a stream of obscenities pouring from his lips. Umpiring crew chief Joe Brinkman intercepted Brett before he reached McClelland, grabbing him around the neck and trying to calm him down. Royals manager Dick Howser and coach Rocky Colavito joined the fray and were soon ejected from the game along with Brett.

Meanwhile, Brett's Kansas City teammate, future Hall-of-Fame pitcher Gaylord Perry, slipped out of the dugout, grabbed the bat, and headed for the clubhouse to hide it. Perry was stopped by stadium security, who took the bat back and ejected Perry from the stadium.

The home run was nullified, and the Yankees won the game 4–3. Or so everyone at the stadium thought. But the Royals protested the decision, arguing that there was no intentional plan to cheat and that they did not violate the spirit of the rules. American League president Lee MacPhail agreed. He overruled the umpires' deci-

The Pine-Tar Rule

Rule 1.10 (c) of the official baseball rulebook states:

The bat handle, for not more than 18 inches from its end, may be covered or treated with any material or substance to improve the grip. Any such material or substance, which extends past the 18-inch limitation, shall cause the bat to be removed from the game.

Following the George Brett pine-tar incident, this rule was amended to read:

NOTE: If the umpire discovers that the bat does not conform to (c) above until a time during or after which the bat has been used in play, it shall not be grounds for declaring the batter out, or ejected from the game.

sion, stating that the game should resume from the point at which the pine-tar incident occurred—in other words, after Brett's home run, which would now count, and give the Royals a 5–4 lead.

Twenty-five days after it began, on August 18 (an open date for both teams), the "pine-tar game" resumed at Yankee Stadium in front of only 1,245 fans. Kansas City's Hal McRae made the final out in the top of the ninth inning, then Royals pitcher Dan Quisenberry set the Yankees down 1-2-3 in the bottom of the ninth inning to give Kansas City the victory.

Following this incident, baseball's rule book was amended to prevent a similar situation from occurring again (see the box on the opposite page).

When Brett was elected to the Baseball Hall of Fame in 1999, the famous pine tar bat went to Cooperstown with him, where it was placed on display.

Martina's First U.S. Open

Continuing her meteoric rise to the top of women's tennis, Martina Navratilova defeated Chris Evert-Lloyd on September 10 to capture her first U.S. Open singles championship. In a match that lasted only 63 minutes, Navratilova crushed Evert-Lloyd 6–1, 6–3. Cementing her stature as the top women's tennis player in the world, Navratilova dominated her opponent, top rival, and friend, rushing the net after nearly every serve, keeping Evert-Lloyd from setting up on the baseline.

The victory was Navratilova's 66th in her last 67 matches. By the end of 1983 she posted a record of 86–1, to follow the

On Top of the World *Martina Navratilova left no doubt that she was the best women's tennis player in the world with an easy, straight-sets victory over Chris Evert in the finals of the U.S. Open.*

90–3 record she put up in 1982. The former Czech defector (now an American) continued to dominate women's tennis throughout the 1980s with an aggressive and intimidating style that changed the face of the game (see box on page 168).

1983

Coaching Giants

The football world lost two of its coaching icons in 1983: On January 26, Alabama's Paul (Bear) Bryant (1913–1983) died at 69; on October 31, the Chicago Bears' George Halas (1895–1983) died at 88.

With 323 career victories, Bryant was the winningest coach in college football history at the time of his death. He had coached through the 1982 season, his 25th at Alabama and his 38th as a major-college coach in a career that began at Maryland in 1945. He also made stops at Kentucky (1946–1953) and Texas A & M (1954–57). It was at Alabama, though, that he really made his mark, wearing his trademark houndstooth hat while leading the Crimson Tide to six national championships and at least a share of 12 conference championships. Bryant died of heart failure only 28 days after he retired as Alabama's coach.

Halas was the founder and owner of the Bears, who were a charter member of the NFL (originally called the American Professional Football Association)

The Changing Face of Women's Tennis

Martina Navratilova's great contributions to the game of tennis can't be limited to her astounding 56 Grand Slam titles. (The Grand Slam is made up of tennis' four major tournaments: the Australian Open, the French Open, Wimbledon, and the U.S. Open.) She also took women's tennis to a new level of excitement and fan interest in the 1980s, bringing speed, power, and strength to the game. Navratilova introduced new training methods and nutritional programs specifically designed for female tennis players.

At age four, in her native Czechoslovakia, Navratilova got her first tennis racquet. At age six, she took her first lesson. When she was eight, she entered her first tournament. By the age of 16, she had become Czechoslovakia's top player.

In 1975, Navratilova defected to the United States, and by the mid-1980s she was well on her way to setting new standards for women's tennis.

She changed the look and style of the women's game, making it faster and more athletic. After winning six Wimbledon titles in a row, from 1982 to 1987, to bring her total to eight, Navratilova returned to the finals in 1990 for her record-breaking ninth Wimbledon victory.

Her success inspired many girls, not only to become tennis players, but also to take part in athletics of many kinds. She had another impact off the court as well, beginning in 1981, when it became widely known, and she confirmed in interviews, that she was gay. Few athletes of her caliber have ever "come out of the closet," and she faced some criticism for her lifestyle. However, she battled against those opinions with the same power that she used to win on the court, and became an important spokesperson for the cause of fair treatment for gay and lesbian athletes.

Other Milestones of 1983

✔ San Diego Padres first baseman Steve Garvey played in his 1,118th consecutive baseball game on April 16, setting a new National League record. Garvey's streak eventually reached 1,207 games before ending in late July.

✔ On May 31, Jack Dempsey (1895–1983), heavyweight boxing champ from 1919 to 1926, died at the age of 87.

✔ Rap music picked up sports culture as a theme when Grandmaster Flash released "The Message," in which he talked about "watching the game or the Sugar Ray fight." Also, rapper Kurtis Blow released the song "Basketball," a tribute to the NBA players he watched in the 1970s.

✔ Evelyn Ashford (b.1957) set a world record for women in the 100-meter run with a time of 10.79 seconds on July 3 at the National Sports Festival in Colorado Springs. The record lasted until 1988, when it was broken by Florence Griffith-Joyner.

✔ Philadelphia Phillies pitcher Steve Carlton picked up his 300th career victory on September 23. Carlton struck out 12 batters in eight innings and beat the St. Louis Cardinals 6–2 to record his milestone win. Carlton went on to win 329 games in a 24-season career that ended in 1988.

✔ Overtime for regular-season NHL games was reinstated for the first time since 1942, with a five-minute time limit. Before then, games simply ended in a tie.

---

in 1920 as the Decatur Staleys. The next year, Halas moved the team to Chicago, still with the name Staleys. In 1922, the club became known as the Bears. Halas coached the franchise for 40 years in four 10-year stints, winning six league championships and 324 games.

Three Royals Head to Jail

For the first time, three active Major League Baseball players were arrested and sent to jail on drug-related charges. On November 17, a federal judge sentenced Willie Wilson, Willie Aikens, and Jerry Martin of the Kansas City Royals to three-month jail sentences for attempting to purchase cocaine. All three had pleaded guilty.

Noting the special place in society he felt professional athletes held, the judge also fined Wilson and Aikens the maximum amount of $5,000, and he fined Martin $2,500. Martin and Aikens were released by the Royals. Wilson, who was the team's starting center fielder, remained with the organization.

Commissioner Bowie Kuhn also suspended the players from baseball for one year, as the growing problem of illegal drug use among professional athletes leapt once again to the front page.

1984

Olympic Gold

On February 16, at the 1984 Winter Games in Sarajevo, Yugoslavia, Bill Johnson became the first American ever to win a gold medal in downhill skiing. That started an avalanche of skiing medals for the United States.

Before the competition ended, the U.S. ski team took gold medals in three of the six downhill events—competition that had traditionally been dominated by European skiers. American brothers Phil and Steve Mahre followed Johnson's performance with gold and silver medal victories in the men's Alpine slalom. And not to be outdone, the American women's downhill team also pulled off a one-two finish.

The 23-year-old Johnson was born in Los Angeles, California, but he learned to ski in Idaho, where his family moved when he was a youngster. He was the U.S. champ in the downhill in 1983. At Sarajevo, Johnson tore down the 3,066-meter course in one minute, 45.59 seconds, beating Peter Mueller of Switzerland by 27-hundredths of a second. Johnson beat Mueller's time with a burst of speed just before he crossed the finish line.

Phil Mahre took the second U.S. downhill gold with a time of one minute, 39.41 seconds in the Alpine slalom, while Steve won the silver.

In the giant slalom, Debbie Armstrong captured the third U.S. downhill gold of the games with a time of two minutes, 20.98 seconds. American Christin Cooper took the silver.

The other notable performance by an American at the Sarajevo Games came from men's figure skater Scott Hamilton, who captured the gold in the men's individual competition. Hamilton became the first American to do so in 24 years.

The United States' ice hockey team was not as successful. The Americans were hoping to build on their "Miracle On Ice" victory at the 1980 Winter Olympics (see page 138), but the team failed to qualify for the medal round in Sarajevo.

Kareem Passes Wilt

There have been a handful of centers in the history of the NBA whose play was so dominant, whose sheer physical ability was so superior, that they changed the way the game is played. Teams had to adjust their strategies to stop these players from scoring, rebounding, or controlling the game on the defensive end of the court.

George Mikan of the Minneapolis Lakers was the first of this breed in the early days of the NBA. Bill Russell of the Boston Celtics helped his team build a championship dynasty in the 1950s and 1960s with his powerful shot blocking, rebounding and defense. In the 1990s and 2000s, Shaquille O'Neal fit the role of the dominant center who could single-handedly change the balance of any basketball game.

Among this elite group, two centers, both of whom began their pro careers elsewhere but eventually came to glory with the Lakers, rose above the rest offensively—Wilt Chamberlain in the 1960s and Kareem Abdul-Jabbar in the 1980s.

On April 5, Abdul-Jabbar hit his trademark skyhook—a high, arcing shot—with eight minutes, 53 seconds remaining in a game against the Utah Jazz. That brought his career scoring total to 31,421 points to surpass Chamberlain as the NBA's all-time leading scorer. (Chamberlain, who retired in 1973, scored 31,419 points during his 14-year NBA career.) The game was stopped and the crowd gave the 7-foot-2 center a long ovation.

While Chamberlain used his sheer size and awesome strength to dominate the league, Abdul-Jabbar used grace and a soft touch to beat his opponents. Following a spectacular college career, during which he led the University of California–Los Angeles (UCLA) to an 88–2 record and three national championships, Abdul-Jabbar joined the Milwaukee Bucks of the NBA and led them to the league championship

Sky Hook *Los Angeles Lakers center Kareem Abdul-Jabbar showcases his signature shot in a game against the Houston Rockets. Abdul-Jabbar became the NBA's all-time leading scorer in 1984.*

171

1984

in 1971. He joined the Lakers in 1975, and helped them win championships in 1980, 1982, 1985, 1987, and 1988.

Pat Riley, Abdul-Jabbar's coach with the Lakers, called his center's skyhook "the greatest weapon of one person who's ever been an athlete in any sport."

Seventh Heaven

The Boston Celtics won the NBA championship for the 15th time, beating the Los Angeles Lakers 111–102 in the seventh and deciding game of the Finals on June 12 in the Boston Garden.

The Celtics had never lost a Game Seven in a championship series—and wouldn't until 2010. They kept that streak going with a dominating performance on the boards against the Lakers. Boston's forwards, Cedric Maxwell and Larry Bird, and its center, Robert Parish, combined to pulled down 36 rebounds, more than the entire Lakers team.

In fact, Boston outrebounded Los Angeles by a commanding 52–33 margin.

Leading throughout, the Celtics scored the last six points of the game to lock up the victory. Maxwell scored 24 points, while Bird poured in 20. Kareem Abdul-Jabbar was the high scorer for the Lakers, with 29 points.

The Celtics and Lakers were familiar foes in the NBA playoffs—it was the eighth time they met in the Finals, and the eighth time the Celtics won—but it was their first meeting in the Magic Johnson–Larry Bird era.

The teams would meet again in the NBA Finals twice more over the course of the next three seasons.

New NBA Commissioner

As the 1980s began, the popularity and reputation of the NBA was at a low. But the "Magic and Bird Show," reigniting the classic Celtics-Lakers rivalry, coupled with the arrival of Chicago Bulls superstar Michael Jordan in 1985, jump-started interest in the league and began its revival.

Then David Stern took over as league commissioner. As it turned out, he was the perfect executive to maximize and capitalize on the league's growing popularity. First, he orchestrated a deal that created an NBA salary cap, setting a limit on how much each team could pay their players. This cap protected owners from endlessly skyrocketing payrolls, while guaranteeing players 53 percent of gross revenues. The agreement helped the NBA avoid the labor disputes that plagued baseball and football (and continue to plague baseball).

Under Stern's guidance, the league started marketing itself to a younger, more ethnically diverse fan base, tapping into hip-hop culture and consciously changing NBA basketball games into sports-and- entertainment events. The annual All-Star Game became All-Star Weekend, with popular slam-dunk and three-point contests, and the televised draft lottery increased fan interest in each year's crop of incoming college players.

With exciting, popular stars already in place, Stern was the final piece of the puzzle that brought the NBA to its greatest popularity in the 1980s and '90s. He entered his 26th season as league commissioner in 2009–10.

Payton Passes Brown

There had never been a football running back like Jim Brown (b.1936). He combined speed, balance, agility, and explosive power, making him almost impossible to tackle. "All you do," said former New York Giants linebacker Sam Huff when asked how he approached tackling Brown, "is grab hold, hang on, and wait for help."

During his nine seasons in the NFL (1957–1965) Brown led the league in rushing eight times, compiling a record 12,312 yards. After winning his second MVP award in 1965, Brown retired, preferring to go out at the top of his game.

On October 7, Brown's nearly 20-year-old career rushing record was shattered by the man they called "Sweetness." In the third quarter of a game against the New Orleans Saints, Chicago Bears

Sweetness

The Chicago Bears' Walter Payton combined amazing balance and power during his 13 years in the NFL (1975–1987) to rack up an astounding 16,726 rushing yards. That was a league record that stood until Dallas' Emmitt Smith surpassed it in 2002.

When a running back picks up 100 yards in a game, it's considered a great day. In a game against the Minnesota Vikings in 1977, Payton soared past 100 yards: He rushed for an NFL-record 275 yards. That mark stood for 23 years.

When faced with the choice between running out of bounds or colliding with a defensive player to try for a few extra yards, Payton put down his shoulder and bashed into his opponent, driving forward with an almost unstoppable force. He was as complete a player as has ever stepped onto a football field. In addition to his unmatched running ability, Payton also was a top-notch blocker and pass receiver. He could throw the ball well, too.

As intimidating as he was on the field, however, Payton earned his nickname "Sweetness" not only for his sweet moves, but also for his kind and playful temperament. Before Michael Jordan became

Walter Payton

Chicago's greatest sports hero, Payton was the most beloved athlete in town.

Sadly, in 1999, the Pro Football Hall of Famer (he was inducted in 1993, his first year of eligibility) was diagnosed with a rare liver disease. He died later that year shaking the entire sports world.

1984

running back Walter Payton took a pitchout (a play where the quarterback tosses the ball underhand to a back who is too far away to hand off to) from quarterback Jim McMahon and ran for six yards. Those yards pushed his 10-year career total past Brown's record.

When the game ended, Payton was mobbed by players from both teams, eager to offer congratulations to one of the most-loved professional athletes of all time (see the box on page 173). He finished that day with 154 yards, bringing his career total at the time to 12,400.

Payton broke another of Brown's records that day as well. He rushed for 100 yards or more for the 59th time of his career—one more than Brown had during his nine years in the NFL.

Colts Leave Town

The ever-tightening grip of business on sports was evident when, in a move that can only be described as sneaky, Baltimore Colts owner Robert Irsay moved his NFL franchise out of Baltimore and into Indianapolis on March 29, in the dead of night.

The secret operation stunned not only fans but also city officials, who, contrary to usual policy, had no idea the team planned to leave. Irsay, unhappy with his stadium lease and declining ticket sales in Baltimore, hired a fleet of vans to sneak over to the team's training facility and clean it out under cover of darkness. The vans then headed for Indianapolis, where Irsay decided to set up shop for the upcoming season. Indianapolis mayor William Hudnut announced the Colts' arrival,

saying the team would play their future NFL games in the yet-to-be-completed, 60,000-seat Hoosier Dome.

It was known that Irsay had been negotiating with city officials in Indianapolis for several months before the move, but the suddenness of the departure caught everyone by surprise. With the entire team's possessions already moved to Indianapolis, there was nothing the state of Maryland could do.

Having lost a court case that allowed the Oakland Raiders to move to Los Angeles in 1982 (see page 161), the NFL decided to keep a low profile and chose to take no action. Fans in Baltimore were outraged, and would remain so until the arrival of the NFL's Ravens in 1996.

Olympic Boycott

In an obvious payback for the U.S.-led boycott of the 1980 Olympics in Moscow, the Soviet Union and 13 of its allies boycotted the 1984 Summer Olympics in Los Angeles in August. Romania was the only Eastern European country in the Soviet bloc to come to Los Angeles. The powerhouse team from East Germany, always among the tops in medals, was among those that stayed away.

A record 140 nations did show up, but without the usual competition from the Soviets and East Germans, the United States won a record 83 gold medals.

The Los Angeles Olympics were the first privately financed games ever, and they made a huge profit of $215 million. *Time* magazine was so impressed that it named organizing president Peter Ueberroth its Man of the Year.

Good as Gold *Sixteen-year-old gymnast Mary Lou Retton (above) and sprinter Carl Lewis starred for the United States at the 1984 Olympic Games in Los Angeles.*

U.S. Men Take Gold

The American men's gymnastic team gave an inspired performance at the Summer Games in Los Angeles, capturing the gold medal in the all-around team competition.

The six-man U.S. squad of Peter Vidmar, Bart Conner, Mitch Gaylord, Tim Daggett, James Hartung, and Scott Johnson edged the world-champion Chinese team, which many thought was unbeatable, by just 0.6 points.

After five of the six events, the Americans held a small lead over the Chinese team. They were trying to win the first gold medal in gymnastics ever by a U.S. squad. Going with riskier but higher-scoring moves, the United States six held

together, finishing the final event, the horizontal bars, with a perfect 10 for Daggett. The gold was finally theirs!

Meanwhile, on the women's team, a 4-foot-9, 94-pound, 16-year-old named Mary Lou Retton led the American women to a silver medal in the team competition. She charmed the fans and instantly became America's sweetheart. Retton then took America's second gymnastics gold medal, becoming the first American woman to do so, by winning the individual all-around competition.

Retton wrapped up her performance with back-to-back perfect scores of 10 on both her vaults. Her inspired performance earned her Woman Athlete of the Year honors from the Associated Press for 1984.

1984

Lewis Wins Four Golds

U.S. track and field star Carl Lewis won gold medals at the Summer Olympics in Los Angeles in the same four events that Jesse Owens had won 48 years earlier at the 1936 Olympics in Berlin.

In the 100-meter sprint, Lewis came from behind to take the event in 9.99 seconds, beating his teammate, Sam Graddy. Next up was the long jump, where he leaped 28 feet, 1/4 inch on his first try. He passed on the remaining four jumps to conserve energy, and his jump held up for another gold. In the 200-meter sprint, Lewis led a United States sweep, winning the gold in 19.80 seconds—an Olympic record. American Kirk Baptiste took the silver with a time of 19.96 seconds, and Thomas Jefferson captured bronze with a time of 20.26 seconds to complete the United States sweep.

Lewis completed his grand slam as part of the 4-by-100-meter relay team, joining Graddy, Ron Brown, and Calvin Smith in setting a world record with a time of 37.83 seconds.

Women's Marathon

The first women's marathon in Olympic history was held at the Los Angeles Games on August 5. American Joan Benoit Samuelson, a two-time Boston Marathon winner and world-record holder in the event, won the inaugural race in two hours, 24 minutes, 53 seconds. Samuelson's gold medal time was not only

Other Milestones of 1984

✔ On April 13, Pete Rose became the second player in baseball history to reach 4,000 career hits. He trailed only all-time hits leader Ty Cobb (1886–1961), who had 4,191 hits in his Major League Baseball career. Rose would pass Cobb in 1985 (see page 182).

✔ Kirk Gibson's World Series home run heroics helped the Detroit Tigers win the Series in five games. In game five on October 14, against the San Diego Padres, Gibson hit two homers and drove in five runs to lead the Tigers to an 8–4 Series-clinching victory.

✔ Powerful lefthander Martina Navratilova continued her dominance of women's tennis, winning 78 of her 80 matches.

✔ The United States Supreme Court ruled that the NFL could not prevent its teams from moving from one city to another.

✔ The United States Supreme Court ruled that the NCAA's exclusive control over television coverage of college football violated the Sherman Antitrust Act, which outlaws monopolies.

✔ Miami Dolphins quarterback Dan Marino set NFL passing records with 5,084 yards and 48 touchdowns.

✔ Brigham Young won college football's national title, capping a 12–0 season with a 24–17 win over Michigan in Holiday Bowl on December 21.

the third best time ever run by a woman in any marathon, but would actually have taken the gold medal in 13 of the previous 20 Olympic marathons run by men.

Amazingly, America's newest golden hero almost didn't make it to the Games. Just before the Olympic trials in May, she injured her right knee and underwent surgery. Intense physical therapy let her to win the Olympic trials just 17 days after her knee surgery.

As the first women's marathon in Olympic history began, many spectators lining the route wept with joy, realizing that the long struggle to achieve recognition for women's long-distance running had finally borne fruit. Just 14 minutes into the race, Samuelson pulled away from the pack and never looked back.

Half a mile from the Los Angeles Coliseum, where the long race would finally end, she passed a large mural depicting her victory at the Boston Marathon. As she entered the tunnel leading to the Coliseum's track, where she would complete her final lap, Benoit Samuelson hoped her achievement would announce to the world that women belonged among the ranks of great long-distance runners.

As she appeared in the stadium and took her final lap around the track, 50,000 screaming fans rose and cheered the lone figure who finished the race 400 meters (and more than minute) ahead of the rest of the field. The world of long-distance running would never be the same.

Women's Firsts

Ten years after Little League Baseball officially opened its game to girls as well as boys, the first girl played in the Little League World Series. She was Victoria Roche, a backup outfielder for the team from Brussels, Belgium, that made it to Williamsport, Pennsylvania.

Women made their mark in the Naismith Memorial Basketball Hall of Fame in 1984, too. Senda Berenson Abbott, Bertha Teague, and Margaret Wade were the first women elected to the shrine.

Abbott was a native of Lithuania who immigrated to the United States. In 1899, she modified men's basketball rules for women, and in 1901 she wrote the first *Basketball Guide for Women*.

Teague was a legendary coach who was known as "Mrs. Basketball of Oklahoma." As coach at Byng High School in Ada, Oklahoma, from 1927 to 1969, she guided her teams to eight state championships, seven runner-up finishes, and an amazing winning percentage of .910 (1,157 wins and only 115 losses).

Wade was a star player and coach at both her prep (Cleveland, Mississippi, High School) and college (Delta State University) alma maters. While coaching at Delta State in the mid-1970s, her teams won three consecutive Association for Intercollegiate Athletics for Women (AIAW) national championships and forged a 51-game winning streak.

1985

"Sneaker Wars"

On the court, Chicago Bulls rookie Michael Jordan established himself as the NBA's hot new star. He averaged 28.2 points per game on his way to winning the Rookie of the Year award. Off the court, Jordan signed an endorsement deal for a new line of Nike shoes called Air Jordans. Sports marketing, endorsement dollars, and urban fashion would never be the same.

Naming an athletic shoe after a top professional athlete ushered in the age of big-time athlete endorsements. As a pro player—particularly a basketball player—rose in fame or entered the league as a touted rookie, marketing gurus and sneaker companies engaged in fierce competition to sign him up.

Every shoe company wanted to be associated with the next big star. Over the next decade, every company from Reebok to Adidas got into the act, scrambling to sign the big names. The so-called "Sneaker Wars" had begun. By the 1990s, big-time rookies were signing endorsement contracts that were even more lucrative than their sky-high NBA salaries.

Very quickly, owning Air Jordans, or whatever the latest athlete-endorsed shoe was, became a major status symbol among American youth. Even those who could not afford the high-priced shoes felt they had to have them. This led to incidents of boys and young men being robbed for their pricey sneakers.

For Jordan, the journey from simply being a great basketball player to becoming his own worldwide marketing brand had begun.

Joe Knows Super Bowls

The AFC-champion Miami Dolphins featured record-setting quarterback Dan Marino, but the NFC-champion San Francisco 49ers had a pretty good quarterback of their own in Joe Montana when the teams met in Super Bowl XIX at Stanford Stadium in Palo Alto, California on January 20. Montana was the difference in the game, earning MVP honors after passing for three touchdowns and running for one in his team's 38–16 victory.

It was another chapter in Montana's growing football legend. He finished the day with 331 passing yards, and he was not intercepted. Running back Roger

Ty-breaking Hit   *Cincinnati Reds first baseman Pete Rose singles to left field in a game in September. With the hit, his 4,192nd, Rose surpassed Ty Cobb as baseball's all-time leader (see page 182).*

Craig helped out by scoring a Super Bowl-record three touchdowns.

Meanwhile, the tough 49ers' defense swarmed all over Marino—who in the 1984 regular season became the first man to pass for more than 5,000 yards in one year—forcing him to rush passes and throw two interceptions. Marino completed 29 of his 50 passes for 318 yards, but Miami could muster little other offense.

1985

Eight Is Enough *After losing to the Boston Celtics in all eight of their previous meetings in the NBA Finals, the Los Angeles Lakers, led by guard Earvin (Magic) Johnson, finally subdued their long-time rivals.*

Lakers Finally Beat Celtics

For the ninth time, the Boston Celtics and Los Angeles Lakers met in the NBA Finals. And for the first time, the Lakers won. Los Angeles prevailed in six games, taking the deciding game 111–100 in front of a hostile crowd at Boston Garden on June 9.

The Celtics were trying to become the first team to win back-to-back NBA championships since they did it themselves in 1967–68 and 1968–69. But this year, Magic Johnson, Kareem Abdul-Jabbar, James Worthy, and the rest of the Lakers proved to be too much for Larry Bird, Kevin McHale, Robert Parish, and their teammates.

Heading into the sixth game in Boston, the Lakers held a 3–2 advantage in the Finals. The Celtics were hoping to tie the series and force a seventh and deciding game—something they had never lost. But Jabbar poured in 29 points and Worthy, who averaged 23.6 points and shot 56.4 percent from the field in the series, added 28. Johnson, who averaged 18.3 points, 14 assists, and 6.8 rebounds in the series, ran the offense.

The game was tied at halftime. The Lakers opened the second half by hitting their first six shots, putting them in control, despite 32 points from McHale and 28 from Bird. What made this victory even sweeter was the fact that the Celtics had crushed the Lakers 148–114 in the series opener, setting the stage for yet another Celtics' championship. But this year, it was not to be.

Thirty-eight-year-old Jabbar, the oldest player in the NBA, was just 12 in 1959, when the Lakers' (who were based in Minneapolis at the time) Finals drought against the Celtics began.

In 1985, Jabbar was the big factor in finally shattering the Celtics' long-time grip on the Lakers.

1985 NBA Finals

GAME	LOCATION	SCORE
1	Boston	Celtics, 148–114
2	Boston	Lakers, 109–102
3	Los Angeles	Lakers, 136–111
4	Los Angeles	Celtics, 107–105
5	Los Angeles	Lakers, 120–111
6	Boston	Lakers, 111–100

Knight's Chair Toss

Indiana University basketball coach Bobby Knight was always known as much for his hot temper as for his success on the court. During a game against University of Illinois, which Indiana lost 66–50, Knight broke a chair in a fit of rage, then made an obscene gesture at the referee—a frequent target of Knight's outbursts.

Later, in a game against Purdue University on February 23, which Indiana also lost, Knight picked up a chair and hurled it across the court, then shouted at the referee as Purdue's Steve Reid was getting ready to shoot a technical foul shot. Knight was immediately ejected from the game.

A few days later, Knight apologized, saying his action was an embarrassment to the university. He explained that he was frustrated by the officiating and lost his temper. This pattern of major tantrums and verbal abuse was repeated throughout his tenure at Indiana.

Knight's most infamous explosion occurred when he was coaching the United States team in the Pan American Games in 1979. During that tournament, Knight hit a policeman in Puerto Rico, creating an international incident. That same year, Knight threw a student newspaper photographer into the bushes because the student took his picture while he was having an argument with a bicyclist about who had the right of way.

Finally, after 29 years at Indiana, during which time he led his teams to 763 victories and three national championships, Knight was fired in September of

Magic Johnson: The First Triple Threat

Magic Johnson blurred the lines between the three positions in basketball: guard, forward, and center. He was the tallest point guard (the guard who brings the ball down the court and runs the offense) in the history of the NBA. He also excelled at forward and center. In game six of the NBA Finals in 1980, Johnson's rookie year, he filled in at center for future Hall-of-Fame teammate Kareem Abdul-Jabbar and dominated the game, helping his team win the championship (see page 141).

Johnson quickly became the master of the triple-double—achieving double figures in points, rebounds, and assists in the same game—another demonstration of his versatility. But perhaps his biggest contri-bution was that he brought a team concept to the NBA at a time when most players were concentrating on their individual performances.

Johnson had enough talent to be a one-man show, but he preferred to make his teammates look good and to use his abilities to forge a winning team. His five NBA titles prove he did just that.

In 1991, Johnson's impact moved beyond the world of sports when he announced to a startled world that he had tested positive for HIV, the virus that causes AIDS. He put a familiar, trusted, beloved, celebrity face on the disease, helping to bring greater acceptance and understanding of the people who live with it.

2000 for allegedly grabbing a student by the arm because he addressed the coach as "Knight," and Knight felt that was dis-respectful. In truth, it was the last straw in his long list of offenses.

Gretzky Breaks 200 Again

Wayne Gretzky broke the 200-point mark for the third time in his NHL career, scoring 73 goals and dishing out 135 assists, for a total of 208 points. He also won his unprecedented sixth con-secutive MVP Award.

Most important, though, he led the Edmonton Oilers to their second straight Stanley Cup Championship, beating the Philadelphia Flyers in five games. In the deciding game on May 30, Gretzky scored a goal and had three assists in the Oilers' 8–3 victory. He got help from defenseman Paul Coffey, who added two goals.

Edmonton's Jari Kurri scored early in the first period. Thirty-five seconds later, Willie Lindstrom knocked in a shot to give the Oilers a two-goal cushion. Two more goals by Coffey in less than three minutes pushed the lead to 4–0. By the end of the second period, the Oilers were up 6–1.

Gretzky scored in the final period to finish the postseason with 47 points (17 goals, 30 assists), an NHL playoff record. The Oilers were on top again, thanks to the Great One.

Rose: All-Time Hits Leader

On September 11, Pete Rose became baseball's all-time hits leader when he picked up his 4,192nd career hit, pass-ing legendary Hall-of-Famer Ty Cobb's career record.

Rose, who earned the nickname "Charlie Hustle," only played the game one way: hard. He pushed himself in the field, on the bases, and at bat. When the Cincinnati Reds needed a hit, there was Rose to slap the ball the other way, slashing it into the corner from either side of the plate, not bothering to slow down at first base, diving headlong into second.

With two balls and one strike on Rose, San Diego Padres pitcher Eric Show threw a fastball and Rose swung the familiar swing baseball fans had seen so many times before, and hit a clean single to left field. Baseball had a new hits leader. Rose had finally caught Cobb, who retired from baseball in 1928. In fact, Rose got his record-breaking hit 57 years to the day after Cobb's final major-league game.

Rose dashed from the batter's box, as he always did, rounding first swiftly, then scooting back to the bag. The game was stopped as flashbulbs went off all over Riverfront Stadium in Cincinnati.

Rose's 15-year-old son, Petey, reached his dad first, as players from both teams poured from the dugouts and gathered around the 44-year-old Cincinnati native. Tears streamed down his face, as he looked skyward and thought of two men who could not be there with him that day: his father, a semi-pro football player who was the biggest influence on Rose's life and his career in sports; and Cobb, whose achievement had haunted Rose through more than 20 major-league seasons.

Royals Win By Decision

The Kansas City Royals beat the St. Louis Cardinals in seven games to win a wild World Series that turned on an umpire's pivotal call in game six.

The Great One *Hockey star Wayne Gretzky celebrates after helping the Edmonton Oilers win their second consecutive Stanley Cup.*

Kansas City had reached the Series in dramatic fashion. First, the Royals edged the California Angels to win the American League West by a single game. Then, they rallied from a three games to one deficit by winning three consecutive games and beating the Toronto Blue Jays in seven games in the American League Championship Series (ALCS).

In the National League, the Cardinals won a big-league-best 101 games in the regular season, then qualified for the Fall Classic when Jack Clark belted a three-run home run in the ninth inning to win the sixth, and final, game of the National

1985

League Championship Series (NLCS) against the Los Angeles Dodgers.

The drama carried over to the World Series. St. Louis won a taut opening game, then scored four times in the ninth inning of game two to rally for a 4–2 victory and take a commanding lead in the Series. The Cardinals still held a three-games-to-two lead and were three outs away from a championship when they carried a 1–0 lead into the bottom of the ninth inning of game six at Kansas City.

Frontier Woman *Libby Riddles became the first woman to win the grueling Iditarod Trail Sled Dog Race.*

Pinch-hitter Jorge Orta led off the ninth inning for the Royals and quickly fell behind no balls and two strikes. Then he grounded to Clark at first base, who threw to pitcher Todd Worrell covering for an apparent out. But umpire Don Denkinger ruled Orta safe—though television replays clearly indicated it was the wrong call. The Cardinals then came unglued. Clark misplayed a foul pop that should have been caught, and a single, a passed ball, and Dane Iorg's single won the game for the Royals, 2–1.

Game seven the next night was no contest. The Royals scored twice in the second inning and three more times in the third to open a 5–0 advantage. In the fifth, the Cardinals lost their composure. Pitcher Joaquin Andujar was ejected during a six-run outburst by the Royals, who went on to win 11–0.

Dominant "D"

The Chicago Bears wreaked havoc on the NFL in 1985 with an intimidating defense that turned in one of the most dominating performances of all time. Head coach Mike Ditka's Bears rolled to 15 wins in 16 games during the regular season, then outscored three postseason opponents by a combined 91–10 to win their ninth NFL championship, but their first of the Super Bowl era.

The success of the 1985 Bears was tied to the 46 Defense. Defensive coordinator Buddy Ryan crowded eight players near the line of scrimmage and confounded opposing offenses with pressure from multiple areas. Ryan installed the 46 in 1981, but it wasn't 1985 that the unit

Other Milestones of 1985

✔ The 45-second shot clock was added to college basketball to help speed up the game.

✔ On July 11, Nolan Ryan became the first pitcher in baseball history to strike out 4,000 batters. Ryan was just getting warmed up, though. By the time he retired following the 1993 season, he had a record 5,714 career strikeouts.

✔ On August 4, the Chicago White Sox's Tom Seaver, the former longtime Mets ace, became the 17th player in Major League Baseball history to win 300 career games.

✔ On August 21, Mary Decker set a new women's record, running the mile in 4 minutes, 16.71 seconds. She broke the old mark of 4 minutes, 17.44 seconds by Maricica Puica of Romania.

✔ Grambling State University football coach Eddie Robinson passed Paul "Bear" Bryant, with his 324th victory on November 23, to become the winningest coach in the history of college football.

✔ The North American Soccer League, the latest unsuccessful attempt at a pro soccer league in the United States, suspended operations after 18 years.

---

achieved near perfection. That season, the Bears' opponents managed a meager 12.4 points per game during the regular season. Chicago allowed 10 or fewer points in 14 of 19 games (including postseason).

By the way, the name of the 46 had nothing to do with the way the players lined up. Instead, it was the uniform number of Doug Plank, a hard-hitting safety who was one of the keys to Ryan's original innovative defense in the early 1980s. By 1985, however, Plank was out of the league, having retired after playing in only one game in 1982.

In the 2009 season, Plank became an assistant on the New York Jets' staff of rookie head coach Rex Ryan, the son of Buddy Ryan.

Women's Pioneer

The Women's Sports Foundation named Libby Riddles its Professional Sportswoman of the Year for 1985. Riddles had made history earlier in the year, on March 20, when she became the first woman ever to win the Iditarod Trail Sled Dog Race in Alaska.

The Iditarod is a grueling test of endurance in which competitors guide a team of dogs more than 1,050 miles through beautiful, but rugged, terrain that includes mountain ranges, rivers, and forest, often in the harshest weather. Riddles, in fact, had to navigate through a deadly blizzard across Norton Sound en route to her victory.

1986

Baseball Suspends Seven

Drug use continued to invade the world of sports—this time Major League Baseball. Baseball commissioner Peter Ueberroth handed out one-year suspensions to seven players, saying that they had used drugs themselves or aided in spreading drugs within baseball.

Keith Hernandez (New York Mets), Dale Berra (New York Yankees), Joaquin Andujar (Oakland Athletics), Dave Parker (Cincinnati Reds), Jeffrey Leonard (San Francisco Giants), Lonnie Smith (Kansas City Royals), and Enos Cabell (Los Angeles Dodgers) were all suspended without pay.

All seven players chose an alternative penalty offered by Ueberroth, which resulted in the lifting of the suspensions. The players agreed to give 10 percent of their salaries for the 1986 season to drug-prevention programs and to put in up to 200 hours of community service over the next two years. They also agreed to undergo drug tests for the remainder of their major-league careers.

The players either testified or were implicated during the 1985 investigations and trials of seven men charged with distributing cocaine. Although none of the players was charged in those trials, six of the seven gave incriminating testimony. The seventh, Andujar, was named by several players as a cocaine user.

In an attempt to stem the spreading tide of drug use, Ueberroth also gave out lesser penalties to 14 other players.

Celtics Back on Top

Forward Larry Bird posted a "triple-double," scoring 29 points, grabbing 11 rebounds, and handing out 12 assists to lead the Boston Celtics to a 114–97 win over the Houston Rockets in the sixth, and deciding, game of the NBA Finals on June 8 at the Boston Garden. The championship was the Celtics' second in three seasons, and their record 16th overall.

During the regular season, Bird ranked among the league leaders in scoring (25.8 points per game), rebounding (9.8 rebounds per game), steals (2.02 steals per game), free-throw percentage (89.6 percent), and three-point-field-goal percentage (42.3 percent). He won his third straight NBA Most Valuable Player award, joining former Celtics' great Bill Russell and former Celtics' archrival Wilt

Celtic Pride *Forward Larry Bird (33) and Celtics brought another NBA championship to Boston.*

Chamberlain as the only players in NBA history to win the award three years in a row. And he helped Boston take back the NBA championship.

One of the main reasons for Bird's and the Celtics' success was a trade that brought veteran center Bill Walton to Boston. This gave the Celtics' already strong front court of Bird, Kevin McHale, and Robert Parish another top scorer,

passer, rebounder, and defender. The addition of Walton also gave Parish some much-needed rest at center. Walton was an unselfish and team-oriented player— much like Bird. When the two were on the court together, the ball seemed to fly everywhere, always eventually finding an open man.

In the regular season the team won 67 games, the most ever for the famous

Watch the Birdie! *Jack Nicklaus starts to celebrate as his putt drops for a crucial birdie on the 17th hole of the final round of the Masters golf tournament. At 46, Nicklaus won the title for the sixth time.*

Major Achievement

Jack Nicklaus watched intently as his 18-foot putt rolled toward the 17th hole during the final round of the Masters at the Augusta National Golf Club on April 13. As the putt neared the hole, Nicklaus raised his club in triumph. "Yes, sir!" announcer Verne Lundquist exclaimed to a national television audience. Nicklaus, the greatest golfer of his (and perhaps, any) generation, had just taken the lead in one of golf's most prestigious tournaments.

Nicklaus went on to close out a final-round 65—he shot an incredible six-under-par 30 on the back nine—to edge Tom Kite and Greg Norman by one shot and win the tournament.

At 46, Nicklaus became the oldest man ever to win one of golf's major championships (now defined as the Masters, U.S. Open, British Open, and PGA Championship). It was his record sixth green jacket as the winner of the Masters, and his 18th major championship in all (another record).

Star Dies From Cocaine

Twenty-two year old Len Bias, an All-American basketball star at the University of Maryland, died on June 19 from using cocaine—just two days after being selected by the Boston Celtics as the number-two pick in the NBA draft.

The 6-foot-8 Bias was Maryland's all-time leading scorer, with 2,149 points during his college career. He averaged 23.3 points per game, pulled down 224 rebounds, and was voted the Atlantic Coast

Celtics. At home, they were nearly unbeatable, posting a regular-season record of 40–1 at the Boston Garden. Then they went 10–0 at home in the playoffs.

The Rockets, led by a pair of seven-footers—Ralph Sampson and Hakeem Olajuwon—beat the defending-champion Los Angeles Lakers in the final round of the Western Conference playoffs but were no match for Boston in the NBA Finals.

Conference's Player of the Year during his final season.

After an exciting day in Boston, during which Bias was introduced as the Celtics' next great star, Bias returned to the Maryland campus. The following night, he was with two teammates when he died suddenly. Autopsy reports showed that he died of intoxication from cocaine, which he most likely snorted only minutes before his death. The sports world was shocked at the tragic loss of a young life and a potential NBA great.

USFL Closes Shop

After three years as a professional football league, trying to compete with the NFL for players and fans, the United States Football League (USFL) disbanded, calling off its 1986 season.

The league began in 1983 with 12 teams, and for three years had played a spring schedule to avoid going head-to-head with the NFL's fall games. But in 1986, the USFL decided to switch to a fall schedule and compete directly with the older league.

After trying unsuccessfully to get a television contract—a must for the survival of any professional sports league—the USFL filed a lawsuit against the NFL, claiming that it monopolized the television networks and prevented the younger league from getting a contract to broadcast their games. The USFL asked for more than $1 billion in damages.

Following a long trial, a jury ruled that although the NFL was a professional monopoly, it had done nothing to keep the USFL off the air. That decision had been made by the networks themselves. Damages were awarded to the USFL in the amount of $1.

Without big money from the lawsuit or a television contract, USFL team owners felt they could not continue operating. The league had already lost more than $150 million in its first three seasons. Six days after the lawsuit ended, the league's remaining eight teams voted to cease operations.

Running back Herschel Walker, the USFL's biggest star and greatest hope for

Bird Flies

At a time in the NBA when high-flying schoolyard moves and flashy slam dunks were the norm, forward Larry Bird stepped onto the parquet floor at the Boston Garden and did something that had not been seen in the league in awhile. He made his teammates better.

After a stunning college career at Indiana State University, capped by a college player of the year award in his senior year and a memorable showdown in the NCAA championship game against Magic Johnson's Michigan State team (won by Johnson and Michigan State), Bird joined the Boston Celtics.

The once-great NBA dynasty was struggling through a low period. In his rookie season, Bird led his team to 32 more victories than the previous year. He went on to win three NBA championships, three consecutive Most Valuable Player awards, and, along with Magic Johnson, reinvigorate interest in the NBA.

After playing with the United States Olympic "Dream Team" in Barcelona, Spain in 1992, Bird retired as a player, due to a bad back. He went on to become a successful professional coach with the Indiana Pacers. In 1998, he was enshrined in basketball's Hall of Fame.

1986

success, signed a five-year contract with the NFL's Dallas Cowboys. In 1989, he was the centerpiece in the largest trade in NFL history, when he was dealt to the Minnesota Vikings as part of a deal involving 18 players or draft picks.

Joyner Sets Record

Jackie Joyner (b.1962), who won the silver medal in the heptathlon at the 1984 Olympics and went on to take the gold in the event in 1988, set a new world record in the heptathlon at the Goodwill Games in Moscow on July 7, smashing individual event records along the way.

Closing Time *The United States Football League made a splash by signing big-name stars such as Herschel Walker (34), but too many empty seats spelled its doom. The league folded in 1986 (see page 189).*

Joyner totaled 7,148 points, becoming the first woman to break the 7,000-point mark in the grueling seven-event competition, and beating the record set by Sabine Paetz of East Germany in 1984 by 202 points.

The heptathlon is a two-day competition made up of seven events: the 100-meter hurdles, the shot put, the high jump, the 200-meter race, the long jump, the javelin, and the 800-meter race.

Joyner set a first-day record by scoring 4,151 points in four events. She ran the 100-meter hurdles in 12.85 seconds, a new American heptathlon record. Then she leaped 62 inches in the high jump; threw the shot put 48 feet, 5 1/4 inches; and ran the 200 meters in 23 seconds.

The second day of competition began with Joyner setting a heptathlon world record by jumping 23 feet in the long jump, her favorite event. She then tossed the javelin 163 feet, 4 inches.

In the final event, Joyner ran the 800-meter race in 2 minutes, 10.02 seconds to capture the heptathlon record. Despite the United States' boycott of the Olympics in Moscow in 1980 and the Soviet boycott of the Games in Los Angeles in 1984, the American was cheered wildly by Goodwill Games fans in Moscow as she set the new standard in her sport.

One Strike Away

The 1986 Major League Baseball playoffs—the American League Championship Series (ALCS), the National League Championship Series (NLCS), and the World Series—were among the most exciting and memorable in baseball history.

Boston Red Sox fans cheered their team to a great regular season, but October 12 they appeared to once again be watching their beloved Sox get eliminated in the postseason. The California Angels led the ALCS three games to one, and led game five by a score of 5–4 in the top of the ninth inning.

Boston center fielder Dave Henderson, faced the Angels' top relief pitcher, Donnie Moore. Henderson worked the count to two balls and two strikes, then drove a pitch into the stands in left field for a two-run homer that gave Boston the lead, 6–5. Although the Angels came back to tie the game in the bottom of the ninth inning, the Red Sox scored again in the 11th inning to win 7–6.

The Angels never recovered. Boston won the next two games easily to earn a spot in the October Series.

Meanwhile, in the NLCS, the New York Mets battled the Houston Astros, who were led by pitcher Mike Scott. Scott won 18 games during the regular season while leading the league with 306 strikeouts and a 2.22 earned run average (ERA—the average number of runs charged to the pitcher per nine innings). He was named the National League Cy Young Award winner and the NLCS Most Valuable Player in 1985, despite the fact that his team lost the playoff series.

Scott dominated the Mets, shutting them out 1–0 in game one, then taking a 3–1 victory in game four. Heading into game six in Houston on October 15, the Mets led the series three games to two. If they lost game six, they would have to face Scott again in a deciding game seven—a fate they were hoping to avoid.

No Rush Hour in New York

Game six of the NLCS began at 3:06 p.m. New York time, and finally ended at 7:48. There was no rush hour in usually busy New York City that night, as office workers stayed in their offices to catch the end of this seemingly endless game.

Buses and subways were half empty, though announcements at Grand Central Station kept the few commuters who did head home updated on the score. People on the street gathered around anyone who had a radio or huddled outside the windows of appliance stores that had TV sets on, unable to leave for fear of missing the latest twist or turn.

The great city slowed down to linger and learn the fate of its beloved Mets.

The Astros jumped out to a 3–0 lead in the first inning, then Houston pitcher Bob Knepper shut down the Mets for eight innings. New York finally scored three times in the top of the ninth to tie the game and send it into extra innings.

The Mets scored a run in the top of the 14th inning, but Houston tied it in the bottom of the 14th. Then, in the top of the 16th inning, New York scored three runs to grab what seemed to be a commanding 7–4 lead. Houston came back to score two in the bottom of the 16th, and had the tying run on second base when Mets relief pitcher Jesse Orosco struck out Houston right fielder Kevin Bass to end the marathon and send the Mets to the World Series.

But the exciting ALCS and NLCS were only prelude to the astounding World Series still to come.

The Red Sox won the first two games in New York, then the Mets returned the favor, taking the next two in Boston. The Red Sox jumped out to a three-games-to-two lead, winning game five 4–2 in Boston.

1986

The series returned to New York for game six on October 25, with the Red Sox one win away from capturing their first World Series since 1918. The game was tied 3–3 after nine innings, but Boston took the lead in the top of the 10th, scoring two runs.

The first two Mets to bat in the bottom of the 10th inning were easily retired by Boston relief pitcher Calvin Schiraldi. Then Gary Carter and Kevin Mitchell both hit singles. The next batter, Ray Knight, fell behind in the count 0–2. Just as they were one strike away from elimination in the ALCS, the Red Sox were

An American in Paris *Greg LeMond became the first man from the United States to win the Tour de France, cycling's most important event and one of the most famous athletic competitions in the world.*

now one strike away from winning the World Series.

Knight singled to center, scoring Carter and cutting the Boston lead to 5–4. Mitchell moved to third base. The Red Sox brought in a new pitcher, Bob Stanley, to face Mookie Wilson.

Wilson worked the count to 2–2, and once again Boston was one strike away from victory. But Wilson kept fouling off pitches. Stanley's seventh pitch was wild, scoring Mitchell from third and tying the game at 5–5.

Three pitches later, Wilson hit a ground ball that dribbled through the legs of Boston first baseman Bill Buckner, scoring Knight with the winning run, setting off a wild celebration among the Mets' players, and tying the Series at three games apiece.

The 36-year-old Buckner normally would have been removed from the game in favor of a defensive replacement. But he had played such an important role in the Red Sox's success that Boston manager John McNamara left him in the game so he could enjoy the presumed victory celebration.

Stunned, the Red Sox lost game seven by a score of 8–5 and the Mets won the World Series, capping off an unforgettable postseason.

Sports Marketing Grows

As a direct result of the increasing connection between professional sports and athlete-endorsed products, sneaker manufacturer Nike topped the billion-dollar mark in revenue for the first time in its history.

Other Milestones of 1986

✔ The Chicago Bears concluded a dominating season with a record-setting, 46–10 rout of the New England Patriots in Super Bowl XX at the Louisiana Superdome on January 26. On offense, the Bears set a record (since broken) for points in a Super Bowl; on defense, they allowed a record-low 7 rushing yards.

✔ Following their overwhelming victory against the New England Patriots in the Super Bowl, the Chicago Bears released the first sports music video, "The Super Bowl Shuffle."

✔ In Switzerland in March, Debi Thomas became the first African-American figure skater to win the world championship.

✔ Bill James published his *Historical Baseball Abstract*, a groundbreaking book with insightful statistical analysis.

✔ Boston Red Sox pitcher Roger Clemens struck out 20 Seattle Mariners' batters during his team's 3–1 victory at Fenway Park on April 29, setting a new single-game record (a decade later, in 1996, Clemens tied his own mark by striking out 20 Detroit Tigers in a game). The old mark of 19 was held by four players. Clemens also won both the Cy Young and AL MVP awards in 1986.

✔ Nancy Lieberman became the first woman ever to play in a men's pro basketball league when she joined the United States Basketball League's Springfield Fame.

✔ The three-point field goal was introduced in college basketball.

✔ The NFL approved the use of instant replay as a tool to aid officials, who could reverse their decisions on certain calls after reviewing visual evidence.

✔ Wayne Gretzky scored his 500th goal on November 22 while breaking his single-season scoring record of 212 points; he racked up 214 points.

✔ Also on November 22, 20-year-old boxer Mike Tyson knocked out Trevor Berbick to become the youngest heavyweight boxing champion in history.

Nike, makers of the famous Air Jordan basketball shoe, extended its product line and its enormous sports marketing reach beyond sneakers and into the apparel business. The company introduced clothing collections endorsed by NBA star Michael Jordan and tennis great John McEnroe.

American Wins in France

It is considered by many to be the largest, most important, and most difficult sporting event in the world. The Tour de France is a grueling 21-day bicycle race in which cyclists ride between 100 and 150 miles each day, often up steep and winding mountain roads.

On July 27, Greg LeMond, a 25-year-old who was born in 1961 in Los Angeles, California, became the first American to win this contest of strength, endurance, skill, and willpower. Battling teammate Bernard Hinault, LeMond pedaled triumphantly into Paris and became an immediate media celebrity and American sports hero.

1987

Simms Leads Giants

The New York Giants rallied in the second half to defeat the Denver Broncos 39–20 in Super Bowl XXI on January 25 in Pasadena, California. It was the Giants' first Super Bowl victory (in their first appearance) and sent the Broncos to the first of their three Super Bowl losses in a four-season span.

New York trailed 10–9 at halftime, but rode the pinpoint passing of game MVP Phil Simms to win. For the game, Simms completed 22 of his 25 passes for 268 yards and three touchdowns. His completion rate of 88 percent remains a Super Bowl record (entering 2010).

After tough defense dominated the first two quarters, Simms tossed a 13-yard touchdown pass to Mark Bavaro early in the third quarter. He then led the Giants down the field for a short field goal, followed by another drive capped by Joe Morris' one-yard touchdown run. Simms also threw a six-yard touchdown pass to Phil McConkey in the fourth quarter, putting the game out of reach at 33–10.

Denver quarterback John Elway passed for 304 yards, but much of it came with the game out of hand.

Sugar Ray Is Back

In 1982, welterweight boxing champion Sugar Ray Leonard retired due to a detached retina in his left eye. Doctors told him that if he kept boxing, there was a chance he could lose vision in the eye.

On April 6, Leonard came out of retirement to battle World Boxing Council (WBC) middleweight champion Marvelous Marvin Hagler. The time away did not seem to diminish Leonard's great boxing skills. He danced, spun, and jabbed his way through the first few rounds, then stood toe-to-toe with Hagler, outslugging the champ as the fight drew to a close.

When it was over, the scores were close, but Leonard took a 12-round, split decision to capture the middleweight title. The more than 15,000 fans in the Las Vegas arena chanted his name, as Leonard earned his 34th victory in 35 fights. Hagler's record was 63–3, with 52 knockouts.

Dodger VP Resigns

Seventy-year-old Al Campanis (1916–1998), vice president in charge of player personnel for baseball's Los Angeles Dodgers, resigned on April 8, fol-

Almost Perfect *Quarterback Phil Simms was nearly flawless while earning game MVP honors in the New York Giants' victory over the Denver Broncos in Super Bowl XXI.*

lowing national outrage over remarks he made on the ABC television show *Nightline* two days earlier.

Campanis appeared on the show, hosted by Ted Koppel, to help celebrate the 40th anniversary of Jackie Robinson breaking baseball's color barrier. Koppel asked Campanis why he thought the major leagues had no black managers, general managers, or owners. Campanis

1987

replied, "I truly believe that they may not have some of the necessities to be, let's say, a field manager, or perhaps a GM."

When Koppel asked him if he really believed that, the Dodgers' vice president said, "Well, I don't say all of them, but they are short. How many quarterbacks do you have, how many pitchers do you have, that are black?" Then Campanis added, "Why are black men or black people not good swimmers? Because they don't have any buoyancy."

These comments set off a storm of controversy, forcing Campanis to apologize.

He claimed that his statements were taken the wrong way and that he did not think blacks are less intelligent than whites. Two days after the remarks, however, Campanis resigned from the Dodgers.

He had been with the Dodgers' organization for 46 years, including seven games as a player in 1943. After serving in World War II, Campanis worked as a manager in the Dodgers' minor-league system. He became a scout in 1950 and director of scouting from 1957 to 1968, before finally settling in as a club vice president in 1969.

Queen of the Iditarod

In March, Susan Butcher won the Iditarod Trail Sled Dog Race. The Iditarod is one of the few sporting events in which men and women compete straight up against each other. Butcher not only beat out the 61 men and 1 other woman in the 1987 race, but she also did it in record time: In finishing in 11 days, 2 hours, 5 minutes, and 13 seconds, she shattered the old Iditarod record by 13 hours.

This was the second year in a row that Butcher won the grueling, 1,150-mile race through the snowy Alaskan wilderness, and she went on to win it again in 1988. After placing second in 1989, she returned to the top in 1990. Her four wins in five years made it the most dominant stretch for any dogsled driver in Iditarod history.

Susan Butcher

Butcher was not the first woman to win the Iditarod. That honor belonged to Libby Riddles in 1985 (see page 185). Together, their success helped spur T-shirt slogans such as, "Alaska: Where Men Are Men and Women Win the Iditarod."

In 2002, Butcher was faced with her biggest challenge yet when she faced a severe blood disorder that eventually was diagnosed as leukemia. She fought the disease with the same determination and toughness that characterized her performances in the Iditarod. In August of 2006, though, she died. She was 51.

Since 2008, Alaskans have celebrated Susan Butcher Day on the first Saturday of March. Traditionally, that's also the day the annual Iditarod starts.

Campanis had actually played as a minor leaguer with Robinson 41 years earlier, and helped to sign minority players such as Roberto Clemente and Tommy Davis, but his questionable comments on *Nightline* spelled the end of his lengthy baseball career.

Amazing Streak Ends

The most incredible winning streak in the history of track events finally came to an end 10 years after it had begun. Between 1977 and 1987, Edwin Moses won 122 consecutive races in the 400-meter intermediate hurdles (400 IM), setting what may be an unbeatable record.

In 1976, Moses won a gold medal in the event at the Munich, West Germany Olympics. The follow year, after a loss to West German Harald Schmid, his amazing winning streak began. As the streak grew longer, Moses took a track event that had lacked glamour and didn't get much attention, and brought it into the spotlight. Along the way, he became one of the sport's biggest stars.

For 10 years, there was no one even in the same class as Moses, who won another Olympic gold medal in 1984 (he didn't have a chance in 1980 because of the United States' boycott of the Games). He set the world record in the 400 IM at 47.02 seconds, and he also owns the next 10 fastest times in the event.

The mental attitude Moses brought to each of the 122 races was as big a factor in his success as his extraordinary physical ability. "The day I feel nice and relaxed," Moses said in 1984, "is the day I'll know the streak is in danger."

All Four Won *Al Unser, Sr. won the Indianapolis 500 at the "Brickyard," the Indianapolis Motor Speedway. Unser joined A.J. Foyt as the only four-time winners of the world-renowned race (see page 198).*

Three years later, on June 4, 21-year-old American hurdler Danny Harris finally defeated the 31-year-old Moses in a 400 IM race. Harris took the lead at the fifth hurdle and finished with a time of 47.56 seconds. Moses finished right behind him, with a time of 47.69 seconds.

The crowd of 11,000 in Madrid, Spain, stood and chanted Moses' name as he ran a solo lap of honor around the track to celebrate his astounding streak.

1987

Unser Wins Fourth 500

Al Unser, Sr., became the second driver in history to win the India-napolis 500 four times when he captured the world's most prestigious motor race on May 24, winning by a margin of just five seconds. At age 47, Unser also became the oldest driver to win the race.

His previous victories came in 1970, 1971, and 1978. His four wins at Indy tied the record set by A.J. Foyt. Unser's 25-year-old son, Al Unser, Jr., finished fourth in the race.

The senior Unser averaged 162.175 miles per hour in front of the crowd of 400,000 racing fans at the Indianapolis Motor Speedway. The veteran drove in third place for most of the race, with Mario Andretti in the lead for 170 of the

Bo Knows Baseball . . . and Bo Knows Football *Bo Jackson already was a star for baseball's Kansas City Royals when he also signed to play football for the NFL's Los Angeles Raiders. He excelled at both sports.*

200 laps, and Roberto Guerrero in second place, where he finished the race just seconds behind Unser.

During lap number 180, Andretti's engine failed, pulling him out of the race. Guerrero then made a rookie mistake during a pit stop that cost him an extra 55 seconds—enough to allow Unser to take the lead and eventually the race.

Gretzky Leads Oilers

Wayne Gretzky won his unprecedented eighth consecutive Hart Memorial Trophy, the award given annually to the NHL's most valuable player. By decade's end he had won the award nine of 10 years. Gretzky also led his Edmonton Oilers to the Stanley Cup, the team's third NHL championship in four years.

In a well-played, seven-game final series, the Great One had some help in game seven to lock up the cup. Teammates Jari Kurri and Glen Anderson put the Oilers in the lead to stay with second- and third-period goals, respectively, as Edmonton beat the Philadelphia Flyers 3–1 on May 31 to capture the series. The Oilers' superb defensive play helped seal the victory.

Philadelphia goalie Ron Hextall had kept the underdog Flyers alive in the series with outstanding performances after the Oilers jumped out to a three-games-to-one lead. Led by Hextall's excellent goaltending, the Flyers bounced back to win game five 4–3 and game six 3–2 to tie the series, setting up the decisive seventh game.

In game seven, Hextall didn't get much help from his teammates, as he

Two-Sport Superstar

By the time Bo Jackson—the 1985 Heisman Trophy winner as college football's top player—signed his first pro football contract, he had already established himself as an amazingly talented Major League Baseball player. He hit massive home runs nearing 500 feet in distance, made impossible throws from the deepest parts of ballparks, and climbed outfield walls to haul in long fly balls and take back home runs.

During the years that he played both professional sports, from 1987 through 1990, Jackson emerged as one of the most feared hitters in baseball and one of the fastest and most unstoppable running backs in the NFL.

A serious hip injury in 1991 ended his football career and cut short his baseball career. Others have played two sports, but no one has shown such ability in both.

dealt with 43 Oilers' shots on goal, compared to only 20 shots faced by Edmonton goalie Grant Fuhr.

Bo Plays Two Pro Sports

Calling it a "hobby" to get him through the winter, pro baseball player Bo Jackson signed a five-year contract to play pro football with the Los Angeles Raiders. Jackson was already playing Major League Baseball for the Kansas City Royals. The agreement called for Jackson to join the Raiders at the end of the baseball season, which would allow him to play in about half of the team's 16 NFL games.

While at Auburn University in 1985, Jackson won the Heisman Trophy as college football's best player. The following spring, he was the number-one overall pick in the NFL draft but turned down a

1987

lucrative offer from the Tampa Bay Buccaneers. Instead, Jackson signed a deal with baseball's Royals and played with one of their minor-league teams.

His first full season in Major League Baseball was 1987. At the time he signed with the football Raiders—during baseball's All-Star break in July—Jackson was batting .254, with 18 homers and 45 RBI. A hip injury in 1994 ended his two-sport success, but the legend of Bo was assured.

A series of popular commercials for Nike using his "Bo Knows . . ." persona helped rocket Jackson to popularity.

NFL Strike. . . Again

The National Football League Players Association went on strike two games into the 1987 season. The NFL players last staged a strike in 1982, when they shut down the game for 57 days (see page 161). This time, the players were hoping to gain unrestricted free agency—the right to sign with any team when a contract was up. They were also looking for a higher salary scale and increased pension benefits, as well as some minor contractual points.

Other Milestones of 1987

✔ On January 2, the Penn State Nittany Lions won college football's national championship for the 1986 season by beating the top-ranked Miami Hurricanes 14–10 in the Fiesta Bowl in Tempe, Arizona.

✔ Three years after losing the America's Cup to Australia, an American skipper, Dennis Conner, regained it on February 4, sailing the ship *Stars & Stripes*.

✔ Woody Hayes, longtime football coaching great at Ohio State University, died on March 12 at age 74.

✔ Philadelphia Phillies third baseman Mike Schmidt hit his 500th career home run on April 18.

✔ The Atlanta Braves started baseball's trend away from the pullover polyester uniforms of the 1970s and early '80s, going back to traditional button-up jerseys and returning to the team logo they had used 25 years earlier in Milwaukee.

✔ Julius Erving joined Wilt Chamberlain and Kareem Abdul-Jabbar as the only players in NBA history to score more than 30,000 career points.

✔ The Little League World Series celebrated its 40th anniversary in August.

✔ Playoff MVP Magic Johnson led the Los Angeles Lakers over the Boston Celtics in the NBA Finals.

✔ Two years after his Cy Young Award performance, New York Mets pitcher Dwight Gooden tested positive for drugs and entered a rehabilitation program.

✔ In a season that marked the beginning of one of baseball's most controversial careers, slugging first baseman Mark McGwire of the Oakland Athletics set a record for baseball rookies with 49 home runs. Over the next decade-plus, McGwire would amaze fans with his home-run prowess. However, he would also become embroiled in the steroid controversy that would come to mark the era.

The NFL responded by hiring replacement players. Games scheduled for the third weekend of the season were canceled, but the games in weeks four, five, and six were played with the replacement players.

The 24-day strike ended on October 15, and striking players returned for the seventh week of the season without a new contract, a back-to-work agreement, or a new collective bargaining agreement in place. Although some agreements were reached on minor issues, the major questions of free agency, drug testing, and pension funding were left unresolved.

One Catch, Two Records

San Francisco 49ers wide receiver Jerry Rice set two NFL records with a single pass reception, catching a 20-yard TD pass from Steve Young in the third quarter of a game against the Atlanta Falcons on December 20. The reception, Rice's 19th of the year, broke the record for the most touchdown catches in a single season. It also marked the 12th straight game in which Rice had caught a touchdown pass, another NFL record.

By season's end, Rice had 22 touchdown receptions—a remarkable figure, especially given that he reached it in only 12 games because of the players' strike early in the year. But Rice, who was in his third NFL season after being selected in the first round of the 1985 draft, was just getting started. He would go on to become the most prolific touchdown scorer the league has ever known.

Rice played for the 49ers through the 2000 season, then joined the Oakland Raiders in 2001. He helped the Raiders reach the Super Bowl in the 2002 season, then played one more full season in Oakland and part of another before closing his career with the Seattle Seahawks in 2004.

In 20 seasons, Rice caught 1,549 passes for 22,895 yards and 197 touchdowns. All of those are league records—and all by a very wide margin. His 207 total touchdowns is another league mark.

1988

Golden Winter Olympics

At the 1988 Winter Olympics in Calgary, Canada in February—the first Olympic Games of the decade without a boycott of some kind—the United States came away with two gold medals. Both of these medals were hard fought, and both required near-perfect performances.

In men's figure skating, American Brian Boitano captured the gold medal in one of the closest competitions in Olympic history. Boitano beat Canadian Brian Orser by a slim margin, as the Canadian took the silver. Viktor Petrenko of the Soviet Union won the bronze. Boitano had a very narrow lead after the short program, leaving plenty of room for Orser to overtake him. But the American skated with great skill, showmanship, and emotion, delivering a stunning performance in the long program to secure his gold medal.

America's other gold came in women's speed skating. Bonnie Blair set a world record in the 500-meter sprint, capturing the gold with a time of 39.10 seconds. Blair knew she would have to skate a world's best time to win, having watched defending Olympic champion Christa Rothenburger of East Germany break her own world record just moments earlier in the competition. Rothenburger set the new record at 39.12 seconds. With that in mind, Blair skated to the gold, shaving Rothenburger's time by just two one-hundredths of a second.

Lakers Repeat NBA Title

In an exciting, seven-game NBA Finals, the Los Angeles Lakers edged the Detroit Pistons to win the league championship for the fifth time in the 1980s and for the 12th time overall. The Lakers won the decisive game 108–105 in Los Angeles on June 21.

The Lakers' title also marked the first time since 1969 that an NBA team successfully defended its league crown. (Boston won consecutive championships in 1967–68 and 1968–69.) After his team's victory in the 1987 NBA Finals over the Celtics, Lakers coach Pat Riley was asked if his team could win again the following year. "I'll guarantee it," Riley replied.

His team proved to be as good as his word. The Lakers had home-court advantage throughout the playoffs, thanks to a league-best 62–20 regular-season record, and they certainly needed it. Each of their

Close Call *Brian Boitano won gold at the Winter Games by the slimmest of margins.*

other series—hard fought contests against the Utah Jazz and Dallas Mavericks—also came down to a deciding seventh game on their home court.

James Worthy led the way in game seven of the finals with the first triple-double (double figures in points, assists, and rebounds) of his career: 36 points, 16 rebounds, and 10 assists.

Night Games at Wrigley

For 74 years, the Chicago Cubs played by day—the way the game was intended to be played, at least according to purists. Only day games were played at Wrigley Field, the Cubs' home stadium (they also played on real grass, not artificial turf). But on August 9, Wrigley Field

1988

became the last Major League Baseball stadium to get lights, and night games could finally be played.

The 36,399 fans on hand were filled with mixed emotions, happy to be a part of history, but sad at the end of a proud tradition. The Cubs beat the New York Mets 6–4 in the first official Wrigley night game. The ceremony introducing the lights actually took place the night before, on August 8, as a 91-year-old Cubs fan flipped a switch to turn on the 540 lights that had been placed on the stadium's roof. But the game that night against the Philadelphia Phillies lasted only three and a half innings before it was postponed by rain.

After years of debate, the decision to put lights into Wrigley Field was finalized earlier in the year. The Cubs' management gave in to the economic reality that the franchise could fill the stands with bigger crowds for night games. However, only 18 night games were scheduled for the 1988 season.

Dodgers Feats

The Los Angeles Dodgers' Orel Hershiser and Kirk Gibson turned in two of the most memorable individual performances in baseball history in 1988. It was only fitting, then, that the Dodgers won the World Series, beating the favored Oakland Athletics in five games. The decisive game was a 5–2 victory in Oakland on October 20.

Hershiser, a right-handed pitcher, set a big-league record for consecutive shutout innings. In his final start of the regular season on September 28, Hershiser threw 10 shutout innings, bringing his streak of consecutive scoreless innings to 59 and breaking the record set by Dodgers great Don Drysdale in 1968. Hershiser, who was just about unhittable over the final month of the season, won 23 games in all and captured the National League's Cy Young Award.

Hershiser continued his dominance into the postseason. On October 12, he shut out the New York Mets 6–0 in the seventh and deciding game of the National League Championship Series, propelling the Dodgers into the World Series.

In the World Series, Hershiser won two games, including another shutout in game two, then a complete-game victory in the deciding game five.

Hershiser shared World Series heroics with teammate Gibson. In game one of the Series at Dodger Stadium, the Dodgers trailed 4–3 with two outs in the bottom

59 Shutout Innings

Here is how Orel Hershiser set a record for consecutive scoreless innings in 1988:

OPPONENT	SCORE	SCORELESS INNINGS PITCHED
Montreal Expos	4–2	4
Atlanta Braves	3–0	9
Cincinnati Reds	5–0	9
Atlanta Braves	1–0	9
Houston Astros	1–0	9
San Francisco Giants	3–0	9
San Diego Padres	0–0 *	10
Total		59

*Hershiser left the game after 10 innings with the score 0–0. The Dodgers lost the game in 16 innings.

Baseball Under the Lights *After 74 years of playing only day games at Wrigley Field, the Chicago Cubs began playing night games in the summer of 1988 (see page 203).*

of the ninth inning. The A's had their ace closer, Dennis Eckersley, on the pitcher's mound, and it looked as if Oakland was going to jump out in front in the Series.

Eckersley walked Mike Davis. Then, as the crowd stood and roared its approval, Gibson, sidelined with a serious knee injury, grabbed a bat and limped up to the plate. It would be his only at-bat in the series, but it was enough. Gibson, wincing in pain, smacked a 3–2 pitch into the right-field seats for a two-run homer that gave the Dodgers the victory and the momentum to take the Series.

Gibson added this dramatic homer to the one he hit four years earlier to help the Detroit Tigers win the 1984 World Series (see page 176). This home run eventually ranked No. 9 in Major League Baseball's Most Memorable Moments campaign in the 2002 season.

NFL Suspends 19 Players

National Football League commissioner Pete Rozelle wanted the message to be heard loud and clear: The league would not tolerate drug use, even by its top players. Rozelle announced that 19 NFL players were being suspended for substance abuse.

Among the 19 were defensive superstars Lawrence Taylor of the New York Giants, Dexter Manley of the Washington Redskins, and Bruce Smith of the Buffalo Bills. They were among 18 players who received 30-day suspensions. Tony Collins, a running back for the Indianapolis Colts, received a one-year suspension.

NFL guidelines state that a player who fails a drug test for the first time receives a warning and treatment. If a player fails a second drug test, he is

1988

suspended for 30 days. A third failure results in a lifetime suspension, although the player may apply for reinstatement based on good behavior.

Oilers Trade Gretzky

Few cities have ever had a love affair with a professional athlete as intense as the relationship between NHL great Wayne Gretzky and the city of Edmonton, Ontario, in Canada. So it was a complete shock when Peter Pocklington, owner of the Edmonton Oilers, announced one of the most startling trades in sports history. Gretzky (along with two other players) had been traded from the Oilers to the Los Angeles Kings (for two

Magnificent Seven *Jackie Joyner-Kersee won the gold medal in the heptathlon—a seven-event competition to identify the world's best female athlete—with a record-setting performance at the Olympics.*

players, three first-round draft choices, and $14.4 million). The details of the trade hardly mattered to Edmonton hockey fans. The Great One (as Gretzky was known) was leaving.

"It's like ripping the heart out of the city," said Edmonton mayor Laurence Decore. Hockey fans in the town agreed. In his nine seasons with the Oilers, Gretzky set 43 NHL scoring records, won eight consecutive Most Valuable Player trophies, captured seven straight scoring titles, and led his team to four Stanley Cup championships. No wonder Canadians felt as if their national treasure had been stolen from them by the United States.

As it turned out, Gretzky himself had requested the trade. In July of 1988, he married American actress Janet Jones. At the time, Canadian hockey fans treated their wedding like a royal affair, tuning in to the event on television and welcoming Jones into their extended "family."

When the trade was announced a month later, though, Canadians blamed Jones for stealing their superstar. Gretzky said Los Angeles offered him a new challenge, to make hockey popular in a city not known for its love of the sport. But he also moved to make it easier for his wife to pursue her acting career.

Gretzky wept openly at the press conference announcing his departure, but Pocklington accused him of acting for the cameras, stating that Gretzky had a huge ego, which is why he requested the trade. The Oilers' owner later refuted the claim, but the damage had been done. The greatest hockey player ever was leaving the country of his birth and the city where he rewrote the NHL record book.

Olympic Sisters-in-Law

After the United States' boycott of the Olympic Games in Moscow in 1980 and the Soviet Union's boycott of the Games in Los Angeles in 1984, the world's two major superpowers finally competed together in the Summer Olympics in the 1988 Games in Seoul, South Korea.

The Soviets dominated these Olympics, winning 132 medals, including 55 gold. But the Americans had numerous memorable performances en route to winning 94 medals, including 36 gold. Chief among them were those by sisters-in-law Jackie Joyner-Kersee and Florence Griffith Joyner.

In some ways, they could not have been more different. Joyner-Kersee was all about hard work, muscle, and sweat, considered by many to be the finest female athlete of the second half of the 20th century. Griffith Joyner (known as "Flo Jo"), also a world-class athlete, combined her great physical abilities with a flashy style and fashion savvy. The two American women teamed up to dominate the track-and-field events in Seoul. They combined to win five gold medals.

Joyner-Kersee broke her own world record in the heptathlon on her way to Olympic gold, shattering the rarely surpassed 7,000-point mark in the event by scoring 7,291 points, almost 400 points ahead of her nearest competitor. (The heptathlon is a seven-event competition made up of the 100-meter hurdles, the shot put, the high jump, the 200-meter race, the long jump, the javelin, and the 800-meter race). She followed up her victory in the heptathlon by setting an Olym-

pic record in the long jump, leaping an amazing 24 feet, 3 1/2 inches to earn her second gold medal. Until Joyner-Kersee did it, no one thought it was possible to win the grueling two-day heptathlon, and then come back and win an individual event. Bruce Jenner, the 1976 Olympic decathlon gold medalist, said of Joyner-Kersee, "She's the greatest multi-sport athlete ever, man or woman."

Flo Jo captured three golds. She won the 100-meter sprint, setting an Olympic record with a time of 10.54 seconds. In the 200-meter race, she set a world record with a time of 21.34 seconds. Her third gold medal came as part of the United States' 400-meter relay team.

The United States also was strong in the swimming and diving events. Seventeen-year-old Janet Evans set a world record on her way to winning the 400-meter freestyle swimming event. She also won gold medals in the 800-meter freestyle and 400-meter individual medley. Matt Biondi won seven swimming medals, including five gold.

Fashion Statements

In addition to her great athletic achievements at the 1988 Summer Olympic Games, Florence Griffith Joyner made some of the most memorable fashion statements of the 1980s.

From her catchy nickname (Flo Jo) to her glittering, sexy track outfits, from colorful, one-legged unitards to outrageous six-inch fingernails and make-up, Flo Jo was style personified. She made no apologies for breaking the rules of how a track star should dress, look, or carry herself.

Flo Jo later went on to design new uniforms for the NBA's Indiana Pacers.

1988

American Greg Louganis (see the box below), arguably the best diver in Olympic history, became the first diver to win two gold medals in two consecutive Olympic Games.

In 1984, at the Games in Los Angeles, Louganis won gold in the platform and springboard events. He repeated those victories in Seoul four years later. In 1988, his victory had added drama when Louganis hit his head on the diving board during a preliminary round of the springboard competition, but still came back to win the event.

Johnson Stripped of Gold

In addition to the success of Jackie Joyner-Kersee and Florence Griffith Joyner, the United States picked up another track and field gold medal—although it didn't appear that way at first. Canadian sprinter Ben Johnson defeated his American rival, Carl Lewis, in the 100-meter sprint, running a world record time of 9.79 seconds. Lewis finished second with a time of 9.92. But three days later, Johnson was disqualified and his gold medal was taken away when he tested

Greg Louganis: Secrets and Success

When United States Olympic gold medal diver Greg Louganis hit his head on the diving board during a preliminary round of the springboard competition at the 1988 Olympic Games, it took five stitches to close the wound. Louganis was very upset, not simply because of the injury, but because Louganis was HIV-positive—a fact only a few of his closest friends were aware of.

Had everyone there been aware of Louganis' illness, panic might have ensued. The pool would likely have been drained, the competition disrupted, and the diver himself exposed to scorn or controversy for putting others in potential danger. (In reality, the chlorine in the pool was enough to kill any virus that may have been shed in his blood.)

Louganis recovered from his fall and captured the gold medal in the event the next day, as well as a second gold in platform diving, but the experience shook him deeply. Louganis was gay, something else

only his closest friends knew. He retired from diving after the 1988 games. In 1994 at the Gay Games in New York City, he announced his homosexuality.

Hiding his homosexuality and his disease for years took its toll. "It's been so difficult with the secret, and asking people to keep the secrets," he said in his autobiography, *Breaking the Surface*, published in 1995. "I was feeling like a fake."

In the book he discussed being gay, living with the secret, and living with HIV. His openness led to a greater comfort with himself, and with his place in diving history. "Being gay and being in sports isn't supposed to mix," Louganis said. "I think I proved that wrong."

Three years later, the growing specter of AIDS in American society would find an even more familiar face when Magic Johnson, one of the dominant athletes of the 1980s, announced that he had tested positive for HIV, the virus that causes AIDS.

Other Milestones of 1988

✔ National League president A. Bartlett Giamatti was chosen to become the new baseball commissioner. Giamatti served until his death from a heart attack in September of 1989.

✔ Jose Canseco of the Oakland A's became the first player in baseball history to hit 40 homers (he had 42) and steal 40 bases in the same season. No other player matched the feat until the San Francisco Giants' Barry Bonds also 42 homers and 40 steals in 1996. Two years later, the Seattle Mariners' Alex Rodriguez hit 42 homers and stole 46 bases.

✔ The Miami Heat and the Charlotte Hornets joined the NBA as expansion franchises.

✔ The catcher's helmet was required in the major leagues for the first time.

✔ The first African-American referee in the NFL, Johnny Grier, made his debut.

✔ Nike's "Just Do It" ad campaign debuted, encouraging everyone to go for their dreams, emulate their sports heroes, and, of course, buy Nike shoes. The phrase quickly became a part of American popular culture.

---

positive for ozolol, an anabolic steroid that was banned by the International Olympic Committee. Johnson was barred from competing on Canada's national team for life and was sent home in disgrace. The gold medal was given to Lewis, who had won four gold medals at the Games in 1984 (see page 176).

Johnson's fall from grace led to increased efforts to eliminate the use of performance-enhancing drugs in the Olympics. More rigorous testing was introduced. Not only were athletes tested immediately after competitions, but also, in some countries, random tests were performed throughout athletes' training periods.

Big-Screen Baseball

Two of the best baseball movies of all time were released in 1988. *Bull Durham*, starring Kevin Costner, Susan Sarandon, and Tim Robbins, was written and directed by Ron Shelton, a former minor-league baseball player. It tells the story of a career minor-league catcher who is asked to whip an up-and-coming pitcher into shape and to teach him the ways of the game.

Eight Men Out, directed by John Sayles, based on the book by Eliot Asinof, tells the story of the 1919 Black Sox scandal, which almost destroyed baseball. John Cusack played Buck Weaver, D.B. Sweeney played "Shoeless" Joe Jackson, and Sayles played writer Ring Lardner. The heavily favored 1919 Chicago White Sox lost the World Series that year, and subsequently were accused of being paid by gamblers to purposely lose. It led to player suspensions and to the appointment of the first baseball commissioner, Judge Kenesaw Mountain Landis, to rid the game of gambling's influence—which was considerable at the time.

1989

On the Air

By the end of the 1980s, the influence of television on sports in America was so strong that it had direct effects on the very structure of the games. Teams moved to new cities because the television markets were larger. Television revenue had become more important than the money collected from fans paying to get into the actual event. Filling the home stadium became less important than local television deals, which more than made up for empty seats.

Entire leagues were restructured and additional tiers of postseason games were added because they made for good television. People who might not follow a particular sport every day throughout the regular season did show an interest in the playoffs. So television gave them more playoff games, which, of course, meant more advertising revenue—charged at much higher rates than during the regular season.

The big television money led to even bigger sponsorship agreements and huge contracts, with dollars reaching into the previously inconceivable millions, for America's professional athletes.

Television's marriage with sports had humble beginnings. The first television broadcast of a Major League Baseball game was on August 26, 1939, when WSBX-TV aired the action between the Brooklyn Dodgers and the Cincinnati Reds at Ebbets Field in Brooklyn, New York. It was seen by a few hundred people watching the approximately 400 television sets in all of New York City. The Dodgers and Reds split a double-header that day.

By the 1950s, sports were a staple of television programming in the still relatively young medium. Friday night boxing matches and Saturday afternoon baseball games became regular parts of the lives of sports-loving Americans.

The 1960s saw big television money just starting to make its way into professional sports. The man most responsible for this was NFL commissioner Pete Rozelle, who brought his league into the television spotlight and into the hearts and living rooms of American sports fans. It was television in the 1960s that catapulted football ahead of baseball—the traditional American national pastime—as the most popular professional team sport in the country.

Joe Cool *Joe Montana helped make the San Francisco 49ers the NFL's team of the decade. He led his team to the winning score late in Super Bowl XXIII (see page 212).*

Rozelle's television contracts in the 1960s brought big money into the league. When CBS began televising NFL games in 1956, the network negotiated a separate contract with each of the 12 teams in the league. Each team got between $35,000 and $185,000 directly from the network for the rights to broadcast its games. In

1989

1962, Rozelle worked out a package deal in which CBS paid the league $4.5 million dollars over two years for the rights to broadcast the games of all the teams.

In 1970, the television networks paid $50 million to broadcast NFL games. In 1985 that figure rose to $450 million. As the 1980s ended, the NFL signed four-year deals with CBS, ABC, ESPN, and Turner Broadcasting for a total of $3.6 billion. In the years between those early deals and the multi-billion-dollar contracts, the NFL expanded from 12 teams to 14, then 16, and finally 28.

In 1950, Major League Baseball signed a deal with the Gillette razor company for $6 million for the rights to the World Series and All-Star Games over a six-year period. Under the terms of the deal, Gillette ads would run exclusively on all television and radio broadcasts of the games. In 1970, the television networks paid $18 million for the rights to broadcast baseball, and in 1985 that amount had grown to $160 million. In 1989, baseball signed a deal with CBS for $1.1 billion, and another deal with ESPN for $400 million.

The huge, ever-expanding flow of money into the pockets of team owners and the leagues did not go unnoticed by the players. They began to demand their fair share of the revenue. Unions were formed, strikes were staged, and restrictive legal clauses binding players to teams for life were challenged and overturned in court. This led to free agency and bidding wars between teams, each club hoping to secure the top players by offering more than the competition. In the end, the players were big winners, commanding salaries unthinkable a few years earlier.

As the 1980s drew to a close, sports and television were as inseparable as a catcher and his face mask. Sports has always been a business, but with big television money leading to huge influence, the realization that in modern sports the bottom line was often of greater interest than the final score became an accepted reality.

Dramatic Super Bowl

With a little more than three minutes remaining in the game and his San Francisco 49ers trailing the Cincinnati Bengals by three points in Super Bowl XXIII in Miami on January 22, quarterback Joe Montana entered the huddle. His team was 92 yards from the most dramatic Super Bowl victory to date, but it could have been a touch-football game in the park for the man they called "Joe Cool."

"Hey, Harris, check it out—there's John Candy," Montana told young offensive lineman Harris Barton, pointing to the actor-comedian in the stands. Barton had been fidgeting nervously during a television time out, but Montana's message was clear: Nothing to worry about.

Cincinnati had forged its lead largely behind a tough defense and a 93-yard, third-quarter kickoff return by Stanford Jennings. San Francisco tied the score early in the fourth quarter on a 14-yard touchdown pass from Montana to his favorite receiver, Jerry Rice, but Cincinnati regained the advantage on a 40-yard field goal by Jim Breech. And so the 49ers trailed 16–13 with three minutes and 10 seconds on the clock and the ball on their own eight-yard line. It was time for Montana, one of the greatest quarterbacks in NFL history at working under pressure, to take things into his experienced hands.

Mixing pass plays and running plays, Montana launched the touchdown drive that gave the 49ers a 20–16 victory. The winning points came on his 10-yard touchdown pass to John Taylor with only 34 seconds left.

Montana finished with a Super Bowl-record (since broken) 357 passing yards, although Rice was named the game's MVP for catching 11 passes for 215 yards.

The victory was San Francisco's third (of four) in the Super Bowl in the 1980s, and it came in Bill Walsh's final game as the 49ers' head coach. Walsh (1931–2007) remains the only man to win a Super Bowl in his final game on the sidelines.

Lemieux Passes Gretzky

For the decade of the 1980s, any talk about the NHL naturally centered around Wayne Gretzky. Fans of hockey in the '80s were lucky enough to have watched the sport as its greatest player dominated the league.

As the decade drew to a close, however, a new star emerged. Twenty-three-year-old Mario Lemieux of the Pittsburgh Penguins won the NHL scoring title, finishing ahead of Gretzky for the second consecutive year. Lemieux, a 6-foot-4, 200-pound native of Montreal, Quebec, scored 85 goals and handed out 114 assists for a total of 199 points—the most ever achieved by anyone other than Gretzky.

Along the way, Lemieux established himself as the league's best player.

Cool Under Pressure

Sometimes all it takes is being told that you're not good enough. Joe Montana was not highly touted heading into the 1979 NFL draft. All he had done in college was work his way up from seventh-string quarterback for the University of Notre Dame to starter, lead the team in staging amazing late-game comebacks, and take the squad to the national championship in 1977.

But he never looked that good on paper. He was too skinny, he couldn't throw the ball all that far, and even his short passes looked a bit wobbly. He didn't have the sculpted body or rocket-launcher arm that seemed to be a requirement for modern quarterbacks. He was more of a throwback to the days of Johnny Unitas, Len Dawson, and Bart Starr, all of whom played in the 1950s.

The San Francisco 49ers picked Montana in the third round of the 1979 draft. By his third year as a pro, he had become the 49ers' full-time starting quarterback. That season, he led San Francisco to a last-minute, come-from-behind victory against the Dallas Cowboys, the team that had dominated the NFL in the 1970s, in the NFC Championship Game (see page 154). He then won the first of his four Super Bowls.

There has never been anyone cooler under pressure. If there was time on the clock and Montana had the ball, the 49ers always had a chance.

1989

Larger and stronger than Gretzky, Lemieux racked up nine hat tricks (scoring three goals in one game) in 1988–89 and set an NHL record by scoring 13 short-handed goals (when your team is short a player because of a penalty). Pittsburgh scored a record 118 power-play goals (when you team has one more player than the opposition because of a penalty), and Lemieux was involved in 109 of those. His 199 points is the fourth-highest total in NHL history.

Giamatti Bans Pete Rose

A. Bartlett Giamatti, former president of the National League, became baseball commissioner on April 1. A lifelong fan, devoted to baseball's traditions, Giamatti earned his reputation for being tough in dealing with unions as president of Yale University.

Giamatti spent most of his first five months as commissioner leading an investigation into the gambling activities of Pete Rose. Rose is baseball's all-time hits leader and was one of the game's best players for more than 20 years.

As a result of the investigation, a huge amount of evidence surfaced, chronicling years of gambling by Rose, including the devastating revelation that he had bet on baseball games. On August 24, Giamatti announced that an agreement had been reached banning Rose from any further involvement with the game of baseball.

Rose signed the agreement, which stated that he accepted the punishment without admitting nor denying his guilt. Rose was also allowed to apply for reinstatement into the game after a year, but

Giamatti would give no guarantee that his position would change at that time.

This painful banishment immediately asserted Giamatti's power as commissioner, though it brought him no joy. Rose would have been a certain selection for baseball's Hall of Fame based on his performance as a player, and to this day he remains out of the Hall and banned from the game.

This sad series of events was immediately followed by a shocking tragedy that stunned the baseball world. On September 1, Giamatti died suddenly of a heart attack while at his summer cottage in Massachusetts—eight days after banning Rose from baseball. Giamatti was just 51 years old.

Earthquake Rocks Series

On October 17, more than 60,000 fans packed Candlestick Park in San Francisco for game three of the World Series between the Giants and their cross-bay rivals, the Oakland Athletics. The Athletics had won the first two games handily, but the Giants' fans on hand were anxious to see the first World Series game at Candlestick in 27 years.

In a flash, though, all concerns about the Giants getting back into the Series were forgotten: At 5:04 P.M., with pregame ceremonies just getting started, a 6.9-magnitude earthquake rocked the San Francisco Bay Area, knocking out power and causing widespread destruction.

Players and fans remained amazingly calm despite swaying press boxes and a sudden loss of power. Live television and radio broadcasts were temporarily knocked off the air. The ballpark had some damage, but mostly held up to the stress, and no one inside was hurt.

Players scrambled to find their families. When broadcasts were restored, viewers who had tuned in for the game saw players holding their children and hugging their wives, all thoughts of a ball game replaced by concern for the safety of loved ones. Anxious fans in the ballpark waited for word of what to do next.

Baseball commissioner Fay Vincent, who had been in the job just a little more than a month, reacted quickly. He postponed the game and began emptying the ballpark before darkness set in.

As fans left the stadium, they had no idea of the extent of the devastation in the surrounding area. When the earthquake ended, 67 people were dead, and roads, bridges, and buildings had collapsed, causing billions of dollars of damage.

Suddenly, the all-Bay-Area World Series had lost its urgency, as people faced the more urgent tasks of rebuilding their city and their lives. Repairs were made to the stadium, and, although some called for the rest of the World Series to be cancelled, Vincent and San Francisco mayor Art Agnos eventually decided to resume the Series beginning October 27. The A's went on to complete their four-game sweep, although the games and final scores all seemed anticlimactic.

San Francisco Giants center fielder Brett Butler put it best. "At the start, I realized what a privilege it was to be in the Series. Now, I realize what a privilege it is to be alive. When people think of the 1989 Series, they're not going to remember who won, but who survived."

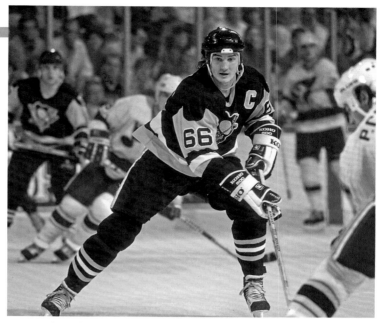

As Good as the Great One? *By the end of the decade, Mario Lemieux may have surpassed Wayne Gretzky as hockey's best player (see page 213).*

Shell Breaks Color Barrier

Art Shell took over as head coach of the Los Angeles Raiders on October 3. He became the NFL's first African-American head coach in 64 years.

Before Shell, the last African-American to coach an NFL team was Fritz Pollard of the Hammond (Indiana) Pros. From 1923 to 1925, Pollard, a running back, was the Pros' player-coach.

Shell was a star tackle in his playing days who was one of the pillars, along with guard Gene Upshaw, of the Oakland Raiders' offensive line in the 1970s. Shell played in 207 regular-season games from 1968 to 1982 and earned eight Pro Bowl selections. He was inducted into the Pro Football Hall of Fame shortly before the start of the 1989 season.

1989

After the Raiders stumbled to a 1–3 start that year, owner Al Davis turned to Shell, who was coaching the offensive line, to succeed young Mike Shanahan as head coach. Under Shell's leadership, the Raiders won seven of their next 10 games, although they failed to make the playoffs. (The next season, however, Shell's team went 12–4 and reached the AFC title game.)

Shell coached the Raiders through 1994, and compiled a 56–41 record (including postseason). He took his team to the playoffs three times. He returned to coach the Raiders in 2006, but did not have the same success, winning only two games in a one-season stint.

Shell's appointment paved the way for other African-American head coaches in the NFL. In 2009, six league teams began the season with African-Americans at the helm, and a seventh black head coach was hired during the season.

Still, the first African-American to coach in the NFL's modern era was a long time coming. By contrast, the NBA hired its first black head coach in 1966, when future Hall-of-Famer Bill Russell became player-coach of the Boston Celtics. Between 1966 and 1989, when Shell broke the NFL coaching color barrier, the NBA had 18 black head coaches.

The first black Major League Baseball manager was hired in 1975, when Hall-of-Famer Frank Robinson became manager of the Cleveland Indians. Between that year and 1989, baseball had four black managers. Hispanics have also made major in-roads in managerial positions since then.

Two Times Ninety

Almost from the moment that wide receiver Jerry Rice joined the San Francisco 49ers as a first-round draft choice in 1985, he dominated headlines with his remarkable play-making ability. During the 49ers' nationally televised 30–27 victory over the Los Angeles Rams on December 11 in Anaheim, however, the incomparable Rice took a back seat to John Taylor. That Monday night, San Francisco's No. 2 wideout became the first NFL player to score two touchdowns of more than 90 yards in the same game.

Taylor turned short passes from Joe Montana into touchdowns of 92 yards and 95 yards. He helped the 49ers rally from a 17-point deficit to beat their NFC West rivals.

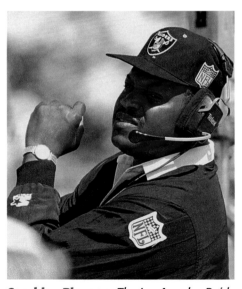

Coaching Pioneer *The Los Angeles Raiders made Art Shell the NFL's first African-American head coach in 64 years.*

Other Milestones of 1989

✔ Bill White was named president of baseball's National League. He became the first African-American to preside over a major sports league in United States history.

✔ Kareem Abdul-Jabbar of the Los Angeles Lakers retired from the NBA as its career leader in points (38,387), games (1,560), and minutes played (56,446).

✔ Greg LeMond won his second Tour de France bicycle race in July. His first win in 1988 had made him teh first American to capture the century-old, grueling month-long bike race.

✔ Jim Abbott, a baseball pitcher with only one hand, played in the major leagues. Abbott went 12-12 for the California Angels. Abbott had won the Sullivan Award during his career at the University of Michigan. His story was an inspiring one, especially for youngsters facing similar physical challenges.

✔ Texas Rangers pitcher Nolan Ryan fanned the 5,000th batter of his career on August 22.

✔ Triple Crown winner Secretariat, considered by many to be the greatest thoroughbred race horse of all time, died on October 4. The mighty horse had captured all three legs of the Triple Crown in 1973 (see page 84).

✔ On October 25, Los Angeles Kings star Wayne Gretzky passed Gordie Howe as the NHL's all-time leading scorer (1,852 points). Gretzky set the mark in Edmonton against the Oilers, the team for whom he had his greatest years.

✔ The International Amateur Basketball Federation opened the Olympics to all professional athletes, including those from the NBA.

✔ American star Chris Evert became the first tennis player, male or female, to win 1,000 career singles matches.

San Francisco, playing under new head coach George Seifert (Bill Walsh's successor), won 14 games during the 1989 regular season to beat out the Rams for the division title. The two teams met again in the NFC Championship Game that year, but that game wasn't so close: San Francisco won in a rout, 30–3.

The 49ers then went on to win their second consecutive Super Bowl by blasting the Denver Broncos 55–24 in game XXIV on January 28, 1990, at the Superdome in New Orleans. Seifert became just the second rookie coach (after the Colts' Don McCafferty in 1970) to win the Super Bowl.

INTRODUCTION
1990–1999

The 1990s was the decade of the Internet revolution, a time when sports and their stars were brought into everyone's homes instantaneously by the wonders of high-speed technology. No longer did sports fans have to wait for the morning paper to see the box scores or read about their favorite teams. They were at their fingertips along the information superhighway at the click of a button (or a mouse).

But even as America hurtled into the digital age, there were nostalgic efforts to cling to the past, such as baseball's new "retro" ballparks that called to mind the fields of earlier years, and the revival of bell-bottom pants in the fashion world.

America enjoyed a period of relative peace and prosperity during the final decade of the 20th century. Alarming news of AIDS, terrorism, and homelessness was often drowned out by the sirens of pop celebrity. Even the Persian Gulf War of 1991 generated an uplifting spin. It was especially evident at the star-spangled Super Bowl XXV in Tampa, Florida, where patriotism packed more punch than the Buffalo Bills' offense.

The first President George Bush couldn't win the battle against economic woes, however, and the nation moved into eight colorful, if controversial, years under Bill Clinton. About the same time that Wall Street's bulls started running wild and the economy skyrocketed, spurred by high-flying dotcom stocks, Chicago's Bulls, behind the gravity-defying feats of Michael Jordan, won the first of their six National Basketball Association (NBA) titles in the 1990s. Reflecting the go-go decade, Air Jordan was equally admired for his commercial endorsements, hugely popular sneaker brand, and ranking atop *Forbes Magazine's* list of richest athletes.

The rite of calling sports a selfish business and referring to athletes as pampered brats dates back to ancient times, when Greek senators cried foul over paying "amateur" Olympians and shut down the original Games because of corruption. In the 1990s, however, the volume of complaints went way up. Free agency, which enabled players to sign with any team, left fans rooting for uniforms rather than the millionaire players in them. The cliché "the best team money can buy" was put to work by George Steinbrenner, Wayne Huizenga, Daniel Snyder, and other wealthy owners. Kids bounded straight from high school to the NBA,

A Windows World *CEO Bill Gates and the Microsoft Corporation were at the forefront of the digital age.*

and underclassmen left college in droves for the National Football League (NFL). And, incredibly—for the first time since 1904—the World Series was cancelled in 1994 because striking players couldn't agree with stubborn owners on how to divvy up billions of dollars.

The thud of sports heroes falling grew louder, too. O.J. Simpson ran from the law instead of tacklers and Mike Tyson

1990– 1999

raged inside a jail cell rather than a boxing ring, reminding us just how fragile are our anointed champions. We may have wagged our fingers, but still, we couldn't turn away. Scandal fed the public's appetite for controversy and the media's rush to cover it. The decade witnessed everything from President Clinton versus Monica Lewinsky to Nancy Kerrigan versus Tonya Harding (see page 257).

In the process, television's reach expanded exponentially. Along with 24-hour general news, sports, weather, and entertainment, cable TV carved such niches as The Golf Channel, SpeedVision, and Court TV. The networks fought tooth and nail for the chance to shell out obscene amounts of money for the broadcast rights to sporting events, regardless of the fact that viewership numbers kept dropping. To pay those bills, and the sports announcers' gigantic salaries, they sold sponsorships to kickoffs, halftime shows, pitching changes, and anything else that could feature a corporate logo.

While cynicism, shame, and greed ran rampant throughout the 1990s, sports fans did have plenty to honestly cheer about. Among the highlights: Bonnie Blair's five Olympic gold medals in speed skating, Cal Ripken Jr.'s streak of consecutive baseball games played, Greg LeMond's three-peat in the Tour de France bicycle race, John Elway's back-to-back Super Bowl wins, Christian Laettner's miraculous basketball shot on the way to the college championship, Dale Earnhardt's first Daytona 500 victory, the New York Rangers' Stanley Cup win to snap a 53-year drought, sprinter Michael Johnson's unprecedented Olympic double, Tiger Woods' obliteration of the Augusta golf course, and Mark McGwire's 70th home run.

Sports and society connected in other ways in the decade. Though American society as a whole had come a long way in addressing racial inequities by 1990, lingering issues gained attention via the sports world. Shoal Creek Country Club's admission of its first African-American

Eye of the Tiger *Tiger Woods eyes a chip during his unprecedented third consecutive United States Amateur championship in 1996. Woods soon took the men's pro golf tour by storm, too.*

member that year—only under extreme pressure—and the fuss over Woods' arrival on the pro golf scene in 1996 only magnified how much the game of golf remained starkly white. On the other hand, just as the O.J. Simpson trial exposed a rift between blacks and whites, baseball's celebration of the 50th anniversary of Jackie Robinson's major league debut provided some healing.

Women overwhelmingly proved their place in sports during the 1990s. Increased opportunities and funding for women's high school and college sports programs, federally mandated by Title IX in 1975, reaped rewards with Olympic championships in soccer, volleyball, and softball. The U.S. soccer team won two of the first three World Cups for women, including a thrilling tournament on American turf in 1999. And women's basketball hit the big time, exemplified by outstanding college teams at the University of Connecticut and the University of Tennessee, where individuals such as Rebecca Lobo and Chamique Holdsclaw gained superstar status. Women literally "got game" when the NBA spun off the Women's National Basketball Association in 1997.

As the country headed into the uncharted waters of the 21st century, it could turn, as past generations always have, to sports and athletes for inspiration. "The spirit, the will to win, and the will to excel are the things that endure," said Vince Lombardi, the late, great football coach and motivator. "These qualities are so much more important than the events that occur."

That indomitable spirit came shining through when one-handed baseball

Women Go Pro *The continuing rise of women in sports was signaled with the debut of the Women's National Basketball Association in 1997. Cheryl Cooper of the Houston Comets was one of several players who gained national stardom.*

pitcher Jim Abbott threw a no-hitter, when speed skater Dan Jansen picked himself up until he won a gold medal, and when cancer survivor Lance Armstrong captured cycling's grueling Tour de France. Their courage and perseverance gave everyone hope that greatness can still be achieved.

1990

Bo Knows Rose Bowl Woes

The University of Southern California (USC) Trojans spoiled the final game of longtime University of Michigan Wolverines coach Glenn "Bo" Schembechler's (1929–2006) career with a 17–10 victory in the Rose Bowl on January 1 in Pasadena, California.

Schembechler coached for 27 seasons at the University of Miami in Ohio (from 1963 to 1968) and at Michigan (1969 to 1989). He compiled a stellar overall record of 234–65–8 and led his teams to 15 conference championships, including 13 Big Ten crowns while at Michigan. But if he had one blip on his résumé, it was a 5–12 record in bowl games, including a 2–8 mark in the Rose Bowl.

Michigan believed it could send Schembechler out on a high note, though, when it took a 10–1 team into Pasadena to face the 8–2–1 Trojans, the champions of the Pacific-10 Conference.

This USC squad featured rookie sensation quarterback Todd Marinovich. His 22-of-31 passing performance, coupled with Pasadena-born running back Ricky Ervins' 126 rushing yards, eventually overcame a valiant Michigan effort.

With 12 minutes remaining in the game, the score was tied at 10–10. Michigan's defense had held USC to 27 third-quarter yards, and now the offense had the ball on its own 46-yard line, with momentum seemingly on Schembechler's side. There was a growing sense among the sold-out crowd of 103,450 that the Wolverines might soon be carrying their coach off the field on their victorious shoulders and into a glorious sunset.

Just like that, though, a holding penalty on a fake punt play nullified a would-be first down for the Wolverines. Michigan was forced to punt—for real. The Trojans chewed up yardage and the clock on their next possession. They marched 75 yards in 13 plays, culminated with a 14-yard, game-winning touchdown run by Ervins with 1:10 left.

Even in his eighth Rose Bowl defeat, Schembechler made the final walk off the football field with his head held high. The Wolverines had their first 10-win season since 1986 and earned their second consecutive outright Big Ten championship. After 21 seasons in Ann Arbor, Schembechler retired as the winningest coach in Michigan football history, with a 194–48–5 record. He went out a winner.

Buster Who? *Mike Tyson (on the mat) was invincible until he ran into the relatively unknown Buster Douglas.*

The Fall of Tyson, Part I

Few people outside the boxing world had ever heard of James "Buster" Douglas (b.1960) before February 11. And even those familiar with the sport didn't give the 6-foot-4, 230-pound fighter much of a chance against heavyweight cham-pion Mike Tyson (b.1966). After all, the ferocious "Iron Mike" was undefeated in 37 bouts, winning 33 by knockouts. His opponents were lucky to last beyond the first round. So when Douglas stepped into the ring that night in Tokyo, Japan, it was no surprise that he was a 42–1 underdog. The surprise came a bit later.

Media Milestones

✔ On January 31, *The National Sports Daily*, America's first all-sports newspaper, made its debut in New York, Chicago, and Los Angeles. Edited by Frank Deford, it folded in 18 months.

✔ NBC did not stand for Notre Dame Broadcasting Company, even though the network signed a five-year, $30-million deal to broadcast 30 University of Notre Dame home football games from 1991 to 1995.

✔ In March, CBS renewed its NFL contract, paying more than $1 billion to telecast National Football Conference (NFC) games for four more years, as well as the 1992 Super Bowl. A day later, NBC paid $752 million for four more years of American Football Conference (AFC) games and the 1993 Super Bowl.

✔ On April Fool's Day, CBS fired broadcaster Brent Musburger after 15 years with the network, but did allow him to broadcast the National Collegiate Athletic Association (NCAA) men's basketball championship game the next day. A month later, he signed a six-year deal with ABC Sports.

✔ Al Michaels became the highest-paid television sportscaster by signing a five-year contract with ABC for $2.5 million a year.

✔ In October, the longtime radio play-by-play broadcaster for professional basketball's Boston Celtics, Johnny Most, retired at the age of 67.

Early on, it became apparent that this fight would not be another typical Tyson demolition job. The much bigger Douglas used his incredible 13-inch reach advantage and lightning jab effectively to stun the 5-foot-11 Tyson. A punishing right wobbled Iron Mike in the fifth round and raised a welt over his left eye. The champ grew increasingly frustrated. Still, he battled back, and late in the eighth round he caught Douglas with a vicious uppercut that dropped the challenger to the canvas. Douglas barely recovered, rising at the count of nine.

The 10th round will go down in history as one of boxing's most memorable. With a relentless combination of punches, Douglas sent Tyson tumbling down. The champ stumbled to his feet, but was clearly dazed. The referee stopped the fight and declared Douglas the winner and new champion. Boxing commentator Larry Merchant said afterward, "The Japanese people came to see Godzilla, only the wrong person turned out to be Godzilla." It remains one of the greatest upsets in sports history—even more so considering that Douglas' unexpected reign ended just eight and a half months later, when he lost his only title defense to Evander Holyfield.

Terrific Twins of Lacrosse

The Gait brothers—identical twins Gary and Paul (b.1967)—carried the undefeated Syracuse University men's lacrosse team to its third consecutive NCAA championship with a 21–9 victory over Loyola (Maryland) on May 28. (The title later was vacated because of NCAA rules violations.)

The tandem talents of the Gait twins, seniors on the Orange lacrosse squad, produced one of the most dynamic duos in collegiate sports history. In that lopsided championship contest—both the goal total and margin of victory set NCAA finals records—they scored eight goals and finished their four-year careers with a combined 319 goals and 146 assists. In the three games Syracuse played in the 1990 postseason, Gary's nine goals established the record for the most ever scored in the NCAA tournament. He also owns another NCAA record for the most goals scored in a single game (nine), in a May 1988 shellacking of Navy.

The Gaits' stick handling, passing, shooting, and overall athleticism dazzled fans and befuddled opponents with moves that had never been seen before. In one, a lacrosse version of basketball's alley-oop play, Paul would lob a high pass to Gary as he streaked across the front of the goal. Gary cradled the ball above his head, and while still airborne and with his back to the mouth of the goal, he would bring his stick down and whip the ball between his legs and into the net.

More spectacular was Gary's jaw-dropping "Air Gait" play, first witnessed during an NCAA championship semifinal match in 1988 against the University of Pennsylvania. Cradling the ball behind the Penn goal and just outside the protective crease, Gary leapt toward the front of the net. He flew over the goal, angled his stick in front of it, and, using the crossbar as a fulcrum, jammed the ball into the net—the equivalent of lacrosse's first slam dunk. (This move is no longer legal.)

Invented centuries ago by Native Americans, lacrosse has a storied history at Syracuse. Jim Brown (b.1936), who played football at Syracuse and later for the Cleveland Browns, also starred on the university's lacrosse team (as well as its track and basketball teams) in the mid-1950s. He is still regarded as one of the best collegiate lacrosse players ever. Since 1971, when the NCAA added lacrosse to its roster of sanctioned sports, Syracuse has won eight championships. A true

dynasty, the Orangemen advanced to the final game every year from 1983 to 2002.

The brothers Gait went on to record-setting careers in professional lacrosse, and remain instrumental in promoting the sport in youth and high school programs.

In the same induction class (of course!) in 2005, both brothers were enshrined in the United States Lacrosse National Hall of Fame.

The Bad Boys Are Good

The Detroit Pistons had finally reached the NBA mountaintop in 1989, winning a championship for the first time in the franchise's 41-year history. Yet critics wondered if their four-game sweep of the Los Angeles Lakers in the best-of-seven-games NBA Finals had more to do with hamstring injuries to L.A.'s Earvin "Magic" Johnson (b.1959) and Byron Scott than a truly outstanding Pistons team. Were they merely a one-year wonder?

The Pistons silenced the critics with a hard-fought defense of their championship in June, beating the Portland Trail Blazers, four games to one. In the process, Detroit joined the Lakers and Boston Celtics as the only teams in NBA history to win consecutive titles.

The 1989–1990 Pistons reflected the tough, hard-working personality of the Motor City. Head coach Chuck Daly (1930–2009) preached defense, and his players heeded his words well—sometimes too well, other teams charged. With an aggressive, hard-fouling, in-your-face style, they became known as the NBA's Bad Boys.

1990

Call them what you will, the Pistons had the league's stingiest defense, holding opponents to 98.3 points per game and a .447 shooting percentage.

Daly made up for the off-season loss of power forward and chief enforcer Rick Mahorn to the expansion Minnesota Timberwolves by moving James Edwards and Dennis Rodman (b.1961) into the starting rotation opposite bruising center Bill Laimbeer. All-star point guard Isiah Thomas (b.1961), Joe Dumars, and

Vinnie "the Microwave" Johnson propelled a lethal outside shooting game. Detroit finished the season with an Eastern Conference-best record of 59–23, highlighted by a 25–1 streak running from January to March.

The Trail Blazers pulled into suburban Detroit's Palace of Auburn Hills for game one of the finals with an identical won-lost record. Led by high-flying scoring machine Clyde Drexler (averaging 23.3 points per game, point guard Terry Porter, and power forward Buck Williams, Portland wasn't about to roll over for the Bad Boys. In fact, their intensity on both ends of the court caught the Pistons by surprise for three quarters, and the Trailblazers led, 90–80, with seven minutes left in the game.

That's the point at which Thomas took over. His offensive outburst, featuring a seven-point barrage, inspired the defense, which made huge stops and forced turnovers. A pair of Thomas three-point baskets sparked a come-from-behind, 105–99 victory.

Game two in Detroit turned into another tight affair. Despite an inspired second-half effort by Laimbeer—he scored 19 points in the last 17 minutes—the game went into overtime. With four seconds left in overtime, Laimbeer hit the last of his six three-pointers, tying an NBA Finals record, to put the Pistons up by one. But Drexler was fouled by Rodman with two seconds remaining and coolly swished both free throws. The Trailblazers escaped with a 106–105 win, taking away Detroit's home-court advantage and sending the series to Portland's Memorial Coliseum for the next three games.

Point Man *Point guard Isiah Thomas (left) was the man who made the Pistons go. He earned MVP honors in Detroit's five-game victory over Portland in the NBA Finals.*

The Pistons hadn't won a game at the Portland Coliseum in 17 years, and they were without the services of NBA Defensive Player of the Year Rodman, who was out with an ankle injury. Those obstacles didn't seem to matter as Detroit's offense caught fire. No one was hotter than Dumars, who scored 33 points. The Microwave sizzled with 21 points, and the home team got smoked, 121–106.

Both teams ran hot and cold in game four. Portland raced to a 32–22 first-quarter lead, but scored only 14 points in the second period and was down 51–46 at the half. Thomas poured in 22 points in the third period, then the Trailblazers countered with a 28–11 run to take a 93–92 lead with 5:20 left in the game. A see-saw battle ensued down the stretch, until the Pistons were up by three points with 1.8 seconds on the clock. A 35-foot shot by Portland's Danny Young went in, but the referees concluded that time had run out before he took the shot.

Portland, trying to become the first NBA team to come back from a 3–1 deficit in the finals, led by eight points with 10 minutes to play in game five. Johnson heated up again, however, scoring 16 points and lifting Detroit to a 90–90 tie in the final seconds. To cap off his scintillating performance, the Microwave sank a 15-footer with 0:00.7 showing on the clock. Portland's goose was officially cooked. The Pistons won, 92–90.

Despite his teammates' heroics, Thomas received the series' Most Valuable Player trophy. Along with sinking 11 of 16 shots from three-point range, he averaged 27.6 points, eight assists, and 5.2 rebounds in the five games.

Like Father, Like Son

Young Ken Griffey Jr. grew up hanging around Riverfront Stadium in Cincinnati, watching the "Big Red Machine" of the Cincinnati Reds dominate baseball for much of the 1970s.

Griffey's dad, Ken Griffey Sr. was a key player on those Reds teams. An outfielder, he was a three-time All-Star who batted a career-best .336 for the Reds' 1976 champs.

Griffey Jr. idolized his dad, and dreamed of becoming a big-leaguer himself, but at six years old in 1975, he never could have foreseen playing in the same outfield with him.

In 1989, though, the younger Griffey made it to the Majors at age 19 with the Seattle Mariners, the team that selected him with the top overall pick of the 1987 amateur draft. In 1990, the elder Griffey signed with Seattle as a free agent on August 29. Two days later, the Griffeys became the first father-and-son combination ever to take the field together when they were in the Mariners' outfield against the Kansas City Royals.

Two weeks later, the elder Griffey homered in the first inning off starter Kirk McCaskill of the Angels. After greeting his dad at home plate, the younger Griffey stepped into the batter's box and hit a home run himself.

1990

Course of a Different Color

Slavery ended in the United States in 1862, yet it took more than 100 years for Congress to pass the Civil Rights Act of 1964, outlawing discrimination based on race, color, religion, or national origin.

It took another 26 years for Shoal Creek Country Club in Birmingham, Alabama, to grant membership to an African American. And that came about only after Shoal Creek's policy of no black members was exposed shortly before the club was set to host the Professional Golfers' Association (PGA) 1990 Championship. The policy sparked a nationwide controversy and forced the change.

Birmingham had been the center of racial upheaval in 1963, when police attacked civil rights demonstrators with dogs and fire hoses. And while race relations in the United States had greatly improved by 1990 in many areas—including education, employment, and business opportunities—private golf clubs throughout the country remained largely whites-only bastions. Many didn't permit women, Jews, Hispanics, or other minorities to join, either. Such exclusionary rules were seldom challenged or even publicized—until Shoal Creek.

In late June, two months before the PGA Championship, the *Birmingham Post-Herald* ran a story about Shoal Creek. Quoted in the article, its founder, Hall Thompson, stated flatly, "This country club is our home and we pick and choose whom we want. . . . I think we've said that we don't discriminate in every other area except the blacks." Thompson apologized later for his remarks, but he didn't retract them.

Overnight, outrage and protest erupted. The word quickly spread, too, that Shoal Creek was hardly alone. Of the 39 PGA Tour events in 1990, at least 17 had been or were to be held at clubs with no black members, the *Charlotte Observer* reported. The United States Golf Association (USGA), which runs the U.S. Open, had scheduled four of the next five Opens at all-white clubs. Suddenly, the golf establishment's dirty laundry was hung out for all to see.

Protests demanding that the PGA move the tournament to another site went unheeded at first, as did calls for Shoal Creek to drop its racist policy. There was only one black professional golfer on the Tour then, so there wasn't much dissent from the players' ranks. That all changed, however, when IBM, Toyota, Sharp Electronics, and other advertisers threatened to pull out of the PGA Championship broadcast on ABC and ESPN. Before long, Shoal Creek admitted its first black member, and the PGA Tour announced that it would no longer hold tournaments at clubs that discriminate. Similar standards were soon adopted by the USGA and the Ladies Professional Golf Association (LPGA).

The actual tournament in August, nearly a footnote amid the turmoil, eventually was won by Wayne Grady. The Australian shot a four-round total of 282 and edged American Fred Couples by three strokes; Couples bogeyed (shot one over par) four straight holes on the last nine holes of the course to see his championship hopes slip away.

Other Milestones of 1990

✔ Super Bowl XXIV on January 28 was a super blow-out, as the San Francisco 49ers corralled the Denver Broncos 55–10. The 49ers set a host of records in the game, including most points and largest margin of victory. Quarterback Joe Montana passed for a record five touchdowns (since broken by San Francisco's Steve Young) and became the first, and still only, player to be named the Super Bowl's Most Valuable Player three times.

✔ Major League Baseball owners locked out players from spring training for 32 days in March and April, delaying the start of the regular season by one week.

✔ Loyola Marymount University's All-America basketball forward Hank Gathers died of heart failure after collapsing on the court during a West Coast Conference tournament game on March 7.

✔ In her professional debut in March, 13-year-old Jennifer Capriati reached the finals of the Virginia Slims tennis tournament.

✔ The University of Wisconsin's Suzy Favor won the 800-meter and 1,500-meter races at the NCAA Track and Field Championships in March, giving her nine individual titles and making her the winningest athlete in NCAA history.

✔ In the most lopsided victory ever in an NCAA men's basketball championship game, the University of Nevada-Las Vegas whipped Duke University on April 2, 103–73.

✔ Oakland A's outfielder Jose Canseco signed a new contract that made him the first baseball player to earn more than $5 million a year.

✔ On June 10, 16-year-old Monica Seles became the youngest player ever to win tennis' French Open. It was the first of her nine career Grand Slam singles titles.

✔ On July 24, baseball's all-time hits leader, Pete Rose, was sentenced to federal prison for five months and fined $50,000 for income tax evasion.

Little Leaguers of the Far East

Baseball may be America's pastime, but don't tell that to Little Leaguers in Taiwan. In Williamsport, Pennsylvania, where the sport's truly world series is played annually among teams from around the globe, the 1990 Little League Championship was won by Taiwan, which shut out the team from Shippensburg, Pennsylvania, 9–0, in the August final.

The win was no fluke, either. Taiwan obliterated its three opponents in the tournament by a combined tally of 43–1. The championship was Taiwan's 14th in the last 22 years. "The game of baseball is very beautiful," said manager Wang Tzyy-Tsann. "You can play it to perfection if you pay attention to the fundamentals."

1991

Wide Right

Super Bowl XXV will forever be summed up by two words: wide right. But depending on whether you're a fan of the New York Giants or the Buffalo Bills, they're famous or infamous. Hearing them will make you either stand up and cheer or break down and cry.

On January 27, with eight seconds left in the closest Super Bowl ever played, the Giants led, 20–19. Bills kicker Scott Norwood, with the ball on New York's 47-yard line, trotted onto the field to attempt a game-winning field goal. Adam Lingner snapped the ball and holder Frank Reich placed it cleanly on the grass. Norwood ran up to it, swung his right leg, and the ball sailed toward the goal posts. As players on both sidelines watched (or couldn't) and prayed (that God really does take sides in sports events), the ball strayed to the right. It wound up wide by several feet. The game was over; the Giants had won. The thrill of victory, the agony of defeat.

This agony-and-ecstasy ending was only fitting, considering the stark contrast between the Giants and the Bills when they arrived at Tampa Stadium in Tampa, Florida, on what was already unlike any previous Super Sunday. The United States was at war with Iraq (see the box on this page), and security at the stadium was extraordinary. So was the outpouring of patriotism among the 73,813 in attendance: American flags waving, chants of "U-S-A" reverberating, fighter jets overhead flying, Whitney Houston's inspiring rendition of the national anthem.

The Giants advanced to the NFL championship game on the strength of their defense, which was the best in the league during the regular season. It would need to be near perfect to counter the NFL's highest-scoring offense, the Bills. New York had given up a total of

The Persian Gulf War

On January 16, Operation Desert Storm went into action in the Middle East. Responding to the surprise invasion of Kuwait by neighboring Iraq and its dictator, Saddam Hussein, on August 2, 1990, an American-led coalition of nations launched a massive air attack aimed at destroying Iraq's military. On February 24, the coalition's ground forces entered Kuwait and southern Iraq. After four intense days of fighting, Iraq was defeated and Kuwait was liberated. There had been some talk of canceling the Super Bowl, but the NFL decided the game should go on.

Near Miss *Buffalo Bills kicker Scott Norwood launches a 47-yard field-goal try in the final seconds of Super Bowl XXV. The kick was just a bit wide to the right, and the New York Giants hung on to win the game 20–19.*

just 16 points in its two National Football Conference (NFC) playoff wins, over the Chicago Bears (31–3) and the San Francisco 49ers (15–13); Buffalo had racked up 95 points in beating the Miami Dolphins (44–34) and the Los Angeles Raiders (51–3) for the American Football Conference (AFC) title.

The Giants' game plan hinged on keeping Bills quarterback Jim Kelly (b.1960) and his no-huddle, quick-strike offense off the field for as long as possible. While its defense had to execute flawlessly, the key really was New York's ball-control offense. That meant efficient drives that took a lot of time—combining short passes from quarterback Jeff Hostetler (pressed into service six weeks earlier when starting quarterback Phil Simms injured his shoulder) and a huge effort from running back Otis Anderson.

The Giants maintained possession of the football for a Super Bowl-record 40 minutes, 33 seconds—more than two-thirds of the 60-minute game. Hostetler completed 20 of 32 passes, and Anderson rushed for 102 yards to earn the Most Valuable Player (MVP) award.

1991

Coach K Gets Big W

After falling short of a national championship in three consecutive trips to the NCAA Final Four, the Duke University Blue Devils men's basketball team beat the University of Kansas Jayhawks 72–65 at Indianapolis on April 1. It was the first national title for Duke and for its successful coach Mike Krzyzewski (b.1947), or Coach K, as he is known (because his name is difficult to say; it is actually pronounced sheh-SHEFFS-key).

When his team took the floor against the Kansas Jayhawks (22–7) in the final game, Coach K wondered if they would have enough energy after an emotional win two nights earlier against defending national-champion Nevada-Las Vegas (UNLV) in the semifinal game. The previous season, UNLV had dispatched the Blue Devils 103–73 in the most lopsided title game ever. In this year's tournament, though, Duke exacted revenge with a thrilling, 79–77 victory. UNLV had entered the game undefeated, ranked No. 1 in the country, and favored to win another title.

The Blue Devils quickly dispelled any doubts, shooting a torrid 59 percent in the first half to take a 42–34 lead at halftime. Hurley and Laettner again propelled the team, with a huge boost off the bench from guard Bill McCaffrey, who scored 16 points.

Kansas, meanwhile, shot inconsistently. Despite a valiant effort in the game's closing minutes, when Duke started to wear down, the Jayhawks couldn't get closer than five points. Duke was crowned national champions, and Coach K won the biggest game of all.

Bittersweet Cup Win

The Pittsburgh Penguins of the National Hockey League (NHL) ended 23 years of frustration by winning the team's first Stanley Cup on May 25 at the Met Center in Bloomington, Minnesota. The Penguins trounced the Minnesota North Stars, 8–0, to capture the Cup in game six of the best-of-seven finals. Pittsburgh superstar Mario Lemieux (b.1965), who had missed the first 50 games of the 80-game regular season due to a back injury, was the MVP of the playoffs.

Lemieux had five goals and seven assists in the finals, despite sitting out game three with back spasms. Since being drafted by the Penguins in 1984, Lemieux had earned the nickname Super Mario by winning two NHL scoring titles and the league's MVP honors in 1988.

As it goes in team sports, though, even the greatest players need support. The Penguins finally surrounded Lemieux with the right mix of talent for the 1990–1991 season, including rookie Jaromir Jagr, Mark Recchi, Paul Coffey, and goaltender Tom Barasso. Then they brought in coach Bob Johnson, who was executive director of USA Hockey and had led the University of Wisconsin to three NCAA hockey titles, to run the team.

Unfortunately, "Badger," as the coach was affectionately known, couldn't be around to help the Penguins defend their long-awaited Stanley Cup championship. In August, the Penguins' beloved coach was diagnosed with brain cancer. On November 26, six months before his team's triumph, he died.

The Bulls Run with Jordan

Michael Jordan (b.1963) had clearly achieved superstardom in the NBA well before the 1990–1991 season. He reigned supreme as the league's leading scorer all four previous seasons, and earned his first MVP award the year before. Yet as high as Jordan soared, there were always doubts and whispers. Could he lead the Chicago Bulls to an NBA championship?

Resounding cheers drowned out the whispers on June 12 when the Bulls claimed the team's very first NBA title by defeating the Los Angeles Lakers, 108–101, at the Great Western Forum in Los Angeles. Chicago lost the first game in the best-of-seven finals at home, then took four straight. Jordan, who averaged 31.2 points, 11.4 assists, and 6.6 rebounds per game for the series, was named the MVP—to go along with another regular-season scoring title and MVP trophy.

The finals included a marquee matchup between Jordan and the Lakers' Earvin "Magic" Johnson, owner of five championship rings. Neither of the two superstars disappointed.

While Jordan performed his MVP feats, Johnson tried to carry the Lakers on his back. The 6-foot-9 point guard posted the 29th and 30th triple-doubles (double figures in scoring, rebounds, and assists) of his career, set a five-game finals record with 62 assists, and averaged 18.6 points and 8 rebounds per game.

Beyond their individual heroics, teamwork made the difference. Scottie Pippen (b.1965), Horace Grant, Bill Cartwright, B.J. Armstrong, and John Paxson

Super Mario *Pittsburgh Penguins star Mario Lemieux holds the Stanley Cup aloft after leading his team to the first National Hockey League championship in franchise history.*

provided the complements to Jordan's aerobatics that had been lacking when the Bulls lost the Eastern Conference Championship the previous two seasons. James Worthy, Byron Scott, A.C. Green, and other aging Lakers, meanwhile, couldn't muster the wizardry that had sparked the Lakers' five NBA titles during the 1980s.

The torch had officially been passed. "I'm not even thinking about any other championships right now," Jordan said during the Bulls' victory celebration. "I just want to enjoy this one for as long as I can."

1991

It's a Bird, It's a Plane . . .

It's Mike Powell (b.1963), soaring to an incredible world record of 29 feet, 4 1/2 inches in the long jump on August 30. By two inches, Powell broke the 23-year-old mark set by Bob Beamon at the 1968 Summer Olympics in Mexico City—a record many track-and-field experts considered unbeatable.

When Powell jogged into a hot and muggy National Stadium in Tokyo for the 1991 World Championships of Track and Field, few expected him to leap into the history books—except Powell, who, for metric-minded Japanese fans, had prophetically signed autographs with "8.95?"—that's meters, and 8.95 meters converts to 29 feet, 4 1/2 inches.

Yet before Powell entertained any thoughts of breaking Beamon's venerable record, he first had to contend with the here and now: the great Carl Lewis (b.1961). Lewis was not only the fastest man in the world (he set a world record in the 100-meter sprint at the same meet on August 25), but also the owner of back-to-back Olympic gold medals in the long jump at the 1984 and 1988 Games. Indeed, he was undefeated over a 10-year, 65-meet stretch. Powell, the Olympic silver medalist in 1988, hadn't beaten Lewis in 15 tries.

This all must have weighed heavily on Powell's mind, because the first four of his six jumps were relatively short compared to Lewis' efforts; three of Lewis' jumps were at least 29 feet (though he was aided by a wind at his back, so the jumps did not count for the record books). But on Powell's fifth jump, he summoned up every ounce of talent, frustration, and determination—and made the jump of his life.

Even as the crowd cheered the incredible eclipse of Beamon's record, Powell stood nervously awaiting Lewis' final jump of the competition. When it came up well short, the world officially had its new long jump superman.

Worst-to-First Double Play

The Minnesota Twins beat the visiting Atlanta Braves 1–0 in 10 innings in Game Seven on October 27 to cap one of the most exciting World Series ever.

Although the Twins were the champions, both teams were winners in a season in which they each executed remarkable turnarounds. Both teams had finished dead last in their respective divisions in 1990. And while hope springs eternal at the start of every baseball season, neither team could have anticipated their historic reversal of fortunes in 1991. There they stood, nonetheless, at the end of the 162-game regular season, alive and well in first place—the Twins atop the American League's West Division, the Braves kings of the National League's Western Division. Never before had any major league team gone from worst to first in consecutive seasons, and now two had done it in the same year.

The two teams then survived their league championship series and squared off in October in one of the most closely contested and entertaining World Series of all time. Four games were decided on the final pitch. Three went into extra innings. Five were decided by a single run.

Rickey Steals the Show

"Mayday" is the international call for help. Many baseball pitchers must have felt like shouting it whenever they saw Rickey Henderson lurking on first base. So it was only appropriate that on May 1—May Day around the world—Henderson became Major League Baseball's all-time stolen base leader, stealing base number 939 for his Oakland A's against the New York Yankees to break Lou Brock's record in a game at the Oakland-Alameda County Coliseum in California.

Born on Christmas Day in 1958 in Chicago, the gifted Henderson lent his unique package of baseball skills to eight different major league teams over a high-speed career that spanned 25 years through 2003. That included four stints with the Oakland Athletics, with whom he moved up from the minor leagues as a 21-year-old rookie in 1979.

Rickey Henderson

Henderson quickly established himself as a complete, five-tool player: He hit for a high average and with home run power, fielded and threw the ball exceptionally well, and was a demon on the base paths. "He's the best lead-off hitter of all time, no question," former Yankees shortstop Tony Kubek told *The Sporting News* in 1986.

The key for the first batter in the lineup is to get on base, and Henderson mastered the art. A .279 lifetime hitter, he had 3,055 career hits. And he was just as happy to draw a walk. He did whatever it took to get on base, as his .401 career on-base percentage testifies.

But it was on base that he was most dangerous. The 10-time All-Star led the American League in stolen bases 12 times, most dramatically in 1982 when he set the single-season record with 130 steals. More than any other major leaguer, he eventually wound up crossing home plate: Henderson holds the record for runs scored, at 2,295. At age 44 in 2003, he played 30 games for the Los Angeles Dodgers. He finished the season at 1,406 career stolen bases. In 2009, he was inducted into the Baseball Hall of Fame.

1991

The finale pitted Atlanta's 24-year-old John Smoltz against 36-year-old veteran Jack Morris, both pitching on just three days' rest. They each came out strong, throwing shutouts into the eighth inning. It looked like the Braves would score in the top half of the eighth inning, when Terry Pendleton smacked a ball into the gap in left-center field with Lonnie Smith on first base and no outs. But Smith hesitated coming around second base and had to hold up at third. The crafty Morris then pitched his way out of the inning.

The game remained scoreless after nine innings, and Morris kept on pitching—holding Atlanta scoreless in the top of the 10th inning. In the bottom of the inning, with one out and the bases loaded, Minnesota's Gene Larkin hit a fly ball over the shallow-playing outfielders, scoring Dan Gladden to win the game—and the World Series.

Morris, who won two of his three starts, was voted MVP of the series. In the end, the worst part was that one team had to lose.

Magic Retires

For many years, activists had raised awareness of the disease commonly known as AIDS (acquired immunodeficiency syndrome), although public per-

---

Other Milestones of 1991

✔ American women skaters swept the World Figure Skating Championships in Munich, Germany, on March 16. Kristi Yamaguchi won the gold medal, Tonya Harding won the silver, and Nancy Kerrigan won the bronze. It was the first of four world championships that Yamaguchi would win in her distinguished career on the ice.

✔ On July 28, the Montreal Expos' Dennis Martinez became the 14th big-league pitcher ever to toss a perfect game: 27 batters up and 27 batters down. Martinez shut down the Dodgers 2–0 in Los Angeles.

✔ On the same day that Rickey Henderson set his stolen base record, May 1, 44-year-old Nolan Ryan pitched his seventh career no-hitter, as the Texas Rangers blanked the Toronto Blue Jays, 3–0, at Arlington Stadium in Arlington, Texas.

✔ Unknown rookie John Daly won the Professional Golfers Association Championship on August 11 at Crooked Stick Golf Club in Carmel, Indiana. As the ninth alternate, the 25-year-old Daly was a long shot even to make it into the field, but he sailed to a three-stroke victory. Daly would become one of the most well-known figures in golf in the next decade, though unfortunately often for his boorish behavior.

✔ On September 13, at the World Gymnastics Championships in Indianapolis, Kim Zmeskal, 15, became the first American in the history of the championships to win the women's all-around title.

✔ On December 14, University of Michigan receiver Desmond Howard was awarded the Heisman Trophy as college football's best player for 1991. He won with the largest margin of votes to that point.

ception remained that only certain segments of the population were at risk. That changed with a shocking announcement from Magic Johnson on November 7. The popular basketball star retired from the sport because he tested positive for HIV, the virus that causes AIDS.

The 31-year-old Johnson, who was still at the top of his game—he averaged 19.4 points, 7.0 rebounds, and 12.5 assists in his final full season in 1990–91—occasionally returned to the basketball court. Even in his retirement, fans voted him to the All-Star Game in the 1991–92 season, and he earned MVP honors in the West's 153–113 rout. He also played for the U.S. Olympic "Dream Team" in 1992, made an aborted comeback attempt in the 1992–93 preseason, coached the Los Angeles Lakers for part of the 1993–94 season, and played 32 games for the Lakers in 1995–96 before retiring for good.

You Goal, Girls!

Half a world away from home, in Tianhe Stadium in Guangzhou, China, the U.S. women's national soccer team scored two historic firsts on November 30. The team won the world's first women's World Cup Soccer Championship. They also became the first United States world champions in soccer since the game was introduced in America 128 years earlier.

The title came after a heart-stopping 2–1 triumph over Norway. With three minutes remaining and the game tied,

On Top of the World *Michelle Akers and the United States team won the first Women's World Cup in soccer.*

United States striker Michelle Akers kicked the decisive goal.

Akers (who scored the game's other goal too, giving her a team-high 10 goals in the six-game tournament) earned high praise from soccer legend Pelé, who led Brazil to three World Cup titles (1958, 1962, 1970). "I like her because she is intelligent, has presence of mind, and is often in the right position," he told reporters at the stadium. "She's fantastic."

1992

The Golden Girls

United States Olympians brought home a total of 11 medals from the Games of the XVI Winter Olympiad, held in Albertville, France, February 8 to 23. American women won nine of them, including all five of the United States' gold medals.

Leading the way was speed skater Bonnie Blair (b.1964) of Champaign, Illinois. The youngest in a family of five speed skating kids, she first laced up a pair of hand-me-down skates at the age of two and began competing when she was four.

At the 1988 Winter Olympics in Calgary, Alberta, she not only edged the defending East German champion in the 500-meter race—by two one-hundredths of a second—for the gold, but also set a world record. Blair won the event again in Albertville, by a more "comfortable" 18 one-hundredths of a second. Blair thus became the first U.S. woman to win a gold medal in two Olympics.

Four days later, with "Blair's Bunch" of 50 or so family and hometown friends, including her sponsors from the Champaign Police Department, cheering her on, she took the gold in the 1,000-meter race.

As did Blair growing up, many speed skaters start out racing in short-track competition, which was added to the Olympic slate of events in 1992. In short track, instead of racing in pairs against the clock, skaters race in a tight, bump-and-grind pack, usually four at a time—like roller derby on ice. The first to cross the finish line wins; elimination heats lead to semifinals and finals. In the finals, American Cathy Turner, who had taken an eight-year break from the sport from 1980 to 1988 to pursue a singing career, won the 500-meter race in a photo finish. With China's Li Yan ahead as they approached the finish line, Turner made a final kick and beat Li by four one-hundredths of a second, or about the length of a skate blade.

Kristi Yamaguchi (b.1971) laced up skates at Albertville, too, in the women's figure skating event. She arrived at the Games as one of two favorites, along with Japan's Midori Ito. The media hyped their contrasting styles: The more athletic Ito's repertoire featured explosive jumps; Yamaguchi was more polished and artistic. A former pairs skater who grew up clutching a Dorothy Hamill doll, Yamaguchi led after the first half of the

Good as Gold *American Kristi Yamaguchi overcame a fall in the freestyle program to win the women's figure skating competition at the Winter Olympic Games.*

competition, the short program, in which required moves are performed. Although she fell in the longer freestyle program, Ito did as well, and Yamaguchi skated away with the gold medal.

America's fifth golden girl, Donna Weinbrecht, won her medal on the snow, in a new Olympic sport: freestyle skiing. In the moguls event, competitors ski a run that is tightly packed with snow

1992

humps called moguls. Besides navigating the obstacle course cleanly, racers have to perform two airborne, or aerial, maneuvers. Weinbrecht grew up in New Jersey and taught herself the bumpy art of mogul skiing during the winter of 1985 in Vermont. At Albertville, racing in a snowstorm to the musical accompaniment of the Ramones' "Rock 'n' Roll High School," she narrowly beat Russian Yelizaveta Kozhevnikova for first place.

Duckpin History Rolls On

A Baltimore-born pastime slightly less well known than baseball celebrated a new icon in 1992. On May 5, Pete Signore Jr. of North Haven, Connecticut, set a new world duckpin record by rolling a 279.

Duckpin is a century-old form of bowling that originated at Diamond Alleys in Baltimore—which happened to be owned by Wilbert Robinson and John J. McGraw, both of whom played for baseball's Baltimore Orioles in the early 1900s (they went on to become Hall of Fame managers with the Brooklyn Dodgers and New York Giants, respectively). Duckpins are sawed-off versions of traditional bowling pins. When the owners saw the way the small pins flew wildly around the alley, one of them remarked that it looked liked a "flock of flying ducks."

Duckpin bowlers use smaller balls (between five and six inches in diameter, versus the standard 8.59-inch bowling ball) and are allowed to roll three balls per turn. Played only in a handful of states, including Maryland, Connecticut, Indiana, and Massachusetts, duckpin and its enthusiasts have yet to bowl the elusive perfect 300 game.

Better Laettner than Never

In what many college basketball observers called the greatest game ever played, on March 28 the Duke University Blue Devils squeaked past the University of Kentucky Wildcats in the East Regional final of the men's NCAA tournament, 103–102. The one-point difference came in the closing 2.1 seconds of double overtime at the Spectrum in Philadelphia, when Duke's Christian Laettner snatched a long in-bounds pass from Grant Hill and nailed a miraculous 17-foot shot. The win sent the Blue Devils back to the Final Four in Minneapolis, where they went on to become the first repeat national champions in 19 years by handily defeating the University of Michigan in the final game, 71–51.

Laettner's magic moment at the Spectrum capped a classic game from the tournament's two best teams. They combined to make a phenomenal 61 percent of their shots. Still, all the precision passing, deft dribbling, and sharp shooting boiled down to the last two nail-biting possessions. After the Wildcats' Sean Woods banked in an off-balance running shot for the lead with 2.5 seconds remaining, it looked as if coach Rick Pitino's Kentucky team would be heading for the finals. But Laettner had other ideas.

The Blue Devils' center had already registered a perfect offensive performance. He was nine for nine from the field and 10 for 10 from the free-throw line. He caught Hill's pass with his back to basket, dribbled once, spun around, stopped, and popped—swish!

Old Is New Again

On April 6, the Baltimore Orioles took baseball back to the future. Hosting the season's home opener, the team christened its new ballpark, Oriole Park at Camden Yards. Besides generating rave reviews and sold-out crowds, the stadium became the prototype for a new generation of "retro" venues around Major League Baseball. (For the record, the Orioles beat the Cleveland Indians 2–0 in that first game behind right-hander Rick Sutcliffe's five-hitter.)

Camden Yards, constructed on 85-acres at a cost of $110 million, has state-of-the-art scoreboards, grandstands, concessions, clubhouses, and other amenities. Yet it is designed in the style of charming, turn-of-the-20th-century, downtown ballparks that were integral centers of their communities. Steel, rather than concrete trusses, an arched brick facade, a sun roof over the sloped upper deck, an asymmetrical playing field, and a natural grass field are some of the nostalgic niceties.

Ebbets Field (Brooklyn Dodgers), Fenway Park (Boston Red Sox), Crosley Field (Cincinnati Reds), Wrigley Field (Chicago Cubs), and the Polo Grounds (New York Giants) were among the ballparks that served as powerful influences in the design of Oriole Park. Other retro parks that followed Camden Yards' lead over the next decade were Jacobs Field (Cleveland Indians), Comerica Park (Detroit Tigers), Safeco Field (Seattle Mariners), Minute Maid Park (Houston Astros), AT&T Park (San Francisco Giants), and Great American Ballpark (Reds).

Magic Moment *Earvin "Magic" Johnson celebrates the U.S. men's basketball team's gold medal at the Olympics. NBA players were allowed to compete in the Games for the first time (see page 242).*

Women in Hoops Hall

Two women who were ahead of their time on the hardwood—Nera White and Lucia Harris-Stewart—were inducted into the Naismith Memorial Basketball Hall of Fame on May 11.

White brought athleticism not often seen in the women's game in the 1950s and 1960s to her Nashville Business College (NBC) team and the United States

1992

National Team. She led NBC to 10 Amateur Athletic Union (AAU) national championships between 1955 and 1969, and was named the Outstanding Player of the tournament 10 times. In 1957–58, she helped the American team win the World Basketball Championship in Rio de Janeiro, Brazil, where she earned tournament MVP honors.

Harris-Stewart was the dominant center of her time (the mid-1970s). In her college career at Delta State, she averaged 25.9 points and 14.4 rebounds per game while helping the school win 109 of 115 games. Delta State won three consecutive Association for Intercollegiate Athletics for Women (AIAW) basketball titles beginning in 1975. Harris-Stewart also was

the leading scorer and rebounder for the United States team that earned a silver medal at the 1976 Olympics.

The Dream Team

Barcelona, Spain, hosted the 1992 Summer Games, July 24 to August 9, with 9,370 of the world's best athletes competing in 257 events. A total of 169 nations competed. They included South Africa, which had been banned since 1960 for its apartheid policy, but had finally abandoned its racist social structure. A single German team appeared for the first time since Word War II, following the tearing down of the Berlin Wall. And there was a Unified Team comprising several former republics of the Soviet Union, which had collapsed in 1991.

This was the last year both the Winter and Summer Olympic Games were held in the same year, as they had been since the modern Olympics began in 1896. After 1992, the games were switched to a staggered schedule. The next Winter Games were held just two years later, in Lillehammer, Norway, and thereafter every four years. The next Summer Games were held four years later in Atlanta, Georgia.

For the first time, the International Olympic Committee opened men's basketball to professional players instead of only amateurs. USA Basketball, the governing body for hoops in the United States, responded by forming the Dream Team. Coached by the Detroit Pistons' Chuck Daly and co-captained by Magic Johnson and Larry Bird (b.1956), the team also starred Charles Barkley (b.1963),

World's Greatest Female Athlete *American Jackie Joyner-Kersee left no doubt about it when she won the heptathlon at the Summer Olympic Games for the second consecutive time (see page 244).*

Dan and Dave and Dollars

Commercialism at the 1992 Olympics wasn't confined to basketball players. A couple of decathletes made financial headlines, too. Reebok International, a maker of sneakers and other sports apparel, signed Dan O'Brien (b.1966) and Dave Johnson to star in a $25 million advertising campaign, which humorously followed their rivalry to qualify for the U.S. Olympic Team. Dan was the reigning world champion in the 10-part, two-day decathlon; Dave held the record for the highest second-day score. One seemed destined to emerge as the world's greatest athlete.

At the qualifying meet for Olympics, however, Dan failed in the pole vault event and didn't make the team—thus suddenly canceling the Dan and Dave rivalry. Dave settled for the bronze medal in Barcelona, while Reebok was forced to revamp its ads. Undaunted, Dan set a new world record a month later at a meet in France.

Clyde Drexler, Patrick Ewing (b.1962), Michael Jordan, Karl Malone (b.1963), Chris Mullin, Scottie Pippen, David Robinson (b.1965), John Stockton (b.1962), and Duke University's Christian Laettner (see page 240).

The presence of Johnson, who had retired from the NBA the previous year after announcing that he was HIV-positive (see page 236), was a boost for people everywhere suffering from the dread disease. The fact that Johnson was still healthy and on his game, and that he still had legions of fans worldwide, did much to lift the sprits of those who had felt shunned and hopeless.

Arguably the greatest basketball team ever assembled, the Dream Team was criticized as being a grandiose display of pampered millionaires—a team that exemplified the big-business and mega-marketing elements that enveloped sports during the 1990s. (Coincidentally, NBA Commissioner David Stern was named 1992's most powerful man in sports in *The Sporting News'* annual top 100 listing.) The fact that the team elected to stay in a $900-a-night luxury hotel rather than the more modest Olympic Village with the rest of the world's athletes only fueled the fire. Four members of the team failed to show up for the Opening Ceremony. "It's very much like traveling with 12 rock stars," Daly remarked.

Wrote Tom Callahan of *U.S. News & World Report* in his post-Games analysis, "At the Olympic Games, where the truest dreamers have been swallowed up by a sensation, the Dream Team represents reality as much as anything else, although it also represents Reebok, Nike, and the United States. Commercialism and professionalism have attended the games for decades—for centuries, truth to tell—but never before have they carried the flag or the day, and the reality is a sensation."

To no one's surprise, the Dream Team dazzled. They went undefeated in eight basketball games, scored more than 100 points in every one, and averaged a record-setting 117.25 points per game. They never called a timeout. The average margin of victory was 43.75 points, and the closest contest was over Croatia, 117–85, for the gold medal.

1992

Jackie of All Trades

It's easy to see why Jackie Joyner-Kersee is considered by many to be the greatest female athlete ever. Just check out her trophy case. Hanging front and center are six Olympic medals, two of them golds won back to back at the 1988 and 1992 Summer Games in the grueling seven-event, two-day heptathlon, and another gold for the long jump in 1988. There are trophies, medals, and newspaper clippings from her days as an All-America basketball star at the University of California at Los Angeles (UCLA), and when she was a three-sport standout at her hometown high school in East St. Louis, Illinois. What makes Joyner-Kersee's accomplishments even

more impressive is that the multi-sport star has asthma.

Born on March 3, 1962, she was named after then President John F. Kennedy's wife, Jacqueline. "If you had asthma, they said you couldn't run or do some of the other things I was doing," said Joyner-Kersee, recalling when she was diagnosed with the disease at age 18. Undeterred, she went on to become the first lady of track and field in the United States, making her first Olympic team in 1984 and earning a silver medal in the heptathlon at the Los Angeles Games that year.

Joyner-Kersee (she married her UCLA track coach, Bob Kersee, in 1986) dominated the event for the next four years, winning all nine heptathlons she

Other Milestones of 1992

✔ On April 8, tennis star Arthur Ashe (1943–1993) revealed that since 1988 he had been HIV-positive and that he now had AIDS.

✔ The University of Arkansas won its ninth consecutive NCAA men's indoor track and field championship on May 14.

✔ In the NBA, the Chicago Bulls successfully defended their league championship from 1991 by beating the Portland Trailblazers in six games in the Finals. The two teams split the opening two games in Chicago, then the Bulls won two of three games in Portland. In the decisive Game Six in Chicago on June 14, the Bulls rallied for a 97–93 win. The Bulls' Michael Jordan was the Finals MVP.

✔ The NBA's Larry Bird retired on August 18. In 13 seasons, all with the Boston Celtics, he made 10 All-Star teams and won three MVP awards.

✔ On September 20, Philadelphia Phillies second baseman Mickey Morandini turned the first unassisted triple play in baseball's National League since May 30, 1927, in a 13-inning, 3–2 loss to the Pirates in Pittsburgh.

✔ The Toronto Blue Jays beat the Atlanta Braves in six games in the World Series. In the final game, on October 24 in Atlanta, Dave Winfield's two-out, two-run double in the 11th inning broke a 2–2 tie and propelled the Blue Jays to a 4–3 victory. It was the first World Series title for a Canada-based team.

entered. The first woman to break the 7,000-point mark, she set world records twice again before eclipsing them all, scoring 7,291 points at the 1988 Games in Seoul, South Korea. She finished her Olympic career at the 1996 Games in Atlanta, where she took the bronze in the long jump.

King Richard Abdicates

Long Live the King *As colorful as he was successful, Richard Petty retired from active NASCAR competition with a host of awards and a legion of fans.*

After a record 200 career race victories, including seven Daytona 500 wins, and seven season points championships (tied for another record), Richard Petty (b.1937) drove in his final NASCAR race at the Hooters 500 on November 15 at Atlanta Motor Speedway.

"The King," as stock car racing's most popular and successful driver had become known, was hanging up his crown (actually, a black cowboy hat, along with dark sunglasses) after a remarkable driving career that spanned 35 years. He finished 35th in his familiar No. 43 car at the Hooters 500 after getting tangled up in a fiery crash with Dick Trickle, Ken Schrader, and Darrell Waltrip. Still, the fans witnessed a great race. At the start, six drivers had a chance to earn enough points to win the season's Winston Cup Championship. It came down to Bill Elliott and Alan Kulwicki. Elliott won the race, but Kulwicki's second-place finish was enough to capture the season championship (determined by finishes in a year's worth of races).

The same day the King bade farewell, a young prince emerged. Finishing 31st in his first Winston Cup event was rookie Jeff Gordon (b.1971). Before the decade was out, Gordon captured three Cup titles and led the series in wins five consecutive years (1995–1999). NASCAR racing had found a new member of its "royal" family.

1993

The Reich Stuff

The Buffalo Bills engineered the largest comeback in NFL history when they overcame a 32-point, third-quarter deficit to beat the Houston Oilers 41–38 in overtime in an AFC Wild-Card Playoff Game (1992 season) at Rich Stadium in Buffalo on January 3.

What's more, the Bills, winners of the last two AFC championships, did it without starting quarterback Jim Kelly, who was injured. Backup quarterback Frank Reich engineered the comeback, though Reich was no stranger to big rallies: He's the guy who led the University of Maryland back from a 31–0 halftime deficit against the University of Miami in 1984 to a 42–40 victory—the greatest comeback in college football history.

Houston, which finished 10–6 during the regular season, and Buffalo, which was 11–5, had just squared off just a week earlier in the last game of the regular season, and the Oilers humiliated the Bills, 27–3. So by halftime in the playoff game, when the Oilers went comfortably into the locker room with a 28–3 lead, it looked like a repeat blowout. Instead, Houston simply blew it.

First, though, the Oilers actually increased their lead with an interception return for a touchdown in the opening moments of the third quarter. With the score 35–3, thousands of the hometown fans began streaming to the exits. They soon wish they had stayed.

Buffalo began its comeback with a 1-yard touchdown run by Kenneth Davis. After the Bills recovered an onside kick, Reich teamed with Don Beebe on a 38-yard touchdown pass. Suddenly, the score was 35–17 with half of the third quarter still remaining.

That was enough time for Reich and Andre Reed to hook up on a pair of touchdown passes to make it 35–31 going into the final period. And when Reed caught another touchdown pass from Reich in the fourth quarter to put the Bills ahead 38–35, their fans were as delirious as the Oilers were dazed. Houston tied the game in the closing moments of regulation time, but in overtime the Bills intercepted a Warren Moon (b.1956) pass, which set up Steve Christie's 32-yard, game-winning field goal.

It was all for naught, though, as the Bills lost their third straight Super Bowl later in January.

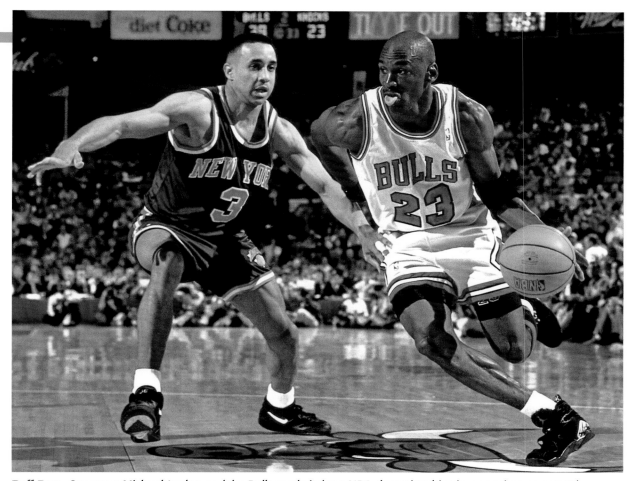

Bull Run *Superstar Michael Jordan and the Bulls made it three NBA championships in a row (see page 249).*

Timing Is Everything

On April 5 in the New Orleans Superdome, with 20 seconds remaining in the NCAA men's basketball tournament final and the University of North Carolina clinging to a 73–71 lead, All-America forward Chris Webber of the University of Michigan rebounded a missed free throw, dribbled down the court, and called for a time-out. Except the Michigan Wolverines were out of time-outs—and now out of luck. Michigan

was assessed a two-shot technical foul and Carolina went on to win, 77–71.

Webber's mistake not only effectively ended the game, but also the run of Michigan's fabled Fab Five. A year earlier, Webber headlined a quintet of highly touted freshman. He and Juwan Howard, Jalen Rose, Ray Jackson, and Jimmy King lived up to the hype and reached the 1992 finals, only to lose to a more experienced Duke University team. The preseason favorites in the 1992–93 college season, Michigan finished its regular schedule

King of the Court

Tennis star Arthur Ashe was just 49 when he died of AIDS on February 6, leaving behind a legacy of on-court achievement, civic contribution, and social justice.

Ashe was the first African American to win the men's singles title at the U.S. Open (in 1968) and at Wimbledon (1975), and he was the first to play in the Davis Cup (in 1963). In all, he won 33 career singles championships, including three Grand Slams, and 18 doubles titles. He compiled a stellar career singles record of 816–260 before suffering a heart attack in 1979 that eventually led to his retirement.

Ashe was much more than a great tennis player, however. Even before being diagnosed with AIDS—he contracted the virus that causes the disease from a blood transfusion—he fought for social causes such as ending South African apartheid (the official practice of racial segregation and discrimination). In his post-playing career, he championed issues such as heathcare, education, and AIDS awareness.

ranked third in the nation, with a 26–4 record and a number-one seed in the NCAA tournament.

It took a pair of overtime wins, against UCLA and the University of Kentucky, but the Fab Five advanced to the finals with UNC coach Dean Smith's (b.1931) 28–4 Tar Heels. It was Webber's final collegiate game. A month later he announced that he would enter the NBA draft. This time, his timing was right: He was the number-one pick.

Lady Jordan

"If Michael Jordan has a clone, it's Sheryl Swoopes." Those lofty words of praise were spoken on April 2 by Vanderbilt University women's basketball coach Jim Foster—and for good reason.

Swoopes had just blistered his top-ranked Commodores for 31 points in leading the Texas Tech Lady Red Raiders to a 60–46 victory in the semifinals of the 1993 NCAA women's Final Four.

In true Jordan-esque fashion, two nights later in the championship game against Ohio State, Swoopes scored more points than the entire Vanderbilt team, racking up 47 points in an 84–82 thriller. Swoopes tallied the most points that any player, male or female, ever managed in an NCAA final.

"When it was over, my first thought was, 'Is this real?'" she said in a post-game interview with the *Washington Post*. "At times, I get it in my mind that there is no way I can miss." Swoopes, a senior, became the second woman ever drafted by the all-male U.S. Basketball League.

Selected by the Daytona Beach Hooters, she opted to go to Europe, where she played 10 games in an Italian league. In 1997, Swoopes joined the Women's National Basketball Association's Houston Comets, where she continued her winning ways.

Jordan's Surprise

 In retrospect, the 1992–93 NBA season might have seemed routine to the guy who had to scale the rafters of Chicago Stadium to hang another banner. Or to whomever made the trophy for the league's leading scorer. Yet the road to the Chicago Bulls' third consecutive championship and Michael Jordan's seventh straight scoring title was anything but routine.

Collectively, the Bulls didn't have much trouble capturing the Central Division title again, with a 57–25 record, although they lost the coveted home-court advantage throughout the playoffs to the New York Knicks, who finished 60–22. Jordan, meanwhile, had to deal with the intense media scrutiny that grew from published reports of his gambling excesses and late-night forays.

The Bulls swept the Atlanta Hawks and the Cleveland Cavaliers in the first two rounds of the playoffs in May, then had their hands full with coach Pat Riley's (b.1945) tough Knicks squad.

Led by center Patrick Ewing (b.1962) and the league's best defense, New York won the first two games of the series at home. The Bulls answered right back and took two in Chicago, with Jordan scoring 54 points in game four.

In the pivotal game five back in New York's Madison Square Garden, Chicago won 97–94. An infamous closing-moments sequence—in which Knicks forward Charles Smith missed several

One-Woman Show *Sheryl Swoopes (center) was an unstoppable force in Texas Tech's march to the NCAA championship.*

1993

point-blank chances to win the game—saved the Bulls' season.

The 4–2 series victory catapulted Chicago back into the NBA Finals, where the Bulls met the Phoenix Suns in June. Behind newly acquired Charles Barkley and sharp-shooters Danny Ainge and Dan Majerle, the Suns had gone 62–20 during the regular season, giving them homecourt advantage. But Jordan and the Bulls reversed that fortune by winning the first two games in Phoenix.

Game three was one of the most memorable postseason games in NBA history, with the Suns prevailing 129–121 in an epic, triple-overtime marathon. But Phoenix couldn't withstand Jordan's 55-point outburst in game four and eventually succumbed in six games. "Winning this championship was harder than anything I've done before in basketball," Jordan said.

His off-the-court life was about to become incredibly harder. On July 23, his beloved father—whom he often called his best friend—was murdered in North Carolina. Three months later, on October 6, still grief-stricken and increasingly disenchanted with the life of a public mega-star, Jordan shocked the sports world by announcing his retirement. At age 30 and with nine years of history-making basketball behind him, he called it quits—for the first time, but certainly not the last—while still at the top of his over-the-top game.

"I feel that at this particular time in my career I have reached the pinnacle of my career," Jordan said in his 1993 retirement press conference. "I have achieved a lot in that short amount of time, but I just feel I don't have anything else for myself to prove."

Ecstasy and Agony

Colonial Affair won the 125th running of the Belmont Stakes in Belmont, New York, on June 5. But the real story wasn't so much the horse as it was the jockey. Colonial Affair was ridden to victory by Julie Krone (b.1963). Krone became the first woman to ride a winner in a Triple Crown race.

The victory was the crowning achievement of Krone's stellar racing career. The winningest female jockey in horse racing history, she had raced hundreds of times at the famous track, including three other Belmont Stakes, so she was familiar with the venue. This time, it counted the most. "I turned for home and told myself, 'Now I'm going to win the Belmont Stakes,'" she said afterward.

In 2000, she became the first woman to be inducted into the National Thoroughbred Racing Hall of Fame. "I wish I could put every one of you here on a race horse at the eighth pole, so you could have the same feeling that I did," Krone said at the ceremony in Saratoga Springs, New York. "I got to do something I love so much every day. And today I know for sure that life doesn't get any better."

The Rarest of No-Hitters

Since St. Louis Brown Stockings righthander George "Grin" Bradley became the first Major League Baseball pitcher to do it, on July 15, 1876, pitching a no-hit baseball game has remained a remarkable personal achievement. But as hard as it is to pitch a complete game with no hits, they're not all that uncommon. At least one no-hitter has been thrown in all

Tall in the Saddle

When he retired from baseball at the end of the 1993 season, Lynn Nolan Ryan, Jr. was 46 years old and still pitching 95 miles per hour. After pitching in the major leagues for 27 years, the gentleman rancher born on January 31, 1947, in Refugio, Texas, rode into the sunset holding more than 50 records, including most no-hitters (seven), most career strikeouts (5,714), and most strikeouts in a season (383 in 1973). Throwing heat over four decades for four teams (the New York Mets, California Angels, Houston Astros, and Texas Rangers), Ryan retired with 324 wins against 292 losses. He started more games (773) than anyone except Cy Young (815). He never won a Cy Young Award, but was inducted into the Baseball Hall of Fame in 1999.

In the May 1993 issue of *Texas Monthly* magazine, Joe Nick Petoski wrote a piece entitled "A Farewell to Arm," a sort of open letter to Ryan. Petoski's prose summed up Ryan, not so much in baseball terms, but in what he meant to the game, those who love it, and the state of Texas.

"I thought I would drop you this thank-you note—not so much for all the records you've shattered and all the milestones you've reached; not for all you've done for baseball in Texas, bringing excitement to the Astros a few years back and respectability to the Rangers today; not for being a walking, talking advertisement for the benefits of rigorous training and clean living; and certainly not for being a celebrity so inextricably tied to our state that two roads—one in Arlington, between Houston and Freeport, near your hometown of Alvin—have been named the Nolan Ryan Expressway. The real reason I wanted to thank you was for being my seven-year-old's first hero. I couldn't have asked for a better role model. It's not just that you are a 46-year-old adult who plays a kid's game for a living, excelling in all aspects of your position—though that would be more than enough. You married your high school sweetheart. You raised your family in

Nolan Ryan

the same town in which you grew up. You're a cattleman—what could be more Texan? And rarely is heard a disparaging word about you. Years from now you may be exposed as a crank and a whiner, a showboat with a big head, or just another money-grubbing jock. But I'm not betting on it. From where I sit in the grandstand, you appear to be a class act, the last in a long line of good guys who seem to have vanished from your profession."

1993

but three major league seasons (1982, 1989, 2000) since 1960. But the 2–0 no-hitter pitched on September 4, 1993, at Yankee Stadium by New York Yankees lefthander Jim Abbott is the only one of its kind.

It's not because Abbott shut down an explosive Cleveland Indians' lineup, featuring such All-Star hitters as Kenny Lofton, Albert Belle, Manny Ramirez, and Jim Thome—who just six days earlier had pounded him for 10 hits and seven runs in an inning and a third. Or because he struck out only three hitters but walked five, and each time wriggled out of trouble. It's because he has only one hand.

His entire life, Abbott had said "no" to accepting pity or being treated differently because he was born without a right hand. And he wouldn't take no for an answer when challenged to prove he belonged on the pitcher's mound. At age 11, in his Little League pitching debut, he threw a no-hitter. He pitched the gold-medal-winning game against Japan in the 1988 Olympics. And without a day in the minor leagues, he jumped directly from the University of Michigan to the California Angels' starting rotation.

"I don't think I'm handicapped," Abbott told *Sports Illustrated for Kids* in 1994. "My hand hasn't kept me from doing anything I wanted to do. I believe you can do anything you want, if you put your mind to it."

Ryding High in England

Golf challenges an individual's physical and mental skills. It's each golfer for himself or herself up and down the fairways and putting greens. But every two years, the top American professional male golfers team up to compete against Europe's best pros in the Ryder Cup. There are no money prizes for the winners, only national pride and transatlantic bragging rights. So when the U.S. team rallied on the last day of the 1993 Ryder Cup—contested at The Belfry in Sutton Coldfield, England, September 24 to 26—the Stars and Stripes unfurled proudly.

Golf is considered a gentlemanly sport, with strictly enforced rules of play and etiquette. There's no trash talking between opponents. Things got a bit testy two years earlier, however, when the matches were held at Kiawah Island in South Carolina (the site alternates between the United States and Europe). Tensions ran high, with the post-Desert Storm Americans feeling patriotic (they donned camouflage caps one day), European charges of cheating, and other back-and-forth head games.

Now, the competition at The Belfry boiled down to the last day. The Americans trailed late in the competition, but Ryder Cup rookie Davis Love III pulled out a critical victory over Constantino Rocca, and the U.S. team won 15-13. America got the Cup back for the first time since 1983. Graciously, both teams accepted the outcome.

Carter's Clout

Almost every kid that grows up watching baseball dreams of one day hitting the home run that wins the World Series for his team. In big-league history, though, only two players ever

Other Milestones of 1993

✔ On February 3, cantankerous Cincinnati Reds owner Marge Schott was suspended from baseball for one year and fined $25,000 for making derogatory racial and ethnic remarks.

✔ President Bill Clinton issued Proclamation 6527, declaring February 4 National Women and Girls in Sports Day. The proclamation recognized the achievements of women in the field of sports and their efforts to break down sexual and racial barriers.

✔ Major League Baseball welcomed two new teams, the Florida Marlins and the Colorado Rockies, on April 5.

✔ On September 7, St. Louis Cardinals outfielder Mark Whiten became the 12th Major League Baseball player to hit four home runs in a single game.

✔ Miami Dolphins head coach Don Shula won his NFL-record 325th game with a 19–14 victory over the Philadelphia Eagles in Philadelphia on November 14.

have hit a walk-off home run to end the World Series. The first was Pittsburgh's Bill Mazeroski, against the Yankees in the Fall Classic in 1960. The next came this year, on October 23, when the Toronto Blue Jays' Joe Carter (b.1960) connected off Philadelphia Phillies reliever Mitch Williams for a three-run home run in the bottom of the ninth inning to win game six 8–6 and give his team a four games to two win in the Series.

The left-handed Williams, the Phillies' hard-throwing closing pitcher, had recorded a career-high 43 saves during the regular season.

But "the Wild Thing" had been living up to his wicked-fastball-shaky-control nickname in the series, saving game two, then blowing game four. On this day, with Philadelphia winning 6–5, Williams walked Rickey Henderson to lead off the ninth inning, induced a fly out, then gave up a single to Paul Molitor (b.1956). Carter worked the count to 2–2 as the raucous Skydome crowd urged him on. Williams wound up, delivered…and so did Carter, sending the ball over the left-field fence. The Blue Jays won!

Toronto, which beat Atlanta in the 1992 World Series (see page 244), thus became the first team to win back-to-back World Series since the New York Yankees in the 1977 and 1978 seasons.

1994

Seminoles Win Two Close Ones

The New Year started out doubly nice for Florida State University's football team. First, the Seminoles pulled out a dramatic, 18–16 victory over the University of Nebraska in the Orange Bowl in Miami on January 1. Then, a day later, the team was voted national champions for the first time in school history.

Florida State won its game when freshman Scott Bentley kicked a 22-yard field goal with 24 seconds left, and Nebraska's Byron Bennett misfired on a 45-yard try as time ran out. The Fighting Irish of the University of Notre Dame also won on New Year's Day, edging Texas A&M University, 24–21, in the Cotton Bowl. What's more, back on November 13, Notre Dame had beaten Florida State. The Irish finished the season with a 11–1 record, Florida State with a 12–1 record. On the strength of their head-to-head win, Notre Dame head coach Lou Holtz (b.1937) complained that the Irish should have been ranked number one.

So it goes in the always-spinning world of sports debates. This one will probably rage forever.

Super Bowl XXVIII: 2–0 vs. 0–4

There are winners and there are losers. And somewhere in between are the Buffalo Bills. Remarkably, they reached the Super Bowl for an unprecedented fourth year in a row. More incredibly, with a 30–13 rout at the hands of the Dallas Cowboys on January 30 at the Georgia Dome in Atlanta, the Bills lost their fourth Super Bowl in a row—also unprecedented.

While Buffalo was left to ponder its triumphs and tragedies, Dallas hoisted the Lombardi Trophy for the second straight year. The Cowboys had whipped these same Bills in Super Bowl XXVII, 52–17. Dallas now joined the Green Bay Packers, Miami Dolphins, Pittsburgh Steelers (who did it twice), and San Francisco 49ers as the only teams to win back-to-back Super Bowls.

The rematch favored the Cowboys. Despite losing their first two regular-season games and overcoming injuries to quarterback Troy Aikman (b.1966) and running back Emmitt Smith (b.1969), the Cowboys went 12–4 to win the NFC East. They sailed through the playoffs, dispens-

Gooooooaaaaaaaaaal! *The United States stunned heavily favored Colombia in soccer's World Cup (see page 259).*

ing the Packers and the 49ers. Buffalo finished 12–4 as well to capture the AFC East, then beat the Los Angeles Raiders and the Kansas City Chiefs in the playoffs. Still, they were considered the underdogs against the reigning NFL champs.

The Bills led at halftime, 13–6, but fell apart from there under the Cowboys' speedy, powerful defense and their massive offensive line. Buffalo turned the ball over three times, including a costly third-quarter fumble by running back Thurman

Thomas that was returned 46 yards for a touchdown. Smith, on the merit of his 132 rushing yards and two touchdowns, was named the game's MVP.

Winter Wonderland

The XXVII Olympic Winter Games were held in idyllic Lillehammer, Norway, February 12 to 27. The friendly, well-organized venue and outstanding athletic achievements combined for one

1994

of the most successful Olympics ever. The United States brought home 13 medals—six gold, five silver, and two bronze—while host Norway doubled that total to win the most medals at the Games.

Although the women's figure skating competition generated the juiciest headlines (see opposite page), the speed skating events best epitomized the genuine Olympic spirit. Norway's own Johann Koss wowed the home crowd by winning three golds—in the 1,500-meter, 5,000-meter, and 10,000-meter races. American skater Bonnie Blair took her third straight Olympic title in the 500-meter sprint and second straight in the 1,000-meter race. Her trove of five gold medals, dating back to the 1988 Calgary Games, are the most won by an American female athlete in either summer or winter.

Unlike Blair, Dan Jansen (b.1965) appeared to be cursed in Olympic competition. One of the greatest sprinters in speed skating history, he had won the world sprint championship twice, won seven overall World Cup titles, and set seven world records. Yet he failed to win any medal at the 1984 Olympics. Four years later, at the Winter Games in Calgary, Jansen was distraught over the death of his sister the day of the 500-meter final, and he slipped and fell during the race. The same thing happened in the 1,000-meter race.

Jansen finished out of the medals again at the 1992 Albertville Games. Unbelievably, he slipped in the 500-meter in Lillehammer and finished eighth. His last chance came in the 1,000-meter race. Powered by what he would later describe in his autobiography, *Full Circle*, as "a jolt

of energy" in his legs, Jansen not only finished in first place, but set a world record. With fans of every nation cheering, he skated a victory lap around the Viking Ship oval with his infant daughter, named after his late sister, Jane, in his arms—and a hard-earned gold medal around his neck.

A comparatively unknown American came out of nowhere to win the gold medal in the men's downhill skiing event. Tommy Moe, a skiing prodigy from Montana, had never even won a World Cup race before hitting the slopes in Lillehammer. Thirty thousand Norwegians watched in agony as Moe edged native son Kjetil Andre Aamodt by four one-hundredths of a second for the gold medal. The blow was later softened when it was learned that Moe's great-great grandfather was Norwegian.

Gretzky's Number One

On March 23, before a packed house at The Forum in Inglewood, California, Los Angeles Kings star Wayne Gretzky officially became the greatest goal scorer in the history of the National Hockey League.

It had been obvious for some time that Gretzky eventually would pass the great Gordie Howe—his boyhood idol—atop the league's all-time goal-scoring chart. Gretzky already had passed "Mr. Hockey" as the top points scorer (goals plus assists) several seasons earlier. His pursuit of the goals record became hockey's version of Hank Aaron chasing Babe Ruth for baseball's all-time career home-run record.

On March 20, Gretzky tied Howe with career goal No. 801, in a game against the San Jose Sharks. The next time the Kings took the ice was three nights later, against the Vancouver Canucks.

In the second period, Gretzky took a pass from long-time teammate Marty McSorley and shot the puck past Canucks' goaltender Kirk McLean for the historic goal.

Gretzky, whose career began in the World Hockey Association in 1978, would go on to play through the 1998–99 season and finish with 894 career goals.

Rangers End a 53-Year Freeze-Out

The New York Rangers won the Stanley Cup in 1940. Not until June 14 of this year did they again possess the National Hockey League's championship trophy. No NHL team or fans had ever waited so long, and the Rangers ended their drought in thrilling fashion.

Haunted by its cursed past, the team began a serious rebuilding effort in 1991 by acquiring Mark Messier (b.1961), who had been captain of the Edmonton Oilers

As the Skates Turn

You can't make this stuff up, unless perhaps for a sleazy soap-opera script. That's pretty much what the sordid Olympic tale of archrival figure skaters Tonya Harding and Nancy Kerrigan seemed like.

Scene 1: Our story opens just after Christmas 1993. Harding, her ex-husband, and two other shady characters conspire to attack and injure Kerrigan—the reigning U.S. champion, Olympic favorite, and thorn in Harding's side—to keep her from competing in the upcoming U.S. Skating Championships.

Scene 2: On January 6, following a practice session in Detroit, Kerrigan is clubbed on her right knee. The unknown attacker flees. Two days later, Harding wins the national title, from which the injured Kerrigan has had to withdraw. Kerrigan is named to the team anyway.

Scene 3: Several witnesses come forward and tip off FBI agents about the plot. Arrests follow, though Harding is spared. She denies any knowledge or involvement, until her ex-hubby cuts a deal with the Feds and squeals on her. Harding finally confesses that she knew he was involved, but found out only after the attack. She sues the U.S. Olympic Committee (USOC) to prevent it from kicking her off the Olympic team. The USOC blinks, and the Tonya and Nancy Show shifts to Norway.

Scene 4: Kerrigan leads after the short program, Harding is in 10th place, and CBS basks in the sixth highest-rated television broadcast of all time. On February 25, petite Ukranian teenager Oksana Baiul edges Kerrigan for the gold. On the medal stand, silver-medalist Kerrigan, unaware her microphone is on, makes snotty remarks about Baiul. Harding, who finished eighth, is nowhere to be found.

Epilogue: Kerrigan turns pro, gets involved with a married man, and skates in ice shows. Harding pleads guilty to conspiracy, is banned from competition, and, years later, becomes a celebrity boxer.

O.J. Runs
Out of Bounds

Orenthal James "O.J." Simpson (b.1947) was a marvel to watch on the football field. As an All-America running back for the University of Southern California, he won the 1968 Heisman Trophy. Over 11 seasons in the NFL (1969–1979), the first nine with the Buffalo Bills, he amassed 11,236 rushing yards—including a then-record 2,003 yards in 1973. He won the league's MVP award that year. When he retired from football, Simpson segued from football player to affable broadcaster, actor, and television pitchman.

On June 17, the nation marveled at TV images of O.J. on the run again, only this time in a white Ford Bronco being chased by the Los Angeles Police Department (LAPD). Simpson finally surrendered and was charged with the stabbing murders of his ex-wife Nicole Brown Simpson and her friend Ronald Goldman, whose bodies were found on June 12. From there unfolded one of the most sensational trials of the 20th century.

Simpson's criminal trial didn't begin until the following January. It lasted more than nine months, generating nearly round-the-clock media coverage and public debate. Even late-night comedians routinely tossed O.J. jokes into their monologues. The prosecution presented mounds of potentially incriminating testimony and physical evidence, none more dramatic than DNA that matched Simpson's blood to that found at the crime scene. His defense was built around accusations of a racially motivated frame-up by the LAPD. The jury, after less than four hours of deliberation, returned a not guilty verdict on October 3, 1995, and Simpson was released from prison.

Nearly three weeks later, Simpson went on trial in a separate civil case resulting from a lawsuit by the victims' families. On January 4, 1996, a jury concluded that he had wrongfully caused the deaths of his ex-wife and Goldman. The court ordered Simpson to pay compensatory damages of $8.5 million and punitive damages of $25 million.

The entire saga provided the public with a vivid portrayal of the justice system and of racial divisions in the country, as well as a glimpse into the future trend of reality television.

for five Stanley Cup titles. In April 1993, highly regarded Mike Keenan (b.1949) signed on to coach the team, which, by the start of the 1993–94 season, featured six members of Messier's championship-rich Oilers' squad. The Rangers compiled the league's best record during the regular season (52-24-8, with 112 points), then advanced to the Stanley Cup Finals against the Vancouver Canucks.

The finals went the distance. Messier came to the rescue in game seven at home in Madison Square Garden, scoring the go-ahead goal. Up 3–2, New York survived a furious third-period attack by Vancouver before wildly celebrating the end of their Stanley Cup drought.

Meanwhile, the Knicks' Agony Continues

Unlike the New York Rangers, with whom they shared Madison Square Garden, the New York Knicks just missed their Garden party when they lost game seven of the NBA Finals to the Houston Rockets on June 22 at The Summit in Houston. It would have been the Knicks' first title since 1973.

Seven-foot centers Patrick Ewing of the Knicks and Hakeem Olajuwon were certainly the centers of attention in this rough-and-tumble defensive battle, in which neither team scored more than 93 points in any of the seven games. Even so, it was the play of guards Sam Cassell of Houston and John Starks of the Knicks that ultimately made the difference.

With the series tied at one game apiece, Cassell scored seven points in the final seconds of game three in New

York to preserve a 93–89 Rockets win. The Knicks won the next two and hoped to finish things off in game six in Houston. Starks, pouring in 27 points, nearly made it happen. But he came up just short in two critical possessions in the closing moments, including a 25-footer blocked by Olajuwon with two seconds left and New York down 86–84.

Starks went ice cold in game seven—2 for 18, including 0 for 11 from three-point range. The Rockets won 90–84 and landed their first NBA championship.

The World Cup Runneth Over

Imagine if Major League Baseball held the World Series in Britain. America's national pastime in a country where the game of cricket is far more popular? It could never happen!

But when FIFA, the international organization that governs soccer, announced that the 1994 World Cup Tournament would be staged in the United States, skeptics wondered what it was thinking. Soccer's grandest event—so special that it is only held every four years—in a country where only little kids play the sport?

Well, not only did the U.S. host the 15th World Cup from June 17 to July 17, but it was also a huge success. Teams from 24 nations played a total of 52 games in arenas across the country, including Giants Stadium in East Rutherford, New Jersey, Soldier Field in Chicago, the Cotton Bowl in Dallas, and the Rose Bowl in Pasadena, California. Nearly 3.5 million fans turned out, while a television audience of more than 35 million tuned in.

Youth soccer is tremendously popular in the United States, and high school and college soccer are growing. Still, the U.S. national team has never been a powerhouse. So it was shocking when the United States upset title contender Colombia, 2–1, in the first round before a crowd of 93,194 at the Rose Bowl on June 22. Indeed, it was the first win in World Cup play for the United States since beating England in 1950.

The United States advanced to the Round of 16, where it was beaten by

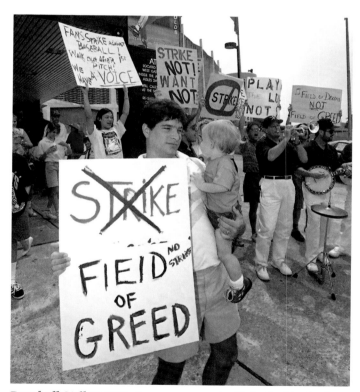

Baseball Strikes Out *Fans were upset with both sides in the labor dispute between owners and players that wiped out much of the 1994 baseball season—including the World Series (see page 260).*

1994

Brazil on July 4 at Stanford Stadium in Stanford, California. Brazil moved on to the finals against Italy on July 17 at the Rose Bowl. The game ended in a tie and had to be decided on a shootout, in which each team alternates in taking five individual shots against the goalie. Brazil won the shootout, 3–2, and the World Cup.

Baseball Strikes Out

For the eighth time since 1972, baseball suffered a work stoppage. And this time, the unthinkable happened: The World Series was cancelled.

San Francisco Treat *Prolific wide receiver Jerry Rice was still going strong in his 10th NFL season in 1994, when he became the NFL's all-time leading touchdown scorer.*

On August 12, the players went on strike. As usual, the main issue was money. This time the owners wanted to institute a cap on salaries, limiting how much teams could spend on their total player payroll—something the players' union strongly opposed.

For the next 34 days, fans kept their fingers crossed that the two sides would come to an agreement and resume one of the best seasons in years. Instead, on September 14, acting Commissioner Bud Selig announced that the remainder of the season was cancelled, including the playoffs and the World Series. The strike did not end until March 31, 1995. In those 232 days, 920 games were missed.

In a League of His Own

On September 5, the San Francisco 49ers' Jerry Rice left little doubt that he was the best wide receiver in the history of the NFL. In a 44–14 wipeout of the Los Angeles Raiders on *Monday Night Football*, he caught three touchdown passes. The last one established an NFL record, pushing him one touchdown past legendary Cleveland Browns fullback Jim Brown for a career total of 127.

Jerry Lee Rice was born on October 13, 1962, in Crawford, Mississippi, where he became a high school star in football, basketball, and track. During four seasons at Mississippi Valley State University (1980–1984), Rice set 18 NCAA Division I-AA records. In his senior year alone, the consensus All-American racked up 1,845 yards and scored 28 touchdowns.

The 49ers traded up for the 16th spot in the 1985 NFL draft specifically to land

Other Milestones of 1994

✔ With a famous Arkansan, President Bill Clinton, in attendance at the Charlotte Coliseum in North Carolina, the University of Arkansas beat Duke, 76–72, to claim the NCAA basketball championship on April 4.

✔ Also on April 4, the Chicago Cubs' Tuffy Rhodes became the first player to homer his first three times up on Opening Day (in a 12–8 loss to the Mets). He had only five more homers the rest of the season.

✔ Sprinter Leroy Burrell set a new world record (9.85 seconds) in the 100-meter sprint on July 6 in Lausanne, Switzerland.

✔ On July 28, Texas Rangers baseball pitcher Kenny Rogers threw a perfect game (no hits, no walks, no runs, and no players to reach first base), blanking the California Angels, 4–0. Rogers' fairy-tale baseball story began when he was first drafted as an outfielder. He had been discovered by a scout who had come to see another player on his high school team..

✔ After rallying from six holes back, Tiger Woods, at age 18, became the youngest winner of the U.S. Amateur Golf Championship on August 28. He would repeat the championship in each of the next two years.

✔ On September 11, Andre Agassi beat Germany's Michael Stich in straight sets to become the first unseeded player to win the men's U.S. Open tennis title since 1966.

✔ The North Carolina women's soccer team continued one of the greatest dynasties ever in college sports, winning their ninth straight NCAA title.

Rice. The rookie wide receiver scored his first touchdown on a 25-yard pass from quarterback Joe Montana on October 6, 1985, and he just got better from there.

Rice played 16 seasons with the 49ers, then four more years with the Oakland Raiders and Seattle Seahawks. He made the Pro Bowl 13 times, played on three Super Bowl-winning teams, and shattered virtually every receiving record there is, including receptions (1,549), receiving yards (22,895), and touchdowns (197). He finished with 207 total touchdowns, another record. In 2010, Rice was inducted into the Pro Football Hall of Fame.

Tar Heels' Dynasty Sticks

The University of North Carolina's women's soccer team won its ninth straight NCAA title on November 20 in Portland, Oregon, shutting out Notre Dame, 5–0. When the North Carolina Tar Heels won their first title, in 1982, there were only 25 women's teams competing on the NCAA Division I level in soccer. In 1994 there were 154, including 24 in the tournament. That was certainly evidence of soccer's growth in the United States, but more so of UNC's utter dominance of the sport.

1995

49ers Mine More Gold

Quarterback Steve Young passed for a record six touchdowns to lead the San Francisco 49ers to a 49–26 rout of the San Diego Chargers in Super Bowl XXIX at Joe Robbie Stadium on January 29. The 49ers became the first team to win five Super Bowls, and made it 11 consecutive wins for NFC teams over AFC teams in the league title game.

The 49ers' first four Super Bowl wins came in the 1980s. Quarterback extraordinaire Joe Montana was the catalyst for their Super Bowl wins during that decade. But in 1993, Montana was traded to the Kansas City Chiefs, leaving Steve Young (b.1961) to fill some big shoes.

Montana had made a career of throwing the ball to All-Pro wide receiver Jerry Rice (see page 260), and Young-to-Rice certainly sounded strange. Yet it produced similarly spectacular results. The new tandem connected on 112 passes for 1,499 yards and 13 touchdowns during the regular season. And that was just a tune-up for the Super Bowl.

San Francisco's biggest postseason challenge was a Dallas Cowboys' team on a quest for its third straight NFL championship. The 49ers got past the Cowboys on November 13, and again two months later in the NFC Championship Game.

That matchup turned out to be the season's pivotal game because the Super Bowl was yet another blowout. Young and Rice teamed on a touchdown pass on the third play of the game, and the 49ers never looked back.

Rice finished with 10 catches for 149 yards and three touchdowns in all, but the game's MVP was Young. He completed 24 of 36 passes for 325 yards. After the game, 49ers head coach George Seifert—who himself knew about replacing a legend after taking over for Bill Walsh in 1989—called Young one of the greatest quarterbacks in league history. "Joe Montana established a standard," he said, "and Steve Young has maintained it."

Twice Is Nice for Marlin

For a NASCAR driver, winning the Daytona 500 is a dream come true. Winning stock-car racing's most prestigious event two years in a row is almost unheard of. But 37-year-old Sterling Marlin joined an elite group of back-to-back Daytona 500 winners when he held off

High Five   *The San Francisco 49ers, led by a record-setting performance from quarterback Steve Young (8), beat the San Diego Chargers in Super Bowl XXIX and became the first team to win the NFL's biggest game five times.*

Dale Earnhardt to win at the Daytona International Speedway on February 19.

Marlin had never won any NASCAR race before taking the checkered flag at Daytona in 1994 in his 279th career start. When he won again this year, he joined Richard Petty and Cale Yarborough as the only drivers to win the race in back-to-back seasons. He also became the first—and still only—driver to make the Daytona 500 his first two career victories.

In all, Marlin has won 10 races in a career that still included a limited schedule of events in 2009.

He's Ba-a-a-a-a-ack!

You're the best basketball player on the planet, so why quit to take up baseball? That question probably crossed Michael Jordan's mind during his 17-month hiatus from the NBA. So after a season of Minor League Baseball, the former outfielder rejoined the Chicago Bulls on March 19.

In his first game back, against the Indiana Pacers—and wearing his baseball number 45 instead of his familiar 23—Jordan scored 19 points.

This Girl's Got Game *Forward Rebecca Lobo and the University of Connecticut soared to the NCAA women's basketball title with a 35-0 record. UConn vanquished University of Tennessee in the title game.*

38-point effort in game two in the next round of the playoffs, against Shaquille O'Neal (b.1972) and the Orlando Magic, the Bulls lost the series in six games.

"We weren't the same team we were 18 months ago," Jordan admitted in the post-game press conference, "but the fun part is trying to live up to the accomplishments of the past."

Perfectly Done

The University of Connecticut's women's basketball team did more than win the NCAA Division I Championship on April 2, defeating the University of Tennessee, 70–64. It even did more than complete the season with a perfect 35–0 record. The Lady Huskies put women's college basketball on the map.

Not that women didn't already have game. Superstars such as Cheryl Miller and Sheryl Swoopes had paved the way at the University of Southern California and Texas Tech University, respectively. And Tennessee's Pat Summit, with 564 wins by season's end, was one of the nation's most accomplished head coaches, man or woman. This UConn squad, though, took the game to a new level.

The poster girl was Rebecca Lobo (b.1973), a 6-foot-4 forward with a great perimeter game and a 4.0 grade-point average—an amazing role model to legions of girls. She and the Huskies earned the number-one ranking in January after knocking off Tennessee, and they never looked back. In the title game, at the Target Center in Minneapolis, Lobo got into foul trouble in the first half, which helped Tennessee's Lady Vols to a 38–32

If there was any rust on the 32-year-old Jordan's game, he shook it off against his old rival, the New York Knicks. On March 28, he set a Madison Square Garden record with 55 points in a 113–111 Bulls' squeaker. He looked pretty much his old self in leading Chicago to a first-round victory in the playoffs against the Charlotte Hornets, averaging 31.5 points in four games. Yet, despite Jordan's vintage

halftime advantage. Lobo and point guard Jennifer Rizzotti led the charge back, though, and UConn completed its dream season in perfect fashion.

They're Ba-a-a-a-a-ack!

Major League Baseball returned from its longest work stoppage on April 25. The shortened season—144 games instead of the normal 162—produced enough goodwill to begin winning back the hearts of disgruntled fans.

The Cleveland Indians, long the doormats of the American League, finished with 100 wins for the first time since 1954. The Seattle Mariners reached the postseason for the first time in team history. Their thrilling, extra-innings victory in game five of the division series in September against the New York Yankees, who hadn't won anything since 1981, lifted them to the American League Championship Series (ALCS). Although the Mariners fell to the Indians, who won the best-of-seven ALCS in six games, the run probably saved baseball in Seattle.

The Colorado Rockies, in just their third season, made the playoffs, but lost to the pitching-rich Atlanta Braves (ace Greg Maddux, thanks to a 19–2 record and a skimpy 1.63 ERA, won his unprecedented fourth straight Cy Young Award). The Braves then swept the Cincinnati Reds and faced the Indians in a World Series in October that confirmed the old saying that good pitching beats good hitting.

As a team, the Indians hit .291 for the season—the best in Major League Baseball. Their lineup featured Albert Belle, who rang up 50 home runs, and veteran Eddie Murray, who whacked his 3,000th career hit on June 30. The Braves' pitching staff had the lowest ERA, at 3.44, in the major leagues.

Maddux opened the Series with a two-hit gem in which he pitched all nine innings; only four balls left the infield. Down two games to none, the Indians won two of three games at home. In game six back in Atlanta, Tom Glavine pitched eight innings and gave up just one hit, David Justice smacked a sixth-inning homer, and closing pitcher Mark Wohlers threw a perfect ninth inning to seal the 1–0 Braves' win. It marked the team's return to baseball's mountaintop after a 37-year absence—and baseball's return to the hearts of its fans.

The Nation Mourns

On April 23, audiences at sports arenas, stadiums, and ballparks across the country observed a moment of silence to honor the victims of what was then the worst terrorist attack ever in the United States. On the morning of April 19, a massive bomb hidden inside a rental truck exploded in front of the Alfred P. Murrah Federal Building in Oklahoma City, killing 168 men, women, and children. Just 90 minutes later, an Oklahoma Highway Patrol officer pulled over 27-year-old Timothy McVeigh for driving without a license plate. Shortly before he was to be released on April 21, McVeigh, an Army veteran, was recognized as a bombing suspect and was charged with the deadly crime. Not long after, an ex-Army friend of McVeigh's, Terry Nichols, was also arrested and charged. The men were tried in two separate, emotional, and highly publicized trials. In June 1997, a jury convicted McVeigh and sentenced him to death. He was executed on June 11, 2001. Nichols was found guilty of involuntary manslaughter and of conspiring with McVeigh. He was sentenced to life in prison.

Baseball's New Iron Man

New York Yankees legend Lou Gehrig (1903–1941) earned the nickname "The Iron Horse" after playing in 2,130 consecutive games. That seemingly insurmountable record was eclipsed at Baltimore's Camden Yards on September 6 in what proved to be baseball's greatest welcome-back gift back to strike-weary fans. On that festive summer evening, Baltimore Orioles shortstop Cal Ripken Jr. (b.1960) played in his 2,131st straight game.

Once the fifth inning of the contest against the California Angels was complete and the game became official, Ripken ran a victory lap around the stadium, stopping and shaking hands with fans and players. The scoreboard read, "Cal, thank you for saving baseball." During a 22-minute, 15-second ovation, Ripken received eight curtain calls from the appreciative crowd.

"I know that if Lou Gehrig is looking down on tonight's activities," he told the throng, "he isn't concerned about someone playing one more consecutive game than he did. Instead, he's viewing tonight as just another example of what is good and right about the great American game."

Ripken began his iron man streak on May 30, 1982, and played in 19,231 out of a possible 19,395

Cal Ripken Jr.

innings. And he went all-out in every single one. Even in this most special of games, he homered to help boost the Orioles to a 4–2 win.

A local boy, born on August 24, 1960, in nearby Havre de Grace, Ripken earned AL Rookie of the Year honors in 1982 and was twice named the league's MVP (1983 and 1991). He started in 17 straight All-Star Games beginning in 1984 (the last three as a third baseman), and hit more home runs than any other shortstop (402).

At 6-foot-4, Ripken was the tallest full-time shortstop, and he set the single-season fielding percentage (a measure of defensive success calculated by dividing the number of successful plays a fielder makes by the total chances he has to play the ball) at the position (.996 in 1990). He recorded the final putout in the 1983 World Series, when the Orioles defeated the Philadelphia Phillies in five games for their first championship since 1970.

Ripken ended his streak at 2,632 games by taking himself out of the lineup on September 20, 1998. He retired at the end of the 2001 season with a lifetime batting average of .297 in 3,001 games. In 2007, he was inducted into the National Baseball Hall of Fame.

Rockets-Powered Sweep

The Houston Rockets swept the Orlando Magic in four games to repeat as NBA champions. While some liked to believe their 1994 title had a lot to do with a Chicago Bulls team that no longer had Michael Jordan, the Rockets put that notion to rest. In fact, after the 113–101 game four on June 14 in Houston, the Rockets became the first team in NBA history to defeat four 50-win teams on the way to a championship.

Before sweeping the Magic, they put away, in order, the Utah Jazz, the Phoenix Suns, and the San Antonio Spurs. And in none of those series did the Rockets have home-court advantage.

X Marks the Sport

The amateur athletes of Generation X (those born between 1965 and 1975) explored new sporting thrills in the 1990s. Shunning tradition, they pioneered alternative sports such as inline skating, snowboarding, mountain biking, and street luge.

ESPN, the all-sports cable channel, quickly saw the potential and seized on a programming opportunity to appeal to a key audience by launching the Extreme Games. Held June 24 to July 1 in Rhode Island and Vermont, the inaugural games featured 27 events, including bungee jumping, barefoot waterski jumping, kite skiing, windsurfing, sky surfing, and bicycle stunt riding.

Not only was the competition gnarly, but it also proved a ratings hit with the all-important group of male TV viewers aged 12 to 34 that advertisers covet. So it was a no-brainer for ESPN to capitalize on the extreme theme every year.

ESPN added a winter version in 1996 and shortened the name to X Games. The snow and ice edition featured such extreme sports as snowboarding, ice climbing, and super-modified shovel racing. Continued success and popularity eventually made the X Games a prime-time event for a new generation of international athletes and TV audiences for years to come. In 2010, ESPN held the Winter X Games 14 and the Summer X Games 16.

X Marks the Spot *ESPN cornered a coveted demographic with the introduction of the Extreme Games. The X Games, as they soon were called, quickly grew in stature and popularity.*

1995

NBC Locks Up Olympics

NBC announced on December 12 that it had purchased the rights to televise each Winter Olympic and Summer Olympic Games through 2008 for $2.3 billion.

The roots for that astounding total date to 1960, the year that Americans got their first look at the Olympics on television. That year, CBS paid the International Olympic Committee $50,000 to air 15 hours of the Winter Games from Squaw Valley, California. On August 7, 1995, NBC paid a whopping $1.25 billion for the U.S. rights to broadcast the 2000 Summer Games from Sydney, Australia, as well as the Winter Games from Salt Lake City, Utah, two years later.

Securing the television rights to sporting events had become a highly competitive business. Viewers never seemed to get enough sports—consider the popularity of cable channel ESPN—and advertisers wanted to reach those audiences. So the networks battled one another and paid millions to air baseball, football, and basketball. (As one example, on November 6, Major League Baseball announced a five-year, $1.7 billion deal with NBC, ESPN, Fox, and Prime Liberty Cable.)

The Olympics, now alternating every two years between Summer and Winter Games, generated huge prime-time television ratings. Although the networks didn't necessarily make money broadcasting them because the expenses of covering them were so high, they benefited from the prestige and the opportunity to promote their other programming.

ABC had dominated Olympics broadcasting through the 1980s, and NBC land-

Other Milestones of 1995

✔ On January 6, Atlanta Hawks coach Lenny Wilkens notched career win No. 939—a 112–90 defeat of the Washington Bullets—to become the NBA's awinningest coach, surpassing the Celtics' Red Auerbach.

✔ Doug Swingley and his nine-dog team finished the Iditarod Trail Sled Dog Race across Alaska on March 14 in record time, completing the 1,160-mile course in nine days, two hours, 42 minutes, 19 seconds.

✔ On June 30, the Cleveland Indians' Eddie Murray collected hit No. 3,000 of his big-league career in a game against the Minnesota Twins.

✔ On June 24, the New Jersey Devils completed their four-game sweep of the Detroit Red Wings to win the NHL's Stanley Cup.

✔ By defeating German Boris Becker on July 9, Pete Sampras became the first U.S. male tennis player to win three consecutive Wimbledon championships.

✔ Dan Marino, quarterback of the Miami Dolphins, completed career pass number 3,687 in a 27–24 loss to the Indianapolis Colts to set an NFL record. He retired in 1999 also holding career records for completions, yards, and touchdowns.

ing the Sydney and Salt Lake Games was considered a coup. The deal involved two rounds of international dealing by NBC Sports president Dick Ebersol. It began with a secret New York-to-Sweden-to-Montreal-to-New York trip in early August, during which he outfoxed Fox Network owner Rupert Murdoch, who had offered the IOC $701 million for the Sydney rights. Ebersol upped the ante to $705 million, and in an unusual move, he got the Salt Lake Games for an extra $545 million—marking the first time the IOC had sold more than one Olympics at a time. Four months later, on December 12, in an even more-stunning move, NBC announced that it had secured the rights to every Summer and Winter Games through 2008 for $2.3 billion.

The Glass Slipper Fits

Who knows how the fairy tale of Cinderella came to be associated with sports teams? But there seems to be one or two Cinderella stories every year—teams relegated to the dust pile who unexpectedly outshine the competition. In 1995, the role fell to the Northwestern University Wildcats football team. For ages a perennial loser in the football-power Big Ten Conference, Northwestern enjoyed one of those when-you-wish-upon-a-star seasons.

It started on September 2 in South Bend, Indiana, when the Wildcats stunned the Notre Dame Fighting Irish, 17–15. Northwestern, a 28-point under-dog, had last beaten the Irish in 1962. On October 7, the Wildcats marched into Ann Arbor and upset the University of Michigan Wolverines, 19–13. A week later, they magically made the University of Wisconsin's Badgers disappear, 35–0! On November 4, the sixth-ranked Wildcats hosted number-12 Penn State University and tamed the Nittany Lions, 21–10. In that game, Northwestern running back Darnell Autry gained 100 yards in his 10th straight game, set a school season rushing record, and scored three touchdowns.

When Michigan spoiled previously unbeaten and second-ranked Ohio State University's hopes of winning the Big Ten by upending the Buckeyes on November 25, Northwestern grabbed the conference title. They were off to the big ball, the Rose Bowl, for the first time since 1947, against the 17th-ranked USC.

Alas, the clock struck midnight on New Year's Day, 1996, in Pasadena, California, where Northwestern's storybook season ended with a 41–32 loss.

1996

Brown Out

The Cleveland Browns long have had some of the most rabid fans in football. Their stadium even has a famous section of fans called the "Dawg Pound." But those loyal followers were left without a team when NFL owners approved the move of the Browns to Baltimore on February 8—well, sort of.

Baltimore indeed would get a new team, called the Ravens, who would take the Browns' place in the AFC's Central Division. And that team would have most of the Browns' old players. But technically, the NFL considered the Ravens a brand new team. Cleveland got to keep the Browns' team name, logos, and history, which dated to 1946, when the team was part of the All-America Football Conference. That wasn't much consolation to the fans, though, who didn't have a team to root for until the new Cleveland Browns were formed in 1999.

Michigan Melts the Ice

College hockey typically has a tough time grabbing the headlines from football and basketball. Not so at the University of Michigan in the early 1990s. From 1993 to 1995, the Michigan Wolverines played to a 93–22–5 record. And when the team scored the winning goal in overtime to seal the 1996 NCAA championship against Colorado College on March 30, it generated even bigger news, because the Wolverines' hopes of skating to a national title had melted away in each of the last three NCAA hockey playoffs—all heartbreaking overtime losses.

The school had been a hockey powerhouse in the 1950s, winning five championships in six years from 1951 to 1956. But its last title had come 32 years ago. So when the 1996 Wolverines faced yet another overtime, in front of a crowd of 13,330 at Riverfront Coliseum in Cincinnati, they hoped recent history would not repeat itself.

At 3:35 into the overtime period, Brendan Morrison, a two-time All-America forward, rebounded a missed shot and fired the puck into the Colorado net. Final score: Michigan 3, Colorado 2.

"We needed this for people to understand just how successful this program is," said Michigan coach Red Berenson. "Winning a national championship isn't easy."

Tiny Athlete, Big Heart *Injured Kerri Strug came to the victory stand in the arms of her coach, Bela Karolyi, after the U.S. women struck gymnastics gold (see page 272).*

Unbelieva-Bulls

Any doubts about Michael Jordan's worth to the Chicago Bulls were laid to rest during the 1995–1996 NBA season. With all due respect to Scottie Pippen, Toni Kukoc, Dennis Rodman, and the rest of the Bulls, they simply weren't the same team without Jordan. Not even close.

Jordan turned 33 in February, and age and the 17-month fling with baseball forced him to alter his game. His gravity-defying dunks went down less frequently, but refinement of a fade-away jump shot and career-best accuracy from three-point range (.427) more than made up for it. Jordan led the NBA in scoring (at 30.4 points per game) for a record eighth time in his career and won his fourth league MVP award.

As great as the Bulls were before Jordan left the first time (see page 249),

271

1996

this edition rewrote the record books. On February 27, with a 120–99 taming of the Minnesota Timberwolves, Chicago became the quickest team in North American professional sports history to reach 50 wins in a season. A come-from-behind victory over the Milwaukee Bucks on April 16 made the Bulls the first NBA team to achieve 70 wins; they finished the regular season at 72–10.

Chicago lost only one game in the first three rounds of the playoffs. Then, in the NBA Finals, the Bulls eliminated the Seattle SuperSonics in six games. The MVP of the best-of-seven championship series? Jordan, of course.

Jordan's greatness might seem almost robotic, yet he demonstrated very human emotion after the final buzzer sounded on June 16 at the United Center in Chicago. As the sold-out crowd cheered another NBA title, he grabbed the game ball and dashed to the Bulls' locker room. This was Jordan's first championship without his late father there to join in the celebration. Overcome with lingering grief, he lay on the floor in tears, clutching the basketball—on Father's Day.

The Atlanta Olympics

Boxing legend Muhammad Ali lit the torch at the Opening Ceremony to officially kick off the XXVI Summer Olympic Games in Atlanta on July 19. Ali, a gold medalist at the 1960 Games in Rome and now a beloved figure worldwide, provided ideal illumination for the brilliant athletic achievements to come over the next two weeks. Although the Games were marred by a bomb at an Atlanta park on July 27 that left one person dead and 100 injured, and complaints of over-commercialization dogged local organizers, these Olympics were otherwise a success.

As with any Olympics, stories aplenty preceded the competition. Among the most compelling was speculation over whether American sprinter Michael Johnson (b.1967) would become the first male Olympian to win both the 200-meter and 400-meter races. He had already pulled off the double at the 1995 world championships, and track and field officials changed the Olympic schedule so he could attempt it again in Atlanta.

Johnson had "owned" the 400-meter event since 1989, winning 54 straight finals. But before the 1992 Olympics in Barcelona, Spain, he contracted a severe case of food poisoning that prevented him from competing. This time, he would not be denied. On July 29, he cruised to the gold medal, crossing the finish line with the largest margin of victory in the event in 10 years.

Two days later, Johnson made Olympic history in shimmering style. Wearing gold-colored running shoes, he stumbled slightly coming out of the starting blocks, but quickly recovered. Johnson already held the world record in the 200-meter race—set at 19.66 seconds in June—and when he kicked into hyperspeed about halfway through this race, he established an astonishing new mark of 19.32.

Gail Devers provided one of the most inspirational stories in Atlanta. A world-class sprinter and hurdler, she had overcome a serious thyroid disorder called Graves Disease, that sidelined her for two years (1989 to 1990) and nearly resulted in having both feet amputated. She not only returned to competition, but won the 100-meter sprint at the 1992 Olympics in a photo finish. At these Games, the same thing happened. Although Devers and Jamaica's Christine Ottey finished with identical times in the 100-meters, the judges declared Devers the gold medalist by the smallest of margins—an infinitesimal two centimeters.

At age 35, Carl Lewis, who had already won eight Olympic gold medals, took an unexpected ninth on July 29. He had won the long jump at the previous three Olympics, but he was not considered a contender this time. Nonetheless, on his third jump in the finals, he leaped into first place and then watched anxiously as the competition failed to beat him.

Americans captured a total of 44 gold medals in Atlanta, though none more heroically than in the team competition in women's gymnastics. The event combines the scores of each team's five athletes on the required apparatus (vault, uneven bars, balance beam, floor exercise). The U.S. team held a slight lead over the Russians as the United States competed on its last apparatus, the vault.

When the teammate before her faltered, 18-year-old Kerri Strug figured the gold depended on her performance. On her first attempt, she fell. Worse than that, she heard a sickening snap in her left ankle. That wasn't going to stop her, though. In excruciating pain and at the urging of her team, coach, and cheering spectators, Strug landed her next vault perfectly—then collapsed in agony. She had to be carried to the medal stand by her coach with a cast around her severely sprained ankle, as the gold medal was hung around her neck. Only later did Strug realize that the team would have won anyway, but that hardly diminished her gutsy feat.

Gymnastics wasn't the only sport in which a U.S. women's team achieved greatness. While the men's more-heralded Dream Team III breezed to the gold in basketball, the women hoopsters proved

MLS Kicks Off

Spurred by the popularity of the 1994 World Cup in America, soccer grew in stature in the decade, culminating with the launch of a new 10-team professional league, Major League Soccer, on April 6. Before a crowd of 31,683 at Spartan Stadium in San Jose, California, the hometown Clash outlasted Washington D.C. United, 1–0.

Fears that the league would fail, as several past attempts in the U.S. had, were soon put to rest when the Los Angeles Galaxy home opener against the New York/New Jersey MetroStars drew 69,255 to the Rose Bowl. For the 16-game season, the MLS attracted 2,786,673 fans, for a respectable average of 17,416 per contest—well over the projected 12,000 figure.

The MLS Cup championship game, on October 20 in front of 34,643 fans at rain-soaked, windswept Foxboro (Massachusetts) Stadium and a national TV audience, provided a thrilling climax to the inaugural season. The Galaxy and D.C. United played to a 2–2 tie at the end of regulation time. A little more than three minutes into the sudden-death overtime, D.C. United's Eddie Pope headed a corner kick for the winning goal. "Soccer fever is alive in the United States," said a jubilant D.C. United captain John Harkes during the post-game revelry, "and it's here to stay."

King of Swing

Pete Sampras dominated men's tennis during the 1990s. He burst onto the scene at the 1990 U.S. Open, one of the sport's four annual Grand Slam tournaments (the others are the Australian Open, the French Open, and Wimbledon). At 19 years, 28 days, he became the Open's youngest male winner, after dispensing with Ivan Lendl, John McEnroe, and Andre Agassi in the last three rounds. Sampras powered his way to 11 more Grand Slam titles during the decade, though perhaps none more memorable than back at the U.S. Open in 1996.

Born on August 12, 1971, in Washington, D.C., Sampras began playing tennis at age seven. He turned professional at 16 in 1988, won his first pro tournament in February 1990, and achieved the number-one ranking for the first of many times in April 1993. By the time he arrived back at the U.S. Open site at the

Pete Sampras

National Tennis Center in Flushing, New York, for the 1996 event, Sampras had already won a half dozen more Grand Slam tournaments, including three straight Wimbledon titles (1993–1995). He also arrived with a heavy heart.

Tim Gullikson, Sampras' longtime coach, mentor, and close friend, had died of brain cancer in May. All year, a grieving Sampras had a hard time concentrating on his game. For the first time since 1992, he failed to win a Grand Slam. Then, on September 5 in the U.S. Open quarterfinal against 22-year-old Spaniard Alex Corretja, he played one of the most inspired matches in the history of the tournament. It went five sets and lasted four hours, nine minutes. Suffering from stomach cramps, Sampras vomited twice during the final set. Barely able to stand, much less serve and volley, he summoned up the energy to defeat Corretja. Three days later—on what would have been Gullikson's 45th birthday—Sampras beat Michael Chang for the title. "I've been thinking about him [Gullikson] all day and all during the match, about things he told me," Sampras said in the post-match press conference. "I still feel his spirit. He is still very much in my heart."

Sampras continued his masterful play over the remainder of the decade, winning four more Grand Slam titles. He also retained his number-one ranking, which he'd held since 1993, for a record six consecutive years, until 1998. (Sampras played through 2002 and finished with a then-record 14 career Grand Slam singles titles.)

After losing to him in the Wimbledon final in 1999, Agassi was asked by the Associated Press whether Sampras was the greatest player ever. Agassi did not hesitate.

"Yes," he said. "He's accomplished more than anybody else has, in my opinion. No question about it. His achievements speak for themselves."

equally impressive. Undefeated in their yearlong pre-Olympic tour (52–0), they won all eight of their games in Atlanta, culminating with a convincing 111–87 victory over Brazil in the gold-medal match-up. The women's soccer team finished 4–0–1 in the first Olympic soccer tournament, including a riveting 2–1 win over China for the gold medal. The U.S. women also beat a strong Chinese team in the inaugural softball tournament final, 3–1. Dr. Dot Richardson, the team's 34-year-old shortstop and an orthopedic surgeon, made the difference with a two-run homer. Several controversial calls against the Chinese led to protests, but video reviews proved the umpires were correct.

American women were golden in the swimming pool, too. Leading the way was the surprising 23-year-old Amy Van Dyken (b. 1973), whose childhood asthma was so bad, she used to collapse just walking up a flight of stairs.

Van Dyken took up swimming to increase her lung capacity, and by high school was a state champion. Her lungs worked just fine in Atlanta. She took individual golds in the 50-meter freestyle and 100-meter butterfly, and was a member of the U.S. teams that won the 4-by-100-meter freestyle and 4-by-100 medley relays.

Van Dyken thus became the first American woman to win four gold medals in one Olympic Games, either Summer or Winter. Teammate Jenny Thompson (b.1973), who brought home two relay gold medals from the 1992 Olympic Games in Barcelona, Spain, picked up three more gold medals in the relays in Atlanta.

Tiger's Tale Grows

He was only two years old when he appeared on television's *Mike Douglas Show*, hitting golf balls with ageless comedian Bob Hope. The knee-high golf prodigy shot a 48 for nine holes at age three and was featured in *Golf Digest* magazine at age five. By 1996, Eldrick "Tiger" Woods (b.1975) had established himself as an emerging star. On August 25, he won an unprecedented third straight U.S. Amateur golf title in a spectacular fashion that would follow him into his record-setting professional career.

At Pumpkin Ridge Golf Club in North Plains, Oregon, Woods found himself five holes down halfway through the 36-hole final match against University of Florida ace Steve Scott. The Tiger clawed his way back to a tie at the end of regulation play, then clinched his historic title on the second extra hole. The comeback capped a phenomenal amateur career in which he won three U.S. Junior Amateur championships. In two years at Stanford University (1995–1996), he won 10 collegiate events, including the NCAA golf title in 1996.

Two days after his smashing performance at Pumpkin Ridge, Woods turned pro by joining the Professional Golfers Association (PGA) tour at the Greater Milwaukee Open. He finished tied for 60th place, but more important, he made his much-anticipated professional debut (he had played in numerous pro tournaments since 1992, including the Masters and the U.S. Open, but with amateur status). The public had become fascinated not just with his amazing game, but also his ethnicity. Woods' father was African-

On Top of the World *Third baseman Charlie Hayes and New York Yankees' fans celebrate the final out of the 1996 World Series. New York beat Atlanta in six games for its first title since 1978.*

Two weeks later, at the Walt Disney World/Oldsmobile Classic in Orlando, he edged Payne Stewart for his second pro victory. Woods earned $940,420 in 11 tournaments worldwide and signed endorsement deals with Nike and Titleist worth $60 million. He was named the PGA Rookie of the Year and *Sports Illustrated's* Sportsman of the Year.

Sports Illustrated managing editor Bill Colson wrote an editorial explaining the choice of Woods over other remarkable athletes of 1996: "It seems clear, to us anyway, that one young man has recently surpassed all the others—perhaps in deeds but certainly in the long ripples those deeds produced. Tiger Woods, all of 20, all of four months as a pro under his belt after he won, in most dramatic fashion, a remarkable third straight U.S. Amateur title, is the only one among the candidates who changed the face of a sport, perhaps more rapidly than any other athlete ever has. In case you blinked and missed it, golf is no longer your father's sport."

Yanks End Slumber

The New York Yankees held off the Atlanta Braves 3–2 at Yankee Stadium on October 26 to win the World Series four games to two. The victory was the Yankees' record 23rd in the Fall Classic, but it marked their first title since 1978. The 18 years between World Series wins was the longest since New York won its first title in 1923.

Under new manager Joe Torre (b.1940), the Yankees finished the regular season in first place (92–70), then beat the Texas Rangers and the Baltimore Orioles

American, his mother is from Thailand. In a predominantly white sport, Woods was being compared to the late, great Jackie Robinson, who broke baseball's color barrier in 1947.

Woods, while confident in his abilities and aspirations, tried to downplay the race issue. "I'm not out just to be the best black player," he said. "I want to be the best golfer ever."

Before the year ended, Woods won two PGA events. On October 6, he held off Davis Love III in a sudden-death playoff to capture the Las Vegas Invitational.

in the playoffs to reach the World Series.

Meanwhile, in the National League, the Atlanta Braves maintained their supremacy by wrapping up their fifth N.L. East title in the last six years (96–66). They beat the Los Angeles Dodgers and St. Louis Cardinals in the N.L. playoffs to reach the Fall Classic.

The Braves burst into Yankee Stadium on October 20 on a roll. They stunned their hosts 12–1 in game one, and, after Atlanta shut out the Yankees 4–0 in game two—behind an 82-pitch, eight-inning gem from Greg Maddux—many wondered if New York was outmatched. Not quite, as the Yankees won three straight games in Atlanta. The Series took a dramatic turn in game four when New York battled back from a 6–0 deficit; the key moment was a three-run home run by Jim Leyritz in the eighth inning to tie the score. The Yanks prevailed, 8–6, in 10 innings.

Game six finally produced a win for the home team, and the Yankees were champs. Said Torre afterward: "Second place is not an option with [owner] George Steinbrenner, which is fine by me."

Other Milestones of 1996

✔ The University of Nebraska Cornhuskers, on the heels of a 62–24 pasting of the number two University of Florida Gators in the Fiesta Bowl on January 2, became the first college football team in 16 years to win back-to-back national championships.

✔ Don Shula, head coach of the Miami Dolphins since 1970, resigned on January 5. His legacy included an NFL-record 347 wins, two Super Bowl titles (VII and VIII), and the only perfect record (17–0 in 1972) in NFL history.

✔ The Dallas Cowboys beat the Pittsburgh Steelers, 27–17, in Super Bowl XXX on January 28 in Tempe, Arizona. Dallas cornerback Larry Brown was the MVP after two second-half interceptions.

✔ The Kentucky Wildcats topped the Syracuse Orangemen, 76–67, to win the NCAA men's basketball championship on April 1. It marked the Wildcats' sixth national title.

✔ In the final round of the Masters golf tournament on April 14, Greg Norman blew a six-shot lead and was overtaken by eventual winner Nick Faldo.

✔ Boxer Evander Holyfield scored a surprising 11th-round technical knockout of Mike Tyson to gain the heavyweight title on November 9.

1997

The Pack Is Back

The Green Bay Packers beat the New England Patriots 35–21 in Super Bowl XXXI at the Louisiana Superdome in New Orleans on January 26. The victory was the Packers' first in the Super Bowl since winning games I and II to cap the 1966 and 1967 seasons.

Balance was the hallmark of this 13–3 Packers team. Quarterback Brett Favre (b.1969) won his second straight NFL MVP award after throwing an NFC-record 39 touchdowns to several receivers. Veteran defensive end Reggie White was the bedrock of the defense.

Less than a minute into the second quarter against the 11–5 Patriots, Favre tossed a Super Bowl-record, 81-yard touchdown bomb to Antonio Freeman. The Packers scored another 10 points before halftime. Undaunted, the Patriots crept to within six points on Curtis Martin's 18-yard touchdown run late in the third quarter, but then Green Bay's Desmond Howard snapped their spirit with a 99-yard return of the ensuing kickoff. A two-point conversion capped off the scoring—and the triumphant back-to-Titletown season for the Packers.

Fresh Prince of NASCAR

Jeff Gordon (b.1971) didn't have the Southern pedigree of Richard Petty, the recently retired King of stock car racing (see page 245). But the clean-cut Midwesterner, like Petty, became a royal pain in the neck to his fellow NASCAR competitors.

Gordon got his engine running right at the start of the Winston Cup season, winning the Daytona 500 on February 14. He promised team owner Rick Hendrick, who was back home in North Carolina fighting leukemia, that he'd win the race. Not only did Gordon, at age 25, become the youngest driver to win NASCAR's most prestigious event, but he led a one-two-three sweep of Hendrick-team cars (Terry Labonte and Ricky Craven finished second and third, respectively).

Less fortunate was Dale Earnhardt (1952–2001), who was still looking for his first Daytona win in 19 tries. Gordon passed Earnhardt for second place with 10 laps to go, and the move set in motion a huge crash that left Earnhardt's car a mess. Instead of taking himself out of the race, though, Earnhardt climbed back inside the wreck and finished 31st.

Sunday Drive   *Tiger Woods left no doubt he was golf's next superstar with a whopping 12-stroke victory at the prestigious Masters tournament (see page 281).*

Gordon went on to post one of the most remarkable seasons in NASCAR history. He took nine more of the 31 races on the Winston Cup circuit, winning $4,201,227 along the way. Plus, he finished first in two of the other four major races: the Coca-Cola 600 and the Southern 500 (the fourth is the Winston 500). That earned him the Winston Million—a cool $1 million bonus—which had only

Boy Wonder *Twenty-five-year-old Jeff Gordon won his first Daytona 500 in 1997 and went on dominate the NASCAR circuit en route to winning driver-of-the-year honors.*

been won once before, by "Million-Dollar" Bill Elliott in 1985. With the princely sum of his season, Gordon was easily crowned Winston Cup driver of the year.

In the 'Zona

The University of Arizona Wildcats finished in just fifth place in the Pacific-10 Conference during the 1996–97 regular season, but head coach Lute Olson's squad hit its stride at just the right time. The Wildcats knocked off three No. 1 seeds en route to winning the NCAA Men's Basketball Tournament, including an 84–79 victory in overtime against Kentucky in the final game March 31 in Indianapolis.

The NCAA tournament featured the usual first-round upsets: number 15 seed Coppin State University surprised second-seeded University of South Carolina; number 14 seed University of Tennessee at Chattanooga upset number three

University of Georgia; number 12 seed College of Charleston beat number five University of Maryland. Even so, three of the number-one seeds advanced to the Final Four at the RCA Dome in Indianapolis. The lone exception was Kansas, which dropped an 85–82 decision to Arizona in the Southeast Region semifinals.

In the national semifinals, defending champion Kentucky beat the University of Minnesota for the right to meet Arizona (which defeated North Carolina) two nights later.

Arizona led by one point at halftime, 33–32. With 61 seconds left in the game, Arizona was up 72–68, seemingly on its way to the school's first national basketball championship. But Kentucky's Ron Mercer and Anthony Epps each hit three-pointers; Arizona could only score two more points for the tie, and the game went into overtime. Kentucky lost its earlier momentum in the five-minute extra period and was forced to foul. Arizona kept its cool, sank enough free throws, and prevailed, 84–79. Arizona became the first school ever to knock off three No. 1 seeds in the tournament en route to winning the title.

Arizona and Kentucky both were composed mostly of freshman and sophomores whose relatively raw talent brought them this far. Yet this tournament, wrote Paul Attner in *The Sporting News*, "provided a wonderful road map to show us where the sport is headed after too many years of losing too many elite underclassmen to the NBA."

Tiger Tames Augusta

The golf world had been waiting for this moment, for Tiger Woods to take on the man-eating course at Augusta National Golf Club in Augusta, Georgia. But with his record-setting 12-stroke victory in the annual Masters Tournament, April 10 to 13, it could be an eternity before we see another such masterful performance. The 21-year-old golf genius made Augusta seem like a miniature golf course.

Woods' incredible golfing performance came on what is considered to be among the most challenging courses in the sport. Augusta's long, narrow fairways, treacherous bunkers, and rolling greens have tested and taunted the best players in the game ever since legendary golfer Bobby Jones created the course and the tournament in 1934.

Woods got off to a shaky start in the four-day tournament. He shot 40 on the first nine holes of the 18-hole course, but then settled into a groove. That's an understatement. Over the next three days and 63 holes, he shot 22 under par, finishing 18 under to break the great Jack Nicklaus' (b. 1940) and Ray Floyd's Masters record. His 12-stroke win was the largest margin of victory in a major tournament since Tom Morris won the 1862 British Open by 13 strokes. (Besides the Masters and the British Open, the two other majors are the U.S. Open and the PGA Championship.)

"He's out there playing another game on a golf course he is going to own for a long time," said Nicklaus, who won the Masters at age 23 and whose six titles are more than anyone else's—so far.

A League of Their Own

The eight-team Women's National Basketball Association (WNBA), an affiliate of the NBA, tipped off its inaugural season on June 21 as the New York Liberty beat the Los Angeles Sparks, 67–57. A crowd of 14,284 at the Great Western Forum, in Inglewood, California, witnessed Sparks guard Penny Toler score the first basket in WNBA history.

A hybrid of the pro and college games, the WNBA features a 30-second shot clock, a 19-foot, nine-inch three-point line, two 20-minute halves, 11-player rosters, and a signature orange-and-oatmeal, collegiate-size basketball (28.5 inches in circumference, one inch smaller than the NBA's regulation ball).

The teams, with recent college stars such as Lisa Leslie, Rebecca Lobo, Sheryl Swoopes, and Cynthia Cooper, played 28 games in 1997. On August 30, the Houston Comets, led by league MVP Cooper's

We've Come A Long Way

The other remarkable aspect of Tiger Woods' phenomenal win at Augusta had to do with his ethnicity (half African-American, half Thai) and its sociological implications. An excerpt from an article written the following day by *Philadelphia Inquirer* sports columnist Bill Lyon poignantly summarized the significance of the occasion:

> Tiger Woods won a tournament of great prestige in one of the most exclusive and restrictive enclaves in the world, a place that, until recent years, he could have gained admission to only by way of the servant's entrance.
>
> The green-coated autocrats of Augusta National would have permitted him to clean their ashtrays and shine their shoes and serve them assorted beverages. But the only way he would have set a shoe onto those lush and fragrant fairways was as a caddy.
>
> Last night, in the gentle Georgia gloaming, those very same men stood to applaud as Tiger Woods slipped into a coat of the very same hue as theirs. They shook the hand of a 21-year-old prodigy, and their grip was sincere. The optimist in you would like to think that at that moment, we edged another inch up the progress chart.
>
> It will be recorded that, two days before the 50th anniversary of Jackie Robinson first playing in a Major League Baseball game, Woods became the first African American to win a Masters or, indeed, any major golf tournament.
>
> But this is too narrow, too constricting. Because through Tiger Woods courses the blood of five nationalities—not only African-American, but Chinese, Cherokee, Thai, and Dutch. Tiger Woods is a melting pot with a wedge.
>
> Better, then, that we celebrate him, and this, for what they are—a triumph for all humankind.

25 points, defeated the Liberty, 65–51, to capture the first WNBA title.

The Fall of Tyson, Part II

By the time he stepped into the boxing ring against Evander Holyfield on June 28, Mike Tyson had experienced a wild range of highs and lows, in and out of boxing. Right from the start of his professional career in 1985, Tyson's power-punching, street-fighting style intimidated opponents. He won 14 fights that year, 11 by first-round knock-outs. A year later, "Iron Mike" won the World Boxing Council (WBC) heavyweight title, becoming the youngest heavyweight fighter, at age 20, to win a world title. By the end of 1987 he held the WBC, World Boxing Association (WBA), and International Boxing Federation (IBF) titles, making him the undisputed heavyweight champion.

In the meantime, his personal life took a beating. A brief and turbulent marriage to actress Robin Givens ended in divorce. In 1992, two years after his shocking loss to relative unknown Buster Douglas, he was convicted of raping an 18-year-old woman and served three years in prison. Tyson regained his WBC and WBA titles in 1996, but then lost the WBA title in November to Holyfield. Now came the rematch, which turned into one of sports' more bizarre spectacles.

The arena at the MGM Grand Garden in Las Vegas was packed for the greatly anticipated fight. Holyfield won the first two rounds on all three judges' scorecards. As Tyson prepared to come out for the third round, Holyfield pointed out that he'd forgotten his mouthpiece. Once the fight resumed, Tyson spit out the mouthpiece, grabbed Holyfield, and bit his right ear. The action had to be halted for four minutes while the ringside doctor tended to Holyfield's bleeding ear. But after the fight started up again, Tyson did the same thing, except this time he bit Holyfield's left ear.

Referee Mills Lane immediately stopped the fight and disqualified Tyson. While Holyfield went to the hospital for treatment, Tyson defended his actions, charging that Holyfield had illegally head-butted him in the first and second rounds. State boxing officials suspended Tyson and withheld his $30 million fee for the fight, pending an inquiry.

On July 9, the Nevada Athletic Commission revoked Tyson's boxing license for one year and fined him $3 million—which meant he ended up making $27 million. Tyson's Nevada boxing license was restored October 19, 1998, and he was back in the ring by January of the following year.

Legends Retire

Two nationally known college coaching legends decided to step down after long and storied careers at their schools. First, basketball's Dean Smith (b.1931) retired on October 9; then, on November 29, it was football's Eddie Robinson (1919–2007).

Smith was the head coach of the University of North Carolina Tar Heels for 36 years beginning with the 1961–62 season. He led his teams to two national championships, 17 Atlantic Coast

Reality Bites *Champion Evander Holyfield grimaces while bitten by challenger Mike Tyson in their heavyweight title fight. Tyson was fined and suspended, but soon was back in the boxing ring.*

Conference titles, and 879 wins in all (a college record that stood until Bob Knight surpassed it in 2007). Twenty-seven of Smith's teams played in the NCAA tournament, including the last 23 in a row. His final team went 28–7 and advanced to the NCAA Final Four.

What Smith was to North Carolina basketball, Robinson was to the Grambling State University Tigers football team. Robinson was the head coach at the predominantly African-American school in Louisiana since 1941. He won 408 games (a record for any NCAA Division I coach) and led his teams to three perfect seasons and eight black national championships.

Both coaches sent dozens of players on to the professional ranks, but both also were equally intent on helping their players graduate.

More Unruly Behavior

Mike Tyson wasn't the only sports personality who couldn't control himself this year:

- In game five of the NBA Eastern Conference semifinals on May 14 in Miami, players from the New York Knicks and Miami Heat got into a bench-clearing brawl. The league suspended the Heat's P. J. Brown and the Knicks' Patrick Ewing, Charlie Ward, and Allan Houston for game six; Brown and the Knicks' Larry Johnson and John Starks were suspended for game seven. The Knicks, up three games to one entering game five, lost that game and the series.

- On September 25, veteran sportscaster Marv Albert pleaded guilty to misdemeanor assault and battery charges. It was revealed during the trial in Virginia that Albert had bitten his female accuser during sex. Hours after the verdict, he was fired from his announcer's job at NBC Sports and resigned as an announcer for the Madison Square Garden Network.

- Latrell Sprewell (b.1970), a guard for basketball's Golden State Warriors, punched and choked his head coach, P.J. Carlesimo, during practice on December 1. Sprewell claimed that he was provoked by ongoing verbal abuse from Carlesimo. In one of the most costly punishments in sports history, the NBA suspended Sprewell for one year and the Warriors terminated the remaining three years of his four-year, $32 million contract.

The One-Year Wonders

By winning the 1997 World Series, team owner H. Wayne Huizenga and his Florida Marlins proved that baseball in the 1990s had unmistakably become a game in which money talks. Following the 1995 season, which the Marlins finished with a record of 67–76, Huizenga devised a two-year upgrade plan. The owner of Blockbuster Video stores opened up his ample wallet to sign top pitchers Kevin Brown and Al Leiter in 1996 and Alex Fernandez in 1997. He bulked up the offense by adding Moises Alou, Darren Daulton, and Bobby Bonilla to the 1997 roster. The critical move, though, was hiring manager Jim Leyland, a proven winner who had navigated the Pittsburgh Pirates to three consecutive National League East titles from 1990 to 1992. Coupled with other complementary acquisitions and its budding homegrown talent, Florida was poised to make a pennant run this year.

Behind strong pitching, Florida won a team-best 92 games during the regular season. That was second in the N.L. East to the 101–61 Atlanta Braves, but enough to qualify as the N.L. wildcard entry in the playoffs. The Marlins swept the San Francisco Giants in three games in the division series, then surprised the mighty Braves by taking the N.L. Championship Series (NLCS), four games to two in September.

The Cleveland Indians won the American League pennant with a power-packed lineup. Sluggers Jim Thome, Matt Williams, David Justice, Manny Ramirez, and Sandy Alomar Jr. led an offense that produced enough runs to overpower a mediocre pitching staff. Cleveland won the A.L. Central with an 86–75 record, knocked off the New York Yankees in the divisional series, and beat the Baltimore Orioles in six games in the ALCS.

The World Series came down to a thrilling seventh game on October 26 in Miami. In the bottom of the 11th inning, with the score tied 2–2, Florida shortstop Edgar Renteria hit a two-out, bases-loaded single off Charles Nagy to score Craig Counsell. Thus the Marlins, in just their fifth season, became the quickest expansion team to win the World Series.

Baseball-wise, Huizenga's investments paid major dividends. Financially, however, the owner complained that he'd lost $30 million and wanted to sell the team. Ironically, to make the sale more attractive—that is, to lower the price of the team—he began unloading players within weeks after the Series. On Opening Day of 1998, an almost entirely new team took the field, leaving dismayed fans with only fleeting memories of glory. The Marlins went on the finish with the worst record in baseball, at 54–108. The following January, the team was sold.

Other Milestones of 1997

✔ Quarterback Danny Wuerffel, the 1996 Heisman Trophy winner, led the University of Florida to its first Division I college football national title following the school's 52–20 trouncing of rival Florida State University in the Sugar Bowl on January 2.

✔ The University of Tennessee's Lady Vols, paced by Chamique Holdsclaw's 24 points, topped Old Dominion University, 68–59, on March 30 to repeat as college basketball national champions.

✔ On June 13, the Chicago Bulls won their fifth NBA title of the 1990s. They beat the Utah Jazz, 90–86, in Chicago to take the series, 4–2. Michael Jordan was the MVP, averaging 32.3 points per game.

✔ On June 30, the Texas Rangers' Bobby Witt hit a home run in an interleague game against the Los Angeles Dodgers. What's so unusual about that? Well, Witt was the first American League pitcher since 1972 to hit a homer. The designated hitter had taken the bat of out of the pitcher's hands. Interleague play sent A.L. pitchers back to the plate.

✔ On December 13, Michigan cornerback Charles Woodson became the first primarily defensive player to win the Heisman Trophy, awarded to college football's best player. Woodson would become the fourth player picked (by the Oakland Raiders) in the NFL draft in the spring of 1998, and would make the Pro Bowl in his first season in the league.

1998

Broncos Kick It Up

Terrell Davis scored a record three rushing touchdowns, including a one-yard run with 1:45 remaining, to lift the Denver Broncos past the Green Bay Packers 31–24 in Super Bowl XXXII on January 25 at San Diego's Qualcomm Stadium. Denver's victory was its first after four losses in as many Super Bowl appearances (dating to the 1977 season), and was the first for an AFC team in the Super Bowl since the 1983 season.

Three of the Broncos' four Super Bowl losses came with John Elway (b.1960) at quarterback. In his fourth try, the 37-year-old Elway at long last had a Vince Lombardi trophy and a championship ring—the missing pieces to go along with reams of spectacular statistics amassed over his 16 NFL seasons.

Elway only needed to be efficient against Green Bay (he passed for 123 yards and ran for a touchdown), thanks to Davis and an offensive line that could make a hole in anything. The AFC's top rusher that season (1,750 yards), Davis tortured the Packers' defense, gaining 157 yards on 30 carries and earning game most valuable player honors.

New Winter Games

From February 7 to 22, the modest mountain city of Nagano, Japan, a little more than an hour northwest of Tokyo, hosted 2,302 athletes from 72 countries as they participated in 68 events in the Winter Olympic Games. Among them were, for the first time as official medal sports, snowboarding, curling, and women's ice hockey. The United States won 13 medals at Nagano: six gold, three silver, and four bronze.

The super-fast Super G (giant slalom) course at the Hakuba downhill skiing venue provided one of the most golden moments of the Games for the United States. That's where Picabo Street turned previous tragedies into triumph. Only 14 months earlier, Street had crashed while training in Vail, Colorado, damaging ligaments, cartilage, and bone in her left knee. She recovered from reconstructive surgery in remarkable time, and began training for Nagano just before Thanksgiving 1997. Then, 11 days before the Olympics began, Street fell on a slope in Sweden and was knocked unconscious.

Her first of two events in Japan was the downhill, in which she took the silver

Curtain Call *Fans at St. Louis' Busch Stadium salute Mark McGwire, the new home-run king (page 292).*

medal at the 1994 Games in Lillehammer, Norway. Though Street finished sixth in the downhill at Nagano, she kept her hopes high for the upcoming Super G.

Wearing a skintight, blazing yellow suit and racing on longer downhill skis, Street had a slight misstep about halfway through her final run, but recovered nicely. Her time of 1:18.02 put her in first place,

though her toughest competitors had yet to ski. Austria's Michaela Dorfmeister crossed the finish line at 1:18.03—giving Street the gold by a scant one one-hundredth of a second, the slimmest margin of victory possible.

Meanwhile, in the figure skating hall, 15-year-old Tara Lipinski skated her short program to a song from the movie *Anas-*

Upside Down *The 1998 Winter Olympics in Nagano, Japan, were host to a number of new medal sports. Among them: the extreme sport of snowboarding, a staple of the X Games.*

nament, which came down to a face-off between the United States and Canada. Throughout the 1990s the Canadians had dominated the sport, especially against the Americans, beating them in four world championships. Canada was fully expected to maintain its mastery in Nagano. But the United States won, 3–1, with clean, hard skating, solid goaltending, and timely goals.

Back on the ski slopes, the United States took three of the four gold medals in freestyle skiing. Eric Bergoust and Nikki Stone won the men's and women's aerials, respectively. Bergoust, with his gravity-defying aerobatics, set a world record with a pair of nearly perfect quadruple twisting triple flips. Stone nailed both her back somersaults to top the 12-woman field. Jonny Moseley, a free-spirited Californian, won the freestyle moguls event on the strength of his trademark helicopter jump—a 360-degree spin in the air while grabbing one of his crossed skis, followed by a pinpoint landing.

Birth of the BCS

It's not often easy breaking with tradition. And in the case of college football's system of bowl games, that tradition has roots that date back more than 100 years. Add to that the millions of dollars in payouts offered by the major traditional postseason bowl games, and the increasing calls for a college football play-off to determine the national champion have gone unheeded.

Nevertheless, the bowl format did undergo tinkering in 1998 in an attempt to decide a true national champion. Pre-

tasia. She did well, but her favored rival, fellow American Michelle Kwan (b.1980), skated slightly better and was in first place going into the decisive long program two nights later. Kwan went first among the six finalists and turned in what appeared to be a winning performance. But Lipinski skated a nearly flawless program. Her squeals of joy, as her scores come up indicating she'd captured the gold medal, echoed throughout the arena.

A lot of women took to the ice for the first Olympic women's hockey tour-

viously, the "champion" was declared by rival polls taken among sportswriters and coaches. Occasionally, those polls disagreed about the national champion, leading to endless debates.

In 1998, in the latest scheme to pair the No. 1 and No. 2 teams in the land in a single "championship" game, officials from the Orange, Sugar, Rose, and Fiesta bowls joined with the Atlantic Coast, Big East, Big 12, Big Ten, Pacific-10, and Southeastern conferences and the University of Notre Dame to form the Bowl Championship Series (BCS). A complex system, using national polls, computer tabulations, and strength of schedules, ranks teams and ultimately determines the bowl match-ups. (The formula has been tweaked several times since the original.) And in the decade-plus existence of the BCS, sometimes it has worked—and sometimes it has only led to more debate.

Beísbol in America

The Hispanic presence in Major League Baseball had been quietly growing since the 1970s. A small handful of players had appeared before that, most notably Hall of Famer Roberto Clemente (1934–1972) from Puerto Rico. In the 1990s, however, their numbers multiplied. In 1998, for instance, for the first time, the MVPs of both leagues were born in Latin American countries: for the National League, Sammy Sosa from the Dominican Republic; for the American League, Puerto Rico native Juan Gonzalez.

From 1990 to 2001, according to Northeastern University's Center for the Study of Sport in Society director, Peter Roby, the number of Hispanic major leaguers swelled to 26 percent from 13 percent; most were born outside the U.S. In the same period, the number of African Americans on Major League Baseball rosters declined to 13 percent from 17 percent and the percentage of white players shrank to 59 from 70. This reflected similar trends in the general U.S. population.

Dating back to the 1860s, baseball has a long and rich tradition in Cuba, the Dominican Republic, Puerto Rico, and other Latin American nations. Some Major League baseball teams used to have spring training camps and play exhibition games there. But not until about the same time Jackie Robinson broke the game's color barrier in 1947, did foreign-born Hispanics catch scouts' eyes. Over the coming decades, some would shine as among baseball's best, including Hall of Famers Juan Marichal (Dominican Republic), Rod Carew (Panama), Orlando Cepeda (Puerto Rico), Tony Perez (Cuba), and Luis Tiant (Cuba).

Hispanics continued to thrive, if not in numbers, then in stature, until the 1990s. That's when economics led to an influx of talented Latin players who could be signed for less money than what U.S. high school and college prospects commanded. By the end of the decade, virtually every major league franchise had opened baseball academies in the Dominican Republic, by far the region's greatest pool of talent. Besides Sosa, the island nation had by then produced such marquee names as Pedro Martinez, Manny Ramirez, Miguel Tejada, Raul Mondesi, and Jose Rijo.

1998

Hispanics on the 1998 All-Star teams included Sosa, Gonzalez, Alex Rodriguez, Ivan Rodriguez, brothers Roberto and Sandy Alomar, Moises Alou, Andres Galarraga, Javy Lopez, and Edgar Renteria. Second baseman Roberto Alomar—on the strength of his home run, walk, stolen base, and superb defensive play—won the MVP Award for the '98 All-Star game, which the A.L. won, 13–8.

Big E for Endurance

NASCAR could not have planned a more perfect beginning for its 50th anniversary season, as the sport's most popular driver won its most prestigious event—finally.

Long Time Coming *Legendary Dale Earnhardt (in the number-3 car) won the biggest race on the NASCAR circuit, the Daytona 500, for the first time on his 20th try.*

After 19 hope-filled tries and 19 frustrating failures, Dale Earnhardt succeeded in taking the checkered flag at the Daytona 500. "The Intimidator," as the hard-driving, highly competitive Earnhardt was known, already had seven Winston Cup driving championships, 70 career Cup wins, and 575 Cup starts under his seatbelt, including 30 on the hallowed, high-banked oval track at Daytona, Florida.

Earnhardt was 46 years old when he climbed into his famous black No. 3 Chevy on February 15, 1998. Since becoming NASCAR's Winston Cup Rookie of the Year in 1979, he had won just about every other race, but was on the brink of becoming one of those sports legends who never wins The Big One.

Earnhardt had been oh-so-close to winning Daytona before. Four times he'd lost the lead with 10 laps to go. He'd come up short twice on the last lap. This year, he had a pack of pesky pursuers on his tail as the 200-lap race neared its exciting conclusion. He held them all off, though, and a long-awaited celebration erupted. To conclude his most memorable victory lap, Earnhardt cruised down pit road (the stretch alongside a racetrack where pit crews are stationed), as drivers and crew members from virtually every team lined up to shake his hand. Then he went into the infield and did a couple of celebratory donuts (spinning his car in circles).

"I wish every race driver that ever runs Daytona could feel what we felt yesterday in Victory Lane," Earnhardt told reporters the following day. "That's one of the greatest feelings in your life, to work that many years and come so close and be so dominant and finally win that race."

The Man in Black

There was little doubt, when he was growing up in tiny Kannapolis, North Carolina, that Dale Earnhardt would some day race cars for a living. His father, Ralph Earnhardt, was one of stock car racing's pioneers during the 1950s, and young Dale soaked up the rough-and-tumble lifestyle. "I wanted to race—that's all I ever wanted to do," he once said. "I didn't care about work or school or anything. All I wanted to do was to work on race cars and then drive race cars. It was always my dream, and I was just fortunate enough to be able to live out that dream."

True to his word, Earnhardt quit school when he was 16 and made his Winston Cup debut in 1975, finishing 22nd in the World 600 at the Charlotte Motor Speedway in North Carolina. He joined NASCAR's "major league" circuit full-time in 1979. Earnhardt took his first Winston Cup win that season at Bristol Motor Speedway in Bristol, Tennessee, and was named Rookie of the Year. A year later, he became the first Winston Cup driver to win Rookie of the Year and Driver of the Year in successive seasons.

Along with six more championships, he claimed victory in nearly every major event on the circuit, including a career-best 11 wins in 1987. In 2000, when some wondered if he'd passed his prime, Earnhardt posted two wins, 13 top five finishes, and 24 top 10s, and came in second behind Jeff Gordon in the final points standings.

On February 18, 2001, Earnhardt started his 23rd Daytona 500 from the seventh position and was racing for third during the last lap. He had himself in position so that his teammate, Michael Waltrip, and his son, Dale Earnhardt Jr., would finish first and second, respectively. Suddenly, Dale Sr.'s No. 3 Chevy was bumped by another car, causing Earnhardt to crash head-on into the wall. He was killed instantly.

Wrote *AutoWeek* managing editor Roger Hart in tribute, "As we found out February 18 at the Daytona International Speedway, even being the best of the best—and make no mistake about it, Dale Earnhardt was the best stock car driver ever—is not always enough. Like many other race fans across the country, I will miss Dale Earnhardt. NASCAR racing will not be the same. He helped make stock car racing what it is today, and if there's any solace in his passing, it's that he loved every minute of it."

Lady Vols, Take Three

Women's sports flourished during the 1990s. From Little League to the Olympics, female athletes participated in ever-increasing numbers at higher and higher levels of competition. The highest profile sport for women was college basketball, which ran a fast break through the decade. And by winning their third straight NCAA national championship on March 29 at Kemper Arena in Kansas City, Missouri, the University of Tennessee's Lady Vols exemplified just how far the sport had advanced.

Coached by the celebrated Pat Summitt, in her 24th year at Tennessee, the Lady Vols steamrolled through the regular season undefeated, with a 33–0 record. They utterly dominated opponents, outscoring teams by an average margin of 30.1 points per game.

Chamique Holdsclaw, the junior forward and national player of the year, solidified her reputation as perhaps the best female college player ever. "Her

Little Guys Pound Big Homers

In a slugfest that would make Mark McGwire and Sammy Sosa proud, the Little League team from Toms River, New Jersey, out-homered the squad from Kashima, Japan, to win the Little League World Series, 12–9, on August 29 in Williamsport, Pennsylvania. This was the first American team to claim the title since Long Beach, California, won back-to-back championships in 1992 and 1993.

A total of 11 homers highlighted the game, six of them for the New Jersey team. Shortstop Chris Cardone hit a pair in consecutive at-bats—the second one a game-deciding two-run shot in the sixth inning. Tetsuya Furukawa belted three of Kashima's five home runs.

Besides several lead changes, the spirited international contest featured Sayaka Tsushima, the sixth girl to play in a Little League World Series, the first in a final, and the first from a Far East champion. She went 0 for 3.

Airness"—as she had become known, borrowing a nickname from Michael Jordan—not only averaged 23.5 points per game (including six NCAA tournament appearances), but demonstrated tremendous leadership to a pair of talented, but raw freshmen, Tamika Catchings and Semeka Randall.

The tournament's field of 64 teams showcased the burgeoning talent found at schools nationwide, but Tennessee was clearly at the head of the class. Its only speedbump along the road to Kansas City came in the Mideast Regional final versus the University of North Carolina, in which the Vols valiantly overcame a 12-point second-half deficit to prevail, 76–70. They played a near-perfect championship game, easily dispensing with Louisiana Tech University, 93–75. Holdsclaw—with 25 points, 10 rebounds, and six assists in the finale—was voted the Final Four's Most Outstanding Player.

Tennessee thus became the first women's team to claim three straight titles, and it was their sixth in 12 years.

"The best team doesn't always win," said Summitt in the post-game press conference, "but tonight, I thought the best team won a championship that they deserved."

Chasing 61

In 1998, the New York Yankees forged one of baseball's best seasons ever. The Bronx Bombers won 114 of 162 regular-season games, breezed through the American League playoffs, and then swept the National League-champion San Diego Padres in four games in the World Series. It was the Yankees' record 24th world championship.

Even still, the most memorable story line of the 1998 season had nothing to do with the Yankees. Instead, it was an epic battle for baseball's single-season home-run record. That chase, waged all summer long between the St. Louis Cardinals' Mark McGwire (b.1963) and the Chicago Cubs' Sammy Sosa (b.1968), captivated the nation, and helped win over the hearts of some fans who felt jilted during the 1994 players' strike.

McGwire smacked 11 homers by the end of April. Sosa had just six home runs by May 1, but went crazy in June, smacking a major league-record 20. At the All-Star break in July, Sosa had 33 home runs to McGwire's 37. The big-league record of 61 home runs by the Yankees (set in 1961) was in sight.

Sosa reached the 50 plateau on August 11; McGwire arrived there on the 20th. By the end of the month, when they both stood at 55 homers, Maris' widow and family were graciously and anxiously awaiting baseball history. They sat proudly in box seats at St. Louis' Busch Stadium on September 7 when McGwire tied the record at 61, and were back there the next day when he hit No. 62. Ironically, the record breaker was his shortest home run of the season.

On September 11, at Wrigley Field, Sosa kept pace with homers 61 and 62. He ended up hitting four more to finish at 66, while McGwire kept up his assault on the record books right up until the last day of the season, blasting two to finish with a phenomenal total of 70 home runs.

Other Milestones of 1998

✔ New Year's Day saw the University of Michigan end a 12–0 season with a 21–16 win over Washington State University in the Rose Bowl. Nonetheless, the Michigan Wolverines shared the number one college football ranking with 13–0 University of Nebraska.

✔ In January, CBS, Fox, and ABC/ESPN committed $17.6 billion from 1998 to 2005 to televise NFL games. Color analyst John Madden signed a five-year deal with Fox worth $8 million per year.

✔ A federal magistrate ruled, on February 11, that under the Americans with Disabilities Act, handicapped pro golfer Casey Martin could use a motorized golf cart in PGA tournaments, despite tournament rules to the contrary.

✔ A couple of baseball pitching gems: On May 6 in Chicago, 20-year-old Cubs rookie Kerry Wood tied a Major League record by striking out 20 Houston Astros in a 2–0 victory in his fifth career start. On May 17 at Yankee Stadium, veteran left-hander David Wells pitched the 15th perfect game ever (27 batters up, and 27 batters down) in a 4–0 win over Minnesota.

✔ In a labor dispute, NBA team owners imposed a player lockout on June 29 that would eventually shorten the 1998–1999 basketball season.

✔ On July 9, Ila Borders became the first female pitcher to start a minor league game. The 24-year-old lefty pitched five innings for the Duluth-Superior Dukes in the Northern League.

✔ Baltimore Orioles shortstop Cal Ripken ended his streak of consecutive games played at 2,632 on September 20 at Camden Yards. Ripken took himself out of the lineup.

1999

Elway Out on Top

Only one NFL player ever was named the Super Bowl's most valuable player in the last game of his career. That player was quarterback John Elway, who guided the Denver Broncos to a 34–19 victory over the Atlanta Falcons in Super Bowl XXXIII at Pro Player Stadium in Miami on January 31.

It was the second consecutive Super Bowl victory for Elway and the Broncos, who beat the Green Bay Packers in game XXXII the previous January (see page 286). Before that, both Denver and its quarterback struggled to overcome the reputation that they couldn't win the Big One. The Broncos had lost the Super Bowl four times, three of them with Elway at quarterback. "You wonder," Elway once said, "if you run out of years."

Elway didn't run out of years, and got to retire on his own terms: after winning a Super Bowl. Against Atlanta, he completed 18 of 29 passes for 336 yards. Early in the fourth quarter, he ran 3 yards for the touchdown that helped put the game out of reach at 31–6. Soon afterward, he was holding aloft the Vince Lombardi Trophy in the Broncos' postgame celebration.

Money Players

On January 6, the Baseball Writers' Association of America (BBWAA) elected three first-time candidates into the National Baseball Hall of Fame in Cooperstown, New York: Nolan Ryan, George Brett, and Robin Yount (players are eligible for induction five years after they retire). The last time that happened was in 1936, and those players—Ty Cobb, Walter Johnson, Christy Mathewson, Babe Ruth, and Honus Wagner—were in the very first group of baseball players enshrined in the Hall of Fame.

The news brought cheers from baseball fans who appreciated the remarkable achievements of each player, although it particularly heartened sports collectors. For as much as money drove athletes, team owners, television networks, and corporate sponsors during the 1990s, the memorabilia and collectibles industry shifted into high gear during the decade, too. Values of trading cards and autographed items—from game-used jerseys to cancelled paychecks—skyrocketed.

The financial significance of the Hall of Fame announcement was the instant increase in price of items related to Ryan,

World Class   *The United States hosted—and won—soccer's Women's World Cup (see page 298).*

Brett, and Yount. Getting into the Hall raises a player's stature, and therefore the worth of his likeness and things connected to him. For example, Ryan's rookie card (1968 Topps #177) rose from about $1,000 to nearly $3,000, practically overnight.

Proof of just how crazy the market had gotten surfaced on January 12, when the baseball that Mark McGwire hit for his historic 70th home run in 1998 sold at auction for slightly more than $3 million. A couple of weeks later, the buyer revealed himself: Todd McFarlane, the creator of *Spawn* and other superhero comic books and toys. In fact, the owner

of the so-called McFarlane Collection had plunked down another $300,000 or so to acquire McGwire's No. 1, 63, 67, 68, and 69 home-run balls, along with Sammy Sosa's No. 33, 61, and 66.

While you chew on that, consider Karen Shemonsky of Clarks Summit, Pennsylvania, who paid $7,475 for Cobb's false teeth—honestly—at a Sotheby's baseball memorabilia auction on September 27. "[Friends] keep calling me, saying, 'Why would you want that?'" Shemonsky told reporters. "My sister goes on cruises. I'd rather have this in my hand." Biting commentary on the times, for sure.

Two Out of Three Ain't Bad   *Jockey Chris Antley rode Charismatic (6) to victory in the Kentucky Derby and the Preakness Stakes, but fell short of the coveted Triple Crown in the Belmont Stakes.*

Every Dog Has His Day

In the 1990s, the University of Connecticut Huskies were heralded from Juneau to Jupiter (Florida) for their outstanding basketball. UConn's men's program, since the arrival in 1986 of head coach Jim Calhoun, rose from the doghouse to the penthouse in the Big East Conference. And coach Geno Auriemma guided the Lady Huskies to national prominence with a perfect season and a national championship in 1995.

It took four years for Calhoun's men to catch up, but they finally won it all in 1999, downing Duke University in the NCAA championship game, 77–74, on March 29 at Tropicana Field in St. Petersburg, Florida. Coming into the tourna-ment, UConn held the unenviable record for most NCAA appearances (20) without reaching the Final Four. What made this championship even sweeter was vanquishing the Blue Devils, who had become UConn's nemesis in recent years. Seven times during the 1990s, UConn had played into the Sweet 16, and each time they'd fallen short—twice to Duke. The most devastating defeat was in the 1990 tournament, when Christian Laettner's last-second shot sent UConn home.

Duke, with only one loss all season and an immaculate 16–0 record in the tough Atlantic Coast Conference, was heavily favored. Yet UConn, with a 28–2 regular-season record, didn't exactly fit the underdog profile. Sure enough, coach Mike Krzyzewski's Blue Devils, powered by 6-foot-8, 260-pound forward Elton Brand—the national player of the year—couldn't stop the sharp shooting of UConn guard Richard "Rip" Hamilton, who went on a game-high 27-point tear. Shortly after Duke's Trajan Langdon was called for traveling while driving to score the potential game-winning basket, the Huskies fell into a celebratory dog pile on the court.

Charismatic, Not Charmed

For the third year in a row, a horse entered the Belmont Stakes with a chance to win thoroughbred racing's Triple Crown. And for the third year in a row, that horse fell short. This year, it was Charismatic that won the Kentucky Derby and the Preakness Stakes before finishing third in the Belmont on June 5 in New York. (In 1997, Silver Charm won the first two legs of the Triple Crown, and in 1998 Real Quiet did it. Through 2010, no horse has won the Triple Crown since Affirmed in 1978.)

After winning the Kentucky Derby at Churchill Downs in Louisville on May 1 and the Preakness Stakes two weeks later at Pimlico Race Course in Baltimore, Charismatic came out of the gate fast and strong at the Belmont. He remained in the lead until about an eighth of a mile was left on the mile-and-a-half racetrack, when a longshot, Lemon Drop Kid, passed him. Vision and Verse, another longshot, also overtook Charismatic.

In the race, Charismatic fractured two bones in his lower left foreleg (an area comparable to the human ankle). He had successful surgery the next day, but his racing days were over.

Won for the Good Guys

The NBA almost didn't happen this year. In the latest round of an ongoing struggle between owners seeking to control costs and players seeking to maximize their salaries, the first three months of the NBA season were cancelled. Without a contract between owners and players, owners locked out the players while negotiations went on between the two sides. The entire preseason and all games through mid-January were cancelled. Finally, to fans' relief, the season began on February 2.

The second edition of the Bulls-without-Jordan NBA Finals (after a shortened regular season of 50 games instead of 82) was a Good Guys versus Bad Guys showdown in June, pitting the angelic San Antonio Spurs against the devilish New York Knicks. The typecasting was a no-brainer, with gentle giants David Robinson and Tim Duncan set to slay New York's surly Marcus Camby and coach-choking Latrell Sprewell (see page 284).

In the end, the Spurs smote the Knicks in five games to gain their first championship in the team's 26-year history. The lopsided outcome, however, had more to do with New York's offensive ineptitude and inability to stop San Antonio's twin seven-foot towers than any clash of virtues. After the title-clincher in New York on June 25, in which Finals MVP Duncan scored 31 points in the 78–77 San Antonio victory, Spurs head coach Gregg Popovich told Knicks head coach Jeff Van Gundy, "I've got Tim and you don't. That's the difference."

When Dallas Froze Over

Until the 1990s, NHL teams had been located almost exclusively in cold-weather cities, with the exception of the Los Angeles Kings. Then ice-challenged places such as Miami, Atlanta, Phoenix, and Dallas landed teams. On June 19 at the Marine Midland Arena in Buffalo, the Dallas Stars—which relocated from Minneapolis, Minnesota, in 1993—became the first Sun Belt team to hoist the Stanley Cup.

It took some effort to lift it over their heads. In game six of the best-of-seven series, the Stars, up three games to two, played the Buffalo Sabres to a 1–1 tie in regulation and two overtime periods. At 14:51 of the third overtime, Dallas rightwinger Brett Hull scored the

1999

winning goal. Or did he? Replays seemed to show that his left skate was illegally in the goal crease before he shot, which would have voided the goal. Despite the Sabres' strong protest, NHL officials let it stand. It went down in the record books as the second-longest overtime game in the history of the Stanley Cup finals, the longest to decide a winner—and, unofficially, the most controversial.

U.S. on Top of the World

On July 10, a crowd of 90,185 at the Rose Bowl in Pasadena, California— the largest ever to watch a women's sporting event anywhere—witnessed the United States outduel China in a thrilling penalty-kick shootout to win the 1999 Women's World Cup soccer tournament. The shootout followed a 0–0 tie after 90 minutes of regulation play and a scoreless 30-minute overtime. United States defender Brandi Chastain blasted the winning shot past Chinese goalkeeper Gao Hong to break a 4–4 deadlock.

World Cup '99 drew record crowds over its three-week, seven-city tournament, held June 19 to July 10.

The American women steamrolled through the first round, outscoring their three opponents 13–1. In the quarterfinals, they outlasted Germany, 3–2, then shut out Brazil, 2–0, to advance to the finals against their archrivals.

The United States had beaten China in both the 1991 World Cup and the 1996 Olympic championship games. This final turned into a grueling stalemate. It boiled down to the final shootout, during which five players from each team

alternate shots on goal from 12 yards out. After China tied it at 3–3, American star Mia Hamm—goalless in her last four games—nailed a pressure-packed kick. China answered, and then came 30-year-old Chastain's date with soccer immortality. When the Rose Bowl exploded with cheers, Chastain dropped to her knees and pulled off one of the more memorable celebrations ever. She ripped off her jersey to reveal a sports bra. The image of Chastain excitedly ripping off her jersey, as the men have long done in soccer, became an icon for tough, exuberant female athletes all over the world.

That wasn't the end of this heroic championship squad. With national attention focused on them, the eight-team Women's United Soccer Association (WUSA) professional league was formed, and all 20 of the '99 Cup players signed on, along with a roster of premier international stars. WUSA launched on April 14, 2001, with Chastain's Bay Area CyberRays facing off against Hamm's Washington Freedom at Robert F. Kennedy Stadium in Washington, D.C. The Freedom defeated the CyberRays, 1–0.

All-Star All-Star Game

Major League Baseball's annual All-Star Game is traditionally a midseason break, where the game's top players shine for a couple of innings apiece to the fans' delight. The 1999 edition, however, played under the lights on July 13 at Boston's vintage Fenway Park, turned into an especially lustrous affair.

Along with some sparkling individual performances, the sport itself put on a spectacular show. As the last All-Star Game of the 20th century, MLB used the occasion to announce the nominees for its All-Century Team in an emotional pre-game ceremony. Onto the diamond trotted such living legends as outfielders Hank Aaron, Stan Musial, and Willie Mays, pitchers Bob Feller, Juan Marichal, Bob Gibson, and Sandy Koufax, and catchers Johnny Bench and Yogi Berra.

The loudest ovation, however, was saved for Ted Williams (1918–2002). Williams played for Boston from 1939 to 1960 and retired in 1960 with 521 home runs and a career .344 average. He earned a reputation as the greatest hitter who ever lived. However, the gruff and un-compromising Hall of Famer actually had not always been a fan favorite during his playing days in Boston.

For this night, though, the 80-year-old Williams, known as "the Splendid Splinter," was universally beloved—by the capacity crowd of 34,187, his fellow All-Century candidates, and the game's all-stars. Two strokes and a broken hip in recent years forced Williams to take the field in a golf cart, which he rode around Fenway to thunderous applause. He climbed out near the pitcher's mound, and, after tossing the ceremonial first pitch, was spontaneously surrounded by players past and present. "There was a baseball love-in on the mound," wrote the Associated Press the next day. "The stars of the night and the stars of the century swamping Ted Williams, gazing at him in awe, reaching over each other to shake his hand."

The game got off to a sizzling start when hometown Red Sox pitcher Pedro

How Sweep It Is

Following the events at the All-Star Game, baseball fell into its predictable pattern. After winning their respective divisions, the New York Yankees and Atlanta Braves powered through two rounds of the playoffs to meet in the World Series, October 23 to 27. It was billed as a showdown to decide not just the best team of the year, but also of the decade. Although the Braves had only captured one World Series since 1990 (defeating the Cleveland Indians in 1997), compared to two for the Yankees (1996 versus Atlanta, 1998 versus the San Diego Padres), the Braves had dominated the National League, winning eight division titles and five league championships.

It didn't turn out to be much of a battle. But for a lone defeat at the right arm of eventual A.L. Cy Young Award winner Pedro Martinez in game three of the A.L. Championship Series, the Yankees went undefeated in the entire postseason, winning 11 of 12 games. In sweeping the Braves in four straight games, the Yankees starting pitchers only gave up seven earned runs and held opposing batters to a paltry .200 average. New York relief pitcher and Series MVP Mariano Rivera pitched 4 2/3 innings, earned two saves, and registered an unblemished earned run average of 0.00.

Martinez struck out all three batters in the first inning—an All-Star Game record. In the bottom of the first, the American League scored two runs off N.L. starter Curt Schilling. Then Martinez came back out and struck out two more batters in the second, including St. Louis' home run king, Mark McGwire. Martinez's two stellar innings earned him the game's Most Valuable Player award.

The Baltimore Orioles' Cal Ripken Jr. and a trio of Cleveland Indians (Kenny Lofton, Manny Ramirez, and Roberto Alomar) each drove in a run in the American League's 4–1 victory.

1999

It's About the Bike

Among the most grueling competitions in sports is the annual Tour de France bicycle race. Even for a world-class athlete in peak condition, biking 2,287 miles around France over 20 days may be the ultimate physical and mental challenge. Now imagine doing it after surviving a near-fatal bout with cancer.

Meet Lance Armstrong. By winning the 1999 Tour de France on July 25—for the first of an amazing seven times in a row—the 27-year-old Texan did more than conquer the brutal course and 179 of the world's top cyclists. He beat death. In October 1996, he was diagnosed with testicular cancer, which rapidly spread throughout his body, including to his lungs and brain. When asked to calculate Armstrong's

odds of survival, the doctor said candidly, "Almost none." After two operations to remove golf ball-sized tumors and extensive chemotherapy, Armstrong launched his courageous comeback early in 1998.

He had shown flashes of brilliance in his racing career, winning the one-day World Championship in 1993 and individual stages of the Tour in 1993 and 1995. Yet his poor showings in the Tour's exhausting mountain climbs had denied Armstrong the chance to join Greg LeMond as the only other American to win cycling's most prestigious event. This year, fueled by the same indomitable spirit it took to overcome his lethal disease, Armstrong annihilated the mountain stages.

Riding with the U.S. Postal Service team, Armstrong won the 86th Tour's opening sprint, which allowed him to begin the race wearing the overall leader's yellow jersey. He lost it, then regained it for good in the eighth stage. He attacked the Alps and Pyrenees with such undaunted strength that the French media wondered if he was using banned performance-enhancing drugs. Armstrong overcame those obstacles, too, when race officials cleared him of any wrongdoing.

By the start of the 20th and final stage, Armstrong held an insurmountable lead of 6:19 minutes over his closest competitor. Resplendent in the yellow jersey, he pedaled triumphantly down Paris' famed Champs Elysees to the finish line, 7:37 ahead of Switzerland's Alex Zuelle. Besides winning four stages, including the toughest of the long mountain stages, Armstrong claimed a victory for cancer survivors everywhere.

Sister, Sister *The Williams sisters (Serena, left, and Venus) became the dominant players in women's tennis at the turn of the century. They teamed to win the U.S. Open doubles title in 1999.*

Other Milestones of 1999

✔ The University of Tennessee won the Fiesta Bowl on January 4, beating Florida State University, 23–16, to gain its first national championship in 47 years. It was the first national title game played as part of the new Bowl Championship Series (see page 288), which took effect in the 1998 college season.

✔ On March 4 in San Jose, the top-ranked Purdue University women's basketball team defeated Duke, 62–45, to claim its first NCAA national title.

✔ At a track and field meet in Athens, Greece, on June 16, Maurice Greene ran the 100-meter sprint in a world record time of 9.79 seconds.

✔ New York Yankees pitcher David Cone recorded the 16th perfect game in baseball history on July 18, shutting out the Montreal Expos, 6–0.

✔ On August 7, a day after baseball star Tony Gwynn of the San Diego Padres collected his 3,000th career hit, Wade Boggs, then with the Tampa Bay Devil Rays, became the first to reach the mark with a home run (against the Cleveland Indians). It turned out to be the last homer of Boggs' 18-year career.

✔ CBS renewed its broadcast rights to the NCAA men's basketball tournament on November 18 by signing a $6-billion, 11-year contract.

Sise Act

While other fathers in his Los Angeles neighborhood were taking their daughters to birthday parties or ballet lessons, Richard Williams watched his two little girls hit tennis balls to each other. Venus (b.1980) and her sister Serena (b. 1981), younger by 15 months, began playing tennis at age four and entered their first tournament when they were nine and eight.

The Williams sisters were 18 and 17 in 1999. They'd both turned pro and had quickly risen in the Women's Tennis Association's world rankings. In September, at the U.S. Open in Flushing, New York, Serena ruled the day.

Seeded seventh in the tournament, she engineered several upsets en route to her first career Grand Slam singles title. Serena not only became the lowest seed to win the women's title in the Open Era (since 1968) but also the second African-American woman ever (after Althea Gibson [b. 1927]) to win a Grand Slam singles title. A day later, she and big sis captured the Open doubles title. The two went on to dominate women's tennis into the new millennium.

INTRODUCTION
2000–2009

The year 2000 saw the beginning of a new year, a new decade, and a new millennium. The entire world held its breath in fear of the "Y2K" problem. That was the worry that computer systems would crash when they suddenly had to read dates that started with 2 instead of 1. As the clocks ticked down to the end of the 1000s, however, other than a few little bugs, Y2K was one crisis that never happened.

If only the rest of the decade had gone so smoothly.

The 2000s ended with *Time* Magazine calling the 10-year span the "decade from hell." Disaster followed disaster around the world, beginning with the sudden, shocking horror of the 9/11/2001 attacks on the United States. A war in Afghanistan began (and continues), followed by a war in Iraq. Hurricane Katrina swamped New Orleans and Gulf Coast Mississippi in 2004, while a series of financial disasters nearly swamped the U.S. economy in the final years of the decade. It was, in short, a rotten way to start a new millennium.

As they had in past decades, people turned their eyes toward America's athletes and teams for entertainment, for relief from the bad news of the "real" world, and for encouragement that things could be brighter.

In sports, they found several inspiring and uplifting individual stories. Cancer survivor Lance Armstrong made the Tour de France his personal showcase. Danica Patrick forged in-roads in the male-dominated world of auto racing. Swimmer Michael Phelps came through with an entire nation pulling for him in the 2008 Olympics.

Team sports thrived, too. Baseball's Boston Red Sox ended a "curse" that spanned the better part of a century. NASCAR sped near the forefront of the American sports consciousness, while pro football stayed there with a couple of classic Super Bowls to close the decade.

Sadly, though, sports weren't immune to the troubles of the 2000s. Perhaps the ambivalence of the decade was best illustrated by its most prominent athlete, Tiger Woods. For almost the entire 10 years, Tiger thrilled fans with incomparable feats on the golf course, including a dramatic U.S. Open for the ages. Suddenly, as the decade came to an end, Tiger made headlines for all the wrong reasons in November of 2009 (see page 384).

Time to Play . . . and Pray *Major League Baseball returned seven days after 9/11, signalling a return to normalcy.*

Other athletes used drugs, cheated, and broke the law in increasing numbers. The massive, unblinking scrutiny of the Internet made it seem even worse than it was, as every tiny twitter of bad news sped around the globe in moments. The amount of money went up and up in sports, leading more people to make more bad choices, while the pressure to excel drove others to cut corners to win.

Still, amid the scandals and arrests, sports did supply more of the events that have cheered Americans for more than a century. In the wake of 9/11, sports venues became national places of remembrance. After Katrina in 2004, the return of sports to New Orleans was seen as a sign of the hard-hit area's rebirth. In the midst of 2008's financial crisis, Olympic glory brought a shine back into people's lives.

As America and the world embark on this new millennium, sports will continue to play a huge part in people's lives, for better or worse.

2000

Two Number Ones

The ongoing controversy about college football's national championship continued—and even grew—as the new millennium began. In 1998, the Bowl Championship Series (BCS) had been created to "fix" the problem of not being able to match up the top two teams at the end of the season in a post-bowl Championship Game. Because all major conferences already had agreements to send their champions to certain bowl games, pitting the number-one team against the number-two team rarely happened. The BCS created a system in which human polls and computers combined to determine the top teams and override the traditional conference tie-ins for a one versus two showdown to determine a true national champion—in theory, anyway.

The biggest impetus for the BCS came in 1997. The University of Michigan Wolverines, ranked number one in both national polls (one voted by coaches, one by writers), won the Rose Bowl on New Year's Day of 1998. But the Nebraska Cornhuskers won the Orange Bowl later that night, and the next day ascended to the top spot in the coaches' poll. Michigan and Nebraska shared the national title. The argument went on for months, with fans and the media crying for clarity. Thus the BCS was born, but its results have been mixed.

In 2000, the BCS computers spit out two top teams: Florida State and Oklahoma. Most fans agreed that undefeated Oklahoma deserved a spot. However, the University of Miami also had only one loss . . . and Miami beat Florida State earlier in the season. Oklahoma ended the controversy by beating Florida State by an unusual 13–2 score. However, the theme of "Who's Number One?" and the issue of just who decides would resonate throughout the decade.

Cinderella Pigskin

Call it coincidence, luck, or a universal leveling of playing fields, but the number of teams winning their first championships as the curtain rose on the new century was unprecedented. Start with the NFL. From Super Bowl XI in 1977, the year the Oakland Raiders won their first NFL title, until Super Bowl XXXII in 1998, when the Denver Broncos at last claimed the Lombardi Trophy, only

He Roared *Tiger Woods destroyed the competition in the U.S. Open, winning by 15 strokes (page 307).*

four teams became first-time champions. Then, following a Broncos' repeat in 1999, came a run of four such teams.

The St. Louis Rams were the first of the four straight first-time Super Bowl winners when they won Super Bowl XXXIV on January 30, 2000. They joined that club in dramatic fashion, capping off one of the best Cinderella stories in recent NFL history.

The Rams' offense became known as "The Greatest Show on Turf" for its high-scoring, pass-happy style. The ringmaster of this football circus was quarterback Kurt Warner, who to everyone's surprise except his own became the league's MVP.

305

Dream Come True *Strong-armed quarterback Kurt Warner was named the Super Bowl MVP as he led the Rams to a surprising Super Bowl victory. His unlikely journey to the top gained national attention.*

starter Trent Green put Warner in the Rams' starting lineup, and he showed everyone what they'd been missing. His rocket arm and calm in the pocket helped the Rams light up scoreboards and storm to its first NFC title since 1979.

After knocking off the Vikings and Buccaneers in the playoffs, St. Louis faced the Tennessee Titans in what proved to be a very entertaining Super Bowl. The Rams jumped to a 16–0 lead, but the Titans charged back to tie the game. Warner hit it big late, though, with a 73-yard touchdown pass to Isaac Bruce that gave the Rams a 23–16 lead. Then, the Titans' Steve McNair led his team down to the 10-yard line with just six seconds left. On the final play of the game, Rams linebacker Mike Jones tackled Titans receiver Kevin Dyson just one yard shy of the end zone, a play that quickly earned the nickname of "The Tackle." Warner was the game's MVP, capping off his storybook season.

McSorley Pays

Pro hockey has always been a tough sport, with on-ice fighting almost as much a part of the game—and the appeal for fans—as slap shots and great saves. It's a game of action and hard hitting. However, in February, one player went too far. Both he and his victim paid the price.

Marty McSorley of the Boston Bruins smashed Donald Brashear of the Vancouver Canucks with just three seconds left in their game on February 21. Brashear fell to the ice and hit his head quite hard. He suffered a concussion and memory loss, though he later recovered fully. However, McSorley's vicious swing shocked players

Warner had played college football at tiny Northern Iowa and was actually working in a supermarket when he finally got a chance with the indoor Arena Football League's Iowa Barnstormers. NFL teams noticed but still thought he needed seasoning, so he was sent to play in the NFL's Europe League. After starting for the Amsterdam Admirals, Warner's odyssey landed him in St. Louis. An injury to

and fans. He was immediately suspended by the National Hockey League (NHL) for the rest of the season. In October 2000, McSorley was convicted of assault, a very rare penalty for actions taken during a sporting event. He was put on probation by the court in Vancouver. The NHL extended his suspension through February 2001, and McSorley retired, never to play in the NHL again.

Hockey remains a rough and dangerous sport, but the McSorley incident drew new attention to fighting and hitting that went beyond the norm, and the NHL, though still not perfect, has been a much safer league in the years since.

Everyone's Chasing Tiger

Golfer Tiger Woods kept proving why he is the real deal (though by the end of the decade, his life would take a major turn; see page 384). Make that unreal. He continued to dominate the PGA Tour into the new millennium, as his impact on the sport reached the status of baseball giant Babe Ruth. Other gifted golfers, such as Ernie Els, Phil Mickelson, David Duval, Jim Furyk, and Sergio Garcia, mounted valiant challenges, yet Tiger beat them all to remain the top-ranked player in the world. Winning tournaments by ridiculous margins, drawing unprecedented galleries and TV ratings, and lifting his game to ever-loftier levels, Woods gained further consideration as perhaps the best golfer ever.

The year 2000 was perhaps the finest of his amazing career. On June 18 at Pebble Beach, California, he captured his first U.S. Open and third major tournament in record-setting fashion. His 15-stroke victory was the largest winning margin ever in a major. (Near the end of the decade, Hall-of-Fame golfer Tom Watson called it golf's biggest achievement.) Just 35 days later, on July 23, Woods wrapped up a 19-under-par performance on the Old Course at St. Andrews, Scotland—the esteemed birthplace of golf—to clinch the British Open. With that, Tiger, at age 24, became the youngest golfer to have won all four majors; the great Jack Nicklaus was two years older when he achieved his career Grand Slam.

Then, on August 20, down by two strokes to Bob May early in the final round of the PGA Championship at Valhalla Golf Club in Louisville, Kentucky, Tiger birdied the last two holes of regulation to force a three-hole playoff. A birdie and two pars later, he had his third major of the year, a feat last accomplished by Ben Hogan (1912–1997) in 1953. "Someday I'll tell my grandkids I played in the same tournament as Tiger Woods," mar-

Signs of Things to Come

After landing on the Women's Tennis Association (WTA) Tour scene in the late 1990s, the Williams sisters, Serena and Venus, ruled the 2000s, especially in the prestigious Grand Slam events. They kicked off their decade of dominance in 2000. Venus defeated her younger sister in the semifinals at Wimbledon en route to her first Grand Slam title, topping reigning champion Lindsay Davenport. Venus beat Davenport again in the U.S. Open final, then capped off a sensational year with the singles crown at the Summer Olympic Games in Sydney, Australia—where she and Serena also collected the doubles gold medal.

Shaq Attack *Powerful center Shaquille O'Neal dominated the boards and joined high-scoring guard Kobe Bryant to lead the Los Angeles Lakers back to the NBA championship.*

veled Watson (b.1949). "We are witnessing a phenomenon here that the game may never, ever see again."

The Lake Show Returns

In the 1960s and again in the 1980s, the Los Angeles Lakers were among the best teams in the NBA, winning numerous championships. In June of 2000, they returned to the top, winning their first title since 1988. The team was led by one of the most powerful one-two punches in sports: slashing guard Kobe Bryant and high-scoring (and quote-spouting) center Shaquille O'Neal.

The two brought enormous talent to the floor, but also big egos off it. It took the addition of super-coach Phil Jackson to pull them together into champions. Jackson had previously led the Chicago Bulls (and Michael Jordan) to six NBA titles. The Lakers stormed through the regular season, with O'Neal earning league MVP honors. He led the league in field goals and field-goal percentage, a testament to his power of getting close to the hoop. (Being 7 feet 2 inches and 325 pounds was helpful in that regard!) Bryant, meanwhile, gave opponents fits with his clutch outside shooting and blazing speed to the hoop.

The Lakers faced the Indiana Pacers in the NBA Finals. Indiana proved to be little competition, with Los Angeles winning in six games. "Shaq Daddy" was the NBA Finals MVP. A few days later, he and Kobe led a boisterous victory parade through downtown Los Angeles. The championship was the first of three straight for the Lakers, with O'Neal earning MVP honors in the Finals each time.

Sampras Is Number One

In tennis, the four Grand Slam tournaments are the Australian, French, and U.S. Opens, and the Wimbledon Championships in England. Since the first Wimbledon in 1886, no one had won more than 12 Grand Slam titles in a career . . . until 2000. With a victory at Wimbledon in July, American star Pete Sampras captured his 13th career Grand Slam tennis title, passing Roy Emerson for the all-time record.

Sampras was not a flashy player, nor blessed with a stunning off-court personality like so many stars of his era. However, he was a superb player, outstanding at the serve-and-volley game that wins on grass at Wimbledon (he won there seven times) and also able to play the power game on hard courts at the U.S. Open, where he was a five-time winner. He would run his record to 14 Grand Slams with a win at the 2002 U.S. Open before retiring in 2003. In 2009, Swiss star Roger Federer would top Sampras' total, but Sampras remains among the greatest stars in world tennis history.

The New Boss *The strong and steady play of Pete Sampras dominated the hard and grass courts and helped him break the all-time Grand Slam record.*

Despite Tarnish, Summer Olympics Shine

Scandal rocked the Olympic movement in November 1998 when it was alleged that International Olympic Committee (IOC) members had been bribed by Salt Lake City, Utah, officials to influence the city's selection as the site for the 2002 Winter Games. An investigation prompted the resignations of two top Salt Lake Olympic Organizing Committee executives and several IOC members, as well as sweeping reforms throughout the IOC, based in Lausanne, Switzerland. (In early 2004, a Utah judge threw out the case against the U.S. official who was charged, citing lack of evidence. However, the IOC reforms remained in place.)

Many worried that the ongoing scandal would affect the 2000 Summer Olympics set for Sydney, Australia, in September. However, with no Olympic athletes accused in the mess, the focus in Australia was on competition, not controversy. Americans brought home the most medals—36 gold, 24 silver, and 31 bronze—while turning in a number of

Golden Women *Lisa Leslie (facing camera) was the star as the U.S. women's basketball team captured the gold medal at the 2000 Summer Games in Australia.*

outshined its Aussie hosts, 14 golds to 5.

Sprinting sensation Marion Jones (b.1975) claimed that she was going to win five gold medals, which would have been an American first for any track athlete. She fell short, but three gold medals and two bronze medals were more than impressive. She and teammate Maurice Greene claimed the title of "World's Fastest Humans" by winning their respective 100-meter races.

The Olympic spirit celebrates underdogs, and there was none more lionized in Sydney than Greco-Roman wrestler Rulon Gardner of the United States. With no major title to his name, the hulking Wyoming native upset legendary Russian Alexander "The Beast" Karelin, who hadn't lost a match in 13 years. Nearly as stunning was the 4–0 upset victory by the American baseball team over the heavily favored Cubans in the championship game.

The Subway Series

In the 1950s, New York City was baseball heaven. Every World Series in the decade except 1959 featured at least one team from the city. In five of those years, two teams from Gotham met up in what were called "Subway Series," after the mode of transportation fans could use to go back and forth to the games. However, the Brooklyn Dodgers and New York Giants moved to the West Coast in 1958. The New York Mets began in 1962, and won the World Series a couple of times. But the Yankees and Mets had never been good at the same time. . . until 2000.

memorable performances. Many came in swimming, a competition that saw 13 new world records and a much-anticipated showdown between the United States and Australian teams. The United States

2000 Summer Olympics Medals

NATION	TOTAL MEDALS	NATION	TOTAL MEDALS
United States	91	France	38
Russia	89	Italy	34
China	59	Cuba	29
Australia	58	Great Britain	28
Germany	56	Netherlands	25

Other Milestones of 2000

✔ In April, American Michelle Kwan won the ladies overall title at the World Figure Skating Championships, the third of five that she would win in her career.

✔ In the Women's National Basketball Association, the Houston Comets won again . . . their fourth consecutive championship. That remains the most WNBA titles ever.

✔ Heavyweight Evander Holyfield became the first boxer to win the world championship four times. He beat John Ruiz August 12 to capture the World Boxing Association (WBA) title.

✔ Controversial University of Indiana head basketball coach Bobby Knight was fired on September 10 after 29 seasons because of a "pattern of unacceptable behavior." On March 23, 2001, he was hired to coach at Texas Tech University. He coached the Red Raiders through 2008, when he resigned and turned over the reins of the team to his son, Pat.

✔ On December 11, All-Star shortstop Alex Rodriguez signed a 10-year, $252 million deal with the Texas Rangers. The enormous contract was the biggest ever signed in sports history. (In 2004, "A-Rod" was traded, at his request, to the New York Yankees for second baseman Alfonso Soriano.) Through mid-2010, the contract remained the largest ever given to an individual player in any major sport.

The first Subway Series in 44 years was cause for celebration all over New York City. The glamour of the Big Apple also excited fans around the country. An incident in Game Two added fuel to the fire. Star pitcher Roger Clemens had taken heat from the Mets for throwing too close earlier in the season. In fact, he had hit Mets star catcher Mike Piazza in a July game. So when, in Game Two, he threw one way inside to Piazza, all sorts of oddness happened. Piazza swung, and the bat broke, with the ball bouncing softly to the infield. The head of the bat, however, bounced toward Clemens, who fielded it cleanly and appeared to then throw the jagged piece of wood at Piazza as he ran down the first-base line. The incident overshadowed the game (neither player was ejected) and added to Clemens' fiery legacy.

The Series itself was decided in Game Five at Shea Stadium, home of the Mets, on October 26. In the top of the ninth with the score tied 2–2, Luis Sojo hit an RBI single off Mets starter Al Leiter, leading to a 4–2 win and the Yankees' record 26th world title.

2001

D and Controversy

The Baltimore Ravens won their first NFL championship, swamping the New York Giants 34–7 in Super Bowl XXXV on January 28. The Ravens' defense was the key, as it did not allow New York an offensive score (the Giants returned a kickoff for their only touchdown). The Ravens also created five turnovers, scored on an interception return, and held the Giants to only 152 total yards.

It was a return to NFL greatness for the city of Baltimore, though it came with a different team. The Ravens used to be the Cleveland Browns, but owner Art Modell moved that team to Baltimore in 1996. The Browns left behind the name and records of the Cleveland franchise and became the "brand-new" Ravens. Baltimore, of course, had a long history of football success, having been home to the Baltimore Colts from 1953 to 1983 before the team moved to Indianapolis (a move not approved by the NFL before it happened in the dead of night!). The multiple-city Ravens were a unique franchise in a league that proved much more stable than other pro leagues in the 2000s.

Another big story during Super Bowl XXXV week revolved around Baltimore linebacker Ray Lewis and events at the previous Super Bowl. In 2000, Lewis had attended the game as a fan. In the early morning after the game in Atlanta, he was involved in a street fight that resulted in the death of a person from a knife wound. Lewis was at first charged with attempted murder for being a part of the incident. However, over the coming months, evidence began to show that Lewis might not have been part of the crime himself. In the end, he pleaded guilty to obstruction of justice (in other words, he admitted that he had not helped police enough with their investigation). He was fined $250,000 by the NFL but was not suspended. It was a huge story at the time

Flag Day *Arizona and Colorado players hold an American flag in memory of the 9/11 attacks (page 316).*

and became a story all over again when he led the Ravens to the Super Bowl and, in fact, was named the game's MVP.

Death of Legend

The sad news continued from the world of sports at the Daytona 500 in February. On the final lap, seven-time NASCAR champion and stock-car racing legend Dale Earnhardt Sr. was clipped from behind. His car swerved to the right and hit the outer wall of the track. It did not seem at the time to be a bad wreck; hundreds of drivers have walked away from much more horrendous crashes. However, in this case, no one walked away.

Earnhardt was pronounced dead, the victim of a broken neck suffered in the crash.

The sports world was stunned. Earnhardt was the face of NASCAR for millions, a hard-driving, tough-talking man who let nothing get in his way on or off the track. He had tied Richard "The King" Petty as the all-time leader with seven NASCAR season championships. Earnhardt's black Number 3 car was far and away the most popular. His death in such a dramatic fashion—it came on the last lap as his teammate Michael Waltrip won and his son Dale Earnhardt Jr. finished second—in NASCAR's most famous race just made the event that much more noteworthy.

2001

After a long mourning period and numerous tributes from around the sports and political worlds, racing continued. In June, Dale Jr. won the Pepsi 400 at the same track on which his father had died. More importantly, the ongoing debate about safety in NASCAR racing received new energy as a result of Earnhardt's death. In the ensuing years, the sport mandated use of special head-and-neck restraints for drivers to prevent the neck-snapping movements. New walls that absorbed some of the energy from crashes were also installed in many tracks. By 2007, NASCAR had redesigned the entire stock car. Beginning in 2008, all racing teams used the same basic car, which was named the Car of Tomorrow and designed from the ground up to increase driver safety.

Finally a Champion

In happier news, another veteran star athlete had a victorious ending to his career. Ray Bourque had been one of the top defensemen in the NHL for 22 years. He had played 1,825 regular-season games and been in the playoffs in 20 other seasons. But he had never held the Stanley Cup, the symbol of the NHL championship. He had never even touched it, since hockey superstition says that a player can't even touch it until he wins it.

Thanks to a furious comeback by his Colorado Avalanche teammates, Bourque got his hands on the Cup this year. The Avalanche overcame a three-games-to-two deficit and beat the New Jersey Devils in seven games in the Stanley Cup Finals.

Bourque had actually left his long-time team, the Boston Bruins, two years earlier with the idea that he had only a few years left to get another shot at the Cup. The move paid off, and he won for the first time in eight tries in the Stanley Cup Finals. Fans and players alike celebrated the win more for Bourque than for the Avalanche.

"In our heart, in our mind, we were playing for Ray," Avalanche coach Bob Hartley said. "This entire community was pulling for Ray. I will remember coaching Ray until the day I close my eyes."

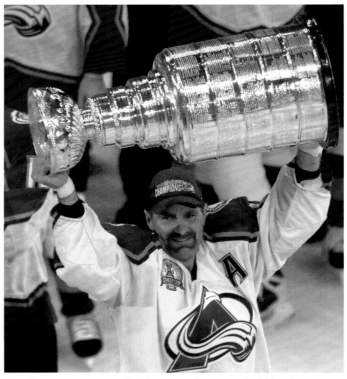

Finally *Ray Bourque finally got a chance to hold hockey's Stanley Cup after leaving his longtime team in Boston to join the Colorado Avalanche.*

Death From Heat

Two events, one in 2001 and another two years later, led to questions about how teams and athletes should deal with heat and with dietary supplements.

On July 31, 2001, the Minnesota Vikings' 335-pound Pro Bowl lineman, Korey Stringer, collapsed during a training-camp session held in the searing heat. His body temperature was 108.8 degrees when he arrived at a hospital, where Stringer died the following day. Eighteen months later, in February 2003, Baltimore Orioles pitching prospect Steve Bechler died of heatstroke suffered during a spring training workout in Florida. The local medical examiner reported that a dietary supplement containing ephedra, which Bechler had been using, played a role in the tragedy. Ephedra was also suspected in Stringer's death, although there was no evidence that he used the substance.

As happened with Earnhardt, it took such tragedies to spur serious action by authorities. Since these events, the NFL, the NCAA, and the International Olympic Committee have banned ephedra, and Bechler's death led to calls for Major League Baseball to do the same. By 2004, President George Bush announced that the Food and Drug Administration was banning it.

Meanwhile, the families of both Bechler and Stringer went to court. Bechler's parents filed a wrongful death suit against the makers of the supplement, arguing that it was unsafe, and that the company was at fault. Stringer's widow sued the Vikings and the team doctor, holding them responsible for her husband's death. A judge dismissed her claims against the team, and she later settled with the doctor for an undisclosed sum.

One-Year Wonder

Since the NFL was born in 1920, several leagues have tried to challenge its dominance in pro football. The All-America Football Conference (AAFC) lasted only four years, 1946–49. The American Football League (AFL) did a bit better, lasting 10 years and ending up merging with the NFL in 1970. The World Football League played only in 1974–75. The United States Football League (1983–85) seemed to get off to a good start but crashed soon after in a pile of debt.

The latest challenger stepped onto the field in 2001. World Wrestling Federation founder Vince McMahon launched the XFL on February 3, 2001. The XFL boasted eight teams and a new idea: Play football in the spring, when the NFL is on vacation. The idea got a lot of atten-

tion but few big-name players. Fans and television revenue did not show up as expected. The league played on, however, and on April 21, the Los Angeles Xtreme dominated the San Francisco Demons 38–6 at the Los Angeles Memorial Coliseum to win the league title in the so-called Million Dollar Game. The Xtreme became the first, and only, XFL champion. McMahon announced on May 10 that the league was folding after just one season. And the NFL remained supreme.

Barry Busts Out

When Mark McGwire and Sammy Sosa chased Roger Maris' single-season home run record in 1998, the saga electrified the sports world. Just three years later, as Barry Bonds set out on a one-man assault on McGwire's new mark

The Day the Earth Stood Still

September 11, 2001, will forever be remembered as the day when life in America underwent a dramatic and deadly change. Early that sunny morning, a horrible terrorist plot unfolded. Two commercial airplanes loaded with passengers were hijacked and deliberately slammed into the twin towers at New York City's World Trade Center. The mighty towers collapsed shortly thereafter. At about the same time, a third hijacked plane was flown into the Pentagon in Washington, D.C. A fourth plane, reportedly targeted for the U.S. Capitol building, crashed in a field in Pennsylvania after passengers overpowered the hijackers. In total, more than 3,000 people were killed as result of the terrorists' actions.

As a shocked nation mourned, everyday activities came to a virtual standstill. Cancellations in the sports world included baseball games for six days, a week of NFL and college football games, NASCAR, golf, and other major events. "At a certain point," said NFL commissioner Paul Tagliabue, "playing our games can contribute to the healing process. Just not at this time." When the action did resume, special homage was paid to the victims at venues nationwide, and strict new security measures were instituted.

Responsibility for the attacks was claimed by members of the Al Qaeda terrorist network, based largely in Afghanistan and led by Osama bin Laden. On October 7, sports broadcasts were interrupted as President George W. Bush announced the beginning of Operation Enduring Freedom, an American-led military action in Afghanistan to overthrow the Taliban government, which supported Al Qaeda's efforts, and to destroy terrorist operations in the country.

The effects of 9/11 continue even to today. "God Bless America" is sung during the seventh-inning stretch at many Major League Baseball games. Servicemen and women are often honored at pro games. Perhaps the most famous sports-related 9/11 story was that of Pat Tillman, an NFL star who was inspired by the events of the day to leave his career behind and join the military (see page 342).

of 70 dingers, the level of attention was quite a bit less. Bonds, though amazingly talented and already a three-time Most Valuable Player (on his way to a record seven MVPs), had a prickly personality and was hard to love.

Still, his home-run power was impossible to ignore. Even as manager after manager intentionally walked him, he still managed to find enough times at bat to hit homers. Bonds had 156 hits that year . . . nearly half were home runs.

Bonds actually started the season slowly, but then hit several hot streaks. He hit an N.L.-record nine homers in five games in May. His 37 homers by the All-Star break were tied for the most ever to that point. By early September, he had cruised past 60. His march was delayed as baseball shut down for a week after 9/11 (see sidebar), but when the sport re-started, he quickly became the focus.

Bonds faced another challenge when the games began again. He did chip away and add homers, but not in bunches. Along with an almost-hostile press and indifferent fans, he battled managers who pitched around him. In one series against the Houston Astros, he was walked intentionally eight times in 14 trips to the plate. In the 15th at-bat of that series, however, he hit his 70th of the season, tying McGwire. In his next game, now back home in San Francisco in front of the only people in America who truly loved him, he set the new mark with number 71 against the archrival Los Angeles Dodgers. He added two more to place the bar, probably out of reach now in the post-steroid era, at 73.

While Bonds earned a spot in the record books, by the end of the decade, he was looking less like a hero and more like the opposite. Looking back at his record season from 2009, it's hard to remember that even back then the issue of steroid use or performance-enhancing drugs was more of a myth or a rumor than full-blown controversy. So as Bonds smashed homer after homer in 2001, people were amazed and thrilled . . . but not really suspicious. That would come later. In 2001, the baseball world simply cheered, though perhaps not as loudly as it could have.

Drama at the World Series

The events of 9/11 were still sadly fresh in America's mind when the World Series began on October 27. The temporary shutdown in baseball had pushed the starting date later than ever before. Along with patriotic songs before and during the games, before Game Three, President George W. Bush famously took the mound to throw out the first pitch at Yankee Stadium, in the same city where the terrorists had struck about two

On Record Pace *San Francisco Giants slugger Barry Bonds connects off a San Diego Padres pitcher for one of what would become an all-time record 73 home runs in the 2001 season.*

2001

months earlier. His appearance was another sign that America was bouncing back from the tragedy, that traditions would continue, and that he and we would show a brave face to terror.

As for the games, the Yankees were facing the upstart Arizona Diamondbacks, the National League champions in only their fourth season of existence. The action on the field proved to be among the most dramatic and memorable in World Series history, adding athletic luster to an emotional event.

Arizona won the first two games at home, led by their one-two starting-pitcher punch of Randy Johnson and Curt Schilling. After Bush's dramatic appear-

ance, the Yankees won Game Three behind Roger "Rocket" Clemens. In Game Four, drama appeared again when Tino Martinez hit a two-run homer in the bottom of the ninth and Derek Jeter hit a solo shot in the 10th to give the Yankees a walk-off win. Game Five provided another hero, Scott Brosius, whose two-run, ninth-inning homer tied the game. The Yankees went on to win in 12 innings.

Game Six was back in Arizona and, perhaps spent from the drama in the Bronx, the Yankees were thumped 15–2, as Arizona tied the Series at three victories apiece.

Game Seven gathered up all the emotion of the week and the games and

Other Milestones of 2001

✔ At the Masters in Augusta, Georgia in April, Tiger Woods held on to win the first major of the year for the second time. Including his victories in the 2000 U.S. and British Opens and PGA Championship, he became the first golfer to hold all four major tournament titles at the same time.

✔ Running great Jim Ryun's 36-year-old high school record in the mile (3:55.3, June 27, 1965) was snapped on May 27 by 18-year-old Alan Webb, who ran the distance in 3:53.43 at the Prefontaine Classic in Oregon.

✔ Ali and Frazier met again on June 8 at Turning Stone Casino in Verona, New York, when the daughters of the boxing rivals (Muhammad Ali and Joe Frazier fought three of the most famous bouts in history in the 1970s) squared off. Laila Ali outlasted Jacqui Frazier-Lyde over eight rounds for the victory.

✔ In July, American cycling star Lance Armstrong won his third straight Tour de France. It continued a run that started in 1999 and would be part of what made Armstrong one of the most famous and successful American athletes of the decade.

✔ Venus Williams successfully defended her Wimbledon and U.S. Open titles in 2001. At the Open, she and runnerup Serena Williams became the first sisters to meet in a Grand Slam final since Wimbledon in 1884. By the end of the decade, Serena would reach a total of 13 major titles, while sister Venus would win seven Grand Slam events.

✔ Major League Lacrosse began play as the first pro U.S. outdoor lacrosse league. MLL, in which all teams are owned by the league itself, had grown to six teams by 2009, mostly in East Coast cities.

ratcheted it up a notch further. Yankees ace Roger Clemens and Schilling locked into a pitcher's duel that left the score 2–1 late in the game. Johnson, the fireballing superstar, came into the game in relief of Schilling. Johnson had pitched and won Game Six the night before, but his team needed some outs. He held the Yankees in check to give the Diamondbacks a chance.

They got their chance and came through in the ninth against New York's ace closer, Mariano Rivera. A lead-off single, a fielder's choice, and an error put a runner on third in a game the Yankees led 2–1. Tony Womack then doubled home the tying run as the Arizona fans went nuts. A few batters later, the bases were loaded with one out. The Yankees' infield came in to cut down a possible winning run. But Luis Gonzalez blooped a single over shortstop Jeter's head, and the Diamondbacks scored, earning their first World Series title in dramatic fashion.

The Series was historic. Johnson set a postseason record with five victories. He and Schilling were named the Series co-MVPs, the first time a pair of pitchers had earned that honor. It was the first time that so many games had ended on walk-off hits. It was the third time that the home team won every game in the Series. In Game Seven, Arizona became the first team to trail going into the bottom of the ninth and win the game and the cham-

Series Winner *Luis Gonzalez of the Arizona Diamondbacks sliced the final, game-winning hit of a dramatic and historic World Series in the bottom of the ninth inning of Game 7.*

pionship. And, of course, this thrilling, positive, exciting event brightened the shadows of tragedy that had darkened the world.

2002

Patriots Days

Less than four months after the tragedy of 9/11, Americans were inspired by a patriotic display of entertainment at Super Bowl XXXVI in the Louisiana Superdome in New Orleans on February. And while no football game ever could make up for the horrifying events of that day in September, the nation's spirits were lifted a bit by a classic Super Bowl that was the first ever to be decided as time ran out. The last play was a 48-yard field goal by Adam Vinatieri that gave upstart New England a 20–17 victory over the heavily favored St. Louis Rams.

The Patriots' surprise ride to their first NFL championship began when Tom Brady, an unheralded sixth-round draft pick from Michigan in 2000, stepped in for injured Drew Bledsoe early in the season. With Brady at the controls, New England overcame an 0–2 start to win 11 of its last 14 games and take the AFC East.

Still, the Patriots' season appeared over when, trailing the Oakland Raiders 13–10 late in the fourth quarter of a divisional playoff game in New England, Brady apparently lost a fumble to end his team's last chance. But in what has come to be know as the "Tuck Rule," the loose ball was ruled an incomplete pass after a replay review because a quarterback that drops a ball, even if in the process of tucking the ball back in to his body, is simulating a throwing motion. The Patriots retained possession, and Vinatieri eventually booted a 45-yard field goal through a driving snowstorm to force overtime. In the extra session, his 23-yard kick won it.

After the Patriots beat the Pittsburgh Steelers in the AFC Championship Game, they faced the Rams in the Super Bowl. St. Louis, which won Super Bowl XXXIV two seasons earlier, featured a high-powered offense that was the first in NFL history to score more than 500 points in three consecutive seasons.

But with the Patriots utilizing a ball-control offense and a bend-but-don't-break defense, the game was tied at 17–17 late in the fourth quarter. Brady, operating without time outs, then needed only 83 seconds to march his team from its own 17-yard line to the Rams' 30. Vinatieri came on with seven seconds remaining to make his winning kick, and set off a celebration of confetti inside the Superdome. Fittingly, the confetti was colored red, white, and blue.

Super Bowl First *Adam Vinatieri's field goal was the first to win a Super Bowl on the final play of the game.*

Salt Lake City Games

Scandals notwithstanding (see box on page 323), the enduring memory of the Winter Olympic Games that began in Salt Lake City February 8 was the gold medal won by 16-year-old American Sarah Hughes in women's figure skating.

Michelle Kwan (b.1980), the holder of four world and six U.S. titles, and the silver medalist at the 1998 Games in Na-

gano, Japan, was expected to finally mine Olympic gold in Salt Lake City. But Kwan fell during the long program and finished with a bronze medal. And just as teenager Tara Lipinski skated away with the gold medal in Nagano, Hughes leapfrogged from fourth place after the short program to win.

Jim Shea claimed a bittersweet victory in the men's skeleton event, which hadn't been in the Olympics since 1948.

2002

After sliding face down on a sleek fiberglass sled along the curvy bobsled track at 80 miles per hour, a triumphant Shea held up a picture of his grandfather to the television cameras. Jack Shea, who won two gold medals in speed skating at the 1932 Olympics in Lake Placid, New York, had died just a few weeks earlier at the age of 91. But his son, Jim Sr.—a cross-country skiing competitor at the 1964 Games in Innsbruck, Austria—was in Salt Lake to congratulate the youngest member of America's first three-generation family of Winter Olympians.

A Golden Smile *American skater Sarah Hughes overcame several more-famous rivals to capture the gold medal at the 2002 Winter Olympics.*

In all, the United States won 10 gold medals at the XIX Winter Games, including an historic victory for Vonetta Flowers in the first women's Olympic bobsled event. When she and teammate Jill Bakken claimed victory, Vonetta became the first black person ever to win an Olympic Winter Games gold medal.

Lakers Three-peat

The Los Angeles Lakers won the NBA championship for the third season in a row, easily beating the Eastern Conference-champion New Jersey Nets in four games. The deciding contest officially was a 113–107 victory in New Jersey on June 12 in a game in which Finals MVP Shaquille O'Neal scored 34 points and grabbed 10 rebounds, and Kobe Bryant added 25 points and 8 assists.

For all intents and purposes, though, the Lakers can point to a game three weeks earlier, on May 26, that really helped earn them their third consecutive title. That night, on the verge of facing an almost-insurmountable three-games-to-one deficit to the Pacific Division-champion Sacramento Kings, forward Robert Horry sank a dramatic buzzer-beating three-point shot for a 100–99 victory at the Staples Center in Los Angeles to even the series at two games apiece. It was the fourth playoff series in a row over a span of two seasons that Horry made a game-winning three-pointer.

To the Kings' credit, they rebounded to win Game Five in Sacramento, but the Lakers took a pair of close decisions in the final two games to win the series and advance to the Finals.

Olympic Scandals

Scandal rocked the Olympic movement in November 1998 when it was alleged that International Olympic Committee members had been bribed by Salt Lake City, Utah, officials to influence the city's selection as the site for the 2002 Winter Games. An investigation prompted the resignations of two top Salt Lake Olympic Organizing Committee executives and several IOC members, as well as sweeping reforms throughout the IOC, based in Lausanne, Switzerland. (In early 2004, a Utah judge threw out the case against the U.S. official who was charged, citing lack of evidence. However, the IOC reforms remained in place.)

The IOC storm had subsided by the time the 2002 Winter Games began in Salt Lake City, but then a different type of problem arose, in the pairs figure skating event. Soon after Russians Elena Berezhnaya and Anton Sikharulidze narrowly won the gold medal over a seemingly superior duo from Canada, David Pelletier and Jamie Sale, a scandal erupted. It was determined that the French judge's vote had been biased—she had allegedly agreed to vote the Russians up in exchange for another judge's vote for a French pair. An unprecedented second set of golds was awarded to the Canadians six days later.

Americans Get Their Kicks

The new and the old came together at soccer's World Cup, held in South Korea and Japan from May 31 to June 30. The new: For the first time, the International Federation of Association Football's (FIFA) premier event was held in Asia. And for the first time, host duties were shared by two countries. The old: For the fifth time in the 17 World Cups to date, it was Brazil, led by brilliant play of striker Ronaldo, that took home the Jules Rimet Trophy as the team champion. Ronaldo scored both goals in Brazil's 2–0 victory over Germany in the final in Yokohama, Japan.

While Brazil clearly was the class of the World Cup, American soccer fans were buoyed by an excellent performance from the U.S. team. After the United States dropped all three of its matches in the 1998 World Cup, little was expected from head coach Bruce Arena's team in Asia. But in their first match, the Americans pulled off a stunning 3–2 upset of Portugal, one of the pre-tournament favorites. That helped propel the United States into the knockout stage, where a 2–0 victory over Mexico earned the Americans a berth in the quarterfinals.

Although their dreams of a World Cup victory were dashed by Germany 1–0 in that round, the Americans had scored another major victory for the visibility of soccer in the United States.

Fit to Be Tied

When the decision was made, Major League Baseball Commissioner Bud Selig could only throw up his hands as if to say, "What else can we do?" Baseball fans could only throw up their hands in disgust. Selig had just declared the All-Star Game at Miller Park in Milwaukee on July 9 a tie.

In 2002, baseball already had fought the bad memories of the long, bitter strike by players in 1994, which cancelled that

2002

year's playoffs and World Series. Those memories resurfaced as another work stoppage threatened to wreck the 2002 season. Luckily, the players and owners agreed on a new collective bargaining agreement just hours before the August 31 deadline.

But then came the All-Star Game. In an exciting, back-and-forth game, the American League scored four runs in the top of the seventh inning to take a 6–5 lead, only to see the National League

counter with two runs in the bottom of the seventh for a 7–6 advantage. After the American League scored again in the eighth to make it 7–7, neither side could push across a tie-breaking run.

After 11 innings, both sides ran out of pitchers, and the umpires consulted Selig. After his decision, fans were outraged. MLB reacted by declaring that the outcome of future games would have real meaning: The winner of the annual Midsummer Classic would determine home-

A Beaming Beem *Rich Beem became the first player to hold off a charging Tiger Woods in a major tournament when he won the 2002 PGA Championship and this gleaming trophy.*

field advantage for the World Series (the advantage previously alternated between leagues each year).

Do a Little Dance

After the final putt dropped, Rich Beem did a little dance, right there on the 18th green. A virtual unknown when the 84th PGA Championship began on August 15 at the Hazeltine National Golf Club in Chaska, Minnesota, the former car-stereo and cell-phone salesman stunned the golf world by holding off Tiger Woods to win the first (and to date, only) major championship of his career.

Beem entered the final round three strokes behind leader Justin Leonard, with Woods lurking two shots behind him. But Beem quickly erased his deficit to Leonard, then took control of the tournament with a brilliant eagle on the 11th hole. On the 16th hole, he drained a 35-foot putt for birdie to hold off the hard-charging Woods, who birdied the last four holes, by one shot.

Then came the hula-like, celebration dance on the final hole. "I probably looked like a total idiot out there," Beem admitted, "but you know what? I won."

Sister, Sister

Venus Williams was the top-ranked women's tennis player in the world in 2001, but all the while she insisted that younger sister Serena was closing in. Sure enough, it was Serena who ascended to the top in 2002.

That year, the sisters met in three consecutive Grand Slam finals—the

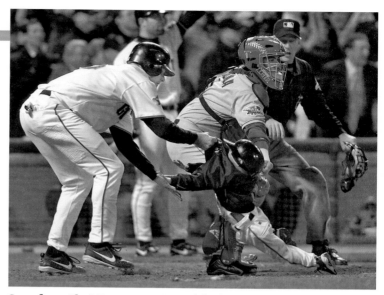

Save for a First Baseman   *One of the biggest plays at the 2002 World Series involved J.T. Snow (left) and batboy Darren Baker (being grabbed), son of the Giants manager.*

French Open, Wimbledon, and the U.S. Open—with Serena winning all three. The 21-year-old Serena ended the season as the top-ranked player in the world, with the 22-year-old Venus second.

Tennis fans would see a lot more of the amazing Williams sisters throughout the decade.

J.T. Snow's Biggest Play

One of the lingering images of the 2002 World Series came in Game Five at PacBell (now AT&T) Park in San Francisco. In the seventh inning of the Giants' 16–4 rout, Kenny Lofton hit a one-out triple with two men aboard. First baseman J.T. Snow scored, with third baseman David Bell in close pursuit.

But when Snow crossed the plate, he noticed the flash of a little Giant near home plate in front of Bell. It was

Running into History *Already a legend for helping the Cowboys win three Super Bowls, Emmitt Smith secured his place in history be becoming the NFL's all-time leading rusher.*

NFL's All-Time Rushing Leaders

Here's the progression of the NFL's all-time rushing mark. Note: The NFL began in 1920, but individual statistics were not kept until 1932.

PLAYER	*YEAR	YARDS
Cliff Battles	1932	3,511
Clarke Hinkle	1940	3,860
Steve Van Buren	1949	5,860
Joe Perry	1958	8,378
Jim Brown	1963	12,312
Walter Payton	1984	16,726
Emmitt Smith	2002	18,355

*The year the player became the NFL's all-time leading rusher.

three-year-old Darren Baker, the son of manager Dusty Baker and the team's batboy that night. Darren was a little too eager to pick up Lofton's bat and was in harm's way with the ball, Bell, and Angels catcher Bengie Molina all converging near the plate.

In one motion, Snow reached back, grabbed Darren by the collar of his Giants' jacket, and lifted him to safety. It may have been the biggest play of Snow's long career.

Heavenly Comeback

The Anaheim Angels were World Series champions for the first time after staging one of the most remarkable comebacks in the history of the Fall Classic to beat the National League-champion San Francisco Giants in seven games.

The Angels were down three games to two and trailed Game Six in Anaheim 5–0 in the bottom of the seventh inning on October 26. No team ever had rallied from five runs down in an elimination game, let alone with only eight outs of life left. But Scott Spiezio's one-out, three-run home run brought the Angels close. Then, Troy Glaus' two-run double was the key hit in a three-run eighth inning that gave Anaheim a 6–5 win.

The next night, rookie John Lackey shut down the Barry Bonds-led Giants on four hits over five innings of a 4–1 victory.

New Rushing King

The Dallas Cowboys, the NFL's dominant team of the 1990s, slogged through their third consecutive five-win

Other Milestones of 2002

✔ Maryland won the NCAA Men's Basketball Tournament for the first time, beating Indiana 64–52 in the final game on April 1 in Atlanta. One night earlier, in San Antonio, Connecticut capped an undefeated season by beating Oklahoma 82–70 for the women's title.

✔ The Detroit Red Wings won the Stanley Cup for the third time in six years, beating the surprising Carolina Hurricanes, who were making their first appearance in the Finals, four games to one. The final game was a 3–1 victory in Detroit June 13. The win marked the record ninth career Stanley Cup win for Red Wings coach Scotty Bowman, who announced his retirement.

✔ On July 30, in a game against the Miami Sol, Los Angeles Sparks star Lisa Leslie became the first player ever to dunk in a WNBA game.

✔ The United States Men's National Basketball Team finished a disappointing sixth at the International Basketball Federation (FIBA) World Championships in Indianapolis in the summer. Yugoslavia, featuring Dallas Mavericks star Dirk Nowitzki, downed the NBA-laden American team in the Knockout Stage and went on to win the title.

✔ Tennis' Pete Sampras won the 14th, and final, major championship of his career when he beat rival Andre Agassi in four sets in the U.S. Open final September 8. At 31, Sampras was the oldest winner of the Open in more than 30 years.

✔ On September 14, American Tim Montgomery set a world record by running the 100 meters in 9.78 seconds in Paris. Three years later, though, the record was vacated after Montgomery was found to be using performance-enhancing drugs.

✔ Boston Red Sox Hall of Famer Ted Williams, one of the greatest hitters in baseball history, died of cardiac arrest July 5. His body was preserved by a method of freezing called cryonics. Other notable deaths in 2002: golfing great Sam Snead (age 89) and football star Johnny Unitas (age 69).

---

season of the 2000s, but did have one major bright spot during a 17–14 loss to the Seattle Seahawks on October 27. That day, 33-year-old Emmitt Smith surpassed Walter Payton as the NFL's all-time leading rusher.

The legendary Payton rushed for 16,726 yards in 13 seasons with the Chicago Bears from 1975 to 1987. Smith, in his 13th season in 2002, entered the game against Seattle 92 yards short of the all-time mark. A little more than five minutes into the fourth quarter, he took a handoff and burst 11 yards up the middle to set the record.

Smith, a first-round draft choice out of Florida who helped lead the Cowboys to three Super Bowl championships in the nineties, played the 2003 and 2004 seasons with the Arizona Cardinals. He finished his 15-year career with 18,355 rushing yards.

2003

Undisputed Champ...Sort Of

For once, there was no arguing that the two best teams in college football were playing for the national championship when the 12–0 and top-ranked Miami Hurricanes played the 13–0 and number-two-rated Ohio State Buckeyes in the Fiesta Bowl in Tempe, Arizona, for the BCS title on January 4. Still, what would college football in the 2000s be without controversy? Ohio State's 31–24 victory in two overtimes was tinged with debate after a crucial pass-interference call in the end zone helped determine the outcome.

The defending-champion Hurricanes took a 24–17 lead in the first overtime on quarterback Ken Dorsey's seven-yard touchdown pass to tight end Kellen Winslow Jr. (In college football, unlike in the NFL, overtime is not sudden death, or "sudden victory." Instead, teams each have one possession beginning at the opponents' 25-yard line to try to break the tie; if the game is still tied after that, they do it again.)

The Buckeyes soon faced a fourth down at the five-yard line on their possession. Quarterback Craig Krenzel threw a pass for receiver Chris Gamble in the end zone. The ball, Gamble, and Miami defensive back Glenn Sharpe all arrived at just about the same time. The ball fell to the ground, and Hurricanes' players began celebrating their victory as fireworks went off above Sun Devil Stadium.

Then, everyone noticed the penalty flag. Sharpe was called for pass interference, and the Buckeyes had a fresh set of downs. They soon tied the game on Krenzel's one-yard run, took the lead on the first possession in the next overtime when Maurice Clarett ran five yards for a touchdown, and won it by stopping Miami on its last chance.

For the Hurricanes, the end to their 34-game winning streak was extra difficult because they thought they already had won. The key penalty flag had been thrown late because, as field judge Terry Porter later explained, "I replayed it in my mind. I wanted to make double sure it was the right call."

To this day, Ohio State fans believe it was the right call. Miami Hurricanes fans do not.

Another Barrier Broken

 Businessman Robert L. Johnson became the first African-American

Hero on Wheels *Lance Armstrong won his fifth Tour de France, equaling an all-time record (page 333).*

majority owner of a major professional sports franchise in the United States when the NBA approved his purchase of the expansion Charlotte Bobcats franchise on January 10. Johnson also became the owner of the WNBA's Charlotte Sting.

Johnson made his fortune as the founder of the cable channel Black Entertainment Television (BET), which debuted in 1980. He sold BET to Viacom for $3 billion in 2001 and became the nation's first African-American billionaire. That year, he also became the first African-American to be named on a *Forbes* magazine "World's Richest" list.

The Bobcats, whose ownership group now also includes legendary basketball star Michael Jordan, began play in the Southeast Division of the NBA's Eastern Conference in the 2004–05 NBA season.

2003

Sound Investment

Tampa Bay Buccaneers owner Malcolm Glazer was so intent on getting Jon Gruden to coach his NFL team that he took the unusual step of obtaining him from the Oakland Raiders (the team Gruden coached from 1998 to 2001) via a trade in 2002. And not only that, but the price was steep: four draft picks, including two first-round selections, and $8 million in cash. But Glazer's investment quickly paid off when Gruden led the Buccaneers to their first Super Bowl victory in game XXXVII on January 26, 2003, in San Diego.

For several years, the Buccaneers had been good but not great. They made the playoffs four times in five seasons beginning in 1997, and never finished below .500 in that span. But they could not make the next step to the Super Bowl, and Glazer did not want the window of opportunity to close on a team that featured stars such as fullback Mike Alstott and linebacker Derrick Brooks. Under Gruden's guidance, Tampa Bay cruised to a division title with 12 victories during the regular season in 2002, then was not challenged much in the playoffs early in the 2003 calendar year.

Even the Buccaneers' victory in the Super Bowl was a rout. Coincidentally, Tampa Bay's 48–21 win came over Gruden's former team, the Raiders.

One Loss Doesn't Hurt

A stunning thing happened to the University of Connecticut women's basketball team in 2003: The Huskies lost a game. Still, that didn't stop them from winning their second consecutive national championship with a 73–68 victory over rival Tennessee in Atlanta on April 8.

Head coach Geno Auriemma's Connecticut team didn't have a senior on the roster, but still cruised through a perfect regular season in which it built its winning streak to a record 70 games entering the Big East Conference Tournament championship game against Villanova. The 14th-ranked Wildcats, however, slowed down the game and stunned Connecticut 52–48, ending the Huskies' long winning streak and a string of nine consecutive Big East Tournament titles.

"Maybe this is the best thing that could happen to us," Auriemma said, as

Taking It to the 'Net

Sports media and fandom began to change in the 1990s with the advent of the personal computer and the Internet. By 2003, virtually every major and minor sport, league, team, and player was represented on multiple Web sites loaded with news, statistics, photos, video clips, history, and everything else ravenous visitors could digest. Fans also gobbled up Web versions of brand names such as ESPN.com and SportsIllustrated.com, as well as online editions of niche sports media. You name it—lacrosse, Olympics, water polo, horse racing, snowboarding, kite surfing, soccer, bass fishing, ad infinitum— you could find it somewhere on the Internet.

The majority of U.S. homes had access to the Internet by then, putting the medium on the verge of replacing newspapers, magazines, and even television as the primary source of sports news and entertainment. High-speed access, via DSL lines or cable modems, promised infinite options for online fans.

Huskies on Top *Coach Gino Auriemma holds up the NCAA trophy just won by his University of Connecticut women's basketball team, capping off one of the best seasons ever.*

the pressure of the win streak was behind his team. That turned out to be a wise prediction. The Huskies still were a top seed in the NCAA Tournament, and they had little trouble reaching the Final Four. There, they overcame Texas and Tennessee in close games to win the title.

Masters Protest

Canadian Mike Weir's one-hole playoff victory over Len Mattiace in the Masters golf tournament April 13 was overshadowed by an attention-getting protest over women's rights outside the exclusive Augusta, Georgia, golf course during the week.

The opening move in the protest was fired in June 2002 when Martha Burk, head of the National Council of Women's Organizations, sent a letter to Augusta National Golf Club chairman William "Hootie" Johnson. Burk's group urged that the men-only club admit women members for the first time in its 70-year history. Johnson steadfastly refused, and a heated national debate ensued. The basic issue: women's rights to equal access versus a private club's right to control its membership.

2003

The controversy came to a head—sort of—on day three of the tournament. Burk led a smaller-than-expected group of protesters outside the club, while a handful of Augusta supporters, curious onlookers, and a CBS television audience (watching the tournament commercial-free after Johnson voided sponsorships) looked on.

In the end, Augusta National remained all-male (and does to this day). Meanwhile, the most effective endorsement for women's equality in golf came, fittingly, on the golf course. In May, Annika Sorenstam became the first woman golfer to play in a men's PGA Tour event since 1945—she missed the cut at the Bank of America Colonial but won the adulation of the galleries. In November, she became the first woman ever to play in the Skins Game, where she finished in second place while earning $225,000 in the annual postseason event.

Historic Sorenstam *Already a superstar on the women's golf tour, Annika Sorenstam made history by taking part in a men's tournament (and later a Skins Game against men). Though she missed the cut in the tournament, she struck a blow for equality in sports.*

The Police Blotter Spreads

In 2003, two major off-the-basketball-court incidents underscored the troubling trend of athletes making headlines for all the wrong reasons. On July 4, Los Angeles Lakers superstar Kobe Bryant was arrested on suspicion of sexual assault. And late in July, former Baylor University basketball player Carlton Dotson was arrested and charged with the murder of a teammate.

In the latter incident, Baylor basketball player Patrick Dennehy was reported missing on June 19, 2003, and foul play was immediately suspected. In late July, two days after friend and teammate Dotson was arrested and charged with Dennehy's murder, the body was found in Waco, Texas.

On July 4, 2003, officials in Eagle County, Colorado, arrested Bryant, 24, on suspicion of sexually assaulting a 19-year-old woman who worked at a resort where Bryant was staying. On July 18, he was formally charged, and in an emotional press conference later that day admitted to having sex with his accuser, with her consent, he believed. (In September of 2004, the charges against Bryant were dropped after his accuser told prosecutors that she was unwilling to testify. Bryant and his accuser also settled a civil lawsuit over the incident.)

Bryant's very public image—as a clean-cut member of three NBA-championship teams with the Lakers and as a highly paid pitchman for McDonald's, Coca-Cola, and Nike—fueled a major media circus, as well as the ongoing debate over the role and treatment of athletes in society.

Facing the Music *Lakers star Kobe Bryant, with his wife Vanessa at this side, faced tough questions about his actions at a Colorado hotel, actions which nearly sent him to court.*

Tour de Lance

As Lance Armstrong took his ceremonial ride along the Champs-Elysees in Paris on July 27, 2003, and crossed the finish line after the 20th and final stage of the world's toughest and most celebrated bicycle race, he joined a very exclusive club. Wearing the leader's yellow jersey, the 31-year-old Texan, racing for the U.S. Postal Service team, had just won his fifth Tour de France. Only four others in the 90 Tours run to that point had won as many (the event was first held in 1903, but was interrupted during both World Wars). Adding to the grandeur of the moment, Armstrong became just the second rider to claim five Tours in a row, joining Spain's Miguel Indurain (b.1964), who dominated from 1991 to 1995. "It's a dream, really a dream," Armstrong said in French from the winner's podium.

All five of Armstrong's victories have been remarkable—they came after a near-fatal fight with cancer in 1996—but this one took on mythical proportions. He suffered through the stomach flu just before the three-week, 2,130-mile race began on July 5; he survived bumps and bruises from two crashes; he narrowly avoided a potentially disastrous spill in the mountains. Plus, the competition had never been so tight.

Armstrong finished a scant 61 seconds ahead of five-time runner-up Jan Ullrich of Germany, whose hopes had tumbled along with his bike on a rain-soaked road during a crucial time trial the day before. The close finish was historic; Armstrong's previous margins of victory had all been more than six minutes. "I think this year I had to rely more on strategy than on physical gifts or physical fitness," he stated.

Armstrong pledged to be back in 2004. "I love cycling, I love my job, and I will be back for a sixth," he said.

The Chicago Curse *When Cubs fan Steve Bartman (in blue hat) reached out for a souvenir in this playoff game, he never imagined what would happen as a result. Moises Alou came down without the ball, and the Cubs left the series without another win.*

Curses, Foiled Again!

With even casual baseball fans eagerly anticipating the matchup, and network TV executives excited about the idea, the American League Boston Red Sox and the National League Chicago Cubs appeared destined to break decades of frustration and disappointment and meet in the World Series in 2003.

Alas, each club's historic curse reared its ugly head at just about the last, and worst, possible moment—in each league's respective championship series—and the dream World Series never came to pass. Instead, the upstart Florida Marlins flouted tradition by whipping the 26-time-champion New York Yankees in six games in the World Series in October. The finale was a five-hit, 2–0 gem by 23-year-old Florida right-hander Josh Beckett.

Boston ended 2003 still trying to shake the Curse of the Bambino: Not long after winning the World Series in 1918, the club sold Babe Ruth to the Yankees and hadn't won a Fall Classic since.

The Red Sox were on the verge of returning to baseball's premier stage for the first time since 1986 when they took a 5–2 lead into the bottom of the eighth inning behind pitching ace Pedro Martinez in game seven of the A.L. Championship Series (ALCS) at Yankee Stadium. But the Yankees rallied to tie the game, then went on to win in the 11th inning on Aaron Boone's solo home run.

Over in the National League, the Cubs still haven't won a World Series championship since 1908 or even a league pennant since the 1945 season— the Cubs' alleged curse involves a goat

Other Milestones of 2003

✔ Ricky Craven beat Kurt Busch at the Carolina Dodge Dealers 400 on March 16 in the closest finish in NASCAR history. Craven won by .002 seconds; he hit the finish line a matter of inches ahead of his rival.

✔ Syracuse, led by freshman sensation (and future NBA star) Carmelo Anthony, beat Kansas 81–78 in the title game in New Orleans on April 7 to win the NCAA Men's Basketball Championship.

✔ Yankees right-hander Roger Clemens reached two of pitching's elite career milestones—300 victories and 4,000 strikeouts—during a 5–2 win over the St. Louis Cardinals in New York on June 13. Clemens became the 21st pitcher to win 300 and only the third to fan 4,000.

✔ After beating the Los Angeles Lakers in the Western Conference semifinals and the Dallas Mavericks in the conference finals, the San Antonio Spurs eliminated the New Jersey Nets in six games in the NBA Finals in June. An 88–77 home-court victory on June 15 at the SBC Center marked the Spurs' second NBA title.

✔ In the first Major League Baseball All-Star Game with home-field advantage in the World Series at stake, the American League beat the National League 7–6 on July 15 at the home of the Chicago White Sox. Texas Rangers third baseman Hank Blalock hit a two-out, two-run home run in the bottom of the eighth inning off Los Angeles Dodgers closer Eric Gagne to make the difference.

✔ Heralded 18-year-old phenom LeBron James made his NBA debut for the Cleveland Cavaliers at Sacramento on October 29. James scored 25 points, grabbed 6 rebounds, and handed out 9 assists, but the Kings won 106–92.

denied admission to the 1945 Series—but new manager Dusty Baker and a talented young pitching staff carried the Cubs to the N.L. Central title in the 2003 season. After beating the Braves in the Division Series, Chicago jumped on Florida, winning three of the first four games and, after dropping Game Five, taking a 3-0 lead into the eighth inning of the potential pennant-clincher at Wrigley Field. That's when Chicago fan Steve Bartman, cheering his beloved team from a front-row seat down the left-field line, instinctively reached for a foul fly ball— and inadvertently kept Cubs left fielder Moises Alou from catching it. There was no official interference (the ball was in the stands) and it should have been a footnote. Instead, batter Luis Castillo, given new life, walked. After four hits, a couple of walks, a critical error, and a sacrifice fly, an astonishing eight runs had crossed the plate. Thousands of fans jammed onto Wavefield and Sheffield Avenues, not to mention the 39,577 inside Wrigley Field, went home stunned. The Marlins won 9–6 the next night to advance to the World Series.

2004

Another BCS Mess

The Bowl Championship Series (BCS) was supposed to settle the argument over who was No. 1 in college football, but it has regularly only added to the debate. That was never more evident than in 2004, when two schools—the Louisiana State Tigers and the Southern California Trojans (USC)—each claimed national championships for the year.

In the weeks leading up to the BCS title game, it appeared as if the top-ranked and undefeated Oklahoma Sooners and No. 2 USC were heading for a showdown. But when Oklahoma was routed by Kansas State 35–7 in the Big 12 Championship Game, the Trojans ascended to the top spot in the polls and prepared to meet the second-ranked Tigers for the national crown.

The complicated BCS formula, however, spit out Oklahoma, now ranked third in the polls, and Louisiana State as the two teams to play for the title, while No. 1 USC went to the Rose Bowl to play the No. 4 Michigan Wolverines.

In Pasadena on January 1, the Trojans easily handled the Wolverines 28–14. Three nights later, at the Sugar Bowl in New Orleans, Louisiana State shut down Oklahoma's high-powered offense in a 21–14 victory.

The Tigers thus were the BCS champions. But the Associated Press kept USC at No. 1 in its final poll and declared the Trojans the national champions.

Twice As Nice for UConn

The University of Connecticut pulled off a rare basketball double by winning both the men's and women's NCAA Basketball Tournaments.

Jim Calhoun's men's team was far from perfect most of the season, but the Huskies were at their best when it counted the most. UConn lost six games during the regular portion of the schedule, but then swept through the rugged Big East Conference Tournament to earn a No. 2 seed at the NCAAs. After breezing through the West region with four victories of at least 16 points each, the Huskies were on the verge of falling to Atlantic Coast Conference power Duke in the national semifinal game on April 3 in San Antonio.

But center Emeka Okafor, who soon would be the No. 2 overall pick in the 2004 NBA draft (by the Charlotte Bobcats),

Victory Dance   *The Boston Red Sox joyously celebrated a World Series title . . . and the end of a curse (page 341).*

asserted himself down the stretch. He scored all 18 of his points in the second half, and the Huskies erased an eight-point deficit in the final minutes to win 79–78. Two nights later, Okafor was a monster, pouring in 24 points and grabbing 15 rebounds in an 82–73 win over Georgia Tech in the title game.

In New Orleans on April 6, head coach Geno Auriemma's UConn women's

2004

team won its third consecutive national title with a 70–61 victory over Tennessee in the championship game. It was the second year in a row that the Huskies beat their biggest rival in the final game. Guard Diana Taurasi earned the Most Outstanding Player award in the Final Four for the second year in a row.

Phinally . . . Phil *Golfer Phil Mickelson exults after his final putt clinched a victory in the Masters, his first victory in a major tournament. He was the first lefthanded player to win the event.*

Stamp of Approval

For a long time, Phil Mickelson was called the "best golfer never to win a Major." He finally shed that undesirable tag with a one-stroke victory at the Masters Tournament at the Augusta (Georgia) National Golf Club on April 11.

The 34-year-old Mickelson, the PGA Tour's most consistent winner this side of Tiger Woods, had teed it up 46 times in golf's most important tournaments—the Masters, the U.S. Open, the British Open, and the PGA Championship—but came up short each time. It looked like it might be another good-but-not-good-enough performance in 2004 when he entered the final round on Sunday tied for the lead, only to shoot two-over-par on the front nine. Beginning on the 12th hole, though, he caught fire. He birdied four of the next six holes and headed to 18 tied for the lead with Ernie Els.

Mickelson's approach shot to 18 landed above the hole, leaving him about an 18-foot downhill putt for a winning birdie. He got a good read from playing partner Chris DiMarco's putt, then curled in his own putt.

Mickelson leaped for joy while the crowd roared its approval. Mickelson arguably has been the most popular golfer of his generation for his aw-shucks attitude and unending willingness to sign autographs and mingle with the fans.

With a major championship finally under his belt, Mickelson finally was rid of one tag, but quickly got another. "Now we can finally stamp him, 'Approved,'" long-time friend and fellow pro Davis Love III quipped.

Hockey's Lost Season

In just their 12th season in the NHL, the Tampa Bay Lightning won hockey's Stanley Cup championship with a 2–1 victory over the visiting Calgary Flames on June 7. That capped a dramatic, seven-game Stanley Cup Finals series in which each of the last four games was decided by only one goal (one of those games went overtime and another into double overtime).

The exciting series, however, would be the last NHL action for quite some time. That's because several months later, on September 15, the Collective Bargaining Agreement (CBA)—the contract between team owners and the players' union—expired. The next day, NHL owners agreed to lock out the players (that is, to prevent them from practicing, playing, or using team facilities) until a new agreement was in place. (A lockout is different from a strike. In a strike, the employees refuse to work.)

As with previous strikes or lockouts in Major League Baseball and the NFL, money was at the heart of the dispute, with the two sides disagreeing over revenue sharing and a salary cap. Revenue is all money earned by an organization. The owners and the players' union did not ratify a new agreement until July 22, 2005, long after the 2004–05 season should have ended. By February of 2005, the league gave up hope of salvaging any part of the season and canceled it altogether.

The NHL thus earned the sad distinction of being the first major pro sports league in North America to lose an entire season because of a labor dispute.

Motor City Mania

The Detroit Pistons beat the Los Angeles Lakers 100–87 in Game Five of the NBA Finals June 15 in Auburn Hills, Michigan, to win the league championship for the third time overall, but for first time since 1990. It also marked the first NBA championship for Hall-of-Fame head coach Larry Brown.

Brown had coached seven ABA or NBA teams in a highly successful, but well-traveled coaching career before arriving in Detroit in the fall of 2003. He guided the Pistons to 54 regular-season wins and a second-place finish in the Central Division behind a balanced team featuring point guard Chauncey Billups, swingman Richard "Rip" Hamilton, and center Ben Wallace.

In the playoffs, Detroit beat Milwaukee and New Jersey before downing Central Division-champion Indiana in six games in an intense Eastern Conference Finals. In the NBA Finals, the Pistons had little trouble dispatching the Western Conference-champ Lakers four games to one.

The series marked the end of an era for basketball in Los Angeles. The Lakers were back in the Finals for the fourth time in five seasons (they won the championship three years in a row beginning in 2000), but superstars Kobe Bryant and Shaquille O'Neal no longer could coexist on or off the court, while veterans such as forward Karl Malone and guard Gary Payton were nearing the end of their careers.

After the season, Los Angeles parted ways with its hulking center, O'Neal,

2004

whom they traded to Miami for three players and a draft choice. Malone retired, and Payton was traded along with forward Rick Fox to Boston. Even coach Phil Jackson, the architect of the team's three titles in the early 2000s, retired. (He eventually came back for the 2005–06 season.) Only Bryant was left in a major rebuilding effort that brought the Lakers back to the top of the NBA before the end of the decade.

Athens Games

For the first time since the modern Olympic Games began in Athens in 1896, the Summer Olympics returned to the Greek capital. More than 10,000 athletes from 201 countries participated. The United States took home the most medals, earning 36 gold and 102 overall.

The lion's share of the American medals came from swimmer Michael

Basketbrawl

A fight that erupted late in a game between the Indiana Pacers and the Detroit Pistons on November 19 carried over into the stands and left the NBA with a big black eye.

Indiana handily was leading defending-champion Detroit on the Pistons' home court in Auburn Hills, Michigan, when an on-court fight broke out in the final minute of the game. (The Pistons, who beat the Pacers in the Eastern Conference Finals in the spring,

sometimes rubbed opponents the wrong way with their rugged style of play.) Left at that, the incident would only have gone down as a minor skirmish.

But when a cup of soda was thrown at Indiana's Ron Artest in the aftermath of that fight, the Pacers' star broke one of the cardinal rules of sports—he charged into the stands. Teammate Stephen Jackson soon followed him, and the incident quickly dissolved into a chaotic scene of players and fans fighting in the stands and some fans moving onto the court to avoid the altercations.

In the end, Artest was suspended for the rest of the season and Jackson for 30 games. Seven other players from both teams were handed smaller suspensions. Players and fans formally were charged with assault or trespassing.

The fight highlighted the increasing need for security at sports events, which had seen several incidents between players and fans in the 2000s—although none as ugly as this one. It also illustrated the increasing disconnect between many millionaire athletes and the fans that idolize them.

Phelps, who earned six gold medals and eight medals overall. Phelps' four gold medals in individual events equaled American swimmer Mark Spitz' feat at the 1972 Summer Olympics, and his eight overall medals marked the first time anyone had done that except for a Russian gymnast at the 1980 Olympics, which the United States and many other countries boycotted. Even still, Phelps' amazing performance was only a warmup act for his incredible run at the 2008 Olympics in Beijing.

Among the other American highlights at the games, the women's softball team overpowered its opponents on the way to a gold medal, and the women's soccer team beat Brazil 2–1 in extra time in an exciting final to win the gold medal. Gymnast Carly Patterson became only the second American woman to win the all-round gold medal in her sport.

It wasn't all good news for the United States, though. For the first time since NBA players were allowed in the Olympics in 1992, the American men's basketball team lost a game, dropping its opener to Puerto Rico by 19 points. Another loss to Lithuania soon followed, and eventual gold medalist Argentina knocked out the Americans in the semifinals. Still, the United States salvaged a bronze medal by beating Lithuania in a rematch.

A Curse Reversed

"Reverse the Curse," Boston Red Sox' fans implored their team when it became apparent it was headed to another trip to the Major League Baseball postseason—its fifth in the past 10 years.

Fastball from Finch *Star pitcher Jennie Finch led the U.S. women's softball team to a dominating gold-medal performance at the Summer Olympics.*

"The Curse" was the Curse of the Bambino, which started after Boston sold Babe "The Bambino" Ruth to the New York Yankees in 1919. In the years since that event, Boston had not won a single World Series. The Yankees had won 26. But 2004 was different. After many agonizing close calls over the years, the Red Sox finally did it. They won their first World Series since 1918. Boston beat the Cardinals October 27 in St. Louis 3–0 to complete a four-game sweep in the Fall Classic.

Other Milestones of 2004

✔ After steadfastly refusing to acknowledge that he ever bet on baseball, former Major League star Pete Rose admitted to doing so in his autobiography called *My Prison Without Bars* (Rodale Press, January 2004). Rose admitted to betting on baseball while managing the Cincinnati Reds. He said he sometimes bet on the Reds, but never against them. Major League Baseball, however, did not lift his lifetime ban from the sport.

✔ The Patriots won the Super Bowl for the second time in three seasons, outlasting the Carolina Panthers in a wild fourth quarter to win game XXXVIII in Houston on February 1, 32–29. Adam Vinatieri, who kicked the game-winning field goal in New England's win in Super Bowl XXXVI , did it again, booting the winning 41-yarder with four seconds left.

✔ Baseball's steroids scandal stayed in the headlines when U.S. Attorney General John Ashcroft announced a 42-count indictment February 12 against individuals involved in the Bay Area Laboratory Cooperative scandal. (BALCO allegedly had provided sports stars with performance-enhancing drugs.) By 2005, all the defendants in the BALCO trial had struck deals with federal prosecutors. Under the agreements, they did not have to reveal the names of any athletes that may have used the illegal drugs.

✔ Former NFL star Pat Tillman, a member of the elite U.S. Army Rangers, was killed while fighting in Afghanistan on April 22. Tillman, 27, played for the Arizona Cardinals from 1998 to 2001 before enlisting in the military in the aftermath of the infamous September 11 terrorist attacks. The true story of Tillman's death would not come out for many months, however, and the controversy about the Army's handling of the event caused anguish in the Tillman family and the sports world. After first reporting that Tillman was killed by enemy fire, though Army officials knew this to be untrue, the Army finally released the real story: Tillman was killed by accident by "friendly fire," when U.S. troops mistook Tillman's squad for the enemy. The process of getting the truth told took many months and called into question the Army's honesty.

✔ Two weeks after winning the Kentucky Derby on May 1, Smarty Jones took the Preakness Stakes by a record 11 1/2 lengths. The three-year-old's bid for horse racing's coveted Triple Crown ended, however, when 36–1 long shot Birdstone beat him in the Belmont Stakes on June 5 with a strong finishing kick. Smarty Jones, who finished second, retired after that, with just the one loss in nine career races.

✔ The Montreal Expos, Major League Baseball's first Canadian team, played its final season north of the border. The Expos, who began as a National League expansion team in 1969, played 39 seasons in Montreal and reached the postseason only one time (1981). The team moved to Washington, D.C. for the 2005 season and became known as the Nationals.

✔ Mia Hamm, who led the United States to a gold medal at the 2004 Summer Olympics, and who was perhaps the most famous American women's soccer player ever, retired from the sport. Hamm had two assists in her last match, a 5–0 victory for the United States over Mexico December 8 in Carson, California.

A big part of the story was how the Red Sox got to the World Series. After winning 98 regular-season games but finishing three games behind the Yankees and earning a wild-card berth in the playoffs, Boston easily dispatched the Anaheim Angels in the A.L. Division Series. In the League Championship Series, though, the Red Sox fell behind the hated Yankees three games to none, and entered the bottom of the ninth inning of Game Four in Boston trailing 4–3.

With their backs to the wall, the Red Sox scratched out the tying run, helped by a key steal from pinch-runner Dave Roberts. In the 12th, slugger David Ortiz won it with a two-run home run.

The next night, Boston rallied from two runs down in the eighth inning to send the game into extra innings. And again, Ortiz delivered the game-winning hit, a single in the 14th inning of a 5–4 victory that sent the Series back to New York.

At Yankee Stadium, the Red Sox jumped out to big leads early in Games Six and Seven and won 4–2 and 10–3 to complete a stunning comeback. Game Six was memorable mostly for the seven strong innings turned in by right-hander Curt Schilling, who pitched with blood seeping through his socks from loosened stitches in his injured ankle. It was the first time that any team in a major American sport had come from that far

Diamond Gems

Two future members of the National Baseball Hall of Fame pitched landmark games during the 2004 season.

On May 18, the Arizona Diamondbacks' Randy Johnson tossed a perfect game—27 batters faced and 27 batters retired—in a 2–0 victory over the Braves in Atlanta. Johnson struck out 13 batters, including the final hitter (Eddie Perez) on a 98 mile-per-hour fastball. At 40, the 6-foot 10-inch lefty was the oldest player ever to toss a perfect game.

On August 7, at San Francisco's SBC (now AT&T) Park, the Chicago Cubs' Greg Maddux won his 300th career game. The right-handed Maddux overcame a shaky start, got some help from his offense—Corey Patterson and Moises Alou slugged two-run homers—and won 8–4. Maddux was the 22nd Major League pitcher (just the 10th since World War II) to reach that magical milestone. He would go on to pitch through 2008, the season he turned 42, and finish with 355 wins.

behind (three games to none) to win a playoff series.

The World Series against St. Louis was almost anticlimactic. Boston scored in the first inning of all four games and never trailed at any time. Outfielder Manny Ramirez batted .412 with 1 home run to earn Series MVP honors.

It had been 86 years since their last championship, but Red Sox fans didn't have to wait long for another. Just to prove 2004 was no fluke—and to dispel any lingering doubts that the curse really was a thing of the past—Boston would win the World Series again in 2007 (see page 368).

2005

Patriots Get Their Kicks

For the third time in four seasons, Adam Vinatieri's field goal made the difference as the New England Patriots won the Super Bowl. And while this one wasn't nearly as dramatic as his final-seconds kicks to win Super Bowls XXXVI and XXXVIII, it was no less satisfying. Vinatieri booted a 22-yard field goal midway through the fourth quarter, and the Patriots held on to beat the Philadelphia Eagles 24–21 in game XXXIX in Jacksonville on February 6.

The game was tied at 14–14 early in the fourth quarter before New England took the lead for good with a 66-yard touchdown march. Corey Dillon scored the go-ahead points on a two-yard run with 13:44 left, but it was versatile rushing-receiving threat Kevin Faulk who made the key plays on the drive. Faulk caught screen passes of 13 and 14 yards, and also had 12- and 8-yard runs.

The next time the Patriots had the ball, Vinatieri kicked his field goal for a 24–14 lead, which held up after the Eagles scored a touchdown with 1:48 remaining. Philadelphia got the ball back one more time after that, but New England safety Rodney Harrison intercepted a pass to seal the victory.

Quarterback Tom Brady passed for 236 yards and two touchdowns for New England. Wide receiver Deion Branch earned game MVP honors after tying a Super Bowl record with 11 catches (for 133 yards). Donovan McNabb passed for three touchdowns for the Eagles, but also was intercepted three times.

With the victory, the Patriots joined the Dallas Cowboys of the 1992 to 1995 seasons as the only NFL teams to win the Super Bowl three times in a four-year span.

MLB Goes to Washington

Baseball's steroid scandal remained firmly in the spotlight as a result of several developments in 2005, none bigger than Congressional hearings in Washington, D.C. beginning on March 17.

Even before that, Major League Baseball and the Players' Association agreed on new, tougher punishment guidelines for players using performance-enhancing drugs, including a 10-day suspension for a first positive test. After the 2005 season, the length of the initial suspension was increased to 50 days.

Top of the World *Tim Duncan of the San Antonio Spurs needs both hands to hold the NBA Finals MVP and NBA championship trophies (page 347).*

Commissioner Bud Selig and several current and former players testified about steroid use before the House Committee on Government Reform in March. Unfortunately, the most memorable testimony did not shed baseball in a positive light. Former slugger Mark McGwire insisted he was "not there to talk about the past." (McGwire eventually admitted to using performance-enhancing drugs, but not until 2010, after

2005

he was hired as a hitting coach by his former team, the St. Louis Cardinals.)

Dominican native Sammy Sosa, whose home-run race with McGwire captivated the nation in 1998, skirted several questions, claiming that he didn't understand them well enough, while the Baltimore Orioles' Rafael Palmeiro steadfastly said that he never took performance-enhancing drugs. That testimony appeared ludicrous when Palmeiro was suspended for 10 days August 1 for testing positive.

After completing his suspension, the 40-year-old Palmeiro went 2-for-26 in seven games before announcing his retirement.

Major Quest

Before he even turned 30 late in the calendar year in 2005, Tiger Woods already had accomplished just about everything there is to accomplish in golf—the biggest amateur events, dozens of professional championships, multiple PGA money titles and Player of the Year awards, and undisputed status as the No. 1-ranked golfer in the world. He has made little secret of his ultimate career goal, however: passing Jack Nicklaus' hallowed record of 18 major golf championships. (The men's golf majors include the Masters, the U.S. Open, the British Open, and the PGA Championship.) Woods took a major step closer toward that objective when he won the Masters and the U.S. Open in 2005.

At the Masters at Augusta (Georgia) National Golf Club beginning April 7, Woods won in part by pulling off one of the most memorable shots in PGA history during the final round. Locked in a tight duel with playing partner Chris DiMarco, Woods missed the green with his tee shot at the par-three 16th hole. His subsequent chip appeared, at first glance, to be way off target. But Woods intentionally chipped above and well left of the pin to let the slope of the green carry the

On the Hot Seat *Baseball superstar Sammy Sosa faced tough questions about the use of performance-enhancing drugs in his sport. His evasive, unspecific answers did not go over well with fans or the media.*

Hurricane Relief

As often happens in the wake of tragedy, people from all walks of life—including the ultra-competitive world of sports—came together to help victims of Hurricane Katrina, which hit the coast of Louisiana and neighboring states on August 29. The most destructive hurricane ever to hit the United States killed at least 1,600 people and caused more than $75 billion in damage.

Individuals, teams, and leagues all pitched in to the relief effort. Athletes such as brother quarterbacks Eli and Peyton Manning, natives of New Orleans, donated their time and money to the cause. The NFL's New Orleans Saints established a Relief Fund that raised more than $1 million to help local causes.

The NHL had players wear special jerseys on opening night in the fall, jerseys that were then auctioned to raise money for relief efforts. The list went on and on.

New Orleans was hit especially hard when its levees gave out, and residents flocked to the Louisiana Superdome (the home of the Saints), which served as a major evacuation center. But the Superdome itself suffered damage, and the Saints spent the 2005 season playing their home games at the Alamodome in San Antonio, Texas, and at Tiger Stadium in Baton Rouge, Louisiana. The Saints did not return to a refurbished Superdome until an emotional Monday-night victory over the Atlanta Falcons early in the 2006 season.

---

ball toward the hole. The ball rolled and rolled until it came to the lip of the cup, stopped for a tantalizing instant, and then fell into the hole. "In your life, have you ever seen anything like that!" announcer Verne Lundquist famously proclaimed to the CBS television audience. The shot gave Woods a two-stroke lead, and he eventually won the tournament on the first hole of a sudden-death playoff with DiMarco.

Woods didn't need such dramatics at the British Open beginning July 14 at The Old Course at St. Andrews in Scotland. He led wire-to-wire and finished five strokes ahead of second-place Colin Montgomerie.

Woods' victories pushed his career total to 10 major championships and vaulted him into third place on the all-time list, behind only Nicklaus and Walter Hagen (11). By decade's end, Woods was up to 14 major titles.

The Quiet Champs

On the list of famous National Basketball Association champions, it's easy to overlook the San Antonio Spurs. Alongside the Boston Celtics' and the Los Angeles Lakers' lengthy list of championships, the Spurs' two titles (entering the 2004–05 season) hardly seemed worth noting. Plus, the Spurs generally have been a team devoid of nationally known players—and devoid of the big egos that sometimes accompany stardom.

NBA championships are all the recognition San Antonio needs, though, and in the 2004–05 season, the Spurs won it all for the second time in three years. (They would make it three titles in five seasons by winning again in 2006–07.)

Led by forward-center Tim Duncan and guards Tony Parker and Manu Ginobili, San Antonio went 59–23 during the regular season to win the inaugural

End of an Era

Jerry Rice, generally considered the greatest wide receiver in NFL history and arguably the greatest player ever, retired shortly before the 2005 season began. He decided against playing a 21st NFL season.

Rice entered the league as the 16th overall pick of the 1985 draft by the San Francisco 49ers. He played his first 16 seasons in San Francisco before finishing his career with three-plus seasons in Oakland and part of his final year in Seattle. He made the Pro Bowl 13 times, was a first-team All-Pro choice 10 times, and was inducted into the Pro Football Hall of Fame in his first year of eligibility in 2010. His final career totals were staggering: 1,549 catches for 22,895 yards and 197 touchdowns, with 207 touchdowns in all. Those are all NFL records, and none figure to be broken for a long time.

As a kicker to his accomplishments, Rice also achieved an unusual feat his final season, when he played in 17 games during the 16-game schedule in 2005. That's because after six games he was traded from Oakland, which had not had its bye week yet, to Seattle, which still had 11 games to play.

Southwest Division championship in the newly realigned NBA. In the playoffs, the Spurs breezed to victories over the Denver Nuggets, Seattle SuperSonics, and Phoenix Suns to reach the NBA Finals.

Defending-champion Detroit provided a tougher test in the Finals, and the series went the full seven games. In the finale, on June 23 in San Antonio, Duncan scored 25 points and grabbed 11 rebounds in the Spurs' 81–74 victory. He was named the Finals MVP.

By the end of the decade, the Spurs had quietly established themselves as the NBA's most consistent winner of the first 10 years of the new millennium. They posted an average of 58 victories during the regular season, made the playoffs all 10 seasons, and won three league championships (to go along with another title won in 1999).

Mr. Versatility

NASCAR's Tony Stewart is one of those drivers who will get behind the wheel of anything, anywhere, anytime. Before he joined NASCAR full-time in 1999, he'd won championships in Karts, Sprint Cars, Midgets, and Indy Cars. By 2002, he added a NASCAR season title to that list.

So when NASCAR instituted a new playoff format called the Chase for the Sprint Cup in 2004 (it's called the Chase for the Nextel Cup now after a sponsor change), that wasn't going to faze the driver in the recognizable orange Home Depot No. 20 car. Stewart finished sixth overall in the first Chase in 2004, in which only the top 10 (now it's the top

Tony the Tiger   *Versatile and talented NASCAR driver Tony Stewart dominated the 2005 season, with 17 top-five finishes helping him claim his second season championship.*

12) drivers can compete for the title over the final 10 races of the season, with the points reset.

In 2005, Stewart was NASCAR's dominant driver. He finished in the top 10 in 25 of 36 races, including a stretch of 13 in a row, and had 17 top 5 finishes. He won five of those times in a seven-race stretch in the summer that vaulted him to the top of the standings. And he won on tracks as varied as the long track at Daytona, the short track at New Hampshire, and the road courses at Sonoma (California) and Watkins Glen (New York).

Fittingly, Stewart became the first—and, so far, only—driver to win NASCAR championships under the season points format and the Chase playoff format.

Seventh Heaven

Even before Lance Armstrong stood on the victory podium on the Champs-Élysées in Paris on July 24, he knew it was time. On the verge of his record seventh Tour de France championship—all of them coming in a row since 1999—he knew it was time to step down and give someone else a chance at the yellow leader's jersey. "There's no reason to continue," he said. "It's time for a new face, a new story. No regrets."

2005

Armstrong's 2005 victory in cycling's biggest competition had been a foregone conclusion for a while. He won in record time, and finished 4 minutes and 40 seconds ahead of his nearest rival, Italian cyclist Ivan Basso.

Number seven, then, was perhaps the easiest of all of Armstrong's victories. The only pressure came from knowing—at least at the time—that it was his last Tour de France (although he later came out of retirement to race again in 2009; see page 381).

"I wanted to go out on top," he said. "That was the only pressure."

Fourth-and-9

Down by three points and nine yards from a first down, No. 1-ranked USC had one shot to hold onto its top ranking. However, the Trojans converted that key play late in the fourth quarter of a 34–31 victory over the Notre Dame Fighting Irish in South Bend, Indiana, on October 15 to extend its school-record winning streak to 28 games.

Notre Dame had taken a 31–28 lead with 2:04 remaining on quarterback Brady Quinn's five-yard touchdown run before the Trojans took over for one last possession beginning at their 25-yard line. On fourth-and-nine from the 26, quarterback Matt Leinart audibled to a pass to Dwayne Jarrett. The wide receiver caught the ball in stride and raced 61 yards to the Irish 13-yard line.

Five plays later—after officials had to clear the field of fans who thought the game ended in a Notre Dame victory on the previous play when the clock operator didn't realize a fumbled ball had gone out of bounds—Leinart sneaked over from the one-yard line with three seconds left to give USC the victory.

Big Catch *USC's Dwayne Jarrett sprints away from Notre Dame defender Ambrose Wooden on a dramatic 61-yard reception late in the fourth quarter that set up the Trojans' winning TD.*

Sox of a Different Color

One season after the Boston Red Sox ended an 86-year championship drought, the American League's Chicago

Other Milestones of 2005

✔ The University of Southern California Trojans (USC) thumped the Oklahoma Sooners 55–19 in a matchup of 12–0 teams in the BCS National Championship Game at the Orange Bowl in Miami on January 4. Still, the arguments continued: unbeatens Auburn and Utah felt they deserved a chance at the Trojans in the title game.

✔ The North Carolina Tar Heels scored the game's final five points to beat the Illinois Illini 75–70 in the NCAA Men's Basketball Tournament final on April 4 in St. Louis. It was the fourth national title for North Carolina. Illinois equaled an NCAA record by winning 37 games (against only two losses), including a thrilling 90–89 victory over Arizona in the Midwest Region final to reach the Final Four.

✔ After the lost season of 2004–05, the NHL returned to the ice with all 30 teams in action on October 5. The Ottawa Senators beat the Toronto Maple Leafs 3–2 on opening night to become the first team to win under the league's new overtime shootout rule. (Games still tied after five minutes of overtime go to a three-man shootout to determine the winner.)

✔ After a one-year retirement, nine-time NBA-championship coach Phil Jackson returned to the Los Angeles Lakers' bench for the 2005–06 season.

White Sox ended their own 88-year championshipless streak by sweeping the National League-champion Houston Astros in four games in the World Series. The final game was a 1–0 victory at Houston on October 26. Four White Sox pitchers combined to shut down the high-scoring Astros on five hits, with Bobby Jenks getting his second save of the Series.

The key game, though, came the night before at Minute Maid Park. Houston, needing a victory after dropping the first two games in Chicago, jumped out to a 4–0 lead through four innings. But the White Sox rallied with five runs in the fifth, and the game eventually went to the ninth inning tied at 5–5. The Astros left the bases loaded in the bottom of the ninth, then stranded two aboard in the 10th and 11th innings. In the top of the 14th, former Astro Geoff Blum broke the tie with a solo home run, and Chicago went on to win 7–5.

The tight contest was similar to the entire Series. Although a sweep appears lopsided on the surface, the White Sox won their four games by a combined total of only six runs. That equaled a 55-year-old big-league record for the smallest run differential in a World Series sweep.

2006

In-Vince-ible

The 2006 Rose Bowl, which also served as college football's national championship game, had everything a fan could want: a perfect setting, a pair of unbeaten teams in Texas and USC—who were also the nation's two highest-scoring squads—the two most recent Heisman Trophy winners (quarterback Matt Leinart and tailback Reggie Bush, both of USC), and the two players who had finished one-two in the season's Heisman race (Bush and Texas quarterback Vince Young). Whew!

USC strutted into Pasadena for the January 4 game boasting a 34-game win streak. The Longhorns countered with a 19-game win streak of their own. Both teams put up about 50 points per game.

The game itself was mesmerizing. Leading 38–33 with 2:13 remaining in the fourth quarter, the Trojans went for it on fourth-and-two from the Longhorns' 45-yard line. Bush, though healthy, was not on the field. The Longhorns stuffed Trojan running back LenDale White.

On the ensuing drive, Texas faced a fourth-and-five from the eight-yard line with less than 30 seconds remain-ing. Young, who had already scored two touchdowns, took a shotgun snap. His receivers covered, the 6-foot 5-inch quarterback won a footrace to the right pylon to score the winning touchdown and se-cure Texas its first national championship since 1970. Many experts immediately called it one of the best games in college football history.

Grand Torino?

The world converged on the north-ern Italian city of Torino (or Turin) for the XX Winter Olympic Games. Every Olympics provides a rich tapestry of win-ners and losers, and heroes and villains. Certainly, these Games fit that model.

Touchdown . . . Title *Texas QB Vince Young dives for the first of his two TDs in the BCS Championship Game.*

The American team seemed more steeped in characters than character at the outset of the Games. Alpine skier Bode Miller, the reigning World Cup champion, claimed that Olympic medals did not mean much to him. Speed skaters Shani Davis and Chad Headrick seemed more intent on undermining each other than on beating anyone skating under a different flag. And the biggest showoff in the group was a male figure skater, Johnny Weir, who missed his bus and then claimed that he'd left his "aura" back at the Olympic Village.

Miller, an overwhelming favorite, failed to win a medal but reportedly had plenty of fun away from the slopes. Weir also missed out on a medal while figure-skater Michelle Kwan, the most renowned talent on the American squad, pulled a groin muscle and dropped out of the Games before her competition began. For Kwan, a five-time world champion, it marked her third Olympics in which she failed to win gold.

The moment that put the American team in the worst light, however, came in the hottest new Olympic event, snowboard cross. In the gold-medal race, Lindsey Jacobellis had a seemingly insurmountable three-second lead over Tanja Frieden of Switzerland heading into

2006

the next-to-last jump. But this was snowboarding, so Jacobellis, 20, chose to reach back and grab the tail of her board—a maneuver known to snowboarders as a method grab—on the jump to showboat for the spectators.

Red = Gold *Flame-haired snowboard superstar Shaun White was a star at the Torino Olympics, winning the half-pipe competition with stunning moves. His youthful joy cemented his status as a rising star in action sports.*

Jacobellis fell on the landing. In a classic tortoise-versus-hare finish, Frieden blew past Jacobellis for gold while the American settled for silver. "Snowboarding is fun," Jacobellis would say in her defense. "I was having fun."

Nobody was having more fun than fellow snowboarder Shaun White. The free-spirited, flame-haired White (aka, "The Flying Tomato") was as refreshing as the Alpine air as he shredded his way to gold in the men's half-pipe. Shani Davis, a speed skater, made history in becoming the first black person to win an individual gold medal in a winter Olympic event (the 1,000 meters). Apolo Anton Ohno, with a cool soul-patch beard to go with his cool name, also took home a gold and two bronzes in short-track speed skating. And lightly regarded Julie Mancuso, who had never won a World Cup race, won gold in the giant slalom.

No athlete in red, white, and blue, though, did more to restore American pride than speed skater Joey Cheek. While the feud between teammates Davis and Headrick raged on at the Oval Lingotto, Cheek earned a gold medal in the 500 meters and a silver medal in the 1,000 meters. The United States Olympic Committee (USOC) handed out bonuses of $25,000 and $15,000, respectively, for those medals, but Cheek donated his winnings to Right to Play, an international humanitarian organization founded by former Olympic gold medalist Johann Olav Koss of Norway.

In an era, and at an event, too far given over to selfish behavior, Cheek's gesture was the fuel that sustained the Olympic flame.

Cinderella Wore Green

When George Mason, a team from the lightly regarded Colonial Athletic Association (CAA) earned an invitation to the NCAA men's basketball tournament (also known as "March Madness" or "The Big Dance"), critics in the basketball media howled. After all, the Patriots had failed even to win the CAA championship.

The Patriots were given a No. 11 seed and little chance to advance beyond an opening-round game with Michigan State. The Spartans, after all, had won the national championship in 2000. George Mason surprised the Spartans, but struggled in the opening moments of their second-round contest against North Carolina. The Tar Heels, the defending national champions, led 16–2 early in the game.

The Patriots, who took their cue from their fun-loving coach, Jim Larranaga, battled back and shocked the heavily favored Tar Heels with a 65–60 victory. That was followed by a defeat of fellow Cinderella mid-major Wichita State. That victory set up a date with No. 1-seed Connecticut, the third opponent Larranaga's no-names would face that had already won a national championship earlier in the decade.

The top-ranked Huskies led by nine points at halftime. In the second half, though, the Patriots were fearless. Despite yielding an average of three to four inches per man, the Patriots would out-rebound Connecticut by a 37–34 margin.

The Patriots actually led 74–70 in the closing moments, but the Huskies fought back to send the game into overtime. In the huddle before the extra period began, Larranaga told his players that there was no place he'd rather be, and no people he would rather be with at that moment. Duly inspired, George Mason went out and won in overtime, 86–84.

In the Final Four the following Saturday, George Mason lost to eventual national-champions Florida and the Cinderella story was over. Few would deny, though, that more fans recall the run that George Mason made in the tourney—beating three former national champions from the past six years—than that the Gators won it all.

Oh, Behave

As was the case for most of the decade, athletes made too many negative headlines.

In March, *San Francisco Chronicle* reporters Mark Fainaru-Wada and Lance Williams released the book *Game of Shadows*, the culmination of their two-year investigation into the alleged use of steroids by Barry Bonds. The San Francisco Giants outfielder was on the verge of breaking the all-time home run record. The evidence detailed in the book showed that other prominent Major League Baseball players, not only Bonds, were involved. The book marked a turning point in baseball's stance on performance-enhancing drugs.

In May, American sprinter Justin Gatlin tied track and field's world record for the 100 meters, at 9.77 seconds. Then he tested positive for a banned substance and was banned from competition for eight years (a sentence that was later commuted to four). His 9.77 performance was also annulled.

In July, American cyclist Floyd Landis stormed back in the final stages to win the Tour de France. Landis, however, tested at almost three times the legal ratio of testosterone to epitestosterone. In September, Landis was disqualified. The title was awarded to Spaniard Oscar Pereiro.

Not Just Americans

Cyclist Floyd Landis' apparent doping skullduggery (see page 355) was not the most abominable act to take place on European soil in the summer of 2006. The World Cup, staged in Germany, had an all-European final pitting France against Italy. In the seventh minute, Zinedine Zidane, the greatest footballer in French annals, scored to put France ahead 1–0. Zidane had already won the Golden Ball award as the top player of this World Cup and that goal, his third in a World Cup final, tied him for the most all-time.

Italy tied the score in regulation. Then, in extra time, Zidane and Italian defender Marco Materazzi got into a heated war of words. The Frenchman lost his composure. With hundreds of millions watching around the world, Zidane got a running start and head-butted Materazzi in the chest. For that, he received a red card and in this, his final match, was kicked out of the game.

Italy won the final on penalty kicks while one of the greatest soccer players of all-time exited on the sourest of notes.

Win Some, Lose Some

On April 9, Phil Mickelson won the prestigious Masters golf tournament at the Augusta (Georgia) National Golf Club for his second consecutive championship in a major—he won the final major of the 2005 season at the PGA Championship in August—and for his third career major title. That was the good news for the popular golfer from San Diego, California. The bad news? Mickelson had a third consecutive major championship in his grasp on June 18 at the U.S. Open at Winged Foot Golf Club in Mamaroneck, New York, before a stunning final-hole collapse handed the title to Australian Geoff Ogilvy.

At the Masters, Mickelson outlasted not only his fellow competitors, but also the elements in a two-shot victory over South Africa's Tim Clark. Mickelson was four shots behind leader Chad Campbell entering the third round on Saturday, which is "moving day," in golf parlance. Mickelson made his move with a two-under-par 70 that day, while many others on the leaderboard, including Campbell (who shot a three-over-par 75) struggled in rainy and windy conditions. Thunderstorms eventually suspended play, but Mickelson picked up where he left off by carding a three-under-par 69 in the final round to win his second green jacket as the Masters champion.

At the U.S. Open, Mickelson entered the 72nd, and final, hole with a one-shot lead over Ogilvy before pushing his tee shot on the par-four well left into the trees. Instead of punching out of the trees and playing for an almost certain bogey, which would have meant an 18-hole playoff the next day, Mickelson went for the green, clipped a tree, and barely advanced the ball. His next shot missed the green, and it took him three more shots to get the ball in the hole. His double-bogey left him tied for second place, one shot behind Ogilvy.

It was a bitter defeat for Mickelson, who always dreamed of winning the U.S. Open, and he berated himself afterward for not playing it safe. "I just can't believe that I did that," he said. "I am such an idiot."

Ironically, Mickelson's final-hole disaster only further endeared him to many golf fans, who long have reveled in his go-for-broke style. Fans equally have cheered the affable lefty's many successes and agonized over his spectacular defeats.

Saga of Barbaro

Twenty-six years. Horse racing's Triple Crown—the Kentucky Derby, Preakness Stakes and Belmont Stakes—had never endured such a drought. Beginning with Sir Barton in 1919, there had been 11 Triple Crown winners. However, no three year-old thoroughbred had done so since Affirmed in 1978.

Barbaro should have ended that drought. The bay colt entered the Kentucky Derby, also known as the "Run for the Roses," having won all five of his races. At Churchill Downs, Barbaro won by 6 1/2 lengths even though his jockey, Edgar Prado, never used a whip. That was the largest margin of victory in the Derby since 1946.

Two weeks later, on May 20 at the Preakness, Barbaro was an overwhelming favorite. As he passed the grandstand shortly after the start, the horse pulled up lame. His right hind leg was broken in 20 places, the foot dangling grotesquely. That moment marked the end of his career, and the start of a nationwide infatuation with Barbaro and an obsession with saving the lame colt's life.

Barbaro was transferred to a veterinary facility in Pennsylvania, where he underwent surgery and the type of round-the-clock care normally reserved for heads of state or celebrities. Thousands upon thousands of "Get Well" cards poured in, including one that measured 7 feet by 72 feet. Updates on his condition transcended the sports pages.

Barbaro developed a disease in his hoof known as laminitis, common among four-legged animals. After several surges and setbacks in his recovery, Barbaro was put to sleep in January of 2007, eight months after first pulling up lame. He was cremated, and his remains, as well as a statue, are located outside the entrance of Churchill Downs.

Tiger, Down and Up

Tiger Woods dealt with mortality and proved he was mortal himself in 2006, but by year's end he reasserted himself as the most dominant athlete of the decade.

Get Well Soon *The great champion horse Barbaro was popular among racing fans. When he was injured in the Preakness, thousands sent in "get well" cards like this one.*

2006

On May 3, Earl Woods, Tiger's father, died after a long bout with prostate cancer. Earl was both Tiger's father and his mentor, the man who had taught him to play golf as soon as he could stand on two feet. The two had always been inseparable, on or off a golf course.

Woods, who had finished in a tie for third place at the Masters a few weeks earlier, took a nine-week hiatus. He re-emerged at the U.S. Open at Winged Foot

Another Kind of Trophy *NFL Hall of Famer Emmitt Smith showed that he could win away from the field. He and partner Cheryl Burke won TV's* Dancing With the Stars.

but shockingly missed the cut. It marked the first time in Woods' career, a span of 40 majors, that he had failed to advance to the weekend.

If grief had led to distraction and poor play, failure was the ideal antidote for the 30-year-old. Woods won the final two major championships of the year, the British Open and the PGA Championship, shooting 18 under par in both. At the former, at Royal Liverpool Golf Club in England, Woods won by two strokes.

Four weeks later, beginning August 17, Woods was dominant at the PGA Championship at Medinah, Illinois. In winning his 12th career major, Woods carded only three bogeys, tying a record for the fewest in a major. That same month, he won his 50th career event on the PGA Tour—the Buick Open—to become, at 30 years and seven months, the youngest golfer ever to do so. Woods would win his final six PGA Tour events of the year and won eight events overall.

Dancing Emmitt

Former Dallas Cowboys superstar Emmitt Smith, the NFL's all-time leading rusher, already had a host of trophies and awards from his playing days, including Super Bowl rings, the Pete Rozelle Trophy as the Super Bowl MVP, and an Associated Press award as the NFL's MVP. To his roomful of impressive hardware, he added an unlikely award on November 15: the Mirror Ball Trophy, presented to the winner of television's *Dancing With the Stars* competition.

Dancing With the Stars is a reality TV series in which a dozen or so celebrities

Other Milestones of 2006

✔ Kobe Bryant scored 81 points for the Los Angeles Lakers in a 122–104 victory over the Toronto Raptors on January 22. Bryant's 81 was the second-highest points total in one game in NBA history after Wilt Chamberlain's 100-point game in 1962.

✔ Ben Roethlisberger, just 23 years of age, became the youngest quarterback to lead a team to Super Bowl triumph when the Pittsburgh Steelers beat the Seattle Seahawks 21–10 in Super Bowl XL in Detroit on February 5.

✔ Japan, led by outfielder Ichiro Suzuki, won the inaugural World Baseball Classic in March. The United States finished with three wins in six games and bowed out in the second round of the 16-nation tournament.

✔ On May 28, San Francisco Giants outfielder Barry Bonds hit his 715th career home run. Bonds' blast, off the Colorado Rockies Byung-Hyun Kim, broke a tie with the legendary Babe Ruth and lifted him into second place on baseball's all-time list, behind only Henry Aaron.

✔ The NHL saw its future as virtuoso talents Alexander Ovechkin (Washington Capitals), 20, and Sidney Crosby (Pittsburgh Penguins), 18, both debuted in the 2005–06 season. Ovechkin, the Russian son of a professional soccer-playing dad and an Olympic basketball gold-medalist mom, won the Calder Trophy as the league's outstanding rookie. Crosby became the youngest player in NHL history to score 100 points in a season.

✔ On November 17, on the eve of "The Game" between the Ohio State Buckeyes and the Michigan Wolverines, legendary retired Michigan football coach Glenn "Bo" Schembechler suffered a fatal heart attack. Ohio State and Michigan were both 11–0 and were ranked one-two in the country entering the annual rivalry game in Columbus, Ohio. The Buckeyes prevailed 42–39.

✔ New York Yankees pitcher Cory Lidle, a licensed pilot, crashed his small plane into a high-rise apartment building on New York City's Upper East Side. Lidle and his co-pilot and flight instructor, Tyler Stanger, died in the crash. Other notable deaths in 2006 included Boston Celtics patriarch Red Auerbach, golfer Byron Nelson, former heavyweight boxing champ Floyd Patterson, and two-time Olympic decathlon gold medalist Bob Mathias.

---

are each paired with one professional dancer. Every week, the couples perform ballroom dance routines, to be judged by a panel of experts and voted on by the television audience. One by one, the teams are eliminated until a champion remains.

In the fall of 2006, Smith was paired with professional dancer Cheryl Burke on the third season of *Dancing With the Stars*.

After nine weeks of competition, the pair reached the finals against actor Mario Lopez and his partner, Karina Smirnoff. Both teams were nearly perfect on the judges' scorecards in the final, but Smith and Burke emerged from the complicated scoring system as the winners.

Four years after he left the NFL, Smith proved he still had winning moves.

2007

Bad News Everywhere

If 2007 was not the worst year in sports, a nadir on and off the fields of play, then it certainly was in contention for such a label. The mishaps and misery began just two hours into New Year's Day with the drive-by-shooting murder of Denver Broncos cornerback Darrent Williams. Only 12 hours earlier, Williams had played in the Broncos' season-ending 26–23 loss to the San Francisco 49ers. As Williams, 24, and friends were driving away from a New Year's Eve party hosted by Denver Nuggets player Kenyon Martin, he was shot once in the neck, killing him instantly.

Williams' murder was a tragedy. It was also foreshadowing for the worst sports year of this decade, if not every other, a year in which the famous were never more infamous. Don't say we didn't warn you.

The bad news continued in February. During the NBA All-Star Game weekend in Las Vegas, NFL cornerback Adam "Pacman" Jones was at the center of a fight at an adult club. He helped start things by tossing money in the air in the crowded club. In the ensuing chaos, gunshots were fired. Three people were hit, including a security guard who was left paralyzed from the waist down from his wounds. In April, NFL commissioner Roger Goodell suspended Jones for the entire 2007 season, a sanction not assessed a player (outside of drug-related issues) by the NFL in 44 years.

College Football Upsets

If only all sports contests could be even half as thrilling as the Fiesta Bowl battle waged between Boise State and Oklahoma on January 1, 2007. The undefeated Broncos, only the second non-Bowl Championship Series school ever to play in a BCS bowl, shocked the Big 12 champions with a 43–42 overtime win that bested any script Hollywood could hope to write.

Three touchdowns were scored in the final 1:26 of regulation. The Broncos converted a fourth-and-18 from midfield via a hook-and-lateral play to tie the score with just 0:07 left. In overtime Adrian Peterson of the Sooners scored on a 25-yard run—the final carry of his brief, but brilliant, college career—but Boise State replied with another fourth-down

The Right Stuff *Venus Williams showed she still had her winning stroke when she won Wimbledon (page 363).*

conversion for a touchdown, this via a halfback pass.

Then, instead of kicking an extra point to send the game into a second overtime, Boise State won it on a Statue of Liberty play handoff from quarterback Jared Zabransky to tailback Ian Johnson. Instead of spiking the ball in celebration,

Johnson got on one knee to propose to his girlfriend, cheerleader Chrissy Popadics.

Seriously.

The Broncos had only been 7 1/2-point underdogs, though. When the '07 season opened the following September, Appalachian State, a Football Championship Subdivision (FCS; formerly known

What a Game! *Using a play seen more often on playgrounds than in top-level college football, Boise State upset Oklahoma in one of the most entertaining games of the decade in any sport.*

as Division I-AA) school, was a 27-point underdog at Michigan.

The Wolverines boasted a No. 5 ranking, the all-time most wins in Football Bowl Subdivision (FBS) history, the following spring's No. 1 overall NFL draft pick in offensive tackle Jake Long, and the Big House, its stadium that overflowed with 110,000 rabid fans.

No matter. The Mountaineers, who had won 14 straight games before arriving in Ann Arbor, won 34–31. It marked the first time an FCS/I-AA school had ever beaten a ranked FBS/I-A school, and it easily would have been the year's most monumental upset if not for . . .

. . . Stanford 24, USC 23. In October, the unranked Cardinal entered Los Angeles Coliseum, where the Trojans had won 35 consecutive home games, as 41-point underdogs. Playing inspired football under first-year head coach Jim Harbaugh, Stanford mounted a late drive behind quarterback Tavita Pritchard, who was making his first-ever start (Pritchard had only attempted three passes in his career beforehand). On fourth-and-goal from the USC 10-yard line, Pritchard connected with Mark Bradford on a fade route for the winning score and the greatest upset, based on the point spread, that college football has ever seen.

Beckham Beckoned

David Beckham, the most iconic figure in soccer, if not all of sport globally, signed in January with the Los

Angeles Galaxy of the MLS. Beckham, whose wife Victoria (aka Posh Spice) is nearly as famous as he, left Spain's Real Madrid for a five-year, $250 million contract with the Galaxy and the faint hope of one day being able to say that he helped make soccer as popular as the big three sports in the United States.

As Beckham was welcomed to great fanfare in front of a big crowd, the move made headlines around the world. Few sports figures in this era were as well-known, in and out of the sports pages, as Beckham. For him to leave soccer-mad Europe to come to America, where soccer is a second-class citizen, was a big gamble for him and for MLS. Most of his money, in fact, was based on sales of soccer gear, not on salary for playing. It was a bold move by the Galaxy and MLS to try to help the 13-year-old league take a big jump ahead.

"In my career, I've played for two of the biggest clubs in the world and for my country, and I've always looked for challenges," said Beckham. "While my family is most important, the second biggest thing in my life is the football, I mean the soccer. I'll get used to saying that! But this is a big challenge. Potentially in the States, soccer could be as big as it is around the world. I'm very proud to be part of that."

A similar experiment in 1975 in the North American Soccer League had brought world superstar Pelé to the New York Cosmos. That lasted only three years, however. By 2009, Beckham was antsy again, spending part of the MLS season "on loan" to Italian club AC Milan. He did play in Los Angeles often enough to help the team make the 2009 MLS Cup, though they lost there on penalty kicks.

Venus and Serena Return to Form

The Williams sisters, Venus and Serena, opted to take tennis seriously again in 2007. That was bad news for the rest of the WTA Tour.

In January, Serena, 25, journeyed Down Under to play in the Australian Open. Injuries and apathy had taken their toll on the younger Williams sibling the past two years. Though she had seven Grand Slam singles championships to her name, Serena was ranked 81st in the world and went unseeded in Melbourne.

It barely mattered, as Serena crushed top-seeded Maria Sharapova 6–1, 6–2 in the final.

Five months later at Wimbledon, older sister Venus, who also had seven Grand Slam singles titles to her credit at the time, was seeded 23rd at the All-England Club. Despite some early hiccups—Venus was one game away from defeat in each of her first two matches—she won her final four matches in straight sets to win the championship, her fourth at Wimbledon.

In doing so, Venus Williams became the lowest-seeded Wimbledon champion in history. That was almost as impressive a feat as that of Serena, who became only the second unseeded woman in the Open era to win a Grand Slam tournament.

Super Colts

For the better part of a decade, the Indianapolis Colts had been good—but not quite good enough to reach the top of the NFL landscape. In the seven

2007

regular seasons from 1999 through 2005, the Colts reached the postseason six times, only to lose in the AFC playoffs each time. Finally, after winning its fourth consecutive AFC South Division title in the 2006 season, Indianapolis carried its success through the postseason, and the Colts beat the Chicago Bears 29–17 in Super Bowl XLI at Dolphin Stadium in South Florida on February 4. It was the franchise's first Super Bowl victory since the Colts, then in Baltimore, beat the Dallas Cowboys in game V following the 1970 season.

The seeds for Indianapolis' championship were sown in the spring of 1998, when the team selected Tennessee quarterback Peyton Manning with the top overall pick of the annual NFL draft. Manning became an immediate starter for the Colts and, after a 3–13 baptism in 1998, engineered an amazing turnaround that had the upstart Colts in the playoffs by 1999.

That year, Manning passed for more than 4,000 yards for the first of six years in a row, and earned the first of 10 Pro Bowl selections in 11 seasons through 2009. In 2004, he set an NFL record (since broken) by passing for 49 touchdowns. By 2006, all that was missing was a Super Bowl championship.

In the AFC title game, the Colts beat the New England Patriots, their playoff nemeses and Super Bowl winners three times in the 2000s, 38–24 as Manning passed for 389 yards and a touchdown. Then, in the Super Bowl, Manning earned game MVP honors after passing for 247 yards and a touchdown. Indianapolis fell behind early when the Bears' Devin Hester returned the opening kickoff 92 yards for a touchdown, but dominated play much of the rest of the way.

Spy Games

Eric Mangini made his coaching debut with the New York Jets on September 9 against the team for whom he had formerly worked as an assistant, the New England Patriots. The Jets lost, 38–14. The following day, Mangini accused the Patriots of having videotaped New York's defensive signals from a sideline location during the game. The Jets had confiscated the video camera used by Patriots assistant Matt Estrella during the game.

The NFL would fine the Patriots $250,000 and force them to forfeit their first-round pick in the 2008 NFL draft. New England coach Bill Belichick was fined a heftier sum of $500,000. Belichick also learned a lesson about double-crossing a former assistant who knows the intricacies of one's operation.

Why was videotaping against the rules? It was not a problem if a team could "steal" such signs during a game; that's why teams often use different signs or decoy signers. However, by taping the signs to be decoded later, the Patriots crossed the line. It was a bigger story because of the star power of the Patriots, too.

Two footnotes, one significant and one trivial, go along with the Colts' victory. Significant: When Indianapolis' Tony Dungy and Chicago's Lovie Smith squared off that day, it marked the first time that the Super Bowl matched two African-American head coaches. Trivial: It was the first time a Super Bowl game ever had been played in the rain.

A Mouth Roars

Milestone Event *With the Vince Lombardi Trophy as their goal, coaches Lovie Smith of the Bears (left) and Tony Dungy of the Colts led their teams into the Super Bowl.*

Don Imus, whose syndicated "Imus in the Morning" radio show was simulcast on MSNBC television, found out just how far you cannot go on the radio. On April 4 (the anniversary of the death of Martin Luther King, Jr., of all days), Imus referred to the Rutgers University women's basketball team in a very offensive way. The evening before, the Scarlet Knights had lost to Tennessee in the women's NCAA basketball championship game.

The dialogue between Imus and his producer, Bernard McGuirk, used inappropriate and racist words to describe the mostly African-American Rutgers team. While Imus probably thought he was just joking around, listeners and other critics were outraged and flooded radio stations with calls and e-mails. The story exploded in the media, and Imus' reputation suffered greatly. Advertisers cut their time on the show, and stations dropped him. Eight days after he made his rude remarks, Imus' show was canceled. Though not directly tied to a sports event or personality, the incident showed how much attention anything related to sports got, especially when controversy was involved.

An Error in Judgment

In June, the FBI contacted the NBA regarding suspicions of wrongdoing by referee Tim Donaghy, a 13-year veteran. Donaghy would soon plead guilty to wire fraud and transmitting wagering information through interstate commerce. In short, Donaghy, a "pathological gambler," admitted to sharing information, as well as wagering on NBA games. Donaghy, in other words, was helping gamblers by his actions during games or by providing them with information he should not have revealed.

NBA commissioner David Stern swiftly labeled Donaghy, who would be sentenced to 15 months in prison, a "rogue, isolated criminal." Yet his indictment opened up questions about the integrity of NBA officials and the games themselves. All those calls—and missed calls—that fans had seen in key moments of playoff games? They wondered if maybe there actually was something more than an honest mistake going on there.

The controversy raged for weeks, as other referees worried that they would be swept up with Donaghy. No others were officially included in the investigation, but the suspicion raised by Donaghy's actions has taken a long time to fade away. Almost nothing harms a sport more than the suspicion of cheating by officials.

Vick Goes to the Dogs

Michael Vick was one of the most dynamic players in the NFL. The first quarterback ever to rush for 1,000 yards in a season, he had signed the richest contract in league history in 2005 when he agreed to a 10-year, $130 million deal with the Atlanta Falcons. In 2007, Vick threw it all away.

In July, Vick was indicted by a federal grand jury for owning and operating Bad Newz Kennels, which bred dogs specifically for fighting. Those that performed poorly were put to death by Vick and his associates, the 19-page indictment alleged.

Public reaction was swift and certain: Vick was a villain. Animal-rights groups demanded further justice, and the case received national attention for weeks. In August, NFL commissioner Roger Goodell suspended Vick indefinitely. The Falcons' dual-threat quarterback would plead guilty to the charges. Four months later, he was sentenced to 23 months in prison.

The fall from grace of such a big star was another piece of bad news for the NFL and the sports world, reeling as they were from ongoing drug investigations and a series of off-field violence. Vick himself took a little while to realize the gravity of his situation, at first stonewalling but then coming clean as he realized his position. After serving his time, he was allowed to return to the NFL, signing with the Eagles as a backup quarterback in 2009.

Solo Act

Hope Solo was unbeatable in goal for the U.S. women's soccer team through the first four games of the Women's World Cup in September. Solo recorded three shutouts as the U.S. advanced to a semifinal match against Brazil.

That is when the coach, Greg Ryan, replaced her with 36 year-old Brianna Scurry (a heroine from the 1998 World Cup and the Olympics). The Brazilians won 4–1. "It was the wrong decision, and I think anybody that knows anything about the game knows that," said Solo. "There's no doubt in my mind I would have made those saves. And the fact of the matter is it's not 2004 anymore."

Ryan was widely criticized for the switch. When his contract expired on the last day of the year, U.S. Soccer made a switch of its own, opting not to extend Ryan's contract.

The move raised a lot of questions. Many said that Solo was wrong to criticize the decision publicly, and that she had broken an unwritten rule by saying that her teammate (Scurry) was not up to the job. Ryan hurt his status with the team by his actions, too, and was punished for it. The interaction of coaches and players, and players' increasing public voice was a big reason that the Solo story made headlines. One footnote: In 2009, Solo was named the player of the year by the U.S. Soccer Association.

Baseball's Dirty Laundry

Throughout the decade of the 2000s, the story of drug use in sports became bigger and bigger. Public and government outcry led to the pro leagues doing more and more to try to investigate and combat the problem. Baseball's answer was to hire former United States Senator George Mitchell to prepare a report for Commissioner Bud Selig. Mitchell took almost two years to complete the job.

In December, the 409-page document, nicknamed The Mitchell Report, came out. It reported the rampant use of anabolic steroids and human growth hormone (HGH) in Major League Baseball. The report named 89 players who were alleged to have used performance-enhancing substances. While those names were supposed to remain confidential, certain high-profile ones (such as Roger Clemens and Andy Pettitte) were later leaked to the media.

A New Home Run Champ?

Earlier in the year, baseball got a dose of positive news, though even it came with baggage. On August 7, Barry Bonds hit a full-count pitch from Mike Bacsik of the Washington Nationals over the right-center field wall in San Francisco. It was Bonds' 756th career home run, breaking Henry Aaron's 33-year-old record. The moment was awkward—neither Aaron nor commissioner Bud Selig witnessed the feat in person—due to the strong, even overwhelming, evidence that Bonds used performance-enhancing drugs for much of the second half of his career. Bonds bowed out at season's end with 762 career home runs.

2007

The report created a firestorm of discussion and anger. For years, fans had seen the evidence of drug use, especially those designed to increase a player's size or performance. There had been isolated incidents of players caught using the stuff. However, the Mitchell Report, for the first time, brought names and details into the public eye. As a result, baseball wound up with a black eye, though some did praise it for at least trying to come clean.

However, for many, it was too little, too late. Critics blasted the players named, including some who had previously and vigorously denied using such substances. Many careers were tainted while hundreds of others not named were called into question. The report started a chain reaction of other revelations, as more and more players were revealed to have tested positive for some of these substances in the previous decade.

Finally, Some Good News

You might have guessed that when the Boston-based movie *The Departed* won four Oscars, including Best

---

Other Milestones of 2007

✔ For the first time, the same two schools (Florida and Ohio State) met to decide the national championship in college football and college basketball in the same calendar year. The Gators defeated the Buckeyes in each sport.

✔ At the U.S. Men's Olympic Marathon Trials in New York November 3, Ryan Shay collapsed just past the 5 1/2-mile mark. One of the premier U.S. marathoners of the decade, Shay suffered a massive heart attack due to an enlarged heart condition and died instantly. Most of his fellow competitors, including the winner, Ryan Hall, had no idea what had happened to Shay until they crossed the finish line.

✔ On September 13, the New York Mets were 83–62 and in first place in the National League East by seven games. New York proceeded to lose 12 of its final 17 games, including 6 of its final 7, to miss the playoffs. The epic collapse was punctuated by an 8–1 loss at Shea Stadium on the final day of the season to the last-place Florida Marlins. With a win, the Mets would have made the postseason.

✔ As stunning as the collapse of the Mets was the revival of the Colorado Rockies. Colorado won 13 of its last 14 games, including a one-game showdown with the San Diego Padres, to earn a wild-card berth in the postseason. Then the Rockies won all seven of their games in the N.L. playoffs before losing to the Red Sox in the World Series.

✔ Jimmie Johnson repeated as NASCAR's Nextel Cup champion.

✔ Deaths: NFL All-Pro safety Sean Taylor, 24, died of a gunshot wound while confronting burglars in the middle of the night in his home. Also passing: baseball's Phil Rizzuto, football's Bill Walsh, and college football coaching legend Eddie Robinson.

Picture and Best Director (Martin Scorsese), it was going to be a banner year for Boston. The Red Sox swept the Colorado Rockies four games to none in the World Series in October. It was the Red Sox's second championship in the decade. In the 2000s, the Sox would go 8–0 in World Series games.

Meanwhile, in Foxboro, the New England Patriots became the first NFL team to finish a regular season 16–0. While the 1972 Miami Dolphins had also gone undefeated in the regular season (and postseason), the league played a 14-game schedule back then. Sure, there was that nasty little matter of the Patriots' SpyGate (see page 364) in the season opener against the New York Jets, but the Patriots and their GQ-caliber quarterback, Tom Brady, who was only dating one of the world's most beautiful women (supermodel Gisele Bündchen) seemed to enjoy the world's disdain.

Victory was infectious around the Hub. Even the long dormant Celtics, whose last NBA title had come in 1986, were suddenly dominant. Behind the trio of Ray Allen, Kevin Garnett, and Paul Pierce, the parquet predators were an astounding 26–3 on New Year's Eve.

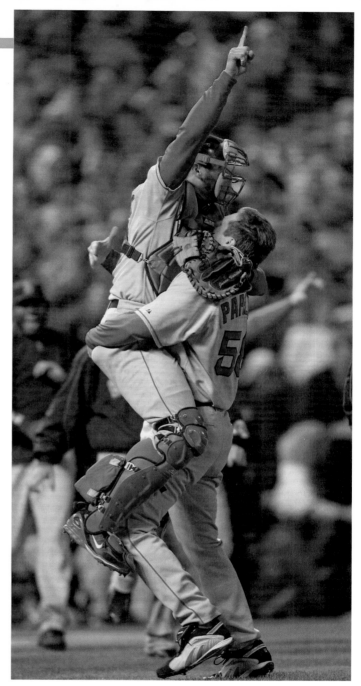

No Curses Here   *Boston Red Sox pitcher Jonathan Papelbon lifts catcher Jason Varitek after the Red Sox swept the Colorado Rockies to win their second World Series in four years.*

2008

The Best Year Ever?

If 2008 was not the greatest year ever in sports, it was indeed the cure for the disappointing one that preceded it. From a football stadium in Glendale, Arizona, to a golf course outside San Diego, from a grass-layered tennis court in London to the Bird's Nest in Beijing, witnesses were left in slack-jawed wonder all over the globe.

A few "greatest" nominees from 2008: Super Bowl play (David Tyree's catch), U.S. Open golf finish (Tiger Woods), tennis match (Wimbledon men's final), Olympic performance (Michael Phelps), and Olympic performance lasting less than 10 seconds (Usain Bolt).

America seemed to agree, as television viewers watched in record numbers. Tiger Woods' 18-hole (make that 19-hole) playoff win at the U.S. Open was the most-watched golf event on cable in history. The New York Giants' 17–14 victory over the New England Patriots was the most-watched Super Bowl ever. The Beijing Summer Olympics, the superlative event in this most superlative of years, became the most-watched global event of all time, with 4.7 billion viewers.

Super Game, Super Catch

The New England Patriots entered Super Bowl XLII on February 3 with an 18–0 record. Only the 1972 Miami Dolphins had finished an undefeated season with a Super Bowl triumph, finishing 17–0. The Patriots, behind head coach Bill Belichick and NFL Most Valuable Player QB Tom Brady, had a chance to join them.

Their opponent? The New York Giants, whose quarterback, Eli Manning, was no better than the second-best quarterback (if not third-best, if you consider his dad, Archie) in his own family, behind the Indianapolis Colts' Peyton Manning. The Giants' march to the Super Bowl had been a three-game road trip that included nail-biting victories at Dallas and Green Bay.

New York's last loss, in fact, had been a 38–35 thriller in the regular-season finale to . . . the Patriots. When the two teams met again in Glendale, Arizona, the Giants' fierce pass rush, led by defensive ends Osi Umenyiora and Michael Strahan (playing his final game), harassed Brady all game, sacking him five times.

With 2:42 to play, the Patriots took a 14–10 lead on Brady's six-yard touchdown pass to Randy Moss. On the ensuing drive,

Splish, Splash *When you set a record for Olympic gold medals, you get to shout like Michael Phelps (page 373).*

the Giants faced a third-and-five from their own 44-yard line with 1:15 remaining. That is when Manning and David Tyree, a wide receiver who was primarily a special-teams player, created perhaps the most spectacular play in Super Bowl lore.

Manning, in the pocket, appeared to be in the grasp of Patriots defender Jar-vis Green. Not known for being mobile, Manning eluded Green's clutches, spun away, and heaved a pass 35 yards down the center of the field. Tyree leaped up to make the catch and pinned the football to the crown of his helmet with both hands as safety Rodney Harrison, one of the fiercest hitters in the NFL, strained to

2008

separate the ball from his grasp. All three entities—Tyree, Harrison and the football—landed together with the pigskin still firmly in Tyree's paws.

The reception defied description, if not physics. A few plays later, Manning found Plaxico Burress for the game-winning touchdown pass. The Patriots were denied their perfect season, while David Tyree etched his name into sports history.

No, He Didn't! *Yes, he did! In one of the NFL's most spectacular plays ever, Giants wide receiver David Tyree (85) clutched the football to his helmet and came down with a Super Bowl-saving grab.*

Wounded Tiger Still Dangerous

The U.S. Open, staged at Torrey Pines in San Diego, came down to an 18-hole playoff on June 16 between two men. There was Rocco Mediate, who at 45 looked as if he were barely in good enough shape to take down the storm windows. Mediate, who had six career PGA Tour wins, had to survive a sudden-death playoff just to qualify for the Open.

Then there was the indomitable Tiger Woods, seeking his 14th career major. Mediate himself had described his adversary, who had buried a 12-foot putt on the 72nd hole on Sunday to force the playoff, as a "monster."

Woods took a three-shot lead onto the 11th hole. Mediate, as if writing the plot for the sequel to the golf movie *Tin Cup* (featuring an out-of-nowhere challenger for a major win), stormed back to take a one-shot lead heading into the 18th hole. In fact, he had a 20-foot putt on 18 to win it. Few golfers ever came so close to slaying Tiger.

It was not to be. Mediate missed his putt, while Tiger sank his for birdie. That forced a 19th hole on the playoff—the 91st overall—and Woods took that by one stroke.

"I'm glad I'm done," said Woods, who walked the final 19 holes with a slight limp of his left leg. "I really don't feel like playing any more."

And who could blame him? It was later revealed that Woods, who had needed pain-killing medicine during the final round, had played with a double stress fracture to his left tibia. He would also shortly need to undergo knee surgery. This, the grittiest win of Woods' career, was also his final tournament of the year.

Beijing

At the outset of the Beijing Summer Olympics, it appeared that everyone's worst fears would be realized. A few days before the Opening Ceremony, a few American cyclists stepped off the plane wearing surgical masks as a precaution against the Chinese city's notoriously polluted air. On the day of the Ceremony itself—8/8/08, since eight is a lucky number in China—as world leaders filed into the Beijing National Stadium (dubbed "The Bird's Nest" for its exterior design), Russia invaded Georgia. Less than 24 hours later, the father-in-law of Hugh McCutcheon, the U.S. men's volleyball team coach, was fatally stabbed at a tourist attraction, the Drum Tower. The assailant, a deranged Chinese man, then leapt to his death.

Then the competitions began. What followed over the next two weeks was instead the realization that we were watching the greatest athletic spectacle of our lifetimes. The highlights:

Michael Phelps

The U.S. swimmer won all eight races that he entered, setting a new gold standard to which all future Olympians must aspire. Performing under the weight of extraordinary expectations, Phelps bested by one Mark Spitz's 36-year-old record for most gold medals (seven) at a single Olympics while also setting seven world records in the process.

Phelps' march to immortality, as dramatic as it was historic, almost ended in his second race. In the 4 x 100 meter relay, anchor Jason Lezak made up a body-length deficit in the final 50 meters against the French world record holder in the event. To do so, Lezak swam the fastest relay leg in history.

After that moment, it was clear that these Games were imbued with a certain magic. In Phelps' seventh race, the 100-meter butterfly, he trailed down to the final stroke, out-touching his Serbian rival by the slightest of margins: one one-hundredth of a second.

Dara Torres

At age 41, Dara Torres was hardly slowing down. In Beijing, the California native became the first American swimmer to compete in five Olympics, and was the first female swimmer above age 40 to participate in an Olympics.

But Torres, whose chiseled body garnered as much attention as her body of work, was there to win. She earned two silver medals in relays. In her final race, the splash-heavy 50-meter freestyle, she lost out on gold by a mere one-hundredth of a second. At another point in her career, Torres might have been crushed, but perhaps knowing how she'd been cheating Father Time for so long, she was able to grin at the irony.

Asked what she was thinking afterward, Torres replied, "I'm thinking I shouldn't have filed my nails last night."

Other American Highlights

More memorable moments from Beijing: The lightly regarded U.S. men's volleyball

Golden Spikes *Clayton Stanley (in red) and the rest of the U.S. men's volleyball team were inspired by the tragic death of their coach's father-in-law early in the Games and rallied to win gold.*

team, which had to deal with the murder of their coach's father-in-law on the opening day of competition, went undefeated to win gold. In shooting, American Matt Emmons, for the second Olympics in a row, squandered a sure gold medal with a disastrously off-target effort on the last of his 10 shots.

The U.S. men's basketball and women's soccer teams, after disappointing finishes in world competition dating back to 2004, both won gold. Japan stunned the United States in the gold-medal game in softball, ending the Americans' 22-game win streak and denying them a fourth gold in as many Olympics. It would be the final Olympic softball game for at least eight years, as the sport was voted off the 2012 program in large part due to, ironically, American domination.

Lightning Bolt

At any other Olympics, Jamaican sprinter Usain Bolt's trio of world-record dashes would have been the story of the Games. As it was, he still got a lot of well-deserved world attention. In the 100-meter final the 6-foot 5-inch Bolt ran the 100 in a world-record 9.69 seconds despite easing up in the final five to ten meters. After being heavily criticized for "showboating," the aptly named Bolt again electrified the Bird's Nest audience by running the fastest 200 meters in history at 19.30 seconds. No other sprinter had ever set world records in both races at the same Olympics.

As an encore, Bolt ran the third leg for Jamaica in the 4 x 100-meter final, lending an assist to yet another world-record-setting (37.10 seconds) gold-medal performance.

Danica on Top . . . Finally

Danica Patrick won the Indy Japan 300, taking the lead from pole-sitter Helio Castroneves with two laps to go, to become the first female to win an IndyCar race. It was the 50th race of the 26-year-old Patrick's career.

Although Patrick had made inroads in the male-dominated world of auto racing, and even had earned IndyCar's Rookie of the Year award for 2005, she was known mostly for the good looks that landed her numerous endorsement opportunities and in many commercials even before taking any checkered flags.

Patrick's April 20 victory in Motegi, Japan, in the annual IndyCar stop there validated her status as one of the top IndyCar drivers. By year's end, speculation mounted that she also might also one day make the jump to stock cars on the more popular NASCAR circuit.

Of Rays and Rain

The World Series pitted the Philadelphia Phillies, who had only won one World Series in their previous 125 seasons, and the Tampa Bay Rays, who had never advanced to the postseason in their brief, 10-year history. The Rays were led by American League Rookie of the Year Evan Longoria, while the Phillies had a deep roster led by sluggers Ryan Howard and Chase Utley, as well as Gold Glove fielders in shortstop Jimmy Rollins and center fielder Shane Victorino.

Philly held a three games to one lead in the series when it began raining heavily in the middle of Game Five. Had this occurred in St. Petersburg, Florida, where the Rays' domed stadium is located, the weather would not have mattered. The contest, however, was taking place in Philadelphia.

With the score tied 2–2 in the middle of the sixth inning, the game was suspended—the Rays had tied it on a two-out single moments earlier. It marked the first time a World Series game was not played through to completion or rendered a tie. Rain continued the next day. It was not until two days later, more than 50 hours after the series-clinching game had begun, that the Phillies stormed—excuse the pun—the diamond to celebrate a 4–3 victory and the city's first major sports championship of any kind since 1983.

Heroes of Another Kind

Finally, there was the uplifting (literally) tale of Western Oregon softball

Other Milestones of 2008

✔ On New Year's Day, an NHL-record crowd of 71,217 fans watched the Pittsburgh Penguins play the Buffalo Sabres outdoors—and in a driving snow-storm—in Orchard Park, New York. The "Winter Classic" was decided in an overtime shootout. The Penguins won 2–1 when star Sidney Crosby scored the game-winning goal.

✔ In March, American alpine skier Bode Miller atoned for his abysmal showing at the 2006 Winter Olympics by winning his second World Cup champi-onship in four years. Compatriot Lindsey Vonn, 23, completed the U.S. sweep by winning the women's overall title.

✔ For the first time, all four No. 1 seeds advanced to the Final Four in the men's NCAA basketball tourna-ment. In the final on April 7, Kansas recovered from a nine-point deficit in the final few minutes—thanks to some poor free-throw shooting by Memphis—and forced overtime via Mario Chalmers' three-pointer with two seconds left. The Jayhawks won 75–68 in overtime for their first NCAA title in 20 years.

✔ The Tennessee Lady Vols basketball team beat Stanford 64–48 on April 8 to win its second NCAA championship in as many years and eighth overall under Pat Summitt. A month earlier, the sport's all-time winningest coach (983 victories at season's end) had dislocated her shoulder shooing a raccoon off her back deck.

✔ Belgian tennis star Justine Henin, 25, retired May 14 even though she was the world's No. 1-ranked player at the time. Henin's news came two weeks before the French Open, which she had won four times.

✔ After winning both the Kentucky Derby and Preak-ness Stakes, 3-10 favorite Big Brown finished in last place in the Belmont Stakes on June 7. Big Brown became the fourth thoroughbred in seven years to win the first two legs of the Triple Crown and then fall short at Belmont.

✔ The Boston Celtics won their NBA-record 17th championship, and first in 22 years, by defeating their old nemeses, the Los Angeles Lakers. The Celtics clinched the title in Boston on June 17 with a 131–92 victory in Game Six. The 39-point margin of victory was the NBA's largest ever in a series-clinching win.

✔ St. Louis Cardinals first baseman Albert Pujols earned the first of back-to-back, N.L. MVP awards after batting .357 with 37 homers and 116 RBI. Pujols arguably was the greatest player in baseball in the opening decade of the 2000s. In 10 seasons beginning in 2001, he was an All-Star nine times and the league MVP three times. (He finished in the top 10 in the balloting for the annual in each of his first nine seasons.)

✔ Annika Sorenstam of Sweden, 38, retired from the LPGA Tour. The dominant golfer of her generation, Sorenstam finished with 72 Tour victories (third all time), including 10 majors.

✔ In December, the Arena Football League sus-pended operations after 22 seasons of pinball-style, indoor pigskin entertainment.

✔ Manny Pacquiao defeated Oscar De La Hoya De-cember 8 on an eighth-round TKO in a hugely popu-lar welterweight bout.

player Sara Tucholsky. In a playoff game against Central Washington, Tucholsky belted the first home run of her career. As she rounded first base, Tucholsky's knee buckled. She was unable to walk.

College softball rules said that teammates were not allowed to assist Tucholsky. If the coach chose to put in a pinch-runner, the home run would not count and the runner would start on first base. The situation was a tough one for Tucholsky, playing in her final season, and for the Western Oregon coach.

In a display of sportsmanship that would cheer the world, two players from Central Washington moved over to Tucholsky. They put down their mitts and picked up the injured home-run hitter. They then carried her around the bases, making sure she stopped to touch each base. The home run counted and, in fact, it helped Western Oregon beat Central Washington, ending its season, too. The image of the two players carrying their injured opponent showed that amid all the bad and weird stuff that was happening in sports and with athletes that there was still a lot of good that could come from competition.

"In the end, it is not about winning and losing so much," said Mallory Holtman, one of the two players who hoisted Tucholsky. "She hit it over the fence and was in pain, and she deserved a home run."

Now That's Sportpersonship *After she hurt her knee running out a home run, Western Oregon's Sara Tucholsky was carried around the bases . . . by her opponents from Central Washington.*

2009

III for XLIII

One team, the Pittsburgh Steelers, already had five Super Bowl championships, tied for the most ever. The other team, the Arizona Cardinals, hadn't been in a championship game since 1947. Together, these two unlikely opponents put together one of the most entertaining and nail-biting Super Bowls yet.

The game on February 1 was a back-and-forth affair, but Pittsburgh seemed to have the upper hand, thanks to the first of three remarkable plays. The Steelers had gained a 17–7 halftime lead with the longest play in Super Bowl history. Pittsburgh linebacker James Harrison intercepted a pass by Kurt Warner and returned it 100 yards as the first half expired.

However, with three minutes left in the game, the Cardinals took the lead. Star receiver Larry Fitzgerald, who would set NFL postseason records for touchdown catches and receiving yards, teamed up with Warner for a stunning 64-yard score. All of a sudden, the surprising Cardinals had a trophy almost in their grasp.

But Pittsburgh quarterback Ben Roethlisberger got one more chance. He teamed with receiver Santonio Holmes and others to drive the Steelers to the six-yard line. With just 35 seconds left, Holmes made an amazing, fingertip, toe-tapping catch. The Steelers hung on to win 27–23 and capture their record sixth Super Bowl title.

Steroids Scandals Continue

Baseball took two more big hits in the ongoing steroid scandal that had distracted players and fans for most of the decade. In February, news broke that three-time MVP Alex Rodriguez had used steroids during his time with the Texas Rangers. He later admitted that he had let his cousin inject him with what he thought were vitamin supplements starting in 2001 and continuing for two years. "I didn't think they were steroids," Rodriguez said. "That's part of being young and stupid. It was over the counter. It was pretty simple. All these years I never thought I did anything wrong." Few people believed his story, but since he had not tested positive during baseball's annual exams, he faced no punishment from the sport. His personal credibility was deeply

It Was a Brees *Amid flying confetti, Saints quarterback Drew Brees helped cap off the decade of the 2000s with the first Super Bowl win for New Orleans (see page 383).*

hurt, however, as he had adamantly denied using drugs during a television interview in 2007.

Further reports from a 2003 test, which was supposed to be secret, said that David Ortiz, star slugger of the Red Sox, had also tested positive. "Big Papi" denied it, and little came of that story.

A much bigger deal came from one of Ortiz's former Red Sox teammates.

2009

Manny Ramirez, who had joined the Los Angeles Dodgers in 2008, was suspended from baseball for 50 games for testing positive for a banned substance. Ramirez did not test positive for steroids. However, his blood showed levels of a drug used by steroid users to rebuild their testosterone, a drug also used by pregnant women. Ramirez returned later in the season, but, like Rodriguez, his public persona was deeply hurt by the admission.

Perfect . . . Catch

In more than 130 years of Major League Baseball, only 18 pitchers have thrown a perfect game. But none of them got as much amazing last-inning help as Mark Buehrle of the Chicago White Sox. On July 23, the left-hander was mowing down the Tampa Bay Rays. He allowed no baserunners of any kind through eight innings and was three outs away from baseball history when Gabe Kapler drove a ball to deep center field.

Center fielder Dewayne Wise was off with the crack of the bat. He jumped at the wall and reached up to snag the ball just before it left the ballpark. As he fell to the ground, the ball popped out of his glove, but Wise grabbed it with his other hand to record the out.

The miraculous catch preserved Buehrle's "perfecto," and he got the final

A Huge Soccer Upset

The U.S. national soccer team rarely dominates the American sports scene, but their success at the Confederations Cup in June earned them well-deserved attention. In a semifinal match, the United States defeated Spain, which was ranked number one in the world at the time, for one of the biggest wins in American soccer history. Young forward Jozy Altidore scored early and veteran Clint Dempsey added a clincher late in the game to cap the upset. In the final game of that tournament, the United States led Brazil 2-0 at halftime. However, the mighty Brazilians stormed back to win 3–2. It was a disappointment, but still a great inspiration for the Yanks.

Later in the summer, the U.S. team qualified for its fifth straight World Cup, which was held in South Africa in June 2010 and was won by Spain.

two outs to add his name to the record book . . . with a little help from a friend.

Armstrong Returns

After winning seven Tour de France bicycle races while also overcoming cancer and becoming an international legend, Lance Armstrong retired from racing in 2005 (see page 349). However, he missed the action, so he came back this year to try again. And he almost added another page to his legend. Armstrong was among the leaders in the race, and in fact wore the leader's yellow jersey for a while. But in the tough mountain stages, Spain's Alberto Contador pulled away to ruin Armstrong's comeback chances. Still, the American did finish third, proving that he still had a lot of gas in the tank . . . even on a bike.

Lightning Strikes Twice

Speaking of leaving gas in the tank: While Jamaican runner Usain Bolt had stunned the world at the 2008 Olympics, winning gold and setting world records, many felt that he still had more to give. He had pulled up slightly in the finals in Beijing, so could he actually post a better time?

The answer was yes, as Bolt proved at the World Track & Field Championships in Berlin in August. The speedster blazed through the 100 meters in 9.58 seconds, shaving 1/10 of a second off his world record. If you think that's not that much time, consider that no one had lowered it by that much in one race in more than 88 years.

He proved to be more than a one-race wonder when he also set a new world record in the 200 meters, at an almost-frightening 19.19 seconds. Bolt has set almost unapproachable standards in the sprint races, but who's to say that his own lightning won't strike again.

U.S. sprinter Tyson Gay set a new American record at 9.71 seconds in that 100-meter race in Berlin, but it was little comfort as he watched Bolt's breathtaking performance ahead of him.

Serena Blows a Gasket

Tennis stars have been known to have emotional outbursts, often in frustration at a missed shot or anger at a blown call. Broken rackets, yelling, pointing, and more are not unknown. In fact, the sport has a system for penalizing players who go too far with such tantrums. At the 2009 U.S. Open, that system, and one star player, got the headlines.

Serena Williams, for more than a decade one of the top players in the world and the 2009 Wimbledon champion, was trailing late in a semifinal match against Kim Clijsters at the U.S. Open in New York City. After Williams made a serve, the back-line judge called her for a foot fault. This very rare foul means that a player stepped on the back line during her serve. Williams went ballistic, screaming and yelling and pointing her racket at the official. The umpire, who is the head official, warned Williams and then awarded her opponent a penalty point. Bad news for Williams, for that penalty point was enough to give the game, set, and match to Clijsters.

2009

The angry tirade damaged Williams's otherwise fine reputation. She was fined more than $80,000 and put on probation for two years. Another such screaming fit and she'll lose more than just a match—it could mean a suspension.

Godzilla Strikes! *Yankees slugger Hideki Matsui, known to his fans back home in Japan as Godzilla, was named the World Series MVP after hitting .615, including this key homer in Game 2.*

Yanks Back on Top

In 1923, Yankee Stadium opened, and the New York Yankees brought home a World Series championship. In 2009, a new Yankee Stadium opened . . . and history repeated itself. The Yankees won their 27th World Series title, more than twice as many as any other team, by defeating the Philadelphia Phillies in six games. The Yanks' championship total is the highest of any pro team in North American sports, ahead of the Montreal Canadiens' 24 Stanley Cups and the Boston Celtics' 17 NBA crowns.

The Yankees were led by a few of the players on whom they lavished more than $400 million in contracts before the season. Pitcher C.C. Sabathia won his start in the Series, while first baseman Mark Teixeira slugged and played great defense. Star third baseman Alex Rodriguez finally shook off a career-long postseason slump and had six homers in the playoffs and World Series combined. In the World Series, Hideki Matsui became the first designated hitter (and first Japanese player) to be named MVP, thanks mostly to his record-tying six RBI in the clinching game.

Four for J.J.

NASCAR has been going around in circles—really, really fast—for more than 50 years, but it has never seen a champion like Jimmie Johnson. He became the first driver ever to win four straight championships when he roared to victory in the Chase for the Nextel Cup in 2009. Johnson continued the consistent, steady success that he has had since his career started in 2001. In fact, he has not finished lower than fifth in any season since 2002. In winning his fourth straight title (topping former record-holder Cale Yarborough, who won three titles in a row beginning in 1976), Johnson won seven races, including three in the playoff-like, 10-race Chase that ends the season.

Johnson's total of four career championships ties him with Jeff Gordon, who actually is a co-owner of Johnson's car and his teammate at Hendrick Motorsports. Both of those drivers are still chasing the all-time record of seven career titles won by Richard "The King" Petty and Dale Earnhardt Sr.

Nearly Perfect Football

The New Orleans Saints were once so bad that fans wore paper bags over their heads at games and the team was known as the "Aints." But like New Orleans itself, rising out of the disaster that was Hurricane Katrina, the Saints showed in 2009 that anything is possible.

The Saints won their first 13 games of the season, with QB Drew Brees heading up a powerful offense. They scored 35 or more points in six of their victories, then whomped Arizona 45–14 in the first round of the playoffs. In the NFC Championship Game, kicker Garrett Hartley sent the Saints to their first Super Bowl with a 40-yard field goal in overtime.

Meanwhile, the Indianapolis Colts were on a pretty hot streak, too. Led by Peyton Manning, who won his record fourth NFL MVP, Indianapolis went 14–2 and faced little trouble in the playoffs.

Athletes on Twitter

Celebrities of all stripes jumped on Twitter in 2009, and sports stars were no exceptions. One web site counted more than 1,100 pro and college stars with Twitter accounts, letting their fans in on just about anything that crossed their minds . . . or their keyboards. NBA star Shaquille O'Neal claimed the most numbers of followers among athletes, with more than 3 million readers as of the end of 2009, while cycling hero Lance Armstrong was read by 2.5 million.

Bengals receiver Chad Ochocinco became well-known for his "tweets," some of which tweaked NFL officials. Some players in college and the pros actually got in trouble for things they wrote. Running back Larry Johnson of the Chiefs criticized his coach and used inappropriate language in some tweets and actually ended up being let go by the team.

While using Twitter to connect with fans was a positive for many athletes, others were learning that sometimes TMI—too much information!—can be a dangerous thing.

These two hot-streak teams met in Super Bowl XLIV in Miami in February 2010. The Saints' offense was on full display, with Brees going 32-for-39 and throwing two touchdown passes. However, it was a big defensive play that cemented the victory for New Orleans. Terry Porter intercepted a pass by Manning and returned it 74 yards for a clinching score in their 31–17 win. The entire city of New Orleans celebrated, pouring out onto the streets to dance and sing. It was the end of a long road for a team that had been playing since 1967 without any sort of title.

For the Colts, even with the loss, the season capped off a record-setting decade. Their 116 wins in the 2000s were the most in any single decade in NFL history. Their 23 consecutive wins over 2008-09

2009

also set a new mark, topping the Patriots' 21 straight in 2002-03. The other big NFL story of 2009 was the second un-retirement for Brett Favre. The NFL's all-time leader in just about every passing statistic had left his longtime team, the Packers, after 2007, only to re-emerge as a New York Jet in 2008. After again "retiring," he was lured out by the Vikings in 2009 and led them to the NFC Central title.

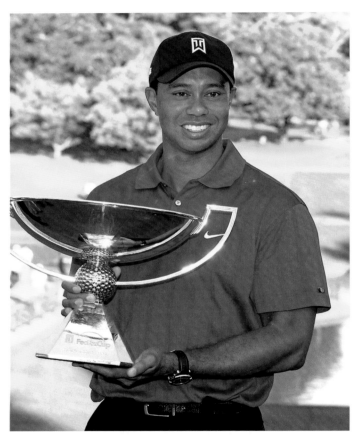

The Last Smile? *Tiger Woods again dominated golf in 2009, winning the FedEx Cup and six other tournaments. By the end of the year, however, his life had taken an ugly turn.*

Tiger Trouble

The final year of the decade came to a bumpy end for the most famous athlete in the world. Golfer Tiger Woods had made positive headlines earlier in 2009 when he bounced back from knee surgery to return to the top of his sport. Though he didn't win any majors, he did capture titles in six other events.

His whole world changed in early December. Very early one morning, word flashed around the world that Tiger had been "seriously injured" in a car accident in front of his Florida home. The first word was that he had been taken to the hospital after his wife had smashed a window to drag him from the car. That report generated sympathy, until details emerged that changed the picture entirely.

Yes, there had been an accident, and yes, Tiger had suffered some minor cuts and bruises. However, his ensuing silence about the event opened up the floodgates of speculation. With no news from Tiger, gossip web sites and bloggers filled the empty space with guesses. Was Tiger fleeing from a fight with his wife? Had they been arguing about whether he had been with other women? Was he under the influence of prescription drugs when he crashed? No one had answers to those questions, and Tiger's reputation crashed. He asked for privacy while he and his family dealt with what he thought was a private matter, but he had not counted on the worldwide fascination with celebrity. For years, he had worked carefully to create a perfect image. With the smash of a fender on a fire hydrant and his evasive answers, that image was smashed.

Other Milestones of 2009

✔ The women's basketball team from the University of Connecticut didn't lose a game all season, going 39–0. It was the third time the school has gone undefeated, and the sixth time it won the NCAA basketball championship.

✔ Everything old was new again at the British Open. At the age of 59, golfing legend Tom Watson came within one stroke of winning the legendary tournament, thrilling fans around the world. Watson, who lost to Stewart Cink in a playoff, had won five British Opens earlier in his career.

✔ In one of the biggest upsets in horse-racing history, 50–1 longshot Mine That Bird won the Kentucky Derby. The horse later won the Preakness Stakes before coming up short in the Belmont Stakes.

✔ Superstar guard Kobe Bryant led the Los Angeles Lakers to their 15th NBA championship. The Lakers defeated the Orlando Magic in five games, and Bryant was named the Finals MVP.

✔ Hockey fans got their wish, as the game's two top stars faced off in the Stanley Cup Finals. In the end, Sidney Crosby's Pittsburgh Penguins overcame Alexander Ovechkin's Washington Capitals to win the Cup.

✔ The New Jersey Nets set a new NBA record for futility. They lost their first 18 games of the 2009–10 season before defeating the Charlotte Bobcats in December. The Miami Heat and Los Angeles Clippers held the old record of 17 straight Ls to start a season. New Jersey ended the season with an NBA-low 12 victories.

As the year was ending, Tiger revealed the truth: He had indeed been unfaithful to his wife. On December 11, he announced that he was taking time off from golf. "After much soul searching, I have decided to take an indefinite break from professional golf. I need to focus my attention on being a better husband, father, and person," Tiger wrote on his Web site.

While Tiger and his family began dealing with the fallout from his bad choices, his decision to step away from the golf course put enormous pressure on the PGA Tour. The entire sport had almost completely depended on Tiger for more than a decade; sure enough, fan interest and television ratings were down early in the 2010 season (at least until Tiger returned to play his first tournament of the new year at the prestigious Masters in April).

Still, the news wasn't all bad: A host of young players stepped to the fore and proved that golf's future was still bright. Among them: the United States' Anthony Kim, Northern Ireland's Rory McIlroy, and Colombia's Camilo Villegas.

RESOURCES

Events and Personalities

Ball Four
By Jim Bouton (New York: World Publications, 1970).
The quintessential "insider" book about pro sports, written by a veteran pitcher, this remains one of the most influential sports books of the last 50 years.

The Book of Basketball: The NBA According to the Sports Guy
By Bill Simmons (New York: ESPN Books, 2009).
A columnist for ESPN.com covers the history of the NBA as seen through his own humorous, intense, and fan-oriented lens.

Coach Wooden's Pyramid of Success
By John Wooden and Jay Carty (Ventura, CA: Regal Books, 2009).
The most successful college basketball coach ever offers up his famous lessons on how to succeed, lessons now used in school districts nationwide.

Koufax: A Lefty's Legacy
By Jane Leavy (New York: HarperCollins, 2000).
One of the best sports books in the past 30 years, in our humble opinion, sheds light on one of baseball's greatest talents and most enduring mysteries.

It's Not About the Bike: My Journey Back to Life
By Lance Armstrong and Sally Jenkins (New York: Berkely, 2003).
The most successful Tour de France rider ever is an American hero and a cancer survivor. His inspiring story thrilled millions in the early 2000s.

Muhammad Ali: His Life and Times
By Thomas Hauser (New York: Simon & Schuster, 1991).
The finest of many biographies of one of the seminal figures in American sports in the past 50 years.

When Pride Still Mattered
By David Maraniss (New York: Simon & Schuster, 2000).
An excellent biography of Vince Lombardi, coach of the Green Bay Packers in the 1960s and the model for many coaches who followed him.

American Sports History

The Complete Book of the Olympics
By David Wallechinsky and Jaime Loucky (London: Aurum Press, 2008)
An extremely detailed look at every Winter and Summer Olympics from 1896 to the present, including complete lists of medal winners and athlete biographies.

Encyclopedia of Women and Sport in America
Edited by Carol Oglesby et al. (Phoenix: Oryx Press, 1998)
A large overview of not only key female personalities on and off the playing field, but a look at issues surrounding women and sports.

Encyclopedia of World Sport
Edited by David Levinson and Karen Christensen (New York: Oxford University Press, 1999)
This wide-ranging book contains short articles on an enormous variety of sports, personalities, events, and issues, most of

which have some connection to American sports history. This is a great starting point for additional research.

The ESPN Baseball Encyclopedia
Edited by Gary Gillette and Pete Palmer (New York: Sterling, 2008, fifth edition)
This is the latest version of a baseball record and stats books, including the career totals of every Major Leaguer. Essays in the book cover baseball history, team history, and articles about the role of women and minorities in the game.

ESPN SportsCentury
Edited by Michael McCambridge (New York: Hyperion, 1999)
Created to commemorate the 20th century in sports, this book features essays by well-known sportswriters as well as commentary by popular ESPN broadcasters. Each decade's chapter features an in-depth story about the key event of that time period.

NFL Record & Fact Book
Edited by Jon Zimmer, Randall Liu, and Matt Marini (New York: Time Inc. Home Entertainment, 2010)
An indispensable reference source for NFL fans and media personnel.

The Sporting News Chronicle of 20th Century Sports
By Ron Smith (New York: BDD/Mallard Press, 1992)
A good single-volume history of key sports events. They are presented as if written right after the event, thus giving the text a "you are there" feel.

Sports of the Times
By David Fischer and William Taafe. (New York: Times Books, 2003)
A unique format tracks the top sports events on each day of the calendar year. Find out the biggest event for every day from January 1 to December 31.

Sports History Web Sites

ESPN.com
www.sports.espn.go.com
The Web site run by the national cable sports channel contains numerous history sections within each sport. This one for baseball is the largest and includes constantly updated statistics on baseball.

Official League Web Sites
www.nfl.com
www.nba.com
www.mlb.com
www.nhl.com
Each of the major sports leagues has history sections on their official Web sites.

Official Olympics Web Site
http://www.olympic.org/uk/games/index_uk.asp
Complete history of the Olympic Games, presented by the International Olympic Committee.

The Sports Illustrated Vault
http://sportsillustrated.cnn.com/vault/
Since its first issue in 1954, Sports Illustrated *has been a must-read for fans everywhere. You can go down memory lane in this trove of features, photos, and covers from the magazine.*

Sports Reference
www.sports-reference.com
By far the most detailed central site, including separate sections on baseball, basketball, football, hockey, and the Olympics. The sections include player stats, team histories, records from all seasons past, and much more.

INDEX

CREDITS

About the Authors

James Buckley, Jr.
One of America's most prolific sports authors, he has written more than 50 books on a variety of sports for adults and young readers, including *Perfect: The Story of Baseball's Perfect Games, The Hall of Fame Collection, Sports Immortals,* and *Classic Sports Rivalries.* He was the editorial director of this book and the *Sports in America* series.

David Fischer
Fischer is the author of several sports books including *Cool Sports Dad: 75 Amazing Sporting Tricks to Teach and Impress Your Kids, The 50 Coolest Jobs in Sports,* and *The New York Times' Sports of the Times.* (1960s)

Jim Gigliotti
A former senior editor at NFL Publishing, Gigliotti has written several books on NASCAR and football, as well as co-written two major books of sports trivia. (1970s, 2000s)

Timothy J. Seeberg
Seeberg is a writer based in Oregon who has written books on outdoor sports for young readers. (1970s)

Michael Teitelbaum
A former editor of Little League Magazine, Teitelbaum is the author of more than 200 books for adults and young readers, including an encyclopedia on the Baseball Hall of Fame and a biography of Jackie Robinson. (1980s)

John Walters
A former staff member at *Sports Illustrated* and NBC Sports, Walters is the co-author of *Basketball for Dummies* and has written for numerous Web sites and blogs. (2000s)

Bob Woods
Woods has written for *Sports Illustrated*, NBC Sports, and several Olympic programs. He is the author of many sports books and biographies for young readers, including titles on baseball and motor sports. He also wrote *The Scooter Book* and edited the *Harley-Davidson 100th Anniversary Magazine.* (1990s, 2000s)

Photo Credits

Sports icons by Bob Eckstein.

Photo Credits:

AP/Wide World: 7, 15, 19, 29, 31, 40, 47, 55, 56, 71, 75, 87, 93, 96, 101, 107, 117, 127, 128, 131, 143, 148, 157, 175 (2), 179, 184, 190, 192, 195, 196, 197, 198 (left), 203, 205, 206, 216, 220, 221, 223, 233, 235, 241, 245, 248, 249, 251, 255, 259, 260, 264, 266, 267, 271, 276, 283, 287, 288, 290, 295, 296, 300, 303, 305, 306, 308, 309, 310, 317, 324, 325, 326, 329, 332, 333, 334, 338, 340, 345, 346, 350, 353, 362, 365, 367, 372, 377, 382

Corbis: 9, 10, 25, 35, 39, 45, 51, 61, 69, 72, 77, 79, 82, 85, 88, 102, 113, 121, 135, 137, 141, 147, 155, 167, 219, 237, 274, 280

Getty Images: 23, 63, 65, 91, 99, 104, 110, 115, 122, 127, 130, 136, 139, 142, 150, 153, 163, 164, 171, 173, 180, 183, 187, 188, 198 (right), 211, 215, 226, 227, 231, 239, 242, 247, 263, 279, 313, 314, 319, 321, 322, 331, 337, 341, 348, 349, 354, 357, 358, 361, 369, 371, 374, 375, 379, 380, 384